KU-004-492

bc

The Letters of

SAMUEL JOHNSON

SAMUEL JOHNSON

by Thomas Trotter. A chalk drawing made shortly before Johnson's death (Hyde Collection)

The Letters of

SAMUEL JOHNSON

VOLUME IV · 1782–1784

Edited by

BRUCE REDFORD

CLARENDON PRESS · OXFORD

1994

Oxford University Press, Walton Street, Oxford OX2 6DP

OXFORD NEW YORK TORONTO
DELHI BOMBAY CALCUTTA MADRAS KARACHI
PETALING JAYA SINGAPORE HONG KONG TOKYO
NAIROBI DAR ES SALAAM CAPE TOWN
MELBOURNE AUCKLAND

AND ASSOCIATED COMPANIES IN
BERLIN IBADAN

OXFORD IS A TRADE MARK OF OXFORD UNIVERSITY PRESS

EDITED AND PRODUCED BY PRINCETON UNIVERSITY PRESS

BRITISH LIBRARY CATALOGUING IN PUBLICATION DATA (DATA AVAILABLE)

ISBN 0–19–811287–4 (vol. 1) 0–19–811951–8 (vol. 4)

LIBRARY OF CONGRESS CATALOGING-IN-PUBLICATION DATA
(REVISED FOR VOLUMES 4 AND 5)

JOHNSON, SAMUEL, 1709–1784. THE LETTERS OF SAMUEL JOHNSON.
INCLUDES BIBLIOGRAPHICAL REFERENCES AND INDEX.
CONTENTS: V. 1. 1731–1772 — [ETC.] — V. 4. 1 JANUARY 1782 TO 10 DECEMBER 1784 — V. 5. APPENDICES AND COMPREHENSIVE INDEX.
1. JOHNSON, SAMUEL—1709–1784—CORRESPONDENCE.
2. AUTHORS, ENGLISH—18TH CENTURY—CORRESPONDENCE.
3. LEXICOGRAPHERS—GREAT BRITAIN—CORRESPONDENCE.
I. REDFORD, BRUCE. II. TITLE.
PR3533.A4 1992 828′.609 [B] 90–8806

PRINTED IN THE UNITED STATES OF AMERICA
BY THE STINEHOUR PRESS, LUNENBURG, VERMONT

CONTENTS

ILLUSTRATIONS

ACKNOWLEDGMENTS

"TIME hovers o'er, impatient to destroy, / And shuts up all the Passages of Joy": the last three years of Johnson's life are robbed of joy by two great calamities, the collapse of his body and the decay of his friendship with Hester Thrale, which breaks off, in July 1784, with two of his most powerful letters. On the whole, however, epistolary aggression is rare during these final years: instead, Johnson constitutes and reinforces community through correspondence, writing against solitude as he fights his rearguard medical action. The majority of the letters collected in this volume provide, in Boswell's description of the *Rambler* essays, *bark and steel for the mind*.

I too have been fortunate in my community of friends, colleagues, and correspondents, who have ministered doses less bitter than quinine and kept at bay the "secret horrour of the last" (*Idler* No. 103). In addition to those singled out in Volume I, chief among them Janet Stern and Marcia Wagner Levinson, I would like to thank Donald Eddy, David Fairer, Alvaro Ribeiro S. J., Richard Sharpe, E. Thorne, and David Weinglass. The translations of Johnson's Latin letters have been examined scrupulously by Michael Murrin, Raphael Newman, Joshua Scodel, and Peter White. To all who have contributed unstintingly: *Nemo sibi placens non lætatur; nemo sibi non placet qui vobis, literarum Arbitris, placere potuit* (To Thomas Fothergill, 7 April 1775).

BRUCE REDFORD

PRINCETON, NEW JERSEY
APRIL 1992

EDITORIAL PROCEDURES

POLICIES of annotation and transcription have been modeled on the style sheet for the Yale Research Edition of the Private Papers of James Boswell. The most detailed version in print appears in the front matter to *The Correspondence of James Boswell with David Garrick, Edmund Burke, and Edmond Malone*, ed. P. S. Baker et al. (1986). The statement that follows adheres closely to this version.

THE TEXTS

Choice and Arrangement of Letters

The letters are presented in chronological order. Letters written for others, as well as public dissertations in the guise of letters, have been excluded. Undated letters that cannot be assigned with confidence to a specific year appear in Appendix I, where they are ordered alphabetically by correspondent. Appendix II gathers together the evidence for letters whose texts have not been recovered. Translations of Johnson's letters in Latin appear in Appendix III.

The copy-text has been the MSS of letters sent, whenever such MSS were available. In the absence of originals, we have used MS copies. When no MSS at all have been recovered, we have used printed texts as copy.

Transcription

In accordance with the policy of the Yale Research Series, "manuscript documents in this edition have been printed to correspond to the originals as closely as is feasible in the medium of type. A certain amount of compromise and apparent inconsistency seems unavoidable, but change has been kept within the limits of stated conventions."

The following editorial conventions are imposed silently: *Addresses.* Elements appearing on separate lines in the MS are run together and punctuated according to modern practice. On franked covers, handwriting is that of the franker unless otherwise specified.

Datelines. Places and dates are joined at the head of the letter regardless of their position in the MS. Punctuation has been normalized.

Salutations. Abbreviations are expanded. Commas and colons after salutations are retained; in the absence of punctuation, a colon is supplied.

Complimentary closes. Abbreviations are expanded. Punctuation has been normalized. Elements appearing on separate lines in the MS are run together. Complimentary closes paragraphed separately in the MS are printed as continuations of the last line of text.

Endorsements. Handwriting is that of the recipient unless otherwise specified.

Punctuation. At the ends of completed sentences periods may replace commas or dashes and are always supplied when omitted. A sentence following a period always begins with a capital letter.

Changes. Substantive additions and deletions in Johnson's hand are recorded in the notes.

Lacunae. Words and letters missing through a tear or obscured by a blot are supplied within angle brackets. Inadvertent omissions are supplied within square brackets. Nonauthorial deletions are not reported unless the reading is in doubt.

Abbreviations, contractions, and symbols. The following abbreviations, contractions, and symbols, and their variant forms, are expanded: abt (about), acct (account), agst (against), Bp (Bishop), cd (could), compts (compliments), Dr (Dear), Ld (Lord), Lop (Lordship), Ly (Lady), Lyship (Ladyship), recd (received), sd (should), Sr (Sir), wc (which), wd (would), yr (your), & (and), &c (etc.). All retained abbreviations and contractions are followed by a period. Periods following ordinals have been removed.

Superior letters. Superior letters are lowered.

Brackets. Parentheses replace square brackets in the text, brackets being reserved for editorial use.

Spelling. The original spelling has been retained, except for obvious inadvertencies, which are corrected in the text and recorded in the notes.

Capitalization and paragraphing. Original capitalization and paragraphing have been retained.

ANNOTATION

Headnotes. Postmarks, although partly illegible on some letters, are left unbracketed when not in doubt. Marks on the wrappers other than addresses, postmarks, endorsements, and stamped and written franks have been ignored.

Footnotes. When an abbreviated source is given, the full citation may be found in the list of cue titles and abbreviations on pp. xvii–xix. All other reference titles in the footnotes are sufficiently complete to enable ready identification; for each letter, these citations are presented in full the first time they occur and are shortened in all subsequent occurrences in the notes to that letter. Except where a work has been directly quoted, no source is given when the information is available in the *Dictionary of National Biography*, an encyclopedia, or other general reference work.

Reference to all letters is made by correspondent and date. *Post* and *Ante* references supplement but do not replace the index, which should be consulted whenever the identity of names or places is in doubt.

CHRONOLOGY

1709	Is born at Lichfield, 18 Sept.
1717–25	Attends Lichfield Grammar School.
1728	Enters Pembroke College, Oxford, in October.
1729	Leaves Oxford in December.
1731	Death of his father Michael.
1732	Usher at Market Bosworth School.
1733	Resides in Birmingham; translates Lobo's *Voyage to Abyssinia.*
1735	Marries Elizabeth Porter; opens school at Edial.
1737	Leaves for London in March; begins work for Edward Cave.
1738	*London.*
1744	*An Account of the Life of Richard Savage*; *Harleian Miscellany.*
1746	Signs contract for the *Dictionary.*
1749	*Irene* produced; *The Vanity of Human Wishes.*
1750	Begins *Rambler.*
1752	Death of Elizabeth Johnson; final *Rambler.*
1755	Oxford M.A.; publication of the *Dictionary.*
1758	Begins *Idler.*
1759	Death of his mother Sarah; publication of *Rasselas.*
1760	Final *Idler.*
1762	Is granted annual pension.
1763	Meets James Boswell.
1764	Founding of The Club.
1765	Meets Henry and Hester Thrale; Dublin LL.D.; *The Dramatic Works of William Shakespeare.*
1770	*The False Alarm.*
1771	*Thoughts on the late Transactions respecting Falkland's Islands.*
1773	Hebridean tour.
1774	*The Patriot*; tour of Wales.
1775	*A Journey to the Western Islands of Scotland*; *Taxation No Tyranny*; Oxford D.C.L.; trip to Paris.

1777	Trial of Dr. Dodd; begins work on *Lives of the Poets*.
1779	First installment of *Lives*.
1781	Death of Henry Thrale; second installment of *Lives*.
1783	Founding of Essex Head Club.
1784	Final break with Hester Thrale; dies 13 Dec.

CUE TITLES AND ABBREVIATIONS

Adam Cat.	R. B. Adam, *The R. B. Adam Library Relating to Dr. Samuel Johnson and His Era*, 4 vols., 1929–30.
Alum. Cant. i	John and J. A. Venn, *Alumni Cantabrigienses*, Part i (to 1751), 4 vols., 1922–27.
Alum. Cant. ii	J. A. Venn, *Alumni Cantabrigienses*, Part ii (1752–1900), 6 vols., 1940–54.
Alum. Oxon. i	Joseph Foster, *Alumni Oxonienses ... 1500–1714*, 4 vols., 1891–92.
Alum. Oxon. ii	Joseph Foster, *Alumni Oxonienses ... 1715–1886*, 4 vols., 1887–88.
Baker	*The Correspondence of James Boswell with David Garrick, Edmund Burke, and Edmond Malone*, ed. P. S. Baker et al., 1986.
Bibliography	W. P. Courtney and David Nichol Smith, *A Bibliography of Samuel Johnson*, 1915, 1925.
Bibliography Supplement	R. W. Chapman and A. T. Hazen, *Johnsonian Bibliography: A Supplement to Courtney*, 1939.
Bloom	E. A. Bloom, *Samuel Johnson in Grub Street*, 1957.
Burke's Correspondence	*The Correspondence of Edmund Burke*, ed. T. W. Copeland et al., 1958–70.
Chapman	*The Letters of Samuel Johnson, with Mrs. Thrale's Genuine Letters to Him*, ed. R. W. Chapman, 3 vols., 1952.
Clifford, 1952	J. L. Clifford, *Hester Lynch Piozzi*, 2d ed., 1952.
Clifford, 1955	J. L. Clifford, *Young Samuel Johnson*, 1955.
Clifford, 1979	J. L. Clifford, *Dictionary Johnson*, 1979.
Croker	James Boswell, *The Life of Samuel Johnson, LL.D.*, ed. J. W. Croker, rev. John Wright, 10 vols., 1868.
SJ's *Dictionary*	Samuel Johnson, *Dictionary of the English Language*, 4th ed., 1773.
DNB	*Dictionary of National Biography.*

Earlier Years	F. A. POTTLE, *James Boswell: The Earlier Years, 1740–1769*, 1966.
Fifer	*The Correspondence of James Boswell with Certain Members of The Club*, ed. C. N. Fifer, 1976.
Fleeman	SAMUEL JOHNSON, *A Journey to the Western Islands of Scotland*, ed. J. D. Fleeman, 1985.
GM	*The Gentleman's Magazine*, 1731–1907.
Greene, 1975	DONALD GREENE, *Samuel Johnson's Library*, 1975.
Hawkins	SIR JOHN HAWKINS, *The Life of Samuel Johnson, LL.D.*, 2d ed., 1787.
Hazen	A. T. HAZEN, *Samuel Johnson's Prefaces and Dedications*, 1937.
Hebrides	*Boswell's Journal of a Tour to the Hebrides with Samuel Johnson, LL.D., 1773*, ed. from the original MS by F. A. Pottle and C. H. Bennett, 1961.
Hendy	J. G. HENDY, *The History of the Early Postmarks of the British Isles*, 1905.
Hill	*Letters of Samuel Johnson, LL.D.*, ed. G. B. Hill, 1892.
Hyde, 1972	MARY HYDE, *The Impossible Friendship: Boswell and Mrs. Thrale*, 1972.
Hyde, 1977	MARY HYDE, *The Thrales of Streatham Park*, 1977.
JB	James Boswell.
Johns. Glean.	A. L. READE, *Johnsonian Gleanings*, 11 vols., 1909–52.
Johns. Misc.	*Johnsonian Miscellanies*, ed. G. B. Hill, 2 vols., 1897.
JN	*Johnsonian Newsletter*.
Later Years	FRANK BRADY, *James Boswell: The Later Years, 1769–1795*, 1984.
Life	*Boswell's Life of Johnson, Together with Boswell's Journal of a Tour to the Hebrides and Johnson's Diary of a Journey into North Wales*, ed. G. B. Hill, rev. L. F. Powell, 6 vols., 1934–50; vols. V and VI, 2d ed., 1964.
Lit. Anec.	JOHN NICHOLS, *Literary Anecdotes of the Eighteenth Century*, 9 vols., 1812–15.
Lit. Car.	F. A. POTTLE, *The Literary Career of James Boswell, Esq.*, 1929.
Lives of the Poets	*Johnson's Lives of the English Poets*, ed. G. B. Hill, 1905.

Lond. Stage — *The London Stage*, Part III (1729–47), ed. A. H. Scouten, 1961; Part IV (1747–76), ed. G. W. Stone, Jr., 1962; Part V (1776–1800), ed. C. B. Hogan, 1968.

Namier and Brooke — SIR LEWIS NAMIER and JOHN BROOKE, *The House of Commons, 1754–1790*, 3 vols., 1964.

OED — *Oxford English Dictionary*.

Piozzi, *Letters* — HESTER LYNCH PIOZZI, *Letters to and from the Late Samuel Johnson, LL.D.*, 2 vols., 1788.

Piozzi — Annotated presentation copy, given to Sir James Fellowes, of H. L. Piozzi's *Letters to and from the Late Samuel Johnson, LL.D.*, 1788 (Birthplace Museum, Lichfield).

Plomer — H. R. PLOMER et al., *Dictionary of Printers and Booksellers, 1668–1725; 1726–1775*, 2 vols., 1922, 1932.

Poems — *The Poems of Samuel Johnson*, ed. David Nichol Smith and E. L. McAdam, rev. J. D. Fleeman, 1974.

Reades — A. L. READE, *The Reades of Blackwood Hill and Dr. Johnson's Ancestry*, 1906.

RES — *Review of English Studies*.

SJ — Samuel Johnson.

Sledd and Kolb — J. H. SLEDD and G. J. KOLB, *Dr. Johnson's Dictionary*, 1955.

Thraliana — *Thraliana: The Diary of Mrs. Hester Lynch Thrale*, ed. K. C. Balderston, 1942.

TLS — *Times Literary Supplement*.

Waingrow — *The Correspondence and Other Papers of James Boswell Relating to the Making of the "Life of Johnson,"* ed. Marshall Waingrow, 1969.

Walpole's Correspondence, Yale ed. — *The Yale Edition of Horace Walpole's Correspondence*, ed. W. S. Lewis et al., 1937–83.

Wheatley and Cunningham — H. B. WHEATLEY and PETER CUNNINGHAM, *London Past and Present*, 3 vols., 1891.

Works, Yale ed. — *The Yale Edition of the Works of Samuel Johnson*, J. H. Middendorf, gen. ed., 1958–.

The Letters of

SAMUEL JOHNSON

Mauritius Lowe

TUESDAY 1 JANUARY 1782

MS: Fitzwilliam Museum.
ADDRESS: To Mr. Lowe.

Sir: Jan. 1, –82

When I desired your company for sunday, I had forgotten that I was myself engaged to another place. I had played Mr. Sastres the same trick.[1] I hope to see you another time. I am, Sir, your humble Servant,

SAM. JOHNSON

1. Francesco Sastres (d. 1822), Italian poet, teacher, and translator, author of *An Introduction to the Italian Language* (1778), settled in London in 1777. Sastres, an original member of the Essex Head Club, became one of SJ's most devoted friends during the last five years of his life (*Life* IV.443; *Lit. Anec.* II.553; E. H. Thorne, "Francesco Sastres," *English Miscellany* 115, 1964, pp. 175–82).

James Boswell

SATURDAY 5 JANUARY 1782

PRINTED SOURCE: JB's *Life*, 1791, II.412–13.

Dear Sir, January 5, 1782

I sit down to answer your letter on the same day in which I received it,[1] and am pleased that my first letter of the year is to you. No man ought to be at ease while he knows himself in the wrong; and I have not satisfied myself with my long si-

1. JB had written "one letter to introduce Mr. Sinclair (now Sir John) [see below, n. 3], . . . and informed him in another, that my wife had again been affected with alarming symptoms of illness" (*Life* IV.136).

lence.[2] The letter relating to Mr. Sinclair,[3] however was, I believe, never brought.

My health has been tottering this last year; and I can give no very laudable account of my time. I am always hoping to do better than I have ever hitherto done.

My journey to Ashbourne and Staffordshire was not pleasant; for what enjoyment has a sick man visiting the sick?[4] Shall we ever have another frolick like our journey to the Hebrides?

I hope that dear Mrs. Boswell will surmount her complaints; in losing her you would lose your anchor, and be tost, without stability, by the waves of life. I wish both her and you very many years, and very happy.

For some months past I have been so withdrawn from the world, that I can send you nothing particular. All your friends, however, are well, and will be glad of your return to London. I am, dear Sir, Yours most affectionately,

SAM. JOHNSON

2. SJ had not been in communication with JB since June of the previous year (*Life* IV.132, 136).

3. John Sinclair (1754–1835), Bt. (1786), of Ulbster and Thurso Castle, Caithness, Scots landowner, barrister, M.P. (1780–1811), and author of the *Statistical Account of Scotland* (1791–99) (Namier and Brooke III.440–41). Sinclair and JB shared an interest in Scots dialect (*Boswell, Laird of Auchinleck*, ed. J. W. Reed and F. A. Pottle, 1977, p. 263 and n. 5).

4. *Ante* To Hester Thrale, 20 Oct. 1781; 27 Oct. 1781; 31 Oct. 1781; 10 Nov. 1781.

Thomas Lawrence

SATURDAY 5 JANUARY 1782

MS: Huntington Library.

T. Laurentio, Medico. S. Nonis Jan. 1782

A corpore pessime habitus ad te confugio, Vir doctissime. Leviora incommoda prætereunda censeo, quod me maxime angit, ut potero, dicam.[1] Ubi in lecto decubui, post somnum

1. "There is general agreement among the twentieth-century doctors who have

brevem, plerumque brevissimum, sensu quodam quasi materiæ intus turgescentis pectus tentatur; ita ut, quanquam nullus dolor aut lacerat aut pungit, somnus prorsus pellatur, et capite de culcitra levato, inter stragula sedere necesse sit. Hinc crebra suspiria, interdum[2] singultus, spirandi labor difficilis. Eo res venit ut lectum horream, neque luce perfrui possim. His malis quo sit modo occurrendum[3] tuum esto judicium. Mihi quidem vena secanda videtur, quod tamen nisi tuo jussu haud libenter fecerim. Quid possit purgatio per alvum, etiam mercurio adhibito, vano experimento satis tentavi. Si sanguis mittendus est, te præsente missum velim, nequid vel metu vel audacia peccetur.[4]

Ad me ne venias; postquam hæc legeris, adero.

---

studied Johnson's case that some, at least, of his symptoms lead without difficulty to a diagnosis of bronchitis, or a chronic bronchial infection. . . . The disease follows an inexorably progressive course, and is accompanied by emphysema" (John Wiltshire, *Samuel Johnson in the Medical World*, 1991, pp. 39–40).

2. MS: "inderdum"

3. MS: "ac" del. before "occurrendum"

4. *Post* To Hester Thrale, 6 Jan. 1782.

Hester Thrale

SATURDAY 5 JANUARY 1782

MS: Current location unknown. Transcribed from photostat in the Hyde Collection.

Dear Madam: Jan. 5, 1782

I have slept in a chair, and am better. When I have b[l]ed, I will do all that the Doctor directs.[1] Your care is a great comfort to me. I am, Madam, Your etc.

SAM. JOHNSON

1. *Ante* To Thomas Lawrence, 5 Jan. 1782; *Post* To Hester Thrale, 6 Jan. 1782.

Hester Thrale

SUNDAY 6 JANUARY 1782

MS: Rylands Library.
ADDRESS: To Mrs. Thrale.

Dear Madam: Jan. 6, 1782

I wrote my complaint to Dr. Laurence,[1] and then went to him. A Chirurgeon was called, and sixteen ounces taken away. I durst not have done so much by myself, but it was right, I had no faintness though I fasted, and had an Elysian night compared to some nights past. I am, Madam, Your most obedient Servant,

SAM. JOHNSON

1. *Ante* To Thomas Lawrence, 5 Jan. 1782.

Thomas Lawrence

THURSDAY 17 JANUARY 1782

MS: Beinecke Library.
ADDRESS: To Dr. Laurence.

Sir: Jan. 17, 1782

Our old Friend Mr. Levett, who was last night eminently cheerful, died this morning. The man who lay in the same room hearing an uncommon noise got up; and tried to make him speak, but without effect, he then called Mr. Holder the apothecary,[1] who though, when he came, he thought him dead, opened a vein but could draw no blood. So has ended the long life of a very useful, and very blam[e]less man.[2] I am, Sir, Your most humble Servant,

SAM. JOHNSON

1. ?Robert Holder (d. 1797), apothecary in the Strand, attended SJ during the many illnesses of his final years; he is described in SJ's will as "my apothecary" (*Life* IV.144 n. 1, 402 n. 2).

2. See SJ's elegy, "On the Death of Dr. Robert Levet" (*Poems*, pp. 233–34).

Thomas Lawrence

MONDAY 21 JANUARY 1782

MS: Huntington Library.
ADDRESS: To Dr. Laurence.

T. Laurentio Medico. S. Jan. 21, 17[82]

Mihi somnus hac nocte fuit sæpe quidem intermissus, ita vero placidus, ut somnijs continuatis, et sibi constantibus otium præberet; neque cubanti quidquam tussis molestiarum fecit. At gravem me sentio et oppleto similem, spiritumque duco solutiorem non tamen liberum. Pectus quodammodo æstuare pergit. Nescio an ausim venam iterum secandam offerre, cum tamen nihil sentiam aut debile aut vacuum, quid sit magnopere extimescendum[1] non video. Te hoc remedium arrepturum non dubito, si quod ego in me sentio, in te ipse sentires. Quod fecisti morbo obstitit, quem tamen non vicit. Vive, valeque.

1. MS: "extimiscendum"

Hester Thrale

MONDAY 28 JANUARY 1782

MS: Hyde Collection.
ADDRESS: To Mrs. Thrale.

Dearest Lady: Jan. 28,[1] 1782

I was blooded on Saturday, I think, not copiously enough, but the Doctor would permit no more.[2] I have however his consent to bleed again to day. Since I left you, I have eaten very little, on Friday, chiefly broath, on Saturday nothing but some bread in the morning, on Sunday nothing but some bread and three roasted apples. I try to get well and wish to see You, but if I

1. MS: "8" altered from "9"
2. *Ante* To Thomas Lawrence, 21 Jan. 1782.

came, I should only cough and cough. Mr. Steevens, who is with me, says that my hearing is returned. We are here all three sick,[3] and poor Levet is gone.[4]

Do not add to my other distresses any[5] diminution of kindness for, Madam, Your most humble servant,

SAM. JOHNSON

3. SJ refers to himself, Anna Williams, and Elizabeth Desmoulins.

4. *Ante* To Thomas Lawrence, 17 Jan. 1782.

5. MS: "any any"

John Perkins

TUESDAY 29 JANUARY 1782

MS: Hyde Collection.

ADDRESS: To Mr. Perkins.

Sir: Jan. 29, 1782

I have been ill, but can now venture out and will call on You this afternoon for a little private conversation, if You are to be at home; Fix what hour You please, I can wait on You any time after dinner. I am, Sir, Your most humble servant,

SAM. JOHNSON

Thomas Lawrence

MONDAY 4 FEBRUARY 1782

MS: Hyde Collection.

ADDRESS: To Dr. Laurence.

Dear Sir: Febr. 4, 1782

This last phlebotomy has, I think, done me good.[1] I had this morning a very kindly sweat.

1. *Post* To Margaret Strahan, 4 Feb. 1782.

Please to send me your papers,[2] which I am sorry that You should mention with an apology, as if You suspected me of forgetting the disproportion between what I can do for You, and what You can do for Me. I am, Sir, your most obliged and most humble servant,

SAM. JOHNSON

2. It is probable that SJ refers to the manuscript of Lawrence's "De Temperamentis," which he was reading the following month (*Works*, Yale ed. 1.313–14).

Margaret Strahan

MONDAY 4 FEBRUARY 1782

MS: Hyde Collection.

ADDRESS: To Mrs. Strahan.

Dear Madam: Febr. 4, 1782

Mrs. Williams showed me your kind letter. This little habitation is now but a melancholy place, clouded with the gloom of disease and death. Of the four inmates one has been suddenly snatched away,[1] two are oppressed by very afflictive and dangerous ilness;[2] and I tried yesterday to gain some relief by a third bleeding from a disorder which has for some time distressed me,[3] and I think myself today much better.

I am glad, dear Madam, to hear that You are so far recovered as to go to Bath.[4] Let me once more entreat You to stay till your health is not only obtained but confirmed. Your fortune is such as that no moderate expence deserves your care, and you have a husband who, I believe does not regard it. Stay therefore till You are quite well. I am, for my part, very much dejected, but complaint is useless. I hope God will bless

1. *Ante* To Thomas Lawrence, 17 Jan. 1782.

2. SJ refers to Anna Williams and Elizabeth Desmoulins (cf. *Ante* To Hester Thrale, 28 Jan. 1782).

3. *Ante* To Thomas Lawrence, 5 Jan. 1782; 21 Jan. 1782.

4. *Ante* To Hester Thrale, 6 Apr. 1780, n. 9.

You, and desire You to form the same wish for me. I am, Dear Madam, Your most humble Servant,

SAM. JOHNSON

Hester Chapone

SATURDAY 9 FEBRUARY 1782

MS: Castle Howard.

ADDRESS: To Mrs. Chapone.

Madam: Febr. 9, 1782

Since I had the honour of receiving this manuscript[1] I know not that I have been otherwise than very ill for a single day. I intended to have written to You, but even that I delayd with the natural expectation of another day. My purpose was to have read the piece as soon as I grew better. You may assure yourself and the authour that since I learned to unlock it, I have never opened it, and that if he does me the honour to send it again when I am better it shall not be again returned unread.[2] I am, Madam, Your most humble Servant,

SAM. JOHNSON

I entreat to see it again.

1. "The Earl of Carlisle having written a tragedy, entitled 'THE FATHER'S REVENGE,' some of his Lordship's friends applied to Mrs. Chapone, to prevail on Dr. Johnson to read and give his opinion of it" (*Life* IV.246). *Post* To Hester Chapone, 28 Nov. 1783.

2. *Post* To Hester Chapone, 28 Nov. 1783.

Charles Patrick[1]

THURSDAY 14 FEBRUARY 1782

1. Instigated by John Thompson, who described himself as a cooper of Hull and a relation of the Levet family, Charles Patrick of Hull (possibly a grocer) had written to inquire after SJ's deceased friend. SJ's response to Patrick provoked a long letter from Thompson, dated 21 Feb. (MS: Hyde Collection; K. J. Allison, *'Hull Gent. Seeks Country Residence,'* 1981, p. 18). See below, n. 4.

MS: Pembroke College, Oxford. A copy in the hand of Thomas Harwood.

NOTE: It does not give the direction; but was in possession of Richard Beatniffe Esq. the Recorder of Hull.

Sir: Bolt Court, Fleet Street, Feb. 14, 1782

Robert Levet, with whom I had been connected by a friendship of many years, died lately at my house.[2] His death was sudden, and no will has yet been found; I therefore gave notice of his decease in the papers, that an heir, if he has any, may appear.[3] He has left very little; but of that little his brother is, doubtless, heir, and your friend may be perhaps his brother.[4] I have had another application from one who calls himself his brother;[5] and I suppose it is fit that the Claimant should give some proof of his relation. I would gladly know, from the Gentleman that thinks himself R. Levet's brother,

In what year, and in what parish R. Levet was born?
Where or how was he educated?
What was his early course of life?
What were the marks of his person; his stature; the colour of his eyes?
Was he marked by the small Pox?
Had he any impediment in his speech?
What relations had he, and how many are now living?[6]

2. *Ante* To Thomas Lawrence, 17 Jan. 1782.

3. "Last week died at the house of his friend, Dr. Samuel Johnson, Dr. Levet, a Practitioner in Physic" (*London Chronicle*, 24–26 Jan. 1782, p. 93).

4. John Thompson was not Robert Levet's brother, but a kinsman who represented "the surviving Brothers and Sister" (Thompson to SJ, 21 Feb. 1782, MS: Hyde Collection).

5. Before Charles Patrick sent his inquiry, Thompson had written to a friend in London, "Mr. Thos. R. Gosnell." In his letter to SJ of 21 Feb., Thompson suggests that it was Goswell who "might be the person refer'd too in your Letter of another Person making a Claim as Brother" (MS: Hyde Collection).

6. In his letter Thompson lists Levet's relations and describes "his person": "about 78 years of age, suppos'd to be about 5 Foot 4 Inch . . . high, rather broad sett, of rather dullish Complexion, nott mark'd with small Pox, his hair and Eyelids Blackish, no Impediment in his speech, his voice not so clear in sound as some are" (MS: Hyde Collection).

His answer to these questions will shew whether he knew him; and he may then proceed to shew that he is his brother.

He may be sure that nothing shall be hastily wasted or removed. I have not looked into his boxes, but transferred that business to a Gentleman in the neighbourhood, of character above suspicion.

SAM. JOHNSON

Hester Thrale

SATURDAY 16 FEBRUARY 1782

MS: Hyde Collection.

Dearest Lady: Febr. 16, 1782

I am better, but not yet well, but Hope springs eternal[1]—As soon as I can think myself not troublesome, You may be sure of seeing [me], for such a place to visit no body ever had. Dearest Madam, do not think me worse than I am, be sure at least that whatever happens to me, I am with all the regard that admiration of excellence and gratitude for kindness can excite, Madam, Your most humble Servant,

SAM. JOHNSON

1. "Hope springs eternal in the human breast" (Pope, *Essay on Man* I.95).

Hester Thrale

SUNDAY 17 FEBRUARY 1782

PRINTED SOURCE: Piozzi, *Letters* II.235.

Dear Madam, Feb. 17, 1782

Sure such letters would make any man well. I will let them have their full operation upon me; but while I write I am not without a cough. I can however keep it quiet by diacodium,[1]

1. *diacodium*: "the syrup of poppies" (SJ's *Dictionary*).

and am in hope that with all other disturbances it will go away, and permit me to enjoy the happiness of being, Madam, Your, etc.

Hester Thrale

THURSDAY 21 FEBRUARY 1782

MS: Hyde Collection.

Dearest Madam: Boltcourt, Febr. 21, 1782

I certainly grow better, I lay this morning with such success, that I called before I rose for dry linen. I believe I have had a crisis.

Last night cal[l]ed Sir Richard Jebb, and many people call or send, I am not neglected nor forgotten. But let me be always sure of your kindness. I hope to try again this week whether your house is yet so cold, for to be away from you, if I did [not] think our separation likely to be short,[1] how could I endure. You are a dear, dear Lady, and your kind attention is a great part of what Life affords to, Madam, Your most obliged and most humble Servant,

SAM. JOHNSON

1. MS: "sho" altered from "?spe"

Edmond Malone[1]

WEDNESDAY 27 FEBRUARY 1782

1. Edmond Malone (1741–1812), editor and biographer, had known SJ since 1764 or 1765, when, as an aspiring barrister, he was studying at the Inner Temple. In 1777 Malone gave up his legal practice in Dublin, moved to London, and began an independent scholarly career with work on Shakespeare. Having grown increasingly intimate with members of the Johnsonian circle, Malone was elected to The Club in Feb. 1782 (James M. Osborn, "Edmond Malone and Dr. Johnson," in *Johnson, Boswell and Their Circle*, 1965, pp. 1–4; Baker, pp. 166–68).

To EDMOND MALONE, 27 *February* 1782

MS: Hyde Collection.

ADDRESS: To Mr. Malone, No. 55 Queen Anne Street East.

POSTMARKS: PENY POST PAYD, [Undeciphered].

ENDORSEMENT: From Dr. Johnson.

Sir: Febr. 27, 1782

I have for many weeks been so much out of order, that I have gone out only in a coach to Mrs. Thrale's, where I can use all the freedom that Sickness requires. Do not therefore take it amiss that I am not with You and Dr. Farmer. I hope hereafter to see you often. I am, Sir, Your most humble servant,

SAM. JOHNSON

Edmond Malone

SATURDAY 2 MARCH 1782

MS: Hyde Collection.

ADDRESS: To Edmund Malone, Esq.

ENDORSEMENT: From Dr. Samuel Johnson.

Dear Sir: March 2, 1782

I hope, I grow better, and shall soon be able to enjoy the kindness of my friends. I think this wild adherence to Chatterton more unaccountable than the obstinate defence of Ossian.[1] For Ossian there is a national pride, [which] may be forgiven though it cannot be applauded; for Chatterton there is nothing but the resolution to say again what has once been said. I am Sir, Your humble servant,

SAM. JOHNSON

1. Malone had sent SJ his *Cursory Observations on the Poems attributed to Thomas Rowley,* which exposed Chatterton's fabrication (*Life* IV.141 n. 1). *Ante* To Hester Thrale, 16 May 1776, n. 9.

Lucy Porter

SATURDAY 2 MARCH 1782

MS: Hyde Collection.

Dear Madam: London, March 2, 1782

I went away from Lichfield ill, and have had a troublesome time with my breath, for some weeks I have been disordered by a cold of which I could not get the violence abated, till I had[1] been let blood three times.[2] I have not, however, been so bad, but that I could have written, and I am sorry that I neglected it.

My dwelling is but melancholy, both Williams, and Desmoulins and myself are very sickly; Frank is not well, and poor Levet died in his bed the other day by a sudden stroke.[3] I suppose not one minute passed between health and death. So uncertain are human things.

Such is the appearance of the world about me; I hope your scenes are more cheerful. But whatever befals us, though it is wise to be serious, it is useless and foolish, and perhaps sinful to be gloomy. Let us therefore keep ourselves as easy as we can; though the loss of Friends will be felt, and poor Levet had been to me a faithful adherent for thirty years.

Forgive me, my dear Love, the omission of writing; I hope to mend that and my other faults. Let me have your prayers.

Make my compliments to Mrs. Cobb, and Miss Adey and Mr. Pearson, and the whole company of my friends. I am, My dear, Your most humble Servant,

SAM. JOHNSON

1. MS: "had had"
2. *Ante* To Margaret Strahan, 4 Feb. 1782.
3. *Ante* To Thomas Lawrence, 17 Jan. 1782.

John Taylor

SATURDAY 2 MARCH 1782

MS: Gerald M. Goldberg.

ADDRESS: To the Reverend Doctor Taylor.

ENDORSEMENT: 1782, 2 March 1782.

Dear Sir: March 2, 1782

I am sorry to hear that You are not well, I have had a very troublesome night myself. I fancy the Weather may hurt us; if that is the case, we may hope for better health as the year advances.

I had a letter last night from Mr. Langley, which I will show you to morrow; which will I believe incline You to doubt Mr. Flints veracity, yet I believe it will be best for the Girls to take the money offered them, but You shall consider it to morrow.[1] I am, Sir, Your etc.

SAM. JOHNSON

I shall come to morrow early in the evening.

1. Thomas Flint had married, as his second wife, Mary Dunn Collier (1733–76), whom SJ claimed as a cousin (*Life* v.581). After her death a disagreement arose between Flint and his two stepdaughters, Mary (b. 1754) and Sophia (b. 1760), concerning the division of their mother's estate. The Misses Collier consulted SJ, who attempted over a period of several years to adjudicate the dispute, in part by gathering precise information from William Langley and others. Ultimately SJ drew up a "Case"—a concise statement of the Colliers' claim (MS: Hyde Collection). The outcome of the dispute has not been determined (*Johns. Glean.* IX.25–39). *Post* To John Taylor, 13 June 1782; 21 Sept. 1782; 3 Oct. 1782; 9 Dec. 1782.

Thomas Lawrence

WEDNESDAY 13 MARCH 1782

MS: Huntington Library.

T. Laurentio Medico. S. Mart. 13, 1782

Malæ valetudinis diuturnitate fatigatus, tuam artem, Vir doctissime, tuamque amicitiam in auxilium iterum voco. Tussis, aliquanto sedatior, me nec sæpe nec graviter vexat, ad minimum tamen frigoris tactum recrudescit. Tanti vero non est ut illi pluribus immorer; longe majores parit molestias spirandi actio laboriosa et[1] impedita, quae quanto fiat taedio, doloris enim nihil habet,[2] latine enarrare haud promptum cuivis est; Mihi enim in lecto recubanti ferenda est pars aliqua diri cruciatus quo tacentis Rei contumaciam aggestis in pectus[3] ponderibus Majores expugnabant. Arteria sæliens interea sæpe interquiescit, cujus moræ quid vel indicent, vel minentur tuum erit reputare.

Hæc omnia incommoda eo gravius fero, quo facilius ea sublevari posse confido. Siquid enim vel sentiendo percipere vel judicando æstimare possim, praesens et tutum remedium in chirurgi cuspide est. Tibi, ut scio, spes est, podagram aliquando auxilio venturam, at quamdiu Podagra erit expectanda quæ fortasse non veniet, et si venerit, fortasse nihil opis est allatura. Ego olim, cum podagra maxime sævijt, et pede et pectore simul laboravi.

Oro igitur, Vir doctissime, atque[4] obtestor, sanguinem mitti ne vetes. Nimis caute res hactenus acta est; nunc vero, ne vel metu peccetur vel temeritate, optarem venam, te præsente, ante meridiem se[c]ari, sanguinemque sisti tuo arbitrio, horis autem pomeridianis te visam, ut judices an sit tuta altera missio, quæ solutâ fasciâ facile fiet.

Hæc scribo primâ nocte ad te cras, mane perferenda; Vale.

1. MS: "and"
2. MS: "habet" superimposed upon undeciphered partial erasure
3. MS: "aggestis in pectus" superimposed upon undeciphered partial erasure
4. MS: undeciphered partial erasure before "atque"

Thomas Lawrence

THURSDAY 14 MARCH 1782[1]

1. Dated with reference to the chronology established by To Thomas Lawrence, 13 Mar. 1782; To Hester Thrale, 14 Mar. 1782; To Thomas Lawrence, 15 Mar. 1782.

MS: Hyde Collection.

ADDRESS: To Dr. Laurence.

Mr. Johnson has sent the volumes that are at hand. The first volume Sir J. Hawkins took back, the third he will send to morrow. Dr. Laurence needs not be in haste to return the books, Sir John will be glad that he reads them.[2]

Mr. Johnson feels no consequence from the loss of blood.

2. Hawkins had lent SJ his five-volume *History of Music* (1776), which SJ in turn was passing on to Lawrence. *Post* To Thomas Lawrence, 15 Mar. 1782.

John Taylor

THURSDAY 14 MARCH 1782

MS: Houghton Library.

ENDORSEMENT: 1782, [1]4 March 82, This relates to a Coffee Pot purchased for Mrs. Fletcher.[1]

Dear Sir: March 14, 1782

To some frames of Mind almost every thing is wrong. You are shocked at refusing what I did not much desire, and I am now so much shocked at seeming to covet what was originally bought as a good bargain for another, that, though I have sent the price (10–7–0) I had rather not have the pot, for I shall have less liking to it for thinking it was not properly bought at first for me. If chance brings another bargain in your way let me have that, otherwise I had rather you took this again.[2]

I have had a tolerable night and Dr. Laurence is now with me. I am, Sir, your most etc.

SAM. JOHNSON

1. Mrs. Fletcher, one of Taylor's Ashbourne friends, described by JB in 1779 as "an ugly widow . . . good, cheerful" (*Boswell in Extremes*, ed. C. M. Weis and F. A. Pottle, 1970, p. 172 n. 4). *Post* To John Taylor, 8 July 1782.

2. SJ thought a silver coffeepot purchased by Taylor had been for him and had accordingly sent Taylor payment. The pot, however, had been purchased for Mrs. Fletcher (*Works*, Yale ed. 1.316; *Post* To John Taylor, 8 July 1782).

Hester Thrale

THURSDAY 14 MARCH 1782

PRINTED SOURCE: Piozzi, *Letters* II.236–37.

Dearest of all Dear Ladies, March 14, 1782

That Povilleri should write these verses is impossible.[1] I am angry at Sastres.

Seven ounces! Why I sent a letter to Dr. Lawrence,[2] who is ten times more *timorsome* than is your Jebb, and he came and stood by while one vein was opened with too small an orifice, and bled eight ounces and stopped. Then another vein was opened, which ran eight more. And here am I sixteen ounces lighter, for I have had no dinner.[3]

I think the loss of blood has done no harm; whether it has done good, time will tell. I am glad that I do not sink without resistance. I am, Dear Madam, Your, etc.

1. According to Giuseppe Baretti, Giovanni Povoleri, a graduate of the University of Padua who taught Italian in London, succeeded him as language tutor at Streatham (*European Magazine* 14, 1788, 93–94). In 1779 Povoleri dedicated to Hester Thrale his edition of Giovanni Rucellai's tragedy, *Rosmunda*; the subscribers included SJ. Earlier in 1782 Povoleri had presented her with a sonnet, whose extravagant praise of "Thrali gentil" may have provoked SJ (*Thraliana* I.529). However, H. L. Piozzi identifies the "verses" in question as a love lyric composed by Gabriel Piozzi and published in her *British Synonymy* (1804, I.25) (Piozzi II.236).

2. *Ante* To Thomas Lawrence, 13 Mar. 1782.

3. "I at last persuaded Dr Laurence on Thursday March 14 to let me bleed more copiously. Sixteen ounces were taken away, and from that time my breath has been free, and my breast easy. On that day I took little food, and no flesh" (*Works*, Yale ed. I.312).

Thomas Lawrence

FRIDAY 15 MARCH 1782

MS: Huntington Library.

T. Laurentio Medico. S. Mart. 15, 1782

Postquam, omnibus rebus benignissime peractis, a me hesternâ die decesseras, tota corporis compages melius habere visa est, spiritus erat facilis, vires minime imminutæ. Vel escæ vel potus perpauxillum sumsi, ne venas vacuas replerem. Prima nocte me tussis creberrima ita exercuit, ut succum papaveris mellitum e pharmacopolio comparandum ducerem; sedata tamen paulo post sine ope papaveris me cubitum dimisit, ubi somnus tantis blanditijs excepit, ut a prima ad octavam horam ne somniasse quidem meminerim. Hinc ut omnia sint et Tibi et mihi fausta et læta faxit Deus. Vale.

Historiæ Musices quod heri ad manum non fuit, nunc mitto; non est ut reddere festines; vix quicquam vidimus aut suavius aut uberius. Vale et fruere.

Ut me visas, nisi tibi commodum fuerit, non est opus.

Hester Thrale

SATURDAY 16 MARCH 1782

MS: Rylands Library.
ADDRESS: To Mrs. Thrale.

Madam: March 16, 1782

This last Phlebotomy has, I think, done what was wanted,[1] and what would have been done at first with a little courage. But a little cold chills me, and a little chill renews the cough. I took diacodium last night, and repented.[2] To night I hope to be wiser, but who can answer for him self till night.

I hear, dear Madam, that You are not well, pray take You care. Set me right with Sir Richard,[3] whom I cannot guess how I offended. I will come back to You as soon as is fit, but I am to be here on Wednesday. I hope however to see You sooner. I am, Madam, Your most humble servant,

SAM. JOHNSON

1. *Ante* To Hester Thrale, 14 Mar. 1782.
2. Cf. *Ante* To Hester Thrale, 17 Feb. 1782 and n. 1.
3. SJ refers to Sir Richard Jebb.

Charles Burney

MONDAY 18 MARCH 1782

MS: Current location unknown. Transcribed from photostat in the Hyde Collection.

ADDRESS: To Dr. Burney.

ENDORSEMENTS: Mar. 18, 1782. From Dr. Johnson, March 18th 1782, No. 8.

Dear Sir: March 18, 1782

I have taken great liberties by shortening your paper but have, I hope, omitted nothing important. A long apology is a tedious thing.[1] I am, Dear Sir, etc.

SAM. JOHNSON

1. At Burney's request, SJ revised the concluding passage of his *General History of Music*, Volume II (published 29 May 1782). In this "apology," the author sets out to appease his subscribers, "who were expecting the *History* to be complete in two volumes and who might resent having to buy a third. . . . Burney concluded with two paragraphs which seem to owe something to Johnson's cheerless view of literary endeavour, in sentences of his own characteristic dignity" (Roger Lonsdale, *Dr. Charles Burney*, 1965, pp. 267–68).

Lucy Porter

TUESDAY 19 MARCH 1782

MS: Hyde Collection.

ADDRESS: To Mrs. Lucy Porter in Lichfield.

POSTMARK: 19 MR.

Dear Madam: Boltcourt, Fleetstreet, March 19, 1782

My last was but a dull letter,[1] and I know not that this will be much more cheerful, I am however willing to write because You are desirous to hear from me.

My disorder has now begun its ninth week, for it is not yet over. I was last thursday blooded for the fourth time,[2] and

1. *Ante* To Lucy Porter, 2 Mar. 1782.

2. *Ante* To Hester Thrale, 14 Mar. 1782.

have since found myself much relieved, but I am very tender and easily hurt, so that since we parted I have had little comfort, but I hope that the Spring will recover me, and that in the Summer I shall see Lichfield again, for I will not delay my visit another year to the end of autumn.[3]

I have by advertising found poor Mr. Levet's Brothers in Yorkshire, who will take the little that he has, left;[4] it is but little, yet it will be welcome, for I believe they are of very low condition.

To be sick, and to see nothing but sickness and death is but a gloomy state, but I hope better times even in this world will come, and whatever this world may withold or give, we shall be happy in a better state. Pray for me, my dear Lucy.

Make my compliments to Mrs. Cobb, and Miss Adey, and my old friend Hetty Bailey,[5] and to all the Lichfield Ladies. I am, Dear Madam, Yours affectionately,

SAM. JOHNSON

3. SJ did not travel to Lichfield again until his valedictory visit in 1784.

4. *Ante* To Charles Patrick, 14 Feb. 1782.

5. Hester Bayley (d. 1785), daughter of Francis Bayley (?1651–1710) of Lichfield by his second wife Ann Hinckley (1659–?1723) (*Johns. Glean.* IV.105 n. *, XI.34, 232).

Bennet Langton

WEDNESDAY 20 MARCH 1782

MS: Hyde Collection.

ADDRESS: To Captain Langton in Rochester.

POSTMARK: 20 MR.

Dear Sir: Boltcourt, Fleetstreet, March 20, 1782

It is now long since we saw one another, and whatever has been the reason neither You have written to me, nor I to You.[1] To let friendship dye away by negligence and silence is certainly not wise. It is voluntarily to throw away one of the great-

1. *Ante* To Bennet Langton, 16 June 1781.

est comforts of this weary pilgrimage of which when it is, as it must be taken finally away, he that travels on alone will wonder how his esteem could possibly be so little. Do not forget me, You see that I do not forget You. It is pleasing in the silence of solitude to think, that there is One at least however distant of whose benevolence there is little doubt, and whom there is yet hope of seeing again.[2]

Of my Life, from the time when we parted, the history is very mournful. The spring of last year deprived me of Thrale,[3] a man whose eye for fifteen years had scarcely been turned upon me but with respect or tenderness, for such another friend the general course of human things will not suffer man to hope. I passed the Summer at Streatham but there was no Thrale, and having idled away the summer with a weakly body and neglected mind I made a journey to Staffordshire on the edge of winter. The season was dreary, I was sickly, and found the Friends sickly whom I went to see. After a sorrowful sojourn I returned to a habitation possessed for the present by two sick women,[4] where my dear old friend Mr. Levet to whom, as he used to tell me, I owe your acquaintance,[5] died a few weeks ago suddenly in his bed. There passed not, I believe a minute between health and death. At night, as at Mrs. Thrale's I was musing in my chamber, I thought with uncommon earnestness, that however I might alter my mode of life, or whithersoever I might remove, I would endeavour to retain Levet about me, in the morning my servant brought me Word that Levet was called to another state, a state for which, I think, he was not unprepared, for he was very useful to the poor. How much soever I valued him, I now wish that I had valued him more.

2. On 21 Mar. Langton replied, "In your very friendly and kind letter, which is this moment come to hand, you do me justice, I hope, when you express an opinion that I preserve an affectionate Remembrance of you in this long continued time of separation" (MS: Hyde Collection).

3. *Ante* To Joshua Reynolds, 4 Apr. 1781.

4. *Ante* To Thomas Lawrence, 17 Jan. 1782; *Ante* To Hester Thrale, 28 Jan. 1782 and n. 3.

5. *Ante* To Bennet Langton, 6 May 1755, n. 1.

I have myself been ill more than eight weeks of a disorder from which at the expence of about fifty ounces of blood, I hope, I am now recovering.

You, dear Sir, have I hope a more cheerful scene. You see George fond of his book, and the pretty Misses airy and lively, with my own little Jenny equal to the best,[6] and in whatever can contribute to your quiet or pleasure You have Lady Rothes ready to concur. May whatever You enjoy of good be encreased, and whatever You suffer of evil be diminished. I am, Dear Sir, Your humble Servant,

SAM. JOHNSON

6. Of the seven Langton children, SJ omits to mention the two youngest, Peregrine (b. 1780) and Algernon (b. 1781) (Fifer, p. lviii n. 29).

Thomas Lawrence

WEDNESDAY 20 MARCH 1782[1]

MS: Huntington Library.

Nugae anapæsticæ in lecto lusæ.
Medico Æger S.

Nunc mihi facilis
Liberiori
Cursu Spiritus
Itque reditque;
Nunc minus acris
Seu thoracem
Sive abdomen
Laniat tussis;
Tantum prodest
Tempore justo
Secare venam;
Tantum prodest

1. Dated with reference to SJ's prose addendum and his diary entries for 20 Mar. and 21 Mar.: "To morrow—To Mrs. Thrale. . . . I went to Mrs. Thrale" (*Works*, Yale ed. 1.315–6). See *Poems*, pp. 231–32.

Potente succo
Dulce papaver.
Quid nunc superest?
Ut modo tentem
Quantum strictam
Mollia laxent
Balnea pellem,
Cras abiturus
Quo revocârit
Thralia suavis.
Hoc quoque superest
Ut tibi, gentis
Medicæ Princeps
Habeam grates;
Votaque fundam
Ne, quæ prosunt
Omnibus, artes
Domino desint.
Vive valeque.

While I was writing this, I had word brought me, that the bath which I had intended to use, is out of order. Is it worth while to look abroad[2] for another, or shall I stay at home. I go to Streatham to morrow.

2. MS: "only" written above "abroad"

Edmund Hector

THURSDAY 21 MARCH 1782

MS: Hyde Collection.[1]

ADDRESS: To Mr. Hector in Birmingham.

POSTMARK: 21 MR.

1. The MS is mutilated: a strip (7½″ by 1¼″) has been removed along the right-hand margin. A note in JB's hand records, "A part of this letter having been torn off, I have from the evident meaning supplied a few words and half words at the ends and beginnings of lines." As several of these conjectural restorations are manifestly inaccurate, I have not felt bound to adhere to them.

London, Boltcourt,
Fleetstreet, March 21, 1782

Dear Sir:

I hope I do not very grossly flatter m⟨yself if⟩ I imagine that You and dear Mrs. Careless will ⟨be glad⟩ to have some account of me. I performed the Jour⟨ney to Lon⟩don with very little inconvenience,[2] and came ⟨safe to my⟩ habitation, where I found nothing but ill health, ⟨and of con⟩sequence very little cheerfulness. I then went to ⟨visit⟩ a little way into the Country, where I got a ⟨complaint⟩ by a cold which has hung eight weeks upon ⟨me and⟩ from which I am at the expence of fifty ou⟨nces of blood⟩ not yet free. I am afraid that I must owe ⟨my recove⟩ry to warm weather, which seems to make no ⟨advance to⟩wards us.

Such is my health which will, I hope soon grow better. In other respects I have no reason to complain. I know not that I have written any thing more generally commended than the lives of the Poets. And ⟨I foun⟩d the world willing enough to caress me, if my ⟨healt⟩h invited me to be in much company; but this ⟨season⟩ I have been almost wholly employed in nursing ⟨mysel⟩f.

When Summer comes I hope to see You again, ⟨and⟩ will not put off my visit to the end of the year.[3] ⟨I have⟩ lived so long in London, that I did not remember the difference of seasons.

Your health when I saw you was much improved ⟨and⟩ You will be prudent enough not to put it in danger. I hope when we meet again we shall all congratulate each other upon fair prospects of longer life, though what are the pleasures of the longest life when placed in comparison with a happy death? I am, Dear Sir, yours most affectionately,

SAM. JOHNSON

Make my compliments to Mr. Loyd.[4]

Mrs. Thrale has been ill, and though she thinks herself bet-

2. *Ante* To Hester Thrale, 8 Dec. 1781.

3. SJ did not visit Birmingham again until Nov. 1784 (*Life* IV.375).

4. SJ refers to Sampson Lloyd.

ter, in my opinion is not well. Her disorder was a rash, an imperfect struggle for a measley eruption.

James Boswell

THURSDAY 28 MARCH 1782

PRINTED SOURCE: JB's *Life*, 1791, II.422.

Dear Sir, London, March 28, 1782

The pleasure which we used to receive from each other on Good-Friday and Easter-day, we must be this year content to miss.[1] Let us, however, pray for each other, and hope to see one another yet from time to time with mutual delight. My disorder has been a cold, which impeded the organs of respiration, and kept me many weeks in a state of great uneasiness, but by repeated phlebotomy it is now relieved; and next to the recovery of Mrs. Boswell,[2] I flatter myself, that you will rejoice at mine.

What we shall do in the summer it is yet too early to consider.[3] You want to know what you shall do now; I do not think this time of bustle and confusion likely to produce any advantage to you.[4] Every man has those to reward and gratify who have contributed to his advancement. To come hither with such expectations at the expence of borrowed money, which, I find, you know not where to borrow, can hardly be consid-

1. During the period 1772–81, SJ and JB spent seven Easters together (*Life* IV.148 n. 2).

2. Margaret Boswell's consumptive condition had worsened in Dec. 1781 (*Boswell, Laird of Auchinleck*, ed. J. W. Reed and F. A. Pottle, 1977, pp. 414, 416).

3. "I wrote to him at different dates; regretted that I could not come to London this spring, but hoped we should meet somewhere in the summer" (*Life* IV.148).

4. On 20 Mar. Lord North had resigned as a consequence of military defeats in America and the ensuing loss of confidence among his administration's parliamentary supporters (Alan Valentine, *Lord North*, 1967, II.291–316). The fall of North's ministry prompted JB, whose hopes for a political career were easily revived, to request Edmund Burke's assistance in procuring an office (*Later Years*, p. 221; Baker, pp. 114–19).

ered as prudent. I am sorry to find, what your sollicitation seems to imply, that you have already gone the whole length of your credit. This is to set the quiet of your whole life at hazard. If you anticipate your inheritance, you can at last inherit nothing; all that you receive must pay for the past. You must get a place, or pine in penury, with the empty name of a great estate. Poverty, my dear friend, is so great an evil, and pregnant with so much temptation, and so much misery, that I cannot but earnestly enjoin you to avoid it. Live on what you have, live if you can on less; do not borrow either for vanity or pleasure; the vanity will end in shame, and the pleasure in regret; stay therefore at home, till you have saved money for your journey hither.

"The Beauties of Johnson" are said to have got money to the collector;[5] if the "Deformities" have the same success, I shall be still a more extensive benefactor.[6]

Make my compliments to Mrs. Boswell, who is, I hope, reconciled to me; and to the young people, whom I never have offended.

You never told me the success of your plea against the Solicitors.[7] I am, dear Sir, your most affectionate,

SAM. JOHNSON

5. *The Beauties of Johnson: Consisting of Maxims and Observations . . . Accurately extracted from the Works of Dr. Samuel Johnson* was published in Nov. 1781 by George Kearsley (d. 1790). A second volume called "Part II" appeared in 1782 (*Bibliography*, pp. 154–55; *Bibliography Supplement*, pp. 160–61). According to L. F. Powell, "Kearsley clearly did very well out of the publications. The name of the editor is not known" (*Life* IV.500). *Post* To Lancelot St. Albyn, 15 May 1782, n. 4.

6. *The Deformities of Dr. Samuel Johnson* (1782), "a scurrilous and witless compilation," was the work of James Thomson Callender (d. 1803) (*Life* IV.499–500). Originally printed and sold in Edinburgh, it was distributed in London, where a second edition appeared later in the year.

7. After the Society of Procurators (viz. Attornies) changed its name to "Society of Solicitors," a mocking paragraph appeared in the *Edinburgh Gazette*. The Society sued the publisher of the *Gazette*, Thomas Robertson, for "intent to injure." When the Court of Session dismissed the action, the Society petitioned for a review. JB, who was Robertson's advocate, persuaded SJ to dictate an argument on behalf of his client. However, in Nov. 1781 Robertson was fined £5 with costs of suit (*Life* IV.128–31, 497; Reed and Pottle, *Laird of Auchinleck*, 1977, p. 407 n. 5).

Elizabeth Aston & Jane Gastrell

SATURDAY 30 MARCH 1782

MS: Pembroke College, Oxford.

London, Boltcourt,
Fleetstreet, March 30, 1782

Dearest Ladies:

The tenderness expressed in your kind letter makes me think it necessary to tell You that they who are pleased to wish me well, need not be any longer particularly solicitous about me.[1] I prevailed on my Physician to bleed me very copiously, almost against his inclination. However he kept his finger on the pulse of the other hand, and finding that I bore it well, let the vein run on. From that time I have mended, and hope I am now well. I went yesterday to Church without inconvenience, and hope to go to morrow.[2]

Here are great changes in the great World, but I cannot tell You more than You will find in the papers.[3] The Men are got in, whom I have endeavoured to keep out, but I hope they will do better than their predecessors; it will not be easy to do worse.[4]

Spring seems now to approach, and I feel its benefit, which I hope will extend to dear Mrs. Aston.

When Dr. Falconer saw me,[5] I was at home only by accident, for I lived much with Mrs. Thrale and had all the care from her that she could take, or that could be taken. But I have never been ill enough to want attendance, my disorder has

1. On 29 Mar. SJ received "a kind letter from Gastrel" (*Works*, Yale ed. I.320).

2. On 29 Mar. (Good Friday) SJ went twice to Church, but there is no record in his diary of attendance on Easter Day (*Works*, Yale ed. I.320).

3. *Ante* To JB, 28 Mar. 1782, n. 4.

4. Lord North's Ministry, which SJ had actively supported in his political tracts, was replaced by a coalition of the Rockingham and Shelburne groups. Although the two factions agreed that the American War should be ended, they disagreed over the details of a prospective peace. Rockingham died later that year and in Feb. 1783 Shelburne resigned (J. S. Watson, *The Reign of George III*, 1960, pp. 242, 258).

5. James Falconer (1737–1809), D.D., Archdeacon of Derby and Prebendary of Lichfield (*Johns. Glean.* I.14; *Alum. Oxon.* II.ii.445).

been rather tedious than violent, rather irksome than painful. He needed not have made such a tragical represen[ta]tion.

I am now well enough to flatter myself with some hope of pleasure from the Summer.[6] How happy would it be if we could see one another, and be all tolerably well. Let us pray for one another. I am, Dearest Ladies, your most obliged and most humble Servant,

SAM. JOHNSON

6. On 28 Mar. SJ recorded in his diary, "The Weather which now begins to be warm gives me great help" (*Works*, Yale ed. I.318–19).

Frances Reynolds

MONDAY 8 APRIL 1782

MS: Hyde Collection.

ADDRESS: To Mrs. Reynolds.

ENDORSEMENT: Dr. Johnson, Ap. 8th 82.

Dearest Madam: Apr. 8, 1782

Your work is full of very penetrating meditation, and very forcible sentiments.[1] I read it with a full perception of the sublime, with wonder and terrour, but I cannot think of any profit from it; it seems not born to be popular.

Your system of the mental fabrick is exceedingly obscure, and without more attention than will be willingly bestowed, is unintelligible.[2] The Ideas of Beauty will be more easily understood, and are often charming.[3] I was delighted with the different beauty of different ages.[4]

I would make it produce something if I could but I have

1. *Ante* To Frances Reynolds, 21 July 1781 and n. 1.

2. The first chapter of Reynolds's *Enquiry* is called "A Sketch of the Mental System respecting our Perceptions of Taste, etc."

3. SJ refers to chapter II, "On the Origin of our Ideas of Beauty."

4. "As the strongest proof that the moral sense is the governing principle of beauty, we may remark, that the human form, from infancy to old age, has its peculiar beauty annexed to it from the virtue or affection that nature gives it, and which it exhibits in the countenance" (*Enquiry*, p. 22).

indeed no hope. If a Bookseller would buy it at all, as it must be published without a name, he would give nothing for it worth your acceptance. I am, my dearest Dear, Your most humble Servant,

SAM. JOHNSON

Hester Thrale

WEDNESDAY 24 *or* THURSDAY 25 APRIL 1782[1]

MS: Hyde Collection.

Madam: Apr.

I have been very much out of order since You sent me away, but why should I tell You, who do not care, nor desire to know. I dined with Mr. Paradise on Monday, with the Bishop of St. Asaph yesterday,[2] with the Bishop of Chester I dine to day,[3] and with the Academy on Saturday; with Mr. Hoole on monday, and with Mrs. Garrick on Thursday the 2d of May, and then—what care You, *what then.*

The news run, that we have taken seventeen French transports[4]—that Langton's Lady is lying down with her eighth child, all alive[5]—and Mrs. Carter's Miss Sharpe is going to marry a schoolmaster sixty two years old.[6]

1. Dated on internal evidence, particularly the reference to the Academy dinner (which took place on Saturday, 27 Apr.).

2. SJ refers to Jonathan Shipley.

3. SJ refers to Beilby Porteus.

4. During a naval engagement off of Ushant, 20–21 Apr., the British fleet under the command of Admiral Samuel Barrington captured twelve French transports, part of a convoy on its way to Mauritius (Robert Beatson, *Naval and Military Memoirs of Great Britain, from 1727 to 1783*, 1804, v.656–59). The number of transports captured was exaggerated by the press: reports ranged from thirteen to twenty-three.

5. On 7 Aug. Lady Rothes gave birth to Isabella, the Langtons' eighth child and fifth daughter. All their children survived "at least through adolescence" (Fifer, pp. lviii–lix and n. 29).

6. Mary Sharpe (*c.* 1753–1807), daughter and heiress of F. W. Sharpe (1729–71), of Enfield Chase, Hertfordshire, was one of Elizabeth Carter's close friends and companions. In 1782 she married Osmund Beauvoir (*c.* 1720–89), D.D., head-

Do not let Mr. Piozzi nor any body else put me quite out of your head, and do not think that any body will love You like, Your humble servant,

SAM. JOHNSON

master of King's School, Canterbury (Namier and Brooke III.427; Montagu Pennington, *Memoirs of the Life of Mrs. Elizabeth Carter,* 2d ed., 1808, I.5 n. *, 457–58 and n. *; *Alum. Cant.* I.i.120; *GM* 1782, p. 502; *GM* 1807, p. 281).

Francesco Sastres

THURSDAY 25 APRIL 1782[1]

MS: Huntington Library.

ADDRESS: To Mr. Sastres at Mr. —— Bookseller in Mortimer Street, Oxford Road. Apr. 26 morning.

POSTMARKS: PENY POST PAYD, T[emple] FR.

Sir: April 25

I am very much displeased with myself for my negligence on Monday. I had totally forgotten my engagement to You and Mr. ⟨Cirillo⟩[2] for which I desire You to make my apology to Mr. ⟨Cirillo⟩[3], and tell him that if he will give me leave to repay his visit, I will take the first opportunity of waiting on him.[4] I am, Sir, Your most humble servant,

SAM. JOHNSON

1. The postmark indicates that this letter was mailed on a Friday. The two possible years (when 26 Apr. fell on a Friday) are 1776 and 1782. SJ did not become friendly with Sastres until after the latter's move to London in 1777.

2. MS: name heavily deleted

3. MS: name heavily deleted

4. Domenico Cirillo (1739–99), F.R.S., Neapolitan physician and botanist, may have been in London to attend the lectures of his friend and colleague Dr. William Hunter (M. D'Ayala, "Vita di Domenico Cirillo," in *Archivio Storico Italiano* s. 3, 11, 1870, p. 144).

Hester Thrale

TUESDAY 30 APRIL 1782

MS: Hyde Collection.

Dearest Madam: Apr. 30, –82

I have had a fresh cold and been very poorly. But I was yesterday at Mr. Hoole's, where were Miss Reynolds and many others. I am now going to the Club. Since Mrs. Garricks invitation I have a letter from Miss Moore to engage me for the evening.[1] I have an appointment to Miss Monkton,[2] and another with Lady Sheffield at Mrs. Way's.[3]

Two or [three] days ago Mr. Cumberland had his third night, which after all expences put into his own pocket, five pounds.[4] He has lost his plume.

Mrs. Sheridan refused to sing at the Dutchess of Devonshire's request, a song to the Prince of Wales.[5] They pay for the playhouse neither principal nor interest;[6] and poor Garrick's funeral expences are yet unpaid, though the Undertaker is broken.[7] Could You have a better purveyor for a little scan-

1. SJ refers to Hannah More.

2. *Ante* To Hester Thrale, 7 May 1780, n. 8.

3. Elizabeth Way's sister-in-law, Abigail Way (*c.* 1746–93), had married John Baker-Holroyd (1735–1821), first Baron Sheffield (1781), later (1816) Earl of Sheffield.

4. Richard Cumberland's play, *The Walloons*, had premiered at Covent Garden on 20 Apr. Following theatrical custom, the proceeds from the third night went to the author, after house expenses had been deducted. The third performance of *The Walloons*, 25 Apr., brought in £110, but the house charge was £105 (*Lond. Stage*, Part v, I.cxciii, 513, 514).

5. Elizabeth Ann Linley (1754–92), daughter of Thomas Linley (1732–95), composer and music teacher, was a gifted singer; however, when she married the fledgling playwright R. B. Sheridan in 1773 she gave up her career (at Sheridan's insistence).

6. In Jan. 1776 David Garrick sold his share of Drury Lane Theatre to R. B. Sheridan, Thomas Linley, and two other investors (G. W. Stone and G. M. Kahrl, *David Garrick*, 1979, p. 605). By 1780, Sheridan had bought all outstanding shares except those owned by his father-in-law. He then found it increasingly difficult to meet the mortgage payment required by these purchases (Stanley Ayling, *A Portrait of Sheridan*, 1985, p. 52).

7. Garrick's funeral (1 Feb. 1779) cost £1,500. The undertaker had still not

dal? But I wish, I was at Streatham. I beg Miss to come early, and I may perhaps reward You with more mischief. I am, Dearest and dearest Lady, Your most humble servant,

SAM. JOHNSON

received payment (Carola Oman, *David Garrick*, 1958, p. 376; cf. *Ante* To Hester Thrale, 27 Oct. 1781 and n. 5).

Thomas Lawrence

WEDNESDAY 1 MAY 1782

MS: Huntington Library.
ADDRESS: To Dr. Laurence.

T. Laurentio Medico. S. Maijs calendis, 1782

Novum frigus, nova tussis, nova spirandi difficultas, novam sanguinosi missionem suadent, quam tamen te inconsulto nolim fieri. Ad te venire vix possum, nec est cur ad me venias. Licere vel non licere uno verbo dicendum est; cætera mihi et Holdero reliqueris. Si per te licet, imperetur nuncio Holderum ad me deducere.

Postquam tu discesseris quo me vertam?[1]

1. Lawrence had already announced his intention to retire to Canterbury later that year.

Hester Thrale

THURSDAY 2 MAY 1782

PRINTED SOURCE: Chapman II.479.
ADDRESS: To Mrs. Thrale.

Dear Madam: May 2—82

No more scandal,[1] but all sorrow. I am very bad. Last night I

1. *Ante* To Hester Thrale, 30 Apr. 1782.

bled 16 ounces. To day more is talked of. I could not go to Mrs. Garrick.[2] Lady Frances not at home.[3] Whether I can go with you to morrow, it is to morrow that must tell. Keep well your dear self. I am, Madam, Your most etc.

SAM. JOHNSON

2. *Ante* To Hester Thrale, 24 or 25 Apr. 1782.

3. It is likely that SJ refers to Lady Frances Montagu (d. 1788), daughter of George Montagu (d. 1739), first Earl of Halifax, and wife (m. 1739) of Sir Roger Burgoyne (*c.* 1710–80), sixth Bt. (*Walpole's Correspondence*, Yale ed. x.352, Table II). In 1782 Lady Frances, whom Hester Thrale had known since childhood, was trying to promote a marriage with her relation, John Montagu (1743–1814), Viscount Hinchingbrooke (*Thraliana* I.286, 555).

Hester Thrale

SATURDAY 4 MAY 1782

MS: Mason City Public Library, Iowa.

Dearest Lady: May 4, —82

I had a quiet night without opium but am not better.[1] Something more is to be done, and I purpose to see Dr. Laurence as soon as I can, and then I hope to be well, and come soon to Streatham. Pray remember me to Miss, if she has not turned me quite out of her heart. I am, Madam, Your most humble servant,

SAM. JOHNSON

1. *Ante* To Hester Thrale, 2 May 1782.

Elizabeth Way

SATURDAY 4 MAY 1782

PRINTED SOURCE: Chapman III.338–39.

Dear Madam: May 4—82

I am compelled by a very frequent and violent cough, with an oppressive and distresful difficulty of breathing to delay the pleasure which I promised myself from your company and that of Lady Sheffield.[1] I am indeed very much disordered, as I have been for several days, but for a time I expected to grow speedily well, and was not in haste to send you notice. I am, Dear Madam, Your most humble servant,

SAM. JOHNSON

1. *Ante* To Hester Thrale, 30 Apr. 1782 and n. 3.

Elizabeth Way

MONDAY 6 MAY 1782

PRINTED SOURCE: Chapman III.339.

May 6—82

Mr. Johnson is truly sensible of dear Mrs. Way's kindness. He hopes that he is now better, but he is still very much disordered.[1]

1. *Ante* To Elizabeth Way, 4 May 1782.

John Perkins

TUESDAY 7 MAY 1782

MS: Hyde Collection.

Dear Sir: May 7, 1782

Having exhausted my coal cellar, I am induced by the present high price of coals,[1] to solicite from You and the other Gentlemen a favour formerly done me by Mr. Thrale, of sending me

1. On 5 May Horace Walpole reported to Sir Horace Mann: "Never was such a spring! After deluges of rain, we have had an east wind that has half starved London, as a fleet of colliers cannot get in; coals were sold yesterday at seven guineas a chaldron: nor is there an entire leaf yet on any tree" (*Walpole's Correspondence*, Yale ed. XXV.274). According to newspaper reports, coals on 4 May cost six pounds per chaldron.

from your store two chaldrons,[2] for which I will pay you. Be pleased to communicate this request with my respects to Mr. Barclay.[3] I am, Sir, Your most humble Servant,

SAM. JOHNSON

2. *chaldron*: "a dry English measure of coals, consisting of thirty six bushels heaped up" (SJ's *Dictionary*).

3. SJ refers to Robert Barclay.

Hester Thrale

TUESDAY 7 MAY 1782

MS: Rylands Library.
ADDRESS: To Mrs. Thrale.

Dear Madam: May 7, 1782

When You left me You knew how I was, and, I hope, You do not think that by leaving me You made me better. I took scarcely any thing but physick, and was troubled with a very frequent and violent cough, my lungs however seem to be set at ease.[1] Barley sugar did me some good, but I took diacodium[2] which gave me quiet but hindred sleep. I think myself upon the whole so much better, that I hope to be soon *sur le pavè*. And then will I try to find Streatham, and then—my dearest Lady—I hope to be better than I have lately been, though I cannot be more, Dear Madam, Your most humble servant,

SAM. JOHNSON

1. *Ante* To Hester Thrale, 30 Apr. 1782.

2. *Ante* To Hester Thrale, 17 Feb. 1782, n. 1.

Hester Thrale

WEDNESDAY 8 MAY 1782

MS: Hyde Collection.
ADDRESS: To Mrs. Thrale.

Madam: May 8, 82

Yesterday I was all so bonny, as who but me?[1] At night my cough drove me to diacodium, and this morning I suspect that diacodium will drive me to sleep in the chair. Breath however is better, and I shall try to escape the other bleeding, for I am of the Chymical sect, which holds phlebotomy in abhorrence.[2]

But it is not plenty nor diminution of blood that can make me more or less, my dearest dear Lady, Your most humble servant,

SAM. JOHNSON

I send my compliments to my dear Queeny.

1. *Ante* To Hester Thrale, 7 May 1782.

2. John Wiltshire suggests that "Johnson is parodying the mystical rhetoric of J.-B. van Helmont, a leader of the iatrochemical school of the seventeenth century" and the author of *Oriatrike* (1662) (Wiltshire, *Samuel Johnson in the Medical World*, 1991, p. 67).

Hester Thrale

THURSDAY 9 MAY 1782

MS: Rylands Library.
ADDRESS: To Mrs. Thrale.

Dearest Lady: May 9, 1782

Since bleeding and a weak opiate I am more at ease,[1] and my present Scheme is to go to the warm bath to morrow, and to Stretham on Saturday.[2]

1. *Ante* To Hester Thrale, 8 May 1782.

2. Hester Thrale conveyed SJ to Streatham on 11 May (*Thraliana* 1.535).

Poor Dr. Laurence followed me home in a chair. He is very bad,[3] but then he can tell of somebody worse.

Keep well, my dearest Lady. I am, etc.

SAM. JOHNSON

3. Lawrence had suffered a stroke, and was "dead on one Side" (*Thraliana* I.535). *Post* To Elizabeth Lawrence, 9 June 1782; 2 July 1782; *Post* To John Taylor, 3 Aug. 1782.

Thomas Lawrence

MID-MAY 1782[1]

MS: Huntington Library.

T. Laurentio Medico. S.

Novum nova mala poscunt auxilium.[2] Post sanguinem tuo jussu nuper missum, meliorem valetudinem sperare coepi; pectus interquievit, spirandique vicibus minus impeditis, omnia erant paulo sedatiora.

Nunc vero omnia retro feruntur. Veteres me morbi exagitant, mitiores forsan quam prius, tales tamen ut ijs ferendis vix sim par. Somnus brevis, interruptus, incertus. Somnolentia tamen gravissima. Mihi quidem iterum videtur a chirurgo remedium petendum. Tu vero, Vir doctissime judicabis.

1. Dated in relation to To Thomas Lawrence, 1 May 1782; To Hester Thrale, 9 May 1782.

2. MS: "auxilia"

Lancelot St. Albyn[1]

WEDNESDAY 15 MAY 1782

PRINTED SOURCE: *GM* 1786, p. 94. Collated with text in JB's *Life*, 1791, II.423.

1. The Rev. Lancelot St. Albyn (*c*. 1722–91), Rector of Paracombe, Devon, and Vicar of Wembdon, Somerset (*GM* 1791, p. 94; *Alum. Oxon.* II.iv.1242; *Life* VI.345; Correspondence between J. M. Osborn and R. G. Sawyer, Osborn Collection, Beinecke Library).

Sir, May 15, 1782

Being now in the country in a state of recovery,[2] as I hope, from a very oppressive disorder, I cannot neglect the acknowledgement of your Christian letter.[3] The book, called "The Beauties of J—n," is the production of I know not whom;[4] I never saw it but by casual inspection, and considered myself as utterly disengaged from its consequences. Of the passage you mention I remember some notice in some paper; but, knowing that it must be misrepresented, I thought of it no more, nor do I now know[5] where to find it in my own books. I am accustomed to think little of newspapers; but an opinion so weighty and serious as yours has determined me to do, what I should, without your seasonable admonition, have omitted; and I will direct my thought to be shewn in its true state. If I could find the passage, I would direct you to it. I suppose the tenor[6] is this: "Acute diseases are the immediate and inevitable strokes of Heaven; but of them the pain is short, and the conclusion speedy: chronical disorders, by which we are suspended in tedious torture between life and death, are commonly the effect of our own misconduct and intemperance. To die,"[7] etc. This, Sir, you see is all true, and all blameless. I hope, some

2. *Ante* To Hester Thrale, 7 May 1782.

3. On 4 May 1782 St. Albyn had written SJ "that in 'The Morning Chronicle' [12 Dec. 1781], a passage in 'The Beauties of Johnson,' article DEATH, had been pointed out as supposed by some readers to recommend suicide"; St. Albyn suggested to SJ "that such an erroneous notion of any sentence in the writings of an acknowledged friend of religion and virtue, should not pass uncontradicted" (*Life* IV.149–50; *GM* 1786, pp. 93–94). The passage in question occurs in *Rambler* No. 85. See below, n. 7.

4. A. T. Hazen argues that *The Beauties of Johnson*, published by George Kearsley, was compiled by William Cooke (Hazen, "The *Beauties of Johnson*," *Modern Philology* 35, 1938, pp. 289–95).

5. "nor do I know" (JB's *Life*, 1791)

6. "tenour" (JB's *Life*, 1791)

7. "Exercise cannot secure us from that dissolution to which we are decreed; but while the soul and body continue united, it can make the association pleasing and give probable hopes that they shall be disjoined by an easy separation. It was a principle among the ancients, that acute diseases are from heaven, and chronical from ourselves; the dart of death indeed falls from heaven, but we poison it by our own misconduct; to die is the fate of man, but to die with lingering anguish is generally his folly" (*Works*, Yale ed. IV.83).

time in the next week, to have all rectified.[8] My health has been lately much shaken; if you favour this with any answer, it will be a comfort to me to know that I have your prayers. I am, Sir, your most humble servant,[9]

SAM. JOHNSON

8. The *Morning Chronicle*, 29 May 1782, reprinted the entire paragraph so "that its true meaning may appear, which is not to recommend suicide but exercise" (*GM* 1786, pp. 94–95). *Post* To The Editor of the *Morning Chronicle*, 27 May 1782.

9. "I am, etc." (JB's *Life*, 1791)

George Kearsley

MONDAY 20 MAY 1782

MS: Beinecke Library. The transcript (in the hand of JB) used as copy for JB's *Life*.

May 20, 1782

Mr. Johnson sends compliments to Mr. Kearsley, and begs the favour of seeing him as soon as he can. Mr. Kearsley is desired to bring with him the last edition of what he has honoured with the name of *Beauties*.[1]

1. *Ante* To Unidentified Correspondent, 15 Oct. 1781, n. 1.

Hester Thrale

TUESDAY 21 MAY 1782

MS: Hyde Collection.

Dear Madam: May 21, 1782

My disorder is, I think, conquered, but it has with the help of its remedies left me in dismal dejection.[1] I have however not totally succumbed, for yesterday I visited Mesdames Reynolds, Horneck, Cholmondely, Biron. It is kind in Miss to come for

1. *Ante* To Hester Thrale, 2 May 1782; 7 May 1782; 8 May 1782; 9 May 1782.

me. I have seen poor dear Laurence on Sunday and to day, without hope.[2] Heberden attends him. Such is this World. I am, Madam, your most etc.

SAM. JOHNSON

2. *Ante* To Hester Thrale, 9 May 1782 and n. 3.

Elizabeth Lawrence[1]

WEDNESDAY 22 MAY 1782

MS: Dennis Katz.

ADDRESS: To Miss Eliz. Laurence.

Madam: May 22, 1782

At a visit yesterday, for want of a fire I caught a fresh cold. I have got no other symptom than a cough, and that not violent, my perspiration is free. Please to ask the dear Doctor (for whom I pray)[2] whether it be fit to still the cough now in its beginning with opium, and send his answer in writing by this Messenger, if it be convenient.

I wish You would write out for me sometime those short lines which I sent to the Doctor, for I have forgotten some of them.[3]

But of this there is no great haste. I am, Madam, Your most humble servant,

SAM. JOHNSON

1. Elizabeth Lawrence (d. 1790), eldest daughter of Dr. Thomas Lawrence (*GM* 1790, p. 478).

2. *Ante* To Hester Thrale, 9 May 1782 and n. 3.

3. *Ante* To Thomas Lawrence, 20 Mar. 1782.

Hester Thrale

SUNDAY 26 MAY 1782[1]

1. SJ's allusion to the influenza epidemic (see below, n. 2), supplemented by his reference to "Sir Richard" Jebb (created Bt. in 1778), establishes 1782 as the only fully credible date.

To HESTER THRALE, 26 *May* 1782

MS: Houghton Library.
ADDRESS: To Mrs. Thrale.

Madam: May 26

When I came home I took physick with good success. In the afternoon came Mr. Langton, whose company was useful. In the Evening came Sir Richard, but directed nothing. I took some buns and negus, and had rather a restless night, but am better today. I am comforted to find that my disorder is epidemical.[2] Pray come soon. I am, Dearest Lady, your most etc.

SAM. JOHNSON

2. The influenza epidemic that had swept through London peaked the last week of May (Theophilus Thompson, *Annals of Influenza*, 1852, pp. 118–20). On 30 May Hester Thrale recorded: "now here is an epidemic Disease which the Drs. not knowing what to call—call an *Influenza*; but every body is sick; Colds, Coughs, and oppression of the Breath seize the stoutest; and Johnson, who besides all this labours under a horribly spasmodick Affection of the Heart, will have much ado to force through it with all his Strength" (*Thraliana* 1.537).

THE EDITOR OF The *Morning Chronicle* MONDAY 27 MAY 1782

PRINTED SOURCE: Chapman II.484–85.

Sir: May 27, 1782

You are right in your opinion that the misrepresentation of the passage about Death should be rectified in the paper in which it appeared;[1] and you are right in your recollection of the paper. Therefore I wish it may now be done.[2]

I have enclosed the letter which I received about it,[3] that you may read it, and return it to me.

1. *Ante* To Lancelot St. Albyn, 15 May 1782, n. 3.
2. *Ante* To Lancelot St. Albyn, 15 May 1782, n. 7.
3. *Ante* To Lancelot St. Albyn, 15 May 1782.

To THE EDITOR OF THE *Morning Chronicle*, 27 *May* 1782

I have been for a long time very ill. I am, Sir, Your humble Servant,

SAM. JOHNSON

Unidentified Correspondent

TUESDAY 28 MAY 1782

PRINTED SOURCE: Hill II.254.

Sir, May 28, 1782

I have collected the dates of our business. I shall be at home to-morrow morning. I am not well, but hope that you are better. Please to make compliments to all the Company of Wednesday. I am, dear Sir, Your most, etc.,

SAM. JOHNSON

James Boswell

MONDAY 3 JUNE 1782

PRINTED SOURCE: JB's *Life*, 1791, II.424–25.

Dear Sir, London, June 3, 1782

The earnestness and tenderness of your letter is such, that I cannot think myself shewing it more respect than it claims by sitting down to answer it the day on which I received it.[1]

This year has afflicted me with a very irksome and severe disorder. My respiration has been much impeded, and much blood has been taken away. I am now harrassed by a catarrhous cough, from which my purpose is to seek relief by change of air; and I am, therefore, preparing to go to Oxford.[2]

Whether I did right in dissuading you from coming to Lon-

1. On 28 May JB had written "in most sincere concern for his illness" (Register of Letters, MS: Beinecke Library).

2. SJ left for Oxford on 10 June and returned on the 19th (*Post* To Sir Richard Jebb, 11 June 1782; *Post* To Hester Thrale, 11 June 1782; 17 June 1782).

don this spring, I will not determine.[3] You have not lost much by missing my company; I have scarcely been well for a single week. I might have received comfort from your kindness; but you would have seen me afflicted, and, perhaps, found me peevish. Whatever might have been your pleasure or mine, I know not how I could have honestly advised you to come hither with borrowed money. Do not accustom yourself to consider debt only as an inconvenience: you will find it a calamity. Poverty takes away so many means of doing good, and produces so much inability to resist evil, both natural and moral, that it is by all virtuous means to be avoided. Consider a man whose fortune is very narrow; whatever be his rank by birth, or whatever his reputation by intellectual excellence, what good can he do? or what evil can he prevent? That he cannot help the needy is evident, he has nothing to spare. But, perhaps, his advice or admonition may be useful. His poverty will destroy his influence: many more can find that he is poor, than that he is wise; and few will reverence the understanding that is of so little advantage to its owner. I say nothing of the personal wretchedness of a debtor, which, however, has passed into a proverb.[4] Of riches, it is not necessary to write the praise. Let it, however, be remembered, that he who has money to spare, has it always in his power to benefit others; and of such power a good man must always be desirous.

I am pleased with your account of Easter.[5] We shall meet, I hope, in autumn,[6] both well and both chearful; and part each the better for the other's company.

Make my compliments to Mrs. Boswell, and to the young charmers. I am, etc.

SAM. JOHNSON

3. *Ante* To JB, 28 Mar. 1782.

4. "I never retired to rest, without feeling the justness of the Spanish proverb, 'Let him who sleeps too much, borrow the pillow of a debtor'" (*Adventurer* No. 41, *Works*, Yale ed. II.354 and n. 3).

5. JB had attended Easter services "in the Church-of-England chapel at Edinburgh" (*Life* IV.152 n. 3).

6. JB did not come to London until Mar. 1783 (*Life* IV.164).

Mary Prowse

TUESDAY 4 JUNE 1782

MS: Hyde Collection.

ENDORSEMENT: Dr. Johnson's receipt for Miss Hearnes 10£. June 1782.

Madam: Boltcourt, Fleetstreet, June 4, 1782

I have thus long omitted the acknowlegement of your letter and bill,[1] not by levity or negligence, but under the pressure of ilness long continued and very distresful. I am now better but yet so far from health, that I have been purposing to seek relief from change of air, by a journey to Oxford.[2]

Your health, Madam, I hope, allows you the full enjoyment of this blooming season, I have yet been able to derive little pleasure from verdure or from fragrance. I am, Madam, Your most humble Servant,

SAM. JOHNSON

1. *Ante* To Mary Prowse, 7 May 1781 and n. 4.

2. *Ante* To JB, 3 June 1782 and n. 2.

Hester Thrale

TUESDAY 4 JUNE 1782

MS: Hyde Collection.

Madam: June 4, 1782, London

Wisely was it said by him who said it first, that this world is all ups and downs. You know, dearest Lady, that when I pressed your hand at parting, I was rather down.[1] When I came hither, I ate my dinner well, but was so harrassed by the cough that Mr. Strahan said it was an extremity which he could not have believed without the sensible and true avouch of his own observation.[2] I was indeed almost sinking under it, when Mrs.

1. SJ returned to London from Streatham 18 May (*Works*, Yale ed. I.321).

2. "I might not this believe / Without the sensible and true avouch / Of mine own eyes" (*Hamlet* I.i.59–61).

Williams happened to cry out that such a cough should be stilled by opium or any means. I took yesterday half an ounce of bark and know not whether opium would not counteract it, but remembering[3] no prohibition in the medical books, and knowing that to quiet the cough with opium was one of Laurence's last orders, I took two grains which gave me not sleep indeed, but rest, and that rest has given me strength and courage.

This morning to my bedside came dear Sir Richard.[4] I told him of the opium, and he approved it, and told me, if I went to Oxford which he rather advised,[5] that I should strengthen the constitution by the bark, tame the cough with opium, keep the body open,[6] and support myself by liberal nutriment.

As to the journey I know not that it will be necessary. Desine mollium tandem querelarum[7]—This day I dined upon Skate, pudding, Goose, and your asparagus, and could have eaten more, but was prudent.

Pray for me, dear Madam, I hope the tide has turned. The change that I feel is more than I durst have hoped, or[8] than I thought possible, but there has yet not passed a whole day, and I may rejoice perhaps too soon. Come and see me, and when You think best upon due consideration take me away. I am, Dear Madam, your most humble servant,

SAM. JOHNSON

3. MS: "remembering" altered from "remember"

4. SJ refers to Sir Richard Jebb.

5. *Ante* To JB, 3 June 1782 and n. 2.

6. "To day [I] have taken a laxative, as Sir Richard directed" (*Post* To Hester Thrale, 5 June 1782).

7. *desine mollium tandem querellarum*: "Cease at length thy weak laments" (Horace, *Odes* II.ix.17–18, trans. C. E. Bennett, Loeb ed.).

8. MS: "at" del. before "or"

Hester Thrale

WEDNESDAY 5 JUNE 1782

MS: Houghton Library.

Dear Madam: London, June 5, 1782

Though Streatham supplies many things[1] which I know not where to find in any other place, you well know it does not answer to change of air. I was yesterday in hope that the poppy would be equivalent to every thing, but having taken it two nights together, I begin to be afraid of it.[2] I have however recovered my appetite and much of my strength. I took my ounce of bark, but to day have taken a laxative, as Sir Richard directed.[3]

I have no mind of a journey but know not whether I can escape it.[4] I shall let you know how we go on. I dined to day on Veal pie. I am, Madam, Your most humble etc.

SAM. JOHNSON

Compliments to dear Queeny Love.

1. MS: "th superimposed upon "gr"

2. "I . . . tried to ease the oppression of my breast by frequent opiates, which kept me waking in the night, and drowsy the next day, and subjected me to the tyranny of vain imaginations" (*Works*, Yale ed. I.312).

3. *Ante* To Hester Thrale, 4 June 1782.

4. *Ante* To JB, 3 June 1782 and n. 2; *Ante* To Hester Thrale, 4 June 1782.

Frances Burney

FRIDAY 7 JUNE 1782

MS: Estate of Sir John Colville.

Madam: June 7, 1782, Boltcourt, Fleetstreet

For some time past there has been often at my House, a young Man whose name is Mara; He is without employment or provision, and therefore is very desirous of going to sea, as a servant of the Captain. His behaviour is without reproach, he is of pleasing manners, and regular conduct, and capable, I suppose, of any business included in cle[r]kship. I have taken an interest in his success, and beg of you, dear Madam, to engage him to Captain Burney, before his number is full.[1] Do for us what you can. I am, Madam, Your most humble Servant,

SAM. JOHNSON

1. According to the muster rolls of Burney's ship, the H.M.S. *Bristol,* a "John Mara" enlisted on 10 June 1782 (P.R.O. MS: Adm. 36: 10469). *Post* To James Burney, 24 June 1782.

Hester Thrale

FRIDAY 7 JUNE 1782

MS: Rylands Library.
ADDRESS: To Mrs. Thrale.

Dear Madam: London, June 7, 1782

I had such a night, that there are few better. My cough is very much abated, but now I am risen, I feel little alacrity, but that may return. I took physick yesterday of the strongest sort, which made me uneasy, but, I think, did me good.

I have no mind of a journey, and had rather not go.[1] If You please to call on me, You will find me, Madam, Your most humble Servant,

SAM. JOHNSON

1. *Ante* To JB, 3 June 1782 and n. 2.

Hester Thrale

SATURDAY 8 JUNE 1782

MS: Houghton Library.
ADDRESS: To Mrs. Thrale.

Dear Madam: Saturday, July[1] 8, 1782

Perhaps some of your people may call to morrow. I have this

1. MS: "July" in error for "June"

day taken a passage to Oxford for Monday. Not to frisk as you express it with very unfeeling irony, but to catch at the hope of better health. The change of place may do something. To leave[2] the house where so much has been suffered affords some pleasure. When I write to You, write to me again and let me have the pleasure of knowing that I am still considered as, Madam, Your most humble servant,

SAM. JOHNSON

2. MS: "leave" superimposed upon undeciphered erasure

Elizabeth Lawrence

SUNDAY 9 JUNE 1782

MS: Hyde Collection.

ADDRESS: To Miss E. Laurence.

Madam: June 9, 1782

Be pleased to let me know the State, whatever it be, of dear Dr. Laurence.[1]

Is he attended by any Clergyman?

Let him know, if it be proper, that I have been much dejected by this long ilness, but think myself slowly recovering. I am going to morrow to Oxford, to try change of place. The Doctor has my prayers, and I desire his. I am, Madam, Your most humble Servant,

SAM. JOHNSON

1. *Ante* To Hester Thrale, 9 May 1782 and n. 3.

Sir Richard Jebb

TUESDAY 11 JUNE 1782

PRINTED SOURCE: Chapman II.491–92.

ADDRESS: To Sir Richard Jebb, Bart., in Westminster.

POSTMARK: 12 IV.

June 11, 1782,
Dear Sir: Oxford, at Mr. Parker's, Bookseller

I came to Oxford yesterday without fatigue in the common coach. I have now more appetite than I venture to gratify, and sleep with very little inconvenience. My cough though very much abated is still troublesome, and takes every opportunity of an open door or a cold blast, to put my breast in motion. If I have any wrong tendency it is to costiveness, though I do not now take the bark, but this indisposition is easily counteracted. My breath is still short and laborious.

This account, dear Sir, I thought it proper to give You, because I have sufficient reason for believing that you have some kindness for me, for which I beg you to accept my sincere thanks. I am, Dear Sir, Your obliged humble servant,

SAM. JOHNSON

Hester Thrale

TUESDAY 11 JUNE 1782

PRINTED SOURCE: Piozzi, *Letters* II.261–62.

Dear Madam, Oxford, June 11, 1783[1]

Yesterday I came to Oxford without fatigue or inconvenience. I read in the coach before dinner. I dined moderately, and slept well; but find my breath not free this morning.

Dr. Edwards, to whom I wrote word of my purpose to come, has defeated his own kindness by its excess. He has gone out of his own rooms for my reception, and therefore I cannot decently stay long, unless I can change my abode, which it will not be very easy to do: nor do I know what attractions I shall find here. Here is Miss Moore at Dr. Adams's, with whom I

1. The subject of the letter (SJ's trip to Oxford and his reception there) makes it clear that "1783" is an error for "1782." Cf. *Ante* To Sir Richard Jebb, 11 June 1782.

shall dine to-morrow.[2] Of my adventures and observations I shall inform you, and beg you to write to me at Mr. Parker's bookseller.

I hope Queeney has got rid of her influenza, and that you escape it. If I had Queeney here, how would I shew her all the places. I hope, however, I shall not want company in my stay here. I am, Dear Madam, Your, etc.

2. "On Wednesday we had here a delightful blue-stocking party. Dr. and Mrs. Kennicott and Miss [Hannah] More, Dr. Johnson, Mr. Henderson, Mr. Davis of Baliol, &c. dined here. . . . Poor Dr. Johnson is in very bad health, but he exerted himself as much as he could; and, being very fond of Miss More, he talked a good deal. . . . He took great delight in shewing Miss More every part of Pembroke College" (Sarah Adams to Mrs. Henry Jones, 14 June 1782, *GM* 1840, p. 17).

Hester Thrale

WEDNESDAY 12 JUNE 1782

MS: Beinecke Library.

Dear Madam: Oxford, June 12, 1782

My Letter was perhaps peevish, but it was not unkind,[1] I should have cared little about a wanton expression, if there had been no kindness.

I find no particular salubrity in this air, my respiration is very laborious. My Appetite is good and my sleep commonly long and quiet. But a very little motion disables me.

I dine to day with Dr. Adams, and to morrow with Dr. Wetherel, and yesterday Dr. Edwards invited some Men from Exeter College whom I liked very well. These variations of company help the mind, though they cannot do much for the body. But the body receives some help from a cheerful mind.

Keep up some kindness for me; when I am with you again, I hope to be less burdensome, by being less sick. I am, Dearest Lady, Your most humble servant,

SAM. JOHNSON

1. *Ante* To Hester Thrale, 8 June 1782.

Elizabeth Way

WEDNESDAY 12 JUNE 1782

PRINTED SOURCE: Chapman III.339.
ADDRESS: To Mrs. Way at the Southsea House, London.
POSTMARK: I–IV.

Dear Madam: Oxford, June 12, 1782

I am much indebted to You for your attention to my health, which is not yet as I wish it. I cannot perceive that I have yet had any other advantage from change of place but the amusement of the journey, and of new company,[1] and believe that my stay here will not be very long.[2] I shall try however for a few days what advantage I can find, and when I return shall perhaps have the gratification of seeing You better. I am, dear Madam, Your most humble Servant,

SAM. JOHNSON

1. *Ante* To Hester Thrale, 12 June 1782.
2. *Post* To Hester Thrale, 17 June 1782.

John Taylor

THURSDAY 13 JUNE 1782

MS: Rare Book and Manuscript Library, Columbia University (Brander Mathews Dramatic Museum Collection).

Dear Sir: [Oxford] June 13, 1782

You will receive in this cover[1] some letters written to me by Miss Collier, to which I really know not what answer to make. The Children are my near relations, and I would not spare any thing that could properly be done. I have not written to her, because I know not if I fully understand the business, and because I was afraid lest Mr. Flint should be made more their enemy by our correspondence.[2] I would write to Mr. Flint but

1. MS: "this cover" written above "another paper" del.
2. *Ante* To John Taylor, 2 Mar. 1782 and n. 1.

that I know not well what topicks to urge. Consider the matter and tell me what to do as soon as You can. I am, Dear Sir, Your most etc.

SAM. JOHNSON

Hester Thrale

THURSDAY 13 JUNE 1782

MS: Johnson House, London.

ADDRESS: To Mrs. Thrale at Streatham, Surry.

POSTMARKS: OXFORD, 14 IV.

Dear Madam: Oxford, June 13, 1782

Yesterday a little physick drove away a great part of my cough, but I am still very much obstructed in my respiration and so soon tired with walking that I have hardly ventured one unnecessary step. Of my long ilness much more than this does not remain, but this is very burthensome. I sleep pretty well, and have appetite enough, but I cheat it with fish.

Yesterday I dined at Dr. Adams's with Miss Moore, and other personages of eminence.[1] To day I am going to Dr. Wetherel, and thus day goes after day, not wholly without amusement.

I think not to stay here long;[2] Till I am better it is not prudent to sit long in the libraries, for the weather is yet so cold, that in the penury of fuel for which we think ourselves very unhappy, I have yet met with none so frugal as to sit without fire.[3] I am, Madam, Your most humble servant,

SAM. JOHNSON

Poor Davies complained that he had not received his money for Boyle.[4]

1. *Ante* To Hester Thrale, 11 June 1782 and n. 2.
2. *Post* To Hester Thrale, 17 June 1782.
3. *Ante* To John Perkins, 7 May 1782, n. 1.
4. SJ had recently been assisting Thomas Davies by securing buyers for his

books (*Works*, Yale ed. I.316, 318). Apparently Hester Thrale had ordered a work by Robert Boyle—perhaps his *Considerations touching the Usefulness of Experimental Natural Philosophy* (1664), to which H. L. Piozzi alludes (*Thraliana* II.830).

Hester Thrale

MONDAY 17 JUNE 1782

MS: Hyde Collection.

ADDRESS: To Mrs. Thrale at Streatham, Surry.

POSTMARKS: OXFORD, 18 IV, [Undeciphered].

Dear Madam: Oxford, June 17, 1782

I have found no sudden alteration or amendment, but I am grown better by degrees. My cough is not now very troublesome to myself nor I hope to others; my breath is still short and encumbred; I do not sleep well, but I lie easy. By change of place, succession of company, and necessity of talking, much of the terrour that had seized me, seems to be dispelled.

Oxford has done, I think, what for the present it can do, and I am going slyly to take a place in the coach for wednesday, and on Thursday You or my sweet Queeney will fetch me on Thursday, and see what You can make of me.

To day I am going to dine with Dr. Wheeler and to morrow Dr. Edwards has invited Miss Adams,[1] and Miss Moore.[2] Yesterday I went with Dr. Edwards to his living.[3] He has really done all that he could do for my relief or entertainment,[4] and

1. Sarah Adams (1746–1804), the only surviving child of William Adams, later (1788) married Benjamin Hyett (1743–1810), of Painswick House, Gloucestershire (*Johns. Glean.* V.181).

2. SJ refers to Hannah More (*Ante* To Hester Thrale, 11 June 1782 and n. 2).

3. Edwards was Rector of Besselsleigh, North Berkshire, about five miles southwest of Oxford.

4. "The [Jesus College] Battel-book for 1784 shows that the average battels or weekly bills were not much over 10*s*. Johnson was there part of two weeks. In the week beginning June 7 the Vice-Principal's battels rose to £2 16*s*. 3*d*., and in the next week to £4 1*s*." (Hill II.261 n. 1).

really drives me away by doing too much. I am, Madam, Your most obedient Servant,

SAM. JOHNSON

When I come back to retirement, it will be great charity in You to let me come back to something else.

James Burney

MONDAY 24 JUNE 1782

MS: Pierpont Morgan Library.

Sir: London, June 24, 1782

The Bearer is the young Man whom I have taken the liberty of recommending to your kindness.[1] He is the son of a Clergyman very regular in his conduct, and decent in his manners. He will serve You I hope with diligence and fidelity, and I shall think myself favoured by your acceptance of his endeavours.

I congratulate You, Sir, upon your fine ship,[2] and sincerely wish You all possible good. You have suffered hardships sufficient, and I hope the time of recompense is not far distant. I am, Sir, Your most humble Servant,

SAM. JOHNSON

1. *Ante* To Frances Burney, 7 June 1782 and n. 1.
2. *Ante* To Hester Thrale, 14 Nov. 1781, n. 2.

William Langley

MONDAY 24 JUNE 1782

PRINTED SOURCE: *GM* 1878, p. 700. A letter from William Langley to SJ, 14 Feb. 1783.

[I have heard very little of Miss Colliers since I rec'd your letter of the 24th of June last, in which you say] that Dr. Taylor has engaged in their affair, and therefore it will be fit to let him act alone. [It certainly might have been settled some months past with equal facility as it is likely to be now or at any time hereafter.][1]

1. *Ante* To John Taylor, 2 Mar. 1782 and n. 1.

Elizabeth Lawrence

TUESDAY 2 JULY 1782

MS: Hyde Collection.

Madam: London, July 2, 1782

My remembrance of the kindness with which I was always treated by dear Dr. Laurence, and of the pleasure which his company has so often afforded me, makes me desirous of knowing from time to time the state of his health and of his mind.[1] That such a mind should be so eclipsed produces very melancholy reflections. Perhaps he may have some happier intervals. Let me know how he goes forward, and let him know, if You can, with how much solicitude[2] I enquire after him, and with how much earnestness I wish him better.

Be pleased to make my compliments to all the Ladies. I am, Madam, Your most humble servant,

SAM. JOHNSON

1. *Ante* To Hester Thrale, 9 May 1782 and n. 3.
2. MS: "citude" repeated as catchword

Richard Chambers[1]

MONDAY 8 JULY 1782

MS: Hyde Collection.

ADDRESS: To Mr. R. Chambers in Newcastle, Northumberland.

POSTMARK: 8 IY.

1. Richard Chambers (1738–1806), younger brother of Sir Robert Chambers, a Newcastle banker who served as sheriff (1786) and mayor (1795–96). In 1796

To RICHARD CHAMBERS, 8 *July* 1782

London, Bolt court,
Fleetstreet, July 8, 1782

Sir:

Your solicitude for your Brother is such as a Brother like him deserves and might expect. I make this haste to tell you that I think the danger over. He will not be recalled this session, and when the parliament meets again, there is likely to be other business.[2] He will doubtless resign the place which has exposed him to censure;[3] and when he no longer offends, there will be no thought of animadversion. He was very well supported, and Smith was forced to confess that the house was generally on his side.[4] He is, by the recal of Impey, now chief Justice,[5] and, I do not see any reason why he may not enjoy his place till he wishes to return unless a new system of government should be formed and even then I know not why he should not be the first man to be consulted and empl[o]yed. I am, Sir, Your humble servant,

SAM. JOHNSON

Chambers went bankrupt; he ended his life as a London ironmonger (information supplied by Professor T. M. Curley).

2. Under the provisions of the Regulating Act of 1773, Sir Robert Chambers was not entitled, as senior puisne justice of the Supreme Court at Bengal, to supplement his income by taking on additional salaried posts. Nonetheless, in 1781 Chambers had accepted the presidency of Chinsura from the Supreme Council at Calcutta. On 18 June 1782 the parliamentary committee investigating the affairs of the East India Company issued a report that criticized Chambers for violating the terms of the Act; on 24 June a motion for censure and recall was introduced in the House of Commons. However, the matter was officially postponed until the next session, and in the interim Chambers's supporters arranged that the motion be dropped (information supplied by Professor Curley).

3. Chambers resigned the presidency of Chinsura in Nov. 1782 (information supplied by Professor Curley).

4. Brigadier-General Richard Smith (1734–1803), chairman of the House of Commons Select Committee (Namier and Brooke III.449–50; Lucy Sutherland, *The East India Company in Eighteenth-Century Politics*, 1952, p. 370).

5. Elijah Impey (1732–1809), Kt., Chief Justice of the Supreme Court at Bengal (appointed 1774), was recalled by the Select Committee to answer the charge that he had violated the provisions of the Regulating Act. Although the Commons failed to impeach Impey, he resigned as Chief Justice in 1789. From 1784 (when Impey returned to England) to 1791 Chambers, who had stayed in India, was Acting Chief Justice; in 1791 he became Chief Justice (P. J. Marshall, *The Impeach-*

ment of Warren Hastings, 1965, pp. 60–62; Sutherland, *East India Company*, p. 384 and n. 3; information supplied by Professor Curley).

John Taylor

MONDAY 8 JULY 1782

MS: Berg Collection, New York Public Library.

ADDRESS: To the Revd. Dr. Taylor in Ashbourne, Derbyshire [*Re-addressed in an unidentified hand*] Market Bosworth, Leicestershire.

POSTMARKS: ASHBORNE, 8 IY, 9 IY.

ENDORSEMENTS: 1782, 8 July 82.

Dear Sir: London, July 8, 1782

You are doubtless impatient to know the present state of the court. Dr. Hunter whom I take to have very good intelligence has just left me, and from him I learn only that all is yet uncertainty and confusion. Fox, you know, has resigned. Burke's dismission is expected. I was particularly told that the Cavendishes were expected to be left out in the new settlement. The Doctor spoke, however, with very little confidence, nor do I believe that those who are now busy in the contest can judge of the event. I did not think Rockingham of such importance as that his death should have had such extensive consequences.[1]

1. Charles Watson-Wentworth (1730–82), second Marquis of Rockingham and First Lord of the Treasury, died 1 July 1782. Rockingham's death upset the precarious balance of power between his own followers and those of William Petty Fitzmaurice (1737–1805), second Earl of Shelburne; these two factions had shared political office since March (*Ante* To Elizabeth Aston and Jane Gastrell, 30 Mar. 1782, n. 4). At the beginning of July, the Cabinet was seriously divided over the issue of unconditional independence for America: Lord Rockingham and Charles James Fox (Secretary of State for Foreign Affairs) favored such an offer, the King and Lord Shelburne (Secretary of State for Home and Colonial Affairs) opposed it. Upon Rockingham's death, Shelburne became First Lord of the Treasury, as a consequence of which Fox resigned (Frank O'Gorman, *The Rise of Party in England*, 1975, pp. 463–65; J. S. Watson, *The Reign of George III*, 1960, p. 578). Other Rockinghamites followed Fox's lead; those quitting the Ministry included Edmund

Have You settle[d] about the silver coffeepot? is it mine or Mrs. Fletcher's,[2] I am yet afraid of liking it too well.

If there is any thing that I can do for Miss Colliers, let me know. But now You have so kindly engaged in it, I am willing to set myself at ease.[3]

When You went away, I did not expect so long absence. If you are engaged in any political business, I suppose your operations are at present suspended, as is, I believe, the whole political movement. These are not pleasant times.

I came back from Oxford in ten days, and was almost restored to health. My breath is not quite free but my cough is gone. I am, Sir, your most etc.

SAM. JOHNSON

Burke, who had served briefly as Paymaster of the Forces, and Lord John Cavendish, Chancellor of the Exchequer—along with his brothers Frederick and George, Taylor's most powerful patron (Namier and Brooke II.203; O'Gorman, *Rise of Party*, p. 466; Watson, *George III*, p. 578). *Post* To John Taylor, 22 July 1782, n. 1.

2. *Ante* To John Taylor, 14 Mar. 1782 and n. 2.

3. *Ante* To John Taylor, 2 Mar. 1782 and n. 1.

Frances Reynolds

SUNDAY 14 JULY 1782

MS: Hyde Collection.

ADDRESS: To Mrs. Reynolds.

ENDORSEMENT: Dr. Johnson, July 82.

Dear Madam: July 14, —82

If You are at home, and desirous of seeing me, I will wait upon You, but it is too late now to carry the letter that we talked of. If it will be equally convenient to You, I will come[1] on Monday about noon. I am, Madam, Your most humble servant,

SAM. JOHNSON

1. MS: "come" superimposed upon undeciphered erasure

Elizabeth Lawrence

MONDAY 22 JULY 1782

PRINTED SOURCE: Chapman II.497.

ADDRESS: To Mrs. Eliz. Laurence in Castle St., Canterbury.

Madam: July 22, 1782, London

I was not without suspicion of the cause why my letter was not answered sooner.[1]

Mr. John Laurence had called and given me part of the account contained in your letter, he has been here today the second time, and has just left me.[2] His cough is abated, but his voice seems hoarse, and I advised him to a mild vegetable diet.

You will easily believe with what gladness I read that you had heard once again that voice to which we have all so often delighted to attend.[3] May you often hear it. If we had his mind and his tongue we could spare the rest.

I am not vigorous, but much better than when dear Dr. Lawrence held my pulse the last time. Be so kind as to let me know from one little interval to another the state of his body. I am pleased that he remembers me, and hope it never can be possible for me to forget him.

Make my compliments to all the ladies. I am Madam Your most humble servant,

SAMUEL JOHNSON

1. *Ante* To Elizabeth Lawrence, 2 July 1782.

2. John Lawrence (d. 1783), son of Dr. Thomas Lawrence (*GM* 1783, p. 542).

3. *Ante* To Hester Thrale, 9 May 1782, n. 3.

John Taylor

MONDAY 22 JULY 1782

MS: Berg Collection, New York Public Library.

ADDRESS: To the Reverend Dr. Taylor at Market Bosworth, Leicestershire.

POSTMARK: 22 IY.

ENDORSEMENTS: 1782, 22 July 82.

Dear Sir: London, July 22, 1782

I do not hear that the Cavendishes are likely to find their [way] soon into publick offices,[1] but I do not doubt of the Duke's ability to procure the exchange for which he has stipulated, and which is now not so much a favour as a contract.[2] Your reason for the exchange I do not fully comprehend, but I conceive myself a Gainer by it, because, I think, You must be more in London.

Mr. Burke's family is computed to have lost by this revolution twelve thousand a year.[3] What a rise, and what a fall.[4] Shelburne speaks of him in private with great malignity.

I have heard no more from the Miss Colliers. Now you have engaged on their side, I am less solicitous about them. Be on their side as much as you can, for You know they are friendless.[5]

Sir Robert Chambers slipped this session through the fingers of revocation, but I am in doubt of his continuance.[6] Shel-

1. *Ante* To John Taylor, 8 July 1782 and n. 1. When the Fox-North Coalition was formed in Apr. 1783, Lord John Cavendish returned as Chancellor of the Exchequer (J. S. Watson, *The Reign of George III*, 1960, p. 579). Lord George, who had been Lord Lieutenant of Derbyshire from 1766 to 1782, never again held a governmental post.

2. Apparently Taylor had proposed a scheme by which his living at Market Bosworth would be exchanged for a living in London. This plan entailed the patronage of the fifth Duke of Devonshire; it also required the approval of Willoughby Dixie (1742–1802), of Market Bosworth, son of the Sir Wolstan (d. 1767) who had briefly employed SJ. Because Willoughby's elder brother had been declared insane in 1769, he controlled the living of Market Bosworth (*Johns. Glean.* VI.112, XI.127; *Post* To John Taylor, 3 Aug. 1782).

3. SJ exaggerates, but not inordinately. Edmund Burke and his family had held offices worth at least £7,500 a year: "In the Pay Office Edmund had a salary of £4000 a year, besides the use of an official residence, while Richard Burke, Jr [Edmund's son], received £500 a year. Richard Burke, Sr [Edmund's brother], as Secretary of the Treasury, was paid £3000 a year" (*Burke's Correspondence* V.10). Furthermore, shortly before he died, Lord Rockingham may have intended to secure the reversion of the Clerkship of the Pells for Richard, Jr.—an office worth about £3,000 a year (*Burke's Correspondence* V.10–14, 12 n. 1).

4. *Ante* To John Taylor, 8 July 1782, n. 1.

5. *Ante* To John Taylor, 2 Mar. 1782, n. 1.

6. *Ante* To Richard Chambers, 8 July 1782 and nn. 2, 3, 5.

burne seems to be his enemy. Mrs. Thrale says they will do him no[7] harm. She perhaps thinks there is no harm without hanging. The mere act of recall strips him of eight thousand a year.[8]

I am not very well, but much better than when we parted, and I hope that milk and summer together are improving you, and strengthening you against the attack of winter. I am, Dear Sir, Your most affectionate,

SAM. JOHNSON

7. MS: "no" altered from "not"

8. Chambers's salary as puisne justice was £6,000 per annum. His monthly stipend from the presidency of Chinsura came to 3,000 sicca rupees—approximately £300 (information supplied by Professor T. M. Curley).

John Perkins

SUNDAY 28 JULY 1782

MS: Hyde Collection.

ADDRESS: To Mr. Perkins.

ENDORSEMENT in JB's hand: 28 July 1782.

Dear Sir: July 28, 1782

I am much pleased that You are going a very long Journey, which may by proper conduct restore your health and prolong your life.[1]

Observe these rules.

1. Turn all care out of your head as soon as you mount the chaise.

2. Do not think about frugality, your health is worth more than it can cost.

3. Do not continue any day's journey to fatigue.

4. Take now and then a day's rest.

1. Perkins was recovering from a severe illness. Hester Thrale had predicted, "the Man will dye; his Nerves, his whole Constitution is so shaken" (*Thraliana* 1.521). However, Perkins survived until 1812, when he was killed on the Brighton racetrack at the age of 83 (*GM* 1812, p. 592).

5. Get a smart seasickness if you can.
6. Cast away all anxiety, and keep your mind easy.

This last direction is the principal; with an unquiet mind neither exercise, nor diet, nor physick can be of much use.

I wish You, dear Sir, a prosperous Journey, and a happy recovery, for I am, Dear Sir, Your most affectionate, humble servant,

SAM. JOHNSON

John Taylor

SATURDAY 3 AUGUST 1782

MS: National Library of Scotland.

ADDRESS: To the Reverend Dr. Taylor in Ashbourne, Derbyshire. [*Readdressed in an unidentified hand*] Market Bosworth, Leicestershire.

POSTMARKS: 3 AV, ASHBORNE.

ENDORSEMENTS: 1782, 4 Augt. 82.

Dear Sir: London, Aug. 4,[1] 1782

The refusal of Mr. Dixie, if it be peremptory and final, puts an end to all projects of exchange.[2] You may however, if your friends get into power, obtain preferment.[3] But do not be any further solicitous about it; leave the world a while to itself.

I now direct to Ashbourne, where, I suppose, you are settled for a while, and where I beg You to do what you can for the poor Colliers.[4]

I have no national news that is not in the papers, and almost all news is bad. Perhaps no nation not absolutely conquered has declined so much in so short a time. We seem to be sinking. Suppose the Irish having already gotten a free trade and an independent parliament should say we will have a King, and

1. The date stamp establishes the correct day.
2. *Ante* To John Taylor, 22 July 1782, n. 2.
3. *Ante* To John Taylor, 22 July 1782.
4. *Ante* To John Taylor, 2 Mar. 1782, n. 1.

ally ourselves with the house of Bourbon, what could be done to hinder or to overthrow them?[5]

Poor dear Dr. Laurence is gone to die at Canterbury. He has lost his speech, and the action of his right side, with very little hope of recovering them.[6]

We must all go. I was so exhausted by loss of blood, and by successive disorders in the beginning of this year that I am afraid that the remaining part will hardly restore me. I have indeed rather indulged myself too much, and think to begin a stricter regimen. As it is my friends tell me from time to time, that I look better, and I am very willing to believe them. Do You likewise take care of your health, we cannot well spare one another. I am, Dear Sir, Yours affectionately,

SAM. JOHNSON

5. Dismayed by the British government's failure to carry out economic reforms, the Irish followed the example of the American colonists and established nonimportation agreements against British goods. The Volunteer Association (a civilian militia) and the opposition leaders in the Irish Parliament joined together to demand free trade for Ireland. Moreover, landowners called tenants' meetings to protest British economic restrictions, while the Irish Parliament refused to pass legislation underwriting government loans. Faced with the real possibility of an uprising, Lord North's government conceded free trade to Ireland in 1780 (J. S. Watson, *The Reign of George III*, 1960, pp. 221–24). Then the defeat at Yorktown (1781) raised hopes of extracting more concessions from Great Britain. In Feb. 1782 the Convention of Volunteers passed resolutions demanding an independent Irish parliament, an end to all controls on Irish trade, and an independent judiciary. On 15 May the government acceded to Irish demands (Watson, *George III*, pp. 245–46; Frank O'Gorman, *The Rise of Party in England*, 1975, pp. 460–61).

6. *Ante* To Hester Thrale, 9 May 1782 and n. 3.

John Nichols[1]

MONDAY 12 AUGUST 1782

MS: Bodleian Library.

1. I follow F. W. Hilles in identifying SJ's correspondent as John Nichols, the printer of the revised edition of SJ's *Lives*, which was to appear early in 1783 (Hilles, "Johnson's Correspondence with Nichols," *Philological Quarterly* 48, 1969, pp. 229–30).

Sir: Aug. 12, 1782

When the sheet that relates the publication of the English Iliad comes to your hand, be so kind as to keep it, till we can talk together. There is a passage in the life of Bowyer upon which we should confer.[2] I am, Sir, Your most humble servant,

SAM. JOHNSON

2. SJ refers to Nichols's *Biographical and Literary Anecdotes of William Bowyer,* published earlier that year. Nichols includes information relating to the printing and sale of Pope's translation of the *Iliad*—information that prompted SJ to modify his account in the *Lives*. "Alterations were made in paragraphs 78, 79, and 90, based on Bowyer, pp. 502f. and in paragraph 87, based on Bowyer, p. 258" (Hilles, "Correspondence," p. 230).

John Taylor

MONDAY 12 AUGUST 1782

MS: Pierpont Morgan Library.

ADDRESS: To the Reverend Dr. Taylor in Ashbourne, Derbyshire.

POSTMARK: 13 AV.

ENDORSEMENTS: 1782, 12 Augt. 82.

Dear Sir: London, August 12, 1782

I calculate this letter to meet You at Ashbourne, whither I hope you are well enough to come according to your purpose. And I write to warn You very earnestly against useless and unnecessary vexation. To be robbed is very offensive, but You have been robbed of nothing that You can feel the want of. Let not the loss, nor the circumstances of the loss take any hold upon your mind. This loss will in a short time repair itself, but you have a greater loss, the loss of health which must be repaired by your own prudence and diligence, and of which nothing can more obstruct the reparation than an uneasy mind.

But how are You to escape uneasiness? By Company and business. Get and keep about you those with whom You are most at ease, and contrive for your mornings something to do, and bustle about it as much as You can. If You think London a place of more amusement come hither, or take any other kind of harmless diversion, but diversion of some kind or other You cannot at present be without. To muse and think will do you much harm, and if you are alone and at leisure, troublesome thoughts will force themselves upon you.

Be particularly careful now to drink enough, and to avoid costiveness;[1] You will find that vexation has much more power over you, ridiculous as it may seem if you neglect to evacuate your body.

I have now had three quiet nights together, which, I suppose, I have not for more[2] than a year before. I hope we shall both grow better, and have a longer enjoyment of each other. I am, Dear sir, yours affectionately,

SAM. JOHNSON

1. *Ante* To Thomas Lawrence, 20 June 1767, n. 2.
2. MS: "eighteen" del. before "more"

John Taylor

SATURDAY 17 AUGUST 1782

MS: Current location unknown. Transcribed from photostat in the Hyde Collection.

ADDRESS: To the Reverend Dr. Taylor in Ashbourne, Derbyshire.

POSTMARK: ⟨17⟩ AV.

ENDORSEMENTS: 1782, 17 Augt. 82.

Dear Sir: Aug. 17, 1782

Though I follow You thus with letters, I have not much to say. I write because I would hear from you the state of your health and of your mind. Upon your mind in my opinion your health will very much depend, and I therefore repeat my injunction of bustle and cheerfulness. Do not muse by Yourself; do not suffer yourself to be an hour without something to do.[1] Suffer nothing disagreeable to approach you after dinner.

1. *Ante* To John Taylor, 12 Aug. 1782.

Of the publick I have nothing to say, there seem to be expectations of a violent session when the factions meet.[2] Nor have I much to say of myself but that I think myself freed from all the supervenient[3] distempers of this year, and as well as when I was with You.[4] My great complaint now is unquietness in the night.

Do not let me write again before I am told how You do. It is reasonable that you and I should be anxious for each other; our ages are not very different, and we have lived long together. I am, Dear Sir, Your affectionate etc.

SAM. JOHNSON

Do not fret.

2. The appointment (upon Rockingham's death) of Lord Shelburne as First Lord of the Treasury exacerbated the personal animosities and disagreements over foreign policy that had plagued the Rockingham-Shelburne coalition since it succeeded Lord North's ministry in Mar. 1782 (*Ante* To Elizabeth Aston and Jane Gastrell, 30 Mar. 1782, n. 4; *Ante* To John Taylor, 8 July 1782, n. 1; J. S. Watson, *The Reign of George III*, 1960, pp. 242–45). Parliament was split into four groups: followers of Shelburne, of Fox, and of North, and the Independents. When in Jan. 1783 Shelburne presented the peace treaties with America and France to the House of Commons, they were met "with an outburst of dissatisfaction" that led directly to Shelburne's resignation on 24 Feb. (Watson, *George III*, pp. 250, 256–58).

3. *supervenient*: "added; additional" (SJ's *Dictionary*).

4. SJ had last stayed at Ashbourne 9–30 Nov. 1781 (*Ante* To Hester Thrale, 10 Nov. 1781; *Ante* To Hester Maria Thrale, 28 Nov. 1781).

George Strahan

MONDAY 19 AUGUST 1782

MS: Berg Collection, New York Public Library.

Sir: Aug. 19, 1782

I have not yet read your letter through and therefore cannot answer it particularly. Of what You say so[1] far as I have read all is I think, true but the application. What I told him[2] of your

1. MS: "s" superimposed upon "m"

2. SJ refers to William Strahan, George's father.

discontent on many occasions was to not provoke him but to pacify him, by representing that discontent of which he complained so much, not as any personal disrespect to him but as a cast of mind which You had always had.[3] Your discontent on many occasions has appeared to me little short of madness, which however I did not tell him. Thus your uneasiness at Oxford was a weak thing which passed for an instance by which I do not see how he could be inflamed. The whole tendency of what I said was this, "He is you say discontented, if he is, it is not by any personale disesteem of you, he is apt to be discontented."

As to the matter of the money I am much of the mind that You have represented. But I did not think nor think now that I said any thing that would hinder Your father from any act of liberality.[4]

You may be sure, I am sure, I had no intention to hurt you, and if I have hurt you, nothing that I can do shall be omitted to repair the hurt.[5]

You may well be at a loss to conjecture Why I should injure you, whom certainly I have no reason to injure, and whom I would suffer much [rather] than injure by design, and shall be very sorry if I have done it by that train of talk which I was drawn into without design and almost without remembrance. If I have really done you harm I shall live in hope of doing you sometime as much good, though good is not so easily done. I am Sir, Your most etc.

SAM. JOHNSON

3. George Strahan's strong disinclination to enter his father William's printing business led him (with SJ's assistance) to Oxford and a clerical career (*Ante* To Henry Bright, 12 Oct. 1762 and nn. 3, 4). Despite George's success in his chosen vocation, relations between father and son remained tense (J. A. Cochrane, *Dr. Johnson's Printer*, 1964, pp. 153, 156).

4. George Strahan, who had been living beyond his means, "looked to his father to make up his stipend [as Vicar of Islington] from the profits of the trade he found so distasteful" (Cochrane, *Dr. Johnson's Printer*, p. 156). *Post* To George Strahan, 10 Oct. 1782.

5. SJ continued to act as intermediary between father and son (*Post* To George Strahan, 10 Oct. 1782; 16 Jan. 1783; ?Jan. 1783; *Post* To William Strahan, 11 Dec. 1782).

James Boswell

SATURDAY 24 AUGUST 1782

PRINTED SOURCE: JB's *Life*, 1791, II.425.

Dear Sir, Aug. 24, 1782

Being uncertain whether I should have any call this autumn into the country, I did not immediately answer your kind letter. I have no call, but if you desire to meet me at Ashbourne, I believe I can come thither; if you had rather come to London, I can stay at Streatham; take your choice.[1]

This year has been very heavy. From the middle of January to the middle of June I was battered by one disorder after another; I am now very much recovered, and hope still to be better. What happiness it is that Mrs. Boswell has escaped.

My "Lives" are reprinting,[2] and I have forgotten the authour of Gray's character: write immediately, and it may be perhaps yet inserted.[3]

Of London or Ashbourne you have your free choice; at any place I shall be glad to see you. I am, dear Sir, your, etc.

SAM. JOHNSON

1. SJ did not visit Taylor, and JB (whose father died 30 Aug.) remained in Scotland.

2. *Ante* To John Nichols, 12 Aug. 1782, n. 1.

3. In his biography of Thomas Gray, SJ had included a "character" of the poet composed by William Johnson Temple (1739–96), Vicar of St. Gluvias, Cornwall, and a lifelong friend and correspondent of JB. In the first edition SJ credits the character to "a nameless writer"; in the edition of 1783 he acknowledges Temple by name (*Lives of the Poets* III.429).

Elizabeth Lawrence

MONDAY 26 AUGUST 1782

MS: Hyde Collection.

ADDRESS: To Mrs. Eliz. Laurence in Castle Street, Canterbury.

POSTMARK: 26 AV.

To ELIZABETH LAWRENCE, 26 *August* 1782

Madam: August 26, 1782

I am much delighted even with the small advances which dear Dr. Laurence makes towards recovery.[1] If we could have again but his mind and his tongue, or his mind and his right hand, we would not much lament the rest. I should not despair of helping the swelled hand by electricity, if it were frequently and diligently applied.

Let me know from time to time whatever happens. I hope I need not tell you how much I am interested in every change.

Please to make my compliments to all the Ladies. I am, Madam, Your most humble servant,

SAM. JOHNSON

I am much better than I was when you last saw me.

1. *Ante* To Hester Thrale, 9 May 1782, n. 3.

James Boswell

SATURDAY 7 SEPTEMBER 1782

PRINTED SOURCE: JB's *Life*, 1791, II.426–27.

Dear Sir, London, Sept. 7, 1782

I have struggled through this year with so much infirmity of body, and such strong impressions of the fragility of life, that death, wherever it appears, fills me with melancholy; and I cannot hear without emotion, of the removal of any one, whom I have known, into another state.[1]

Your father's death had every circumstance that could enable you to bear it; it was at a mature age, and it was expected; and as his general life had been pious, his thoughts had doubtless for many years past been turned upon eternity. That you did not find him sensible must doubtless grieve you; his disposition towards you was undoubtedly that of a kind, though

1. "On the 30th of August, I informed him that my honoured father had died that morning" (*Life* IV.153–54).

not of a fond father. Kindness, at least actual, is in our power, but fondness is not; and if by negligence or imprudence you had extinguished his fondness, he could not at will rekindle it. Nothing then remained between you but mutual forgiveness of each other's faults, and mutual desire of each other's happiness.

I shall long to know his final disposition of his fortune.[2]

You, dear Sir, have now a new station, and have therefore new cares, and new employments. Life, as Cowley seems to say, ought to resemble a well ordered poem;[3] of which one rule generally received is, that the exordium should be simple, and should promise little. Begin your new course of life with the least show, and the least expence possible; you may at pleasure encrease both, but you cannot easily diminish them. Do not think your estate your own, while any man can call upon you for money which you cannot pay; therefore, begin with timorous parsimony. Let it be your first care not to be in any man's debt.

When the thoughts are extended to a future state, the present life seems hardly worthy of all those principles of conduct, and maxims of prudence, which one generation of men has transmitted to another; but upon a closer view, when it is perceived how much evil is produced, and how much good is impeded by embarrassment and distress, and how little room the expedients of poverty leave for the exercise of virtue; its sorrows[4] manifest that the boundless importance of the next life, enforces some attention to the interests of this.

2. The estate of Auchinleck possessed a nominal rent roll of £1,500, a substantial sum, but Lord Auchinleck had imposed on the estate a number of permanent charges in the form of annuities to various relatives. In particular, his liberal bequests to Lady Auchinleck severely curtailed JB's inheritance (*Later Years*, pp. 228, 232).

3. "If Life should a well-order'd Poem be / (In which he only hits the white / Who joyns true Profit with the best Delight), / The more Heroique strain let others take, / Mine the Pindarique way I'le make" (Cowley, "Ode Upon Liberty," in *Several Discourses by way of Essays, in Verse and Prose*, Essay No. 1: "Of Liberty," *The Works of Abraham Cowley*, 1668).

4. "its sorrows" altered to "it grows" in the second edition of JB's *Life* (1793)

Be kind to the old servants, and secure the kindness of the agents and factors; do not disgust them by asperity, or unwelcome gaiety, or apparent suspicion. From them you must learn the real state of your affairs, the characters of your tenants, and the value of your lands.

Make my compliments to Mrs. Boswell; I think her expectations from air and exercise are the best that she can form. I hope she will live long and happily.

I forget whether I told you that Rasay has been here;[5] we dined cheerfully together. I entertained lately a young gentleman from Coriatachat.[6]

I received your letters only this morning. I am, dear Sir, yours, etc.

SAM. JOHNSON

5. SJ refers to John Macleod (*Ante* To Hester Thrale, 14 Sept. 1773, n. 7).

6. The 1791 reading was corrected to "Corrichatachin" in 1793. SJ probably refers to a member of the Mackinnon family of Coirechatachan, Skye (*Ante* To Hester Thrale, 21 Sept. 1773, n. 44).

James Boswell

SATURDAY 21 SEPTEMBER 1782

PRINTED SOURCE: JB's *Life*, 1791, II.427.

One expence, however, I would not have you to spare:[1] let nothing be omitted that can preserve Mrs. Boswell, though it should be necessary to transplant her for a time into a softer climate. She is the prop and stay of your life. How much must your children suffer by losing her.[2]

1. In mid-September JB informed SJ "that he would come to London" to consult him in the aftermath of Lord Auchinleck's death (*Post* To John Taylor, 3 Oct. 1782). In his letter of 21 Sept., from which JB preserves this single paragraph, SJ advised him "to stay at home and ⟨concern⟩ himself with his own affairs" (*Works*, Yale ed. I.333; *Post* To John Taylor, 3 Oct. 1782).

2. On 1 Oct. JB replied from Auchinleck: "While I was still intent on flying away to you, your most excellent letter forcibly dissuading me from *deserting my*

station arrived, and at once settled me. . . . My wife was so affected by your letter that she shed tears of grateful joy, and declared that she would write to you herself. Accordingly you have enclosed the spontaneous effusion of her heart" (*Boswell, Laird of Auchinleck*, ed. J. W. Reed and F. A. Pottle, 1977, p. 481).

John Taylor

SATURDAY 21 SEPTEMBER 1782

MS: Boston Public Library.

ADDRESS: To the Reverend Dr. Taylor in Ashbourne, Derbyshire.

POSTMARK: ⟨21⟩ SE.

ENDORSEMENTS: 1782, 21 Septr. 82.

Dear Sir: Sept. 21, 1782

Your letter about a week ago told me that your health is mended. Health is the basis of all happiness of this worlds giving. Your loss likewise seems to be less than I had feared.[1]

Of the probability of Shelburne's continuance I can make no judgement.[2] Sickness has this year thrown me out of the world; but I think myself growing better.

The proposal of Miss Colliers seems to be wild. If I understand it right, they wish that he should lend them money, that they may sue him for the estate.[3]

Please to let them know that if they send me their Grandfather's will, I will get some opinion upon it.[4] If they want money to procure it from the registry I will repay You what You may advance them as far as ten pounds.

Take great care of your health. Let nothing disturb you. Particularly avoid costiveness, and open no letters of business but in the morning.

1. *Ante* To John Taylor, 12 Aug. 1782.

2. *Ante* To John Taylor, 17 Aug. 1782, n. 2.

3. For the dispute between Mary and Sophia Collier and their stepfather, Thomas Flint, *ante* To John Taylor, 2 Mar. 1782 and n. 1.

4. The inheritance in dispute had descended from the Colliers' mother's father, John Dunn (d. 1757), an innkeeper of Colwich, Staffordshire (*Johns. Glean.* IX.26–28, XI.132).

To JOHN TAYLOR, 21 *September* 1782

If You would have me write to Mr. Langley about the Miss Colliers let me know. I would do any thing for them that is proper. I am, Sir, Yours affectionately,

SAM. JOHNSON

Philip Metcalfe[1]

THURSDAY 3 OCTOBER 1782

PRINTED SOURCE: JB's *Life*, 1791, II.429.

Mr. Johnson is very much obliged by the kind offer of the carriage; but he has no desire of using Mr. Metcalfe's carriage, except when he can have the pleasure of Mr. Metcalfe's company.[2]

1. Philip Metcalfe (1733–1818), F.R.S., later (1784–1806) M.P., a wealthy London brewer and close friend of Sir Joshua Reynolds. SJ "met Mr. Philip Metcalfe often at Sir Joshua Reynolds's, and other places, and was a good deal with him at Brighthelmston this autumn [1782], being pleased at once with his excellent table and animated conversation" (*Life* IV.159–60, 505).

2. Metcalfe reported to JB that he "could not but be highly pleased that his company was thus valued by Johnson, and he frequently attended him in airings" (Waingrow, p. 589).

John Taylor

THURSDAY 3 OCTOBER 1782

MS: Berg Collection, New York Public Library.

ADDRESS: To the Reverend Dr. Taylor in Ashbourn, Derbyshire.

POSTMARK: 3 OC.

ENDORSEMENTS: 1782, 4 Octr. 82, very good.

Dear Sir: London, Oct. 4,[1] 1782

To help the ignorant commonly requires much patience, for

1. The date stamp establishes the correct day (cf. *Ante* To John Taylor, 3 Aug. 1782).

the ignorant are always trying to be cunning. To do business by letters is very difficult, for without the opportunity of verbal questions much information is seldom obtained.

I received, I suppose, by the coach a copy of Dunn's will,[2] and an abstract of Mr. Flint's marriage settlement.[3] By whom they were sent I know not. The copy of the Will is so worn, that it is troublesome to open it, and has no attestation to evince its authenticity. The extract is, I think, in Mr. Flints own hand, and has not therefore any legal credibility.

What seems to me proper to be done, but You know much better than I, is to take an exemplification of the will from the registry.[4] We are then so far sure. This will I entreat You to read, if it be clear and decisive against the Girls, there can be no further use of it. If You think it doubtful send it to Mr. Madox,[5] and I will pay the fee.

When the will is despatched the marriage settlement is to be examined, which if Mr. Flint refuses to show he[6] gives such ground of suspicion as will justify a legal compulsion to show it.

It may perhaps be better that I should appear busy in this matter than You, and if You think it best, I will write to Lichfield that a copy of the will may be sent to You, for I would have You read it. I should be told the year of Mr. Dunn's death.

Both You and I think the generosity of Mr. Flint somewhat suspicious. I have however not yet condemned him nor would irritate him too much, for perhaps the Girls must at last be content with what he shall give them.

My letter, which You showed to Miss Collier, she did not understand, but supposed that I charged her with asking

2. *Ante* To John Taylor, 21 Sept. 1782 and n. 4.

3. *Ante* To John Taylor, 2 Mar. 1782 and n. 1.

4. According to A. L. Reade, "there is no actual evidence of the 'exemplification of the will' having been obtained from Lichfield, either by Johnson or Taylor, and the original will there bears no visible signs of having been inspected or copied before" (*Johns. Glean.* IX.32).

5. ?John Maddox (d. 1794), a lawyer (*Johns. Glean.* XI.308).

6. MS: "he" superimposed upon "it"

money of Mr. Flint, in order to sue him.[7] I only meant that her proposal was to him eventually the same, and was therefore, as I called it, wild.

I hope your health improves. I am told that I look better and better. I am going, idly enough, to Brighthelmston.[8] I try, as I would have You do, to keep my body open,[9] and my mind quiet.

I hope my attention grows more fixed. When I was last at your house I began, if I remember right, another perusal of the Bible which notwithstanding all my disorders I have read through except the Psalms. I concluded, the twenty second of last month.[10] I hope for as many years as God shall grant me, to read it through at least once every year.[11]

Boswels Father is dead, and Boswel wrote me word that he would come to London—for my advice—⟨the⟩[12] advice which I sent him is to stay at home, and ⟨concern⟩ himself with his own affairs.[13] He has a good estate considerably burthened by settlements, and he is himself ⟨deep⟩ in debt. But if his Wife lives I think he will be prudent. I am, Sir, Yours affectionately,

SAM. JOHNSON

7. *Ante* To John Taylor, 21 Sept. 1782.

8. SJ stayed in Brighton with the Thrales from 7 Oct. to 20 Nov. (*Works*, Yale ed. I.339, 351; *Diary and Letters of Madame D'Arblay*, ed. Austin Dobson, 1904, II.128).

9. *Ante* To Hester Thrale, 4 June 1782 and n. 6.

10. On 22 Sept. 1782 SJ read the last eight books of the New Testament (*Works*, Yale ed. I.334).

11. There is no evidence that SJ carried out this resolution in the two years remaining to him.

12. MS: torn along right-hand margin

13. *Ante* To JB, 7 Sept. 1782; 21 Sept. 1782.

James Compton[1]

SUNDAY 6 OCTOBER 1782

1. The Rev. James Compton (b. *c.* 1747), librarian of the Benedictine convent at which SJ stayed in 1775, had resolved to convert to the Anglican church; instrumental in his decision was the promise of support from SJ and the impact of *Rambler* No. 110 (on repentance). Compton arrived in London during the summer of 1782; "very scantily provided with the means of subsistence, he immediately re-

To JAMES COMPTON, 6 *October* 1782

PRINTED SOURCE: JB's *Life*, ed. Malone, 1811, IV.225.

Sir: Oct. 6, 1782

I have directed Dr. Vyse's letter to be sent to you, that you may know the situation of your business. Delays are incident to all affairs; but there appears nothing in your case of either superciliousness or neglect. Dr. Vyse seems to wish you well. I am, Sir, your most humble servant,

SAM. JOHNSON

---

paired to Bolt-court, to visit Dr. Johnson; and having informed him of his desire to be admitted into the Church of England, for this purpose solicited his aid to procure for him an introduction to the Bishop of London" (Hill II.271 n. 4; JB's *Life*, ed. Edmond Malone, 1811, IV.225, Malone's note). On 9 Sept. SJ wrote to William Vyse, asking for his assistance; on the 30th Compton met with Vyse and presented "his letters of ordination, and testimonials" (*Works*, Yale ed. I.330, 335). After an introduction to Bishop Lowth had been arranged, Compton was received into the Church in Jan. 1783. Throughout this period SJ supported Compton, and then helped him to find employment (Malone, *Life*, IV.226; *Post* To The Mercers' Company, 19 Apr. 1783).

John Nichols

THURSDAY 10 OCTOBER 1782

MS: British Library.

ADDRESS: To Mr. Nicol.

Sir: Brighthelmston, Oct. 10, 1782

While I am at Brighthelmston,[1] if You have any need of consulting me, Mr. Strahan will do us the favour to transmit our papers under his frank.

I have looked often into your Anecdotes,[2] and You will hardly thank a lover of literary history for telling You that he has been informed and gratified.

I wish You would add your own discoveries and intelligence

1. *Ante* To John Taylor, 3 Oct. 1782, n. 8.
2. *Ante* To John Nichols, 12 Aug. 1782, n. 2.

to those of Dr. Rawlinson, and undertake the supplement to Wood.[3] Think on it. I am, Sir, Your humble servant,

SAM. JOHNSON

3. Richard Rawlinson (1690–1755), D.C.L., topographer, antiquarian, and non-juring bishop, had collected materials for a continuation of *Athenae Oxonienses* (1691–92), the biographical dictionary by Anthony Wood (1632–95). "In preparing this new edition, on which he was engaged until the time of his death, Rawlinson made voluminous extracts from the official Registers of the University; he wrote to his contemporaries inviting them to supply information about themselves, and circulated a *questionnaire* written in his own hand" (S. and M. A. Gibson, "An Index to Rawlinson's Collections (*circa* 1700–50) for a new Edition of Wood's *Athenae Oxonienses*," *Oxford Bibliographical Society, Proceedings and Papers*, 1924, I.ii.68). Rawlinson bequeathed all these materials to the Bodleian Library.

George Strahan

THURSDAY 10 OCTOBER 1782

MS: Berg Collection, New York Public Library.

ADDRESS: To the Reverend Mr. Strahan at Islington, London.

POSTMARKS: BRIGHTHELMSTONE, 12 OC, [Undeciphered].

Sir: Brighthelmston, Oct. 10, 1782

When I called last week, to do a little business in Newstreet, I found the difference between You and your Father still subsisting,[1] and though I have reason to think you sufficiently prejudiced against my advice, I will, without much anxiety about my reception, suggest some reasons, for which, in my opinion, You ought to make peace as soon as You can.

All quarrels grow more complicated by time, and as they grow more complicated, grow harder to be adjusted.

When a dispute is made publick by references and appeals, which neither your Father nor You have enough avoided, there mingles with interest or resentment a foolish point of honour. Perhaps each part would yield, were not each ashamed.

1. *Ante* To George Strahan, 19 Aug. 1782 and n. 3.

Your dispute has already gone so far, that the first concession ought to come from You, since You may without any disgrace yield to your Father, and your Father will hardly yield to You, but with some dishonour to both.

You might therefore properly make the first advances, even if your Father.were in the wrong, of which, if I understand the question, you will find it difficult to convict him.

When a Man is asked for money which he does not owe he has a right to enquire, why the demand is made.

When You tell him that You ask for money because You want it, he may again very reasonably enquire why you are in want who have already much more than is generally appendant to your station.[2]

To this question it is my advice that You give[3] a calm, decent, and general answer. Neither your Friends wish, nor, I suppose your Father wishes that You should show bills and receipts, though of those you need not be ashamed, for nobody suspects your expences of any thing vitious, but that You should tell in a manly and liberal way why your income falls short of your desires.

With a general account, such as may liberally give him the victory, your Father will probably be satisfied, and this account it will be prudent rather to write than to give in person, though to a written account there may be objection. You will use your discretion.

My serious, and whatever You may think, my friendly advice is that You make haste to reconciliation. Those who encourage either to persist, mean ill to one of you,[4] perhaps without meaning well to the other, or without much malice or any kindness divert themselves with your discord, and are quietly amused by guessing the event. I am, Sir, your most humble servant,

SAM. JOHNSON

2. *Ante* To George Strahan, 19 Aug. 1782, n. 4.

3. MS: "g" superimposed upon "h"

4. MS: "you" altered from "your"

John Nichols

c. OCTOBER 1782[1]

MS: British Library.

This is all that I can think on therefore send it to the press, and fare it well.

1. According to John Nichols, this note refers to the text of "the advertisement prefixed to the second edition" of SJ's *Lives* (1783) (*GM* 1785, p. 11). As F. W. Hilles points out, if the note does indeed refer "to copy for the advertisement, it was written before the letter itself [*Post* To John Nichols, 28 Oct. 1782] in which Johnson alludes to the proof sheets of that advertisement" (Hilles, "Johnson's Correspondence with Nichols," *Philological Quarterly* 48, 1969, p. 230).

Mauritius Lowe

TUESDAY 22 OCTOBER 1782

MS: Hyde Collection.
ADDRESS: To Mr. Lowe.

Sir: [Brighthelmston] Oct. 22, 1782

I congratulate you on the good that has befallen You.[1] I always told You that it would come. I would not however have you flatter yourself too soon with punctuality. You must not expect the other half year at Christmas. You may use the money as your needs require, but save what you can.

You must undoubtedly write a letter of thanks to your benefactor in your own name. I have put something on the other side.[2] I am, Sir, Your most humble servant,

SAM. JOHNSON

1. Apparently SJ's request that the Southwell family restore Lowe's allowance had at long last borne fruit (*Ante* To Lady Southwell, 9 Sept. 1780; see below, n. 2).

2. On the verso SJ supplies the draft of a note to "My Lord," thanking "your Lordship" (presumably the second Viscount Southwell) for "the allowance which you are pleased to make me."

James Compton

THURSDAY 24 OCTOBER 1782

MS: Houghton Library.

ADDRESS: To the Reverend Mr. Compton, to be sent to Mrs. Williams.

Sir: [Brighthelmston] Octr. 24, 1782

Your business, I suppose, is in[1] a way of as easy progress as such business ever has.[2] It is seldom that event keeps pace with expectation.

The Scheme of your book I cannot say that I fully comprehend.[3] I would not have you ask less than an hundred Guineas, for it seems a largo octavo.

Go to Mr. Davies in Russel Street, show him this letter, and show him the book if he desires to see it. He will tell You what hopes you may form, and to what Bookseller You should apply.

If You succeed in selling your book, You may do better than by dedicating it to me.[4] You may perhaps obtain permission to dedicate it to the Bishop of London[5] or to Dr. Vyse, and make way[6] by your book to more advantage than I can procure You.[7]

Please to tell Mrs. Williams that I grow better and that I wish to know how she goes on. You, Sir, may write for her to, Sir, Your most humble servant,

SAM. JOHNSON

1. MS: "i" superimposed upon "a"

2. *Ante* To James Compton, 6 Oct. 1782 and n. 1.

3. This project has not been identified.

4. "What will the world do, but look on and laugh when one Scholar dedicates to another?" (*Ante* To Thomas Patten, 24 Sept. 1781).

5. SJ refers to Robert Lowth.

6. MS: "way" superimposed upon "it"

7. *Post* To James Compton, 7 Nov. 1782.

William Strahan

THURSDAY 24 OCTOBER 1782

MS: Pierpont Morgan Library.

ADDRESS: To William Strahan, Esq., M.P. in London.

POSTMARKS: BRIGHTHELMSTONE, FREE.

Sir: [Brighthelmston] Oct. 24, 1782

I am very much obliged by your kind enquiries. When I came hither I was so breathless and encumbred that I stopped four times to rest between the inn and the lodging,[1] a space perhaps as great as from your house to Black Friers. I can walk better now. We have a deep Well, when I came I suffered so much in letting down the bucket, that I never tried to pull it up. But I have done both to day with little trouble. By such experiments I perceive my own advances. I have likewise much easier nights. I have evacuated much, but without bleeding, and have lived sparingly. The success of my endeavours has really been beyond my hopes. This is a place where one lives much one's own way, and one is not much hindred in a regimen.

I hope dear Mrs. Strahan and You are both well and will long[2] continue well. I am, Sir, your humble servant,

SAM. JOHNSON

1. The travelers arrived at the Ship Tavern, and then proceeded to their quarters on West Street (*Works*, Yale ed. I.339; *Post* To Hester Thrale, 9 Nov. 1782).

2. MS: "l" superimposed upon "c"

John Nichols

MONDAY 28 OCTOBER 1782

MS: British Library.

ADDRESS: To Mr. Nicol.

To JOHN NICHOLS, 28 *October* 1782

Dear Sir: [Brighthelmston] Oct. 28, 1782

You somehow forgot the advertisement for the new Edition.[1] It was not enclosed.

Of Gay's letters I see not that any use can be made, for they give no information of any thing. That he was member of the philosophical Society is something, but surely he could be but a corresponding member.[2] However not having his life here I know not how to put it in, and it is of little importance.

What will the Booksellers give me for this new Edition? I know not what to ask.[3] I would have 24 sets bound in plain calf, and figured with[4] number of the volumes.[5] For the rest they may please themselves.

I wish, Sir, you could obtain some fuller information of Jortin,[6] Markland,[7] and Thirlby.[8] They were three contemporaries of great eminence. I am, Sir, Your most humble servant,

SAM. JOHNSON

1. *Ante* To John Nichols, *c.* Oct. 1782, n. 1.

2. Apparently Nichols had suggested that SJ, in revising his biography of the poet John Gay, draw upon two letters from Gay to Maurice Johnson, a founding member of the Spalding Society. The Society was established in 1712 "for the supporting of mutual Benevolence, and . . . Improvement in the Liberal Sciences and Polite Learning." Gay himself was a member from 1728 until his death in 1732 (*GM* 1785, p. 11; *Lit. Anec.* VI.28–29, 84–85).

3. SJ received £100 for revising the text of his *Lives* for the edition that appeared early the following year (Receipt, 19 Feb. 1783, MS: Beinecke Library).

4. MS: "with with" at page break

5. The revised edition was published in four volumes octavo (*Bibliography*, p. 142).

6. The Rev. John Jortin (1698–1770), D.D., classical scholar, ecclesiastical historian, and homilist, had contributed to the notes that accompanied Pope's translation of the *Iliad*. In revising his account of Pope for the 1783 edition, SJ took the occasion to supplement the reference to Jortin (*Lives of the Poets* III.116 and nn. 4, 5).

7. Jeremiah Markland (1693–1776), classical philologist, editor of Euripides and Statius; "one of the most learned and penetrating Critics of the eighteenth century" (*Lit. Anec.* IV.272). SJ's interest in Markland may have been piqued by the references to him in Nichols's *Anecdotes of William Bowyer* (*Ante* To John Nichols, 12 Aug. 1782 and n. 2).

8. The Rev. Styan Thirlby (*c.* 1692–1753), LL.D., Fellow of Jesus College, Cambridge (1712–53), figures briefly in SJ's biography of Pope. SJ's request for more

information prompted Nichols to write a brief memoir of Thirlby (*GM* 1784, pp. 260–62, 893), almost half of which consists of anecdotes contributed by SJ (MS: Hyde Collection; *Johns. Misc.* II.430–31).

James Compton

THURSDAY 7 NOVEMBER 1782

MS: Hyde Collection.

ADDRESS: To the Reverend Mr. Compton, to be left with Mrs. Williams.

Sir: Brighthelmston, Nov. 7, 1782

You and Mrs. Williams judged right in supposing that I did not mean to refuse your kindness. You are welcome to all the popularity that my name can procure your book. To the dedication which You have written I have some slight objections which we shall have leisure enough to consider.[1] I wish You success in this and all your undertakings. I am, Sir, Your most humble servant,

SAM. JOHNSON

1. *Ante* To James Compton, 24 Oct. 1782.

John Perkins

FRIDAY 8 NOVEMBER 1782

MS: Courage Barclay and Simonds Ltd.

ADDRESS: To Mr. Perkins in Southwark.

POSTMARK: 9 NO.

ENDORSEMENT in an unidentified hand: Dr. Johnson, Sep. 1782.

Dear Sir: Brighthelmston, Sept.[1] 8, 1782

I am sorry that your journey and voyage have not restored your health so much as I thought might be reasonably ex-

1. MS: "Novr." written above "Sept." in an unidentified hand; the date stamp establishes the correct month

pected;[2] continue to use as much exercise as You can, and keep care as much as You can out of your head.

Nothing can be more liberal or more elegant than the manner in which You and Mr. Barclay do me the favour to treat me with respect to this unhappy fellow. What to propose I know not. It seems fit to send some intelligent man to talk with him. If he persists in being a soldier I do not see what remains but to help him to his cloaths and perhaps a little money, and leave him to the consequences of his own choice. Yet it surely moves compassion to see an ignorant unexperienced Highlander inveigled to destruction. I am willing to contribute six Guineas to his preservation, if in your opinion he can be preserved. I must leave the whole to your discretion; be as kind to him as You can.

Your generosity and civility on this occasion can never be forgotten, by, Sir, Your most humble Servant,

SAM. JOHNSON

2. *Ante* To John Perkins, 28 July 1782.

Hester Thrale

SATURDAY 9 NOVEMBER 1782

MS: Hyde Collection.

ADDRESS: To Mrs. Thrale [*added in an unidentified hand*] West Street.

[?Cowdray House, Sussex] Saturday, Nov. 9, 1782

Madam:

Mr. Metcalf has found so many places worthy of curiosity in our way, that we cannot find our way home to day. I hope to wait on You to morow.[1] I am, Madam, Your most humble Servant,

SAM. JOHNSON

1. SJ and Philip Metcalfe took a short tour of western Sussex, 8–10 Nov., stopping at Arundel Castle, Chichester, Cowdray, and Petworth (*Works*, Yale ed. 1.348–49). *Ante* To Philip Metcalfe, 3 Oct. 1782, n. 2.

Joshua Reynolds

THURSDAY 14 NOVEMBER 1782

MS: Hyde Collection.

ADDRESS: To Sir Joshua Reynolds in London.

POSTMARK: BRIGHTHELMSTONE.

Dear Sir: Brighthelmston, Nov. 14, 1782

I heard yesterday of your late disorder, and should think ill of myself if I had heard of it without alarm. I heard likewise of your recovery which I sincerely wish to be complete and permanent.[1] Your Country has been in danger of losing one of its brightest ornaments, and I, of losing one of my oldest and kindest Friends, but I hope You will still live long for the honour of the Nation, and that more enjoyment of your elegance,[2] your intelligence, and your benevolence is still reserved for, Dear Sir, Your most affectionate and most humble Servant,

SAM. JOHNSON

1. Reynolds had suffered a "slight paralytic affection," from which he completely recovered (James Northcote, *The Life of Sir Joshua Reynolds*, 1818, II.131).

2. MS: "gance" repeated as catchword

William Strahan

THURSDAY 14 NOVEMBER 1782

MS: Hyde Collection.

ADDRESS: To William Strahan, Esq., M.P., London.

POSTMARKS: BRIGHTHELMSTONE, 16 NO, FREE.

Sir: Brighthelmston, Nov. 14, 1782

Your kindness gives You a right to such intelligence relating to myself as I can give You.

My Friends all tell me that I am grown much better since my arrival at this place. I do not for my own part think myself well, but I certainly mend.[1]

1. Cf. *Ante* To William Strahan, 24 Oct. 1782.

I shall not stay here above a week longer,[2] and indeed it is not easy to tell why we stay so long, for the company is gone.[3]

Last fryday or saturday there was at this place the greatest take of herrings that has been ever known. The number caught was eight lasts,[4] which at eight thousand a last, make eight hundred thousand.[5] I am, Sir, Your most humble servant,

SAM. JOHNSON

Make my compliments to dear Mrs. Strahan.

2. SJ, the Thrales, and Frances Burney left Brighton 20 Nov. and returned to London (*Works*, Yale ed. I.351).

3. The last ball of the autumn season had taken place on 4 Nov. (*Diary and Letters of Madame D'Arblay*, ed. Austin Dobson, 1904, II.117).

4. *last*: "a commercial denomination of weight, capacity, or quantity, varying for different kinds of goods and in different localities"; in the case of cod and herrings, one last is equivalent to twelve barrels (*OED*).

5. SJ's mathematical ability temporarily deserted him.

Hester Thrale

SATURDAY 30 NOVEMBER 1782

MS: Rylands Library.
ADDRESS: To Mrs. Thrale.

Madam: Nov. 30, 1782

Nothing that You say has any other effect upon my opinion, than to make me rest in the sullen conclusion that what is past is past. You have only turned uncoined silver into silver coined.[1]

Your fathers case and yours have an essential difference which I cannot now explain,[2] but will try to do it if ever you

1. The suit brought against Hester Thrale by Lady Salusbury (*Ante* To Hester Thrale, 3 Nov. 1773, n. 13) was settled when Mrs. Thrale agreed to pay "a Compromise for 7500£" (*Thraliana* I.550). In order to raise this sum, Mrs. Thrale had to part with her silver plate, which was sold on 30 Nov. (*Works*, Yale ed. I.353; *Thraliana* I.551).

2. *Ante* To Hester Thrale, 3 Nov. 1773, n. 13. "See how I am tortured at forty

will hear me. With regard to myself I am obliged to you for thinking my quiet worth an apology. I am, Dearest, dearest, Your most humble servant,

SAM. JOHNSON

Years Distance, by my Father's borrowing Money before I was born" (*Thraliana* I.551, 27 Nov. 1782).

John Perkins

TUESDAY 3 DECEMBER 1782

MS: Hyde Collection.

ADDRESS: To Mr. Perkins.

Dear Sir: Decr. 3, 1782

Macquin[1] had, as I find, two volumes of the Rambler, and two of Burnet's History.[2] They make sets imperfect, and therefore I wish Mr. Scot[3] could be so kind as to enquire after them, and recover them.[4]

I was much delighted to see You so well yesterday. I am, Sir, Your humble Servant,

SAM. JOHNSON

1. SJ refers to the "young gentleman" of the Mackinnon family who was visiting London (*Ante* To JB, 7 Sept. 1782 and n. 6; *Works*, Yale ed. I.328, 353).

2. SJ owned a copy of the four-volume edition (1753) of *History of his Own Times* (originally published in two volumes, 1724–34) by Gilbert Burnet (1643–1715) (Greene, 1975, p. 43).

3. SJ may refer to Thomas Scott (1723–1816), of Shepperton, Middlesex, M.P. for Bridport (1780–90), the second husband (m. 31 Jan. 1782) of Henry Thrale's sister Susanna (Namier and Brooke III.417).

4. On 2 Dec. SJ "visited Perkins and brought home books, apparently some that had been left at Streatham, or in Perkins's care, when Johnson went to Brighton. He seems to have seen Mackinnon, the young Scot, at Perkins's," and learned that Mackinnon had borrowed four of the volumes in question (*Works*, Yale ed. I.353–54).

James Boswell

SATURDAY 7 DECEMBER 1782

PRINTED SOURCE: JB's *Life*, 1791, II.427–28.

Dear Sir, London, Dec. 7, 1782

Having passed almost this whole year in a succession of disorders, I went in October to Brighthelmston, whither I came in a state of so much weakness, that I rested four times in walking between the inn and the lodging. By physick and abstinence I grew better, and am now reasonably easy, though at a great distance from health.[1] I am afraid, however, that health begins, after seventy, and often long before, to have a meaning different from that which it had at thirty. But it is culpable to murmur at the established order of the creation, as it is vain to oppose it. He that lives, must grow old; and he that would rather grow old than die, has God to thank for the infirmities of old age.

At your long silence I am rather angry.[2] You do not, since now you are the head of your house, think it worth your while to try whether you or your friend can live longer without writing, nor suspect after so many years of friendship, that when I do not write to you, I forget you. Put all such useless jealousies out of your head, and disdain to regulate your own practice by the practice of another, or by any other principle than the desire of doing right.

Your oeconomy, I suppose, begins now to be settled; your expences are adjusted to your revenue, and all your people in their proper places. Resolve not to be poor: whatever you have, spend less. Poverty is a great enemy to human happiness, it certainly destroys liberty, and it makes some virtues impracticable, and others extremely difficult.[3]

Let me know the history of your life, since your accession to

1. *Ante* To William Strahan, 24 Oct. 1782; 14 Nov. 1782.

2. JB had not written since 1 Oct. (*Ante* To JB, 21 Sept. 1782, n. 2). However, there is no indication that SJ had responded; it was therefore he who was remiss.

3. Cf. *Ante* To JB, 7 Sept. 1782.

your estate. How many houses, how many cows, how much land in your own hand, and what bargains you make with your tenants.

* * * * * *

Of my "Lives of the Poets," they have printed a new edition in octavo, I hear, of three thousand.[4] Did I give a set to Lord Hailes?[5] If I did not, I will do it out of these. What did you make of all your copy?[6]

Mrs. Thrale and the three Misses are now for the winter, in Argyll-street.[7] Sir Joshua Reynolds has been out of order, but is well again;[8] and I am, dear Sir, your affectionate humble servant,

SAM. JOHNSON

4. *Ante* To John Nichols, 28 Oct. 1782 and nn. 3, 5.

5. A set had indeed been ordered and sent (*Ante* To JB, 13 Mar. 1779; *Ante* To Thomas Cadell, 5 Mar. 1781).

6. *Ante* To JB, 14 Mar. 1781 and n. 3.

7. In Sept. 1782 Hester Thrale had let Streatham Park; after the visit to Brighton, she and Queeney, Susanna, and Sophia occupied a rented house on Argyll Street, Nov. 1782–Apr. 1783 (Clifford, 1952, pp. 211, 214, 220).

8. *Ante* To Joshua Reynolds, 14 Nov. 1782 and n. 1.

Margaret Boswell

SATURDAY 7 DECEMBER 1782

PRINTED SOURCE: JB's *Life*, 1791, II.427.

Dear Lady, London, Sept.[1] 7, 1782

I have not often received so much pleasure as from your invitation to Auchinleck.[2] The journey thither and back is, indeed, too great for the latter part of the year; but if my health were fully recovered, I would suffer no little heat and cold, nor a

1. The correct month is established by SJ's diary entry for 7 Dec.: "I wrote to Mr Mrs Boswel, and Dr Taylor" (*Works*, Yale ed. I.354). The letter arrived 11 Dec. (JB's Register of Letters, MS: Beinecke Library). Margaret Boswell replied 20 Dec. (*Life* IV.157).

2. *Ante* To JB, 21 Sept. 1782, n. 2.

wet or a rough road to keep me from you. I am, indeed, not without hope of seeing Auchinleck again,[3] but to make it a pleasant place I must see its lady well, and brisk, and airy. For my sake, therefore, among many greater reasons, take care, dear Madam, of your health, spare no expence, and want no attendance that can procure ease, or preserve it. Be very careful to keep your mind quiet; and do not think it too much to give an account of your recovery[4] to Madam, your, etc.

SAM. JOHNSON

3. SJ had visited Auchinleck at the conclusion of the Hebridean tour (*Ante* To Hester Thrale, 3 Nov. 1773).

4. Margaret Boswell replied: "I am much flattered by the concern you are pleased to take in my recovery. I am better" (*Life* IV.157).

Richard Clark

SATURDAY 7 DECEMBER 1782

MS: Earl Waldegrave.

ENDORSEMENT in the hand of Laetitia Matilda Hawkins:[1] Dr. Johnson to Richard Clark, Esqr., now Chamberlain of London. Received from Mr. Clark June 19th 1816. L. M. Hawkins.

Dear Sir: Boltcourt, Dec. 7, 1782

If You are not engaged by any previous solicitation, I hope You will be pleased to favour the Bearer —— Collet,[2] in his petition for the place of Tollgatherer on the Bridge.[3] He has

1. Laetitia Matilda Hawkins (1760–1835), daughter of Sir John Hawkins. Her *Memoirs* (1827) included anecdotes about SJ (*Johns. Misc.* II.139–44).

2. Matthew Collet, SJ's barber "for the last twenty-four years of his life" (*Boswell, Laird of Auchinleck*, ed. J. W. Reed and F. A. Pottle, 1977, p. 56 and n. 9). On several occasions SJ loaned money to Collet (*Works*, Yale ed. I.284, 326, 355).

3. In all likelihood SJ refers to Blackfriars Bridge, sponsored by the Corporation of London and opened in 1768. Every pedestrian had to pay a toll of one halfpenny (which was raised to a penny on Sundays). After popular protests, the toll was eliminated in 1785 (Wheatley and Cunningham I.197; John Pudney, *Crossing London's River*, 1972, p. 63).

been long known to me, is an honest Man, and has great difficulty to support his family. I am, Sir, Your most humble servant,

SAM. JOHNSON

John Taylor

SATURDAY 7 DECEMBER 1782

MS: Rosenbach Museum and Library.

ADDRESS: To the Reverend Dr. Taylor in Ashbourne, Derbyshire.

POSTMARK: 7 DE.

ENDORSEMENTS: 1782, 7 Decr. 1782.

Dear Sir: London, Dec. 7, 1782

I went in October to Brighthelmston in a very feeble state, but I grew better, and though not well, have much less to complain of.

I am now willing to resume the offices of life, and particularly to do what I can for my Cousin Colliers. You sent me a will and recommended to me to carry it to Counsel which I am willing to do, but do not, till you have instructed me know what is expected from the will, nor what questions I am to ask.[1]

You will therefore, dear Sir, recollect the affair, and give me what instruction you can, for I am very much in dark, not being used to business, and not having much investigated the case now before us.

Do not let your law come, however, without some account of your health. As You might have suspected of me, I suspect of you, that silence is no good sign, and am afraid that You are not well. Take care of yourself. We have outlived many friends, let us keep close to one[2] another. I am, dear sir, Your most affectionate,

SAM. JOHNSON

1. *Ante* To John Taylor, 2 Mar. 1782 and n. 1; 3 Oct. 1782 and n. 4.

2. MS: "o" superimposed upon "a"

John Taylor

MONDAY 9 DECEMBER 1782

MS: Loren Rothschild.

ADDRESS: To the Reverend Dr. Taylor in Ashbourne, Derbyshire.

POSTMARKS: 9 DE, 10 DE.

ENDORSEMENTS: 1782, 9 Decr. 82.

Dear Sir: London, December 9, 1782

Your letter contained almost an answer to that which You had not received.[1]

Take great care of your health. I am sorry that You are still subject to unprovoked disorders; but now You are better, be very tender of yourself. Had You been costive? or had any thing disturbed You? I have but two rules for You, keep your body open, and your mind quiet.[2]

Sickness concentrates a man's attention so[3] much in himself, that he thinks little upon the affairs of others. Now I have a little gleam of health, I have the business of the Miss Colliers almost to begin.[4] I do not know what it is that Mr. Flint offers. Make me as much Master of the business as You can, yet I am afraid of giving you trouble. I would write to the Miss Colliers if I knew how. Shall I send my letter under cover to You, or to any other person? Miss Collier writes well, and can perhaps tell me something of importance. Let me know what I shall do.

Take a scrupulous and diligent care of your health, that we may yet have a little comfort in each other. I am, Sir, Yours most affectionately,

SAM. JOHNSON

1. *Ante* To John Taylor, 7 Dec. 1782.

2. Cf. *Ante* To John Taylor, 3 Oct. 1782.

3. MS: "to"

4. *Ante* To John Taylor, 2 Mar. 1782 and n. 1; 7 Dec. 1782.

William Strahan

WEDNESDAY 11 DECEMBER 1782

MS: Berg Collection, New York Public Library.

Sir: Decr. 11, 1782

In your letter there is no need of alteration. It may serve its purpose very well as it is, but if you change any thing, I think You may better say nothing of his cloaths, for if you allow him five suits in two years, they will cost near 45£ and the other 25£ will easily go for linen shoes and all other parts of cloathing.[1]

Suppose you concluded your letter with some thing like this.

You express your desire of seeing me, and therefore I think it [right] to let you know, that whenever you bring with you that respect and gratitude to which I am entitled, you shall find[2] me no longer your offended etc.

This is all that occurs, except that perhaps it were as well not to insist on a minute knowledge of the wife's expences, but to blame the first article as indistinct, without requiring it to be reformed. I am, Sir, Your most humble Servant,

SAM. JOHNSON

1. *Ante* To George Strahan, 10 Oct. 1782.

2. MS: "no longer" del. before "find"

Hester Thrale

WEDNESDAY 11 DECEMBER 1782

MS: Pierpont Morgan Library.

Madam: Dec. 11, 1782

You are very kind to think so well of so little as I am doing, or can do. It was not till today at noon that Mr. Norris brought me the writing of which Lord Ashburton required the perusal.[1] He accompanied it however with other papers, I think,

1. SJ refers to John Dunning, who had been raised to the peerage as Baron

very properly. The whole bundle I sent this day to his Lordship, and when he has leisure, shall hear from him; but that leisure it is fit that I should wait.

I am glad of Cator's intelligence, and am inclined to think him right. Therefore, dear Lady, hope the best. The best is indeed very bad, so bad that hope can hardly be joined with it. Let us however remember with gratitude that the worst, is but vexation, it will not be distress.

We had yesterday a very crouded Club. St. Asaph,[2] Fox, Bourke,[3] Althrop,[4] and about sixteen more. And the talk was of Mrs. Siddons.[5] Can You talk skilfully of Mrs. Siddons? I had nothing to say. There was talk of Cecilia,[6]—and I did better.

Then I went to the Painters distribution of prizes. Sir Joshua made his Speech.[7] The King is not heard with more attention.

I have very sorry nights, and therefore but chearless days. But I hope things will mend with us all. Let me continue to be, Dear Madam, your most humble servant,

SAM. JOHNSON

Ashburton earlier that year. The legal papers in question undoubtedly concerned the settlement of the dispute with Lady Salusbury (*Ante* To Hester Thrale, 30 Nov. 1782 and n. 1).

2. SJ refers to Jonathan Shipley.

3. SJ refers to Edmund Burke.

4. George John Spencer (1758–1834), Viscount Althorp, later (1783) second Earl Spencer, had been elected to the Club in 1778 (Fifer, p. xx). SJ's spelling reflects the pronunciation of the name.

5. Sarah Kemble Siddons (1755–1831), the great tragic actress, had retired to provincial theaters after her failure during the season of 1775–76. On 10 Oct. 1782 she made a triumphal return to Drury Lane in the title role of Garrick's *Isabella*. On 1 Dec. Hester Thrale reported, "The Town has got a new *Idol*—Mrs Siddons the Actress" (*Thraliana* 1.554).

6. On 12 June Frances Burney's second novel, *Cecilia*, had appeared to great acclaim, including that of SJ (Joyce Hemlow, *The History of Fanny Burney*, 1958, p. 151).

7. At the biennial prize-giving of the Royal Academy of Arts, 10 Dec., Reynolds delivered his twelfth *Discourse*. SJ was in the audience (*Works*, Yale ed. 1.355).

Hester Thrale

MONDAY 16 DECEMBER 1782

MS: Rylands Library.

ADDRESS: To Mrs. Thrale.

Madam: Monday evening, December 16, 1782

My purpose was to have shared the gayety of this evening,[1] and to have heard, ye Gods! and to have seen, but a very dreadful night has intervened,[2] and[3] as want of sleep has made me very sleepy, it remains for me to dream if I can of Argyle Street.[4] I am, Madam, your most etc.

SAM. JOHNSON

1. "There was a very full assembly at Mrs. Thrale's. . . . The evening proved very gay and very agreeable" (*Diary and Letters of Madame D'Arblay*, ed. Austin Dobson, 1904, II.147).

2. SJ reports generally of this period, "my body much disordered, and opium frequently taken" (*Works*, Yale ed. I.355).

3. MS: "and and"

4. *Ante* To JB, 7 Dec. 1782, n. 7.

Hester Thrale

TUESDAY 17 DECEMBER 1782

MS: Rylands Library.

ADDRESS: To Mrs. Thrale.

Madam: Dec. 17, 1782

I am really very much disordered, and know not how to get better; but am trying the old way.—Thou know'st my *old ward*—[1]I hope You are well after all your fatigue of talking—or of hearing, if of that you suffered any.[2] I am, Madam, your most humble servant,

SAM. JOHNSON

1. "Thou knowest my old ward—here I lay, and thus I bore my point" (*I Henry IV* II.iv.190–91).

2. *Ante* To Hester Thrale, 16 Dec. 1782 and n. 1.

Hester Thrale

WEDNESDAY 18 DECEMBER 1782

MS: Rylands Library.
ADDRESS: To Mrs. Thrale.

Dearest Madam: Dec. 18, 1782

I have been bad, and am something better; perhaps to be worse and better, and never to be well, is what now remains. Perhaps yet a little more.

Mr. Cator was with me this morning to enquire about Lord Ashburton, I told him what I have told you,[1] and let him know that I took care to live within call, but that the hurry into which he must be put by the fire in his chambers would naturally divert his attention.

I have not been wanting. I wrote him a respectful note upon the accident. Our papers are at his House.

I may perhaps not be long before I come[2] and see you. Dum spiro, spero.[3] That's[4] my maxim, what d'ye say to that now?

Mr. Cator still thinks that our adversaries are not eager of more law, and that they may yet accept the six[5] thousand.[6] I am apt to think that he may be right. I am, Madam, most cordially your etc.

SAM. JOHNSON

1. *Ante* To Hester Thrale, 11 Dec. 1782 and n. 1.
2. MS: "co" altered from "ca"
3. *Dum spiro, spero*: "While I breathe, I hope."
4. MS: "That's" superimposed upon "I"
5. MS: "sixt"
6. *Ante* To Hester Thrale, 30 Nov. 1782, n. 1.

Hester Thrale

FRIDAY 20 DECEMBER 1782

MS: Hyde Collection.
ADDRESS: To Mrs. Thrale.

Dear Lady: Dec. 20, 1782

I hope the worst is at last over.[1] I had a very good night, and slept very long. You can hardly think how bad I have been, while You were in all your altitudes, at the opera,[2] and all the fine places, and thinking little of me. Sastres has been very good. Queeney never sent me a kind word. I hope however to be with you again in a short time, and show You a man again. I am, Madam, your most obliged and most humble Servant,

SAM. JOHNSON

1. *Ante* To Hester Thrale, 16 Dec. 1782; 17 Dec. 1782; 18 Dec. 1782.

2. On 19 Dec. Hester Thrale, Queeney, and Frances Burney attended a performance at the King's Theatre of *Il Trionfo della Costanza*, a comic opera by Pasquale Anfossi (*Lond. Stage*, Part v, i.579; *Diary and Letters of Madame D'Arblay*, ed. Austin Dobson, 1904, II.148).

Hester Maria Thrale

SATURDAY 21 DECEMBER 1782

MS: The Earl of Shelburne.

ADDRESS: To Miss Thrale.

Dearest Love: Dec. 21, shortest day, 1782

I am grown better by the old way, but the contest has been very stubborn. I have tasted no land animal since Sunday, but I will venture a little to morrow, and hope to be among you ere long.

You are very kind in writing. Never omit those little ceremonial notices, they nourish friendship, at very small expence. I would therefore have you practice them through life rather superfluously than penuriously.

Please to tell my Mistress that I hear nothing yet from Lord Ashburton, and, after what has happened, do not think it proper to importune him.[1] I am, dearest Sweeting, your most humble servant,

SAM. JOHNSON

1. *Ante* To Hester Thrale, 11 Dec. 1782; 18 Dec. 1782.

Hester Thrale

THURSDAY 26 DECEMBER 1782

MS: Rylands Library.

Dear Madam: Dec. 26, 1782

I had not passed the door since I left You, before yesterday morning. That I dined out was the consequence of a very early invitation and much importunity.[1]

In the afternoon I was seized with a fit of convulsive breathlessness such as I think You have never seen, but I fell asleep[2] before the fire and awaked somewhat better. But my nights are very restless, and life is very heavily burthened. I am afraid of opium and the methods which succeeded so well at Brighthelmston have not now had the same effect.[3]

I have this day seen Mr. Allen, Hoole, Compton, Walker,[4] and Cambridge.[5] But I have not seen those of whom I once hoped never to have lost sight.

This is the time of good wishes. I hope, Ye all know that You have those of, dearest, and dearest Madam, Your most humble Servant,

SAM. JOHNSON

1. On 25 Dec. SJ dined with John Hoole (*Works*, Yale ed. I.356).

2. MS: "at asleep"

3. *Ante* To William Strahan, 24 Oct. 1782.

4. John Walker (1732–1807), lexicographer and specialist in elocution. Two of his numerous treatises on the subject he dedicated to SJ: *Elements of Elocution* (1781) and *Rhetorical Grammar* (1785). Walker's *Critical Pronouncing Dictionary* (1791) was the chief authority on English pronunciation until the publication of the *OED* (*Life* IV.519).

5. Richard Owen Cambridge (1717–1802), amateur poet and essayist, a celebrated host at his villa in Twickenham, where SJ had been a guest (*Life* II.361). According to Horace Walpole, Cambridge, who had "a passion for knowing every person who is in any degree remarkable, . . . solicits eagerly an opportunity to be with such" (*Walpole's Correspondence*, Yale ed. XV.332).

Hester Thrale

SATURDAY 28 DECEMBER 1782

MS: Houghton Library.

Dear Madam: Decemb. 28, 1782

I am very poorly, and am going home.[1] When I get a little better, I will be with You again, in the mean time think on me a little, and be certain that You will think on nobody, who thinks oftener on You. I am, Madam, Your most etc.

SAM. JOHNSON

1. On 26 Dec. SJ had gone to Hester Thrale's house in Argyll Street, but two days later decided to return to Bolt Court (*Works*, Yale ed. 1.356).

John Taylor

TUESDAY 31 DECEMBER 1782

MS: Berg Collection, New York Public Library.

ADDRESS: To the Reverend Dr. Taylor in Ashbourne, Derbyshire.

POSTMARK: 31 DE.

ENDORSEMENTS: 1782, 31 Decr. 82.

Dear Sir: Dec. 31, 1782

Your last little note was very unsatisfactory. That a silly timorous unskilful Girl has behaved improperly, is a poor reason for refusing to tell me, what expectations have been raised by the will, and what questions I must ask the Lawyers.[1] Questions which if You do not like to answer them I must ask elsewhere, and I am unwilling to mingle this affair with any name that You may hear with disgust.[2]

This, my dear Sir, is the last day of a very sickly and melancholy year. Join your prayers with mine, that the next may be

1. *Ante* To John Taylor, 2 Mar. 1782 and n. 1; 3 Oct. 1782; *Post* To John Taylor, 16 Jan. 1783.

2. SJ refers to William Langley (*Post* To John Taylor, 16 Jan. 1783).

more happy to us both. I hope the happiness which I have not found in this world, will by infinite mercy be granted in another. I am, Dear Sir, Yours affectionately,

SAM. JOHNSON

Thomas Wilson

TUESDAY 31 DECEMBER 1782

MS: Hyde Collection.

Bolt court,
Reverend Sir: Fleetstreet, London, Dec. 31, 1782

That I have so long omitted to return You thanks for the honour conferred upon me by your dedication,[1] I entreat you with great earnestness not to consider as more faulty than it is. A very importunate and oppressive disorder has for some time debarred me from the pleasures, and obstructed me in the duties of life. The esteem and kindness of wise and good men is one of the last pleasures which I can be content to lose, and gratitude to those from whom this pleasure is received, is a duty of which I hope never to reproach myself with the final neglect.

I therefore now return You thanks for the notice[2] which I have received from You, and which I consider as giving to my name not only more bulk, but more weight, not only as extending its superficies but as encreasing its value.

Your book was evidently wanted, and will I hope, find its way into the Schools, to which however I do not mean to confine it, for no man has so much skill in ancient rites and practices as not to want it.

As I suppose myself to owe part of your kindness to my excellent friend Dr. Patten, he has likewise a just claim to my acknowledgements which I hope You, Sir, will transmit.[3]

1. *Ante* To Thomas Patten, 24 Sept. 1781, nn. 1, 5.

2. MS: "notice" superimposed upon undeciphered erasure

3. MS: "transmit" superimposed upon "carry" partially erased

There will soon appear a new edition of my poetical biography.[4] If You will accept of a copy to keep me in your mind, be pleased to let me know, how it[5] may be conveniently conveyed to You.[6] The present is small but it is given with good will, by, Reverend Sir, ⟨your most obliged⟩ and most humble Servant,

SAM. JOHNSON

4. *Ante* To John Nichols, 12 Aug. 1782 and n. 1.

5. MS: "it" superimposed upon "they" partially erased

6. SJ carried out his promise to present Wilson with a set of the revised *Lives of the Poets* (*Life* IV.508).

Thomas Wilson

1782

PRINTED SOURCE: *The Works of the Right Reverend . . . Thomas Wilson, D.D.*, ed. C. Crutwell, 2d ed., 1782, xvi.

To think on Bishop Wilson with veneration is only to agree with the whole christian world.[1] I hope to look into his books with other purposes than those of criticism, and after their perusal NOT ONLY TO WRITE, BUT TO LIVE BETTER.

1. Thomas Wilson (1663–1755), D.D., Bishop of Sodor and Man (1698–1755), was the father of SJ's correspondent, Thomas Wilson the younger. Apparently the son had sent SJ a copy of the first edition (1781) of his father's collected theological writings; SJ responded "in the following emphatical terms."

John Perkins

WEDNESDAY 8 JANUARY 1783

MS: Hyde Collection.

ADDRESS: To Mr. Perkins.

Dear Sir: Jan. 8, 1783[1]

I am again in distress for coals and desire You to let me have

1. MS: "8" superimposed upon "5"

another Chaldron.[2] The last coals which I had were too inflammable, and burned away too fast. If You will be pleased to give orders that what are now to come should be of a more durable kind, or a mixture of two kinds, they will accommodate me better. Be so kind as to send them soon, for I hear, I am quite out. I am, Sir, Your humble servant,

SAM. JOHNSON

2. *Ante* To John Perkins, 7 May 1782 and n. 2.

John Nichols

FRIDAY 10 JANUARY 1783

MS: British Library.

ADDRESS: To Mr. Nichol.

Sir: Jan. 10, 1783

I am much obliged by your kind communication of your account of Hinkley.[1] I knew Mr. Carte as one of the Prebendaries of Lichfield, and for some time Surrogate[2] of the Chancellor.[3] Now I will put you in a way of showing me more kindness. I have been confined by ilness a long time, and sickness and solitude make tedious evenings. Come sometimes, and see, sir, Your humble Servant,

SAM. JOHNSON

1. Nichols had presented SJ with a copy of his *History and Antiquities of Hinckley in the County of Leicester* (1782). Nichols notes, "For the account of Hinckley, Dr. Johnson had contributed several hints towards the life of Anthony Blackwall, to whom, when very young, he had been some time an usher at Market Bosworth-school" (*Lit. Anec.* II.551 n. ↓; *History and Antiquities of Hinckley*, p. 178 n. ‡).

2. *surrogate*: "a deputy; a delegate; the deputy of an ecclesiastical judge" (SJ's *Dictionary*).

3. The Rev. Samuel Carte (1652–1740), homilist and antiquarian, Prebendary of Lichfield (1682–1740), had collected materials for a history of Leicester (*Lit. Anec.* I.701, II.471–72, 726–27). It is most probable that the man for whom he served as "surrogate" was either Henry Raynes (?1677–1734), Chancellor of the Diocese from 1713 until his death, or Richard Rider (b. *c.* 1693), who succeeded Raynes and held the diocesan chancellorship until 1740. Rider was a close friend of SJ's father (information supplied by Dr. G. W. Nicholls).

George Strahan

THURSDAY 16 JANUARY 1783

MS: Berg Collection, New York Public Library.

Sir: Thursday, Jan. 16, 1783

I had very lately a visit from Mr. Strahan. Our talk was of You, and I am sure he will tell You that I have never been your enemy.[1] What passed is too long to be written, but if You will call on me to morrow in Bolt court, where I shall be in the afternoon on purpose to receive You, I hope that Peace may be made.[2] I am, Sir, Your most humble servant,

SAM. JOHNSON

1. *Ante* To George Strahan, 19 Aug. 1782 and nn. 3, 5; 10 Oct. 1782.

2. George Strahan's reply (dated from Islington, 16 Jan.) is recorded on the verso: "Mr. G. Strahan presents his best Respects to Dr. Johnson, is much obliged to him for any Service he may have done him, and will wait upon him Tomorrow according to his Appointment" (MS: Berg Collection).

John Taylor

THURSDAY 16 JANUARY 1783

MS: Berg Collection, New York Public Library.

ADDRESS: To the Reverend Dr. Taylor in Ashbourne, Derbyshire.

POSTMARK: 16 IA.

ENDORSEMENTS: 1783, 16 Jany. 83.

Dear Sir: London, Jan. 16, 1783

I have for some time been labouring under very great disorder of Body, and distress of Mind. I wish that in our latter days we may give some comfort to each other.—Let us at least not be angry, nor suppose each other angry. We have no time to lose in petulance. I beg You not to take amiss that I trouble you once more about the Colliers.[1] I have but You and Mr. Langley

1. *Ante* To John Taylor, 2 Mar. 1782 and n. 1.

to consult, and him I never have consulted, because You dislike him.[2]

I would show the Lawyers the papers, but that I know not what questions to ask nor can state the case, till I am informed with regard to some particulars.

What do Miss Colliers suppose will be discovered in the writings?

Had Mr. Flint a son by their Mother? I think he has.[3]

What had he with their Mother? I think about 200£ a year.

What do they ask from Mr. Flint?[4]

What does he offer them?[5] This You have told me, but my memory is not distinct about it, and I know not how to find your letter. Tell me again.

All that has a bad appearance on Flint's part, is his requisition of a discharge from future claims. If they have no claims what is the discharge? Yet this may be only unskilfulness in him.

I think there is no reason to suppose that Mrs. Flints estate could be settled by her father exclusively upon Colliers Children,[6] or[7] that she should be advised at her marriage with Mr. Flint to debar herself from providing for her future children whatever they might be, in their due proportions.

2. *Ante* To John Taylor, 31 Dec. 1782 and n. 2.

3. Thomas Flint had one son by Mary Collier, Thomas the younger (b. 1769) (*Johns. Glean.* IX.29).

4. In Feb. 1783 Mary and Sophia Collier reported to William Langley, who then reported to SJ, that they wished "to have a certain sum of money given or secured to us, the interest of which may procure for us a moderate but decent subsistence" (*GM* 1878, p. 699).

5. According to the two Colliers: "Mr. Flint some time ago offered us seventy pounds a year, which we would willingly have accepted if it would have been secured to us and our heirs. We have been since told that he would give us five hundred pounds each . . . on condition that we entirely excluded ourselves and our heirs from any future claim" (*GM* 1878, p. 699).

6. "At the time of our mother's marriage with Mr. Flint, the estate at Bishton was reserved in her power, and intended for our support. This estate was afterwards sold, but we have been informed from one of the trustees of the marriage settlement that there was an engagement given by Mr. Flint that a specified sum of money should be paid to each of us in lieu of this estate" (*GM* 1878, p. 699).

7. MS: "an" del. before "or"

Do answer this, and add what it is necessary for me to know, and I hope to trouble You no more about it. When I have your answer I will transact with Mr. Flint and Miss Collier, or with as little trouble to you as I can.

You and I have lived on together to the time of sickness and weakness. We are now beginning another year; May the merciful God protect us both. Let us not neglect our Salvation, but help each other forward in our way as well as we can. I am, Dear Sir, Your affectionate,

SAM. JOHNSON

Hester Thrale

FRIDAY 17 JANUARY 1783

MS: Rylands Library.
ADDRESS: To Mrs. Thrale.

Dearest Lady: Jan. 17, 1783

I lay last night at my new lodging but it is inconvenient,[1] I shall not go above once or twice more. But I had eleven hours sleep in it, and my Breath is easy; Of this relief I see no other cause than my compliance with Dr. Pepys's directions. My Life is certainly lightened of great oppression, and, I hope, will be lengthened. You shall see to morrow, Madam, Your most etc.

SAM. JOHNSON

1. Apparently SJ, whose obstructed breathing caused him to have difficulty climbing stairs, had found sleeping quarters on the ground floor (*Post* To Robert Chambers, 19 Apr. 1783).

Joseph Cradock[1]

MONDAY 20 JANUARY 1783

1. Joseph Cradock (1742–1826), F.S.A., man of letters and prominent Leicestershire landowner, whose tragedy, *Zobeide*, was produced at Covent Garden in 1771. Cradock had been an acquaintance of SJ since 1776 (*Life* III.38).

MS: Hyde Collection.

ADDRESS: To Mr. Cradock.

ENDORSEMENT: Dr. Johnson.

Jan. 20, 1783

Mr. Johnson is very glad of any intelligence, and much obliged by Mr. Cradock's favour and attention. The Book which he has now sent shall be taken care of, but of a former book mentioned in the note, Mr. Johnson has no remembrance, and can hardly think he ever received it, though bad health may possibly have made him negligent.[2]

2. The "former book" to which SJ refers was a MS volume of poetry by James I and others. Cradock had borrowed this volume from Lord Harborough and lent it to SJ. When Cradock asked George Steevens for help in recovering the folio, Steevens replied, "That then . . . is the book, which now lies under his [SJ's] inkstand; it is neatly packed up, and sealed; and I never was able to make out what it was" (Joseph Cradock, *Literary and Miscellaneous Memoirs*, 1826, I.243–44).

Joseph Cradock

MONDAY 20 JANUARY 1783

MS: Hyde Collection.

ADDRESS: To Mr. Cradock.

Jan. 20, 1783

Mr. Johnson who suspected his own memory is glad to find himself clear. The Book will probably be found, and when found shall be carefully laid up, and thankfully returned.[1]

1. *Ante* To Joseph Cradock, 20 Jan. 1783 and n. 2.

John Taylor

TUESDAY 21 JANUARY 1783

MS: Berg Collection, New York Public Library.

ADDRESS: To the Revd. Dr. Taylor in Ashbourne, Derbyshire.

POSTMARK: 21 IA.

ENDORSEMENTS: 1783, 21 Jany. 1783.

To JOHN TAYLOR, 21 *January* 1783

Dear Sir: Jan. 21, 1783

I am glad that your friends are not among the promoters of equal representation, which I consider as specious in theory but dangerous in experiment, as equitable in itself, but above human wisdom to be equitably adjusted, and which is now proposed only to distress the government.[1]

An equal representation can never form a constitution because it can have no stability, for whether you regulate the representation by numbers or by property, that which is equal to day, will be unequal in a week.

To change the constituent parts of Government must be always dangerous, for who can tell where changes will stop. A new representation will want the reverence of antiquity, and the firmness of Establishment. The new senate will be considered as Mushrooms which springing in a day may be blasted in a night.

What will a parliament chosen in any new manner, whether more or less numerous, do which is not done by such parliaments as we have? Will it be less tumultuous if we have more, or less mercenary if we[2] have fewer? There is no danger that the parliament as now chosen should betray any of our important rights, and that is all that we can wish.

If the scheme were more reasonable this is not a time for innovation. I am afraid of a civil war. The business of every wise man seems to be now to keep his ground.

I am very glad you are coming. I am etc.

SAM. JOHNSON

1. On 7 May 1782, William Pitt the younger had moved that "a committee be appointed to enquire into the present State of the Representation of the Commons of Great Britain in parliament" (*Parliamentary History of England*, 1814, XXII.1422). The motion was defeated, but only by twenty votes (*Parliamentary History*, XXII.1438). Although emphasizing that he opposed extension of the franchise to all male citizens, Pitt continued to press for parliamentary reform, and placed three new resolutions before the House of Commons in May 1783. These too were defeated, by an even larger majority than in 1782 (*Parliamentary History*, XXIII.827, 830, 834, 875). Taylor's patrons the Cavendishes and other prominent Whigs opposed Pitt's reform program.

2. MS: "we" superimposed upon "they" partially erased

Unidentified Correspondent

WEDNESDAY 22 JANUARY 1783

MS: Houghton Library.

Sir: Jan. 22, 1783

You once gave me hope that You could procure me a large packet sent to me from the East Indies some years ago, which being landed at Lisbon and sent by the packet was charged, as I remember, seven pounds ten shillings, a larger sum than it was convenient for me to pay for intelligence.[1] I have now particular want of it, and if by the great indulgence of your office, it be granted me it will be a high favour to, Sir, Your most humble servant,

SAM. JOHNSON

1. "A curious incident happened to-day [5 Apr. 1776]. . . . Francis [Barber] announced that a large packet was brought to him [SJ] from the post-office, said to have come from Lisbon, and it was charged *seven pounds ten shillings*. He would not receive it, supposing it to be some trick, nor did he even look at it. But upon enquiry afterwards he found that it was a real packet for him, from that very friend in the East-Indies of whom he had been speaking; and the ship which carried it having come to Portugal, this packet, with others, had been put into the post-office at Lisbon" (*Life* III.22–23). The friend in question was Joseph Fowke (*Life* III.20 n. 1).

George Strahan

JANUARY 1783[1]

MS: Berg Collection, New York Public Library.[2]

ADDRESS: To the Reverend Mr. Strahan.

Sir:

You seem to suppose that your Father had some influence on

1. I follow Hill (II.283) and Chapman (III.3) in assigning this letter conjecturally to Jan. 1783, on the basis of the sequence of letters relating to the troubled relations between William and George Strahan. *Ante* To George Strahan, 19 Aug. 1782; 10 Oct. 1782; 16 Jan. 1783; *Ante* To William Strahan, 11 Dec. 1782.

2. MS: mutilated; approximately one and three-quarters inches missing from top of sheet

my Letter. You are utterly mistaken. He knows nothing of it. My reason for writing was, if I had done any mischief to undo it as far as I could by good counsel. You have done what I wished to be done, and I have nothing more to recommend. Of promises I know nothing, and have nothing to say.

The conference may perhaps as well be forborn, but if it must be, it will probably be made by the presence of others shorter and more moderate; and may therefore do less harm, if it does no good.

⟨ ⟩

Debts of kindness there may be, but[3] surely those debts are not very niggardly paid, when nothing is required but to show that they are wanted.

I flatter myself that by this time peace and content are restored among You, if not, I wish I could recal them. I am, Sir, Your humble Servant,

SAM. JOHNSON

3. MS: "but" superimposed upon "and" partially erased

Elizabeth Lawrence

TUESDAY 4 FEBRUARY 1783

MS: Hyde Collection.

ADDRESS: To Mrs. Eliz. Laurence in Castle Street, Canterbury.

Madam: Bolt court, Fleetstreet, Febr. 4, 1783

Though the account with which You favoured me in your last letter could not give the pleasure that I wished, yet I was glad to receive it, for[1] my affection for my dear friend makes me desirous of knowing his state, whatever it be.

I beg therefore that You continue to let me know from time to time all that You observe.[2]

Many fits of severe ilness have for about twelve months past

1. MS: "f" superimposed upon "I"
2. Cf. *Ante* To Elizabeth Lawrence, 26 Aug. 1782.

forced my kind Physician often upon my mind. I am now better, and hope gratitude as well as distress can be a motive to remembrance.

I am afraid to ask questions, yet I am very desirous to know what You think of his memory and his judgement, and whether he is silent for want of words, or by having lost the power of utterance. Does he grow stronger or weaker? is he more or less attentive to things about him? Dear Madam let me know what is to be known; write at leisure and write at large. I am, Madam, Your most humble servant,

SAM. JOHNSON

James Boswell

c. TUESDAY 4 FEBRUARY 1783

PRINTED SOURCE: JB's *Life*, 1791, II.431.

I am delighted with your account of your activity at Auchinleck, and wish the old gentleman, whom you have so kindly removed, may live long to promote your prosperity by his prayers.[1] You have now a new character and new duties; think on them, and practise them.

Make an impartial estimate of your revenue, and whatever it is, live upon less. Resolve never to be poor. Frugality is not only the basis of quiet, but of beneficence. No man can help others that wants help himself; we must have enough before we have to spare.[2]

I am glad to find that Mrs. Boswell grows well; and hope that to keep her well, no care nor caution will be omitted. May you long live happily together.

1. JB had sent SJ "a full account of what I was doing at Auchinleck, and particularly mentioned what I knew would please him, —my having brought an old man of eighty-eight from a lonely cottage to a comfortable habitation . . . where he had good neighbours near to him" (*Life* IV.163). John Colville, a retired servant on the Auchinleck estate, praised his new quarters as "the best house he had ever been in" (*Boswell: The Applause of the Jury*, ed. I. S. Lustig and F. A. Pottle, 1981, p. 50 and n. 7).

2. Cf. *Ante* To JB, 7 Sept. 1782.

When you come hither, pray bring with you Baxter's Anacreon.[3] I cannot get that edition in London.

3. When SJ examined the library at Auchinleck, 2 Nov. 1773, he "found here Baxter's *Anacreon*, which he told me he had long enquired for in vain, and began to suspect there was no such book" (*Life* v.376). Because SJ's undergraduate book collection included "Anacreon per Baxter," it seems likely that the rarity he sought was the corrected edition of 1710 (*Johns. Glean.* v.229). William Baxter (1650–1723) had brought out the first edition in 1695.

Herbert Croft

MONDAY 10 FEBRUARY 1783

MS: British Library.
ADDRESS: To Mr. Crofts.

Dear Sir: Febr. 10, 1783

It was not insensibility of your kindness, I hope, that made me negligent of[1] answering your letter, for which I now return you thanks, and which I consider as a strong proof of your regard.

I am better, much better, and am now in hope of being gradually well and of being able [to] show some gratitude for the kindness of my friends. I do not despair of seeing Oxford in the Summer,[2] and, in the mean time, hope now and then to see you here. I am, Dear Sir, Your most obliged,

SAM. JOHNSON

1. MS: "of" superimposed upon "in"
2. SJ did not visit Oxford until June 1784 (*Post* To Edmund Allen, 7 June 1784).

Thomas Cadell

FEBRUARY 1783[1]

1. See n. 2 below. The postulated link to payment for the revised *Lives* is reinforced by the handwriting, which is that of SJ's last few years.

MS: Hyde Collection.

ADDRESS: To Mr. Cadel, Bookseller.

ENDORSEMENT: Dr. Johnson.

Sir:

I shall be glad to see You and Mr. Nicol on tuesday morning.

Be pleased to return my respectful thanks to the proprietors, to whom I wish that success in all their undertakings which such liberality deserves.[2] I am, sir, your very humble servant,

SAM. JOHNSON

2. On 19 Feb. SJ received £100 for revising the text of his *Lives of the Poets* for the edition of 1783 (*Life* IV.35 n. 3; J. D. Fleeman, *A Preliminary Handlist of Documents and Manuscripts of SJ*, 1967, p. 32).

Hester Maria Thrale

MONDAY 17 FEBRUARY *or* MARCH 1783

MS: Hyde Collection.

ADDRESS: To Miss Thrale, No. 37 Argyle Street, Monday nine in the morning.

POSTMARKS: PENY POST PAYD, T MO, [Undeciphered].

Dearest Love: Monday, 17th

I am engaged to dinner to morrow, of which I forgot to tell You, but I hope You will favour me with a call early on Wednesday. I am, dearest, Your most humble servant,

SAM. JOHNSON

Joshua Reynolds

WEDNESDAY 19 FEBRUARY 1783

MS: Yale Center for British Art.

ADDRESS: To Sir Joshua Reynolds.

Sir: Febr. 19, 1783

Mr. Mason's address to You deserves no great praise it is lax without easiness, and familiar without gayety. Of his Translation I think much more favourably,[1] so far as I have read, which is not a great part, I find[2] him better than exact, he has his authours distinctness and clearness, without his dryness and Sterility.

As I suspect You to have lost your Lives, I desire You to accept of these volumes and to keep them somewhere out of harm's way; that You may sometimes remember the writer.[3] I am, Sir, Your most humble servant,

SAM. JOHNSON

1. *The Art of Painting of Charles Alphonse du Fresnoy . . . with Annotations by Sir Joshua Reynolds, Knt,* William Mason's verse translation of du Fresnoy's *De Arte Graphica* (1668), had been published earlier that year. Mason dedicated the work to Reynolds, who presented a copy to SJ (J. D. Fleeman, *A Preliminary Handlist of Copies of Books associated with Dr. Samuel Johnson,* 1984, p. 54, No. 235).

2. MS: "f" superimposed upon "th"

3. In fact Reynolds had not lost SJ's gift: the presentation set of *Prefaces* (1779–81) which descended through the family is now at the Yale Center for British Art. Also at the Yale Center are "these volumes": Sir Joshua's set of the revised 1783 edition.

William Richardson

SUNDAY 23 FEBRUARY 1783

PRINTED SOURCE: *Edinburgh Magazine or Literary Miscellany,* 1791, XIV.357.

Sir, Feb. 23, 1783

You will do me a favour, by returning my respectful thanks to Dr. Ogilvie, for the kind present of his book; and let him know, that I take amiss to be suspected of having forgotten him.[1] I hope we shall never forget each other. I am, Sir, Your humble servant,

SAM. JOHNSON

1. The Rev. John Ogilvie (1733–1813), D.D., Scots homilist and poet, promi-

nent in both Edinburgh and London literary circles, had been introduced to SJ in 1763 by JB (*Life* I.423). Ogilvie had sent SJ (via William Richardson) a copy of his *Inquiry into the Causes of Infidelity and Scepticism*, published earlier that year. Accompanying the book was a letter that reminded SJ of their first meeting "as an event that might have been erased from his memory" (*Edinburgh Magazine* XIV.357 n. *).

Frances Reynolds

MARCH 1783

MS: Society of Antiquaries, London.
ADDRESS: To Mrs. Reynolds.
ENDORSEMENT: Dr. Johnson believe in March 83.

Dear Madam:

I have not been at Mrs. Thrales since I saw You, and therefore have not the papers.[1] I am going to day.

For saturday I have engaged company. Please to let it alone to the saturday following, or some other day. I am, Madam, Your most etc.

SAM. JOHNSON

1. SJ may refer to the manuscript of Reynolds's "Enquiry Concerning the Principles of Taste." *Ante* To Frances Reynolds, 21 July 1781 and nn. 1, 2.

Joshua Reynolds

TUESDAY 4 MARCH 1783

MS: Hyde Collection.
ADDRESS: To Sir Joshua Reynolds.

Sir: March 4, 1783

I have sent You back Mr. Crabb's poem which I read with great delight.[1] It is original, vigorous, and elegant.

1. The Rev. George Crabbe (1754–1832), clergyman and poet, author of *The Village* (1783) and *The Borough* (1810), had been introduced by his patron Edmund Burke to Joshua Reynolds. Reynolds in turn had introduced Crabbe to SJ, who

The alterations which I have made, I do not require him to adopt, for my lines are perhaps not often better [than] his own, but he may take mine and his own together, and perhaps between them produce something better than either.[2]

He is not to think his copy wantonly defaced. A wet sponge will wash all the red lines away, and leave the page clear.

His dedi[c]ation will be least liked, it were better to contract it into a short spritely address.[3]

I do not doubt of Mr. Crabbe's success.[4] I am, Sir, Your most humble servant,

SAM. JOHNSON

"consented to read and give his opinion of the *Village*" (*Life* IV.509; Crabbe, *Poems*, 1808, p. xii).

2. According to JB, who saw the revised manuscript of *The Village*, SJ "had taken the trouble not only to suggest slight corrections and variations, but to furnish some lines, when he thought he could give the writer's meaning better than in the words of the manuscript" (*Boswell: The Applause of the Jury*, ed. I. S. Lustig and F. A. Pottle, 1981, p. 85; *Life* IV.175).

3. When *The Village* appeared in May, it contained neither a dedication nor an address, "the lines to the memory of Lord Robert Manners being perhaps intended as a substitute" (George Crabbe, *The Complete Poetical Works*, ed. Norma Dalrymple-Champneys and Arthur Pollard, 1988, I.664).

4. "The son says that the success of the poem exceeded his father's utmost expectations and that his reputation was now 'by universal consent greatly raised and permanently established.' . . . The reviewers, however, although on the whole favourable, were not of one mind about the truth of Crabbe's sombre picture of rural life" (Dalrymple-Champneys and Pollard, *Complete Poetical Works*, I.664).

William Scott

TUESDAY 4 MARCH 1783

PRINTED SOURCE: Christie's Catalogue, 5 June 1888, Lot No. 52.

[Asking him to give employment to a young man for whom he is interested; and says,] He is not without literature, and I hope he will be diligent.[1]

1. According to G. B. Hill, "it is very likely that the young man was Crabbe" (Hill II.288). However, as R. W. Chapman observes, "'not without literature' is

faint praise," and SJ "was much struck with C's literature" (Chapman III.10). At this time, moreover, Crabbe, who was serving as chaplain to the fourth Duke of Rutland, was hardly "a man in great distress" (*Post* To William Scott, 17 Mar. 1783; *Selected Letters and Journals of George Crabbe*, ed. T. C. Faulkner, 1985, pp. 20 n. 4, 24).

William Scott

MONDAY 17 MARCH 1783

PRINTED SOURCE: Sotheby's Catalogue, 21 Mar. 1966, Lot No. 254, p. 74.

Whether you have received my letter, or have forgotten it I know not.[1] . . . if you know any business, in which a man not without literature, and accustomed to write for Lawyers can be employed, you would be pleased to make trial of my friend, by which you will have the satisfaction of helping a man in great distress . . .[2]

1. *Ante* To William Scott, 4 Mar. 1783.
2. *Ante* To William Scott, 4 Mar. 1783 and n. 1.

Hester Thrale

SUNDAY 23 MARCH 1783

MS: Rylands Library.
ADDRESS: To Mrs. Thrale.

Dear Madam: March 23, 1783

I hope You did not take cold with me, and however You took it, I hope it will be soon better. I have already taken all Dr. Pepys's pills, which have acted only as opiate, and have not exerted that power in any great degree. Ask his leave that if I find a cathartick necessary I may take it.

I am, I think, recovering. Mr. Langton is in town with Lady

Rothes. I am invited to meet them to morrow, but will not venture.

I hope, Harriet is well,[1] and all of you. I am, Dear Madam, etc.

SAM. JOHNSON

Dr. Hunter is dying.[2]

1. Henrietta Sophia, Hester Thrale's youngest child, had been ill, successively, with swollen glands, whooping cough, and measles (Hyde, 1977, p. 237). *Post* To Hester Thrale, 1 May 1783.

2. On 15 Mar. William Hunter went to bed, suffering from the gout that had afflicted him for several years; on the 20th he insisted on delivering a lecture, but fainted toward its conclusion. On the night of 21–22 Mar. he suffered a stroke, and he died on the 30th (S. F. Simmons and John Hunter, *An Account of the Life and Writings of the Late William Hunter, M.D.* [1783], ed. C. H. Brock, 1983, pp. 26–27).

Hester Thrale

SUNDAY 30 MARCH 1783

MS: Rylands Library.

ADDRESS: To Mrs. Thrale.

Madam: March 30, 1783

Pray let me know how my dear little Miss does.[1] That is the most pressing question, but as an Episode You may let me know how any of You do.

My *Arthritical* complaints, there's a nice word, rather encrease, but are not yet, as the Scotch say, *ferious*.[2] I took the poppy last night, and slept so well this morning, as I have not done for some time past. Such a sleep I had as I wish You to have, whenever You are in good humour with, Your humble servant,

SAM. JOHNSON

1. *Ante* To Hester Thrale, 23 Mar. 1783, n. 1.

2. *feerious*: "furious" (*Scottish National Dictionary*).

Hester Thrale

MONDAY 31 MARCH 1783

MS: Rylands Library.

ADDRESS: To Mrs. Thrale.

Dear Madam: Boltcourt, March 31, 1783

I hope to hear again that my dear little girl is out of danger.[1] It will now be pleasing to consider that she and her sister have past two of the ambushes of life, and that you may leave them at a distance with less anxiety.[2]

I am willing to think that lightened, as You are, of part of your load, you will bear the rest with less difficulty, and recover your health as you recover your quiet.[3]

My foot is neither better nor worse, the rest of me is rather better. I am, Madam, Your humble servant,

SAM. JOHNSON

1. *Ante* To Hester Thrale, 23 Mar. 1783, n. 1.

2. Cecilia Thrale had contracted whooping cough, and her mother, fearing contagion, placed her with a nurse at Streatham. By 1 Apr., however, she appeared to have recovered sufficiently for Hester Thrale to proceed with her plans for Bath (see below, n. 3).

3. A settlement having been reached with Lady Salusbury, Hester Thrale resolved to move to Bath, where she could live economically and escape the rumors circulating about her attachment to Gabriel Piozzi (Clifford, 1952, pp. 219–20; *Thraliana* I.561–62). On 5 Apr. she and SJ met for what may well have been the last time (*Works*, Yale ed. I.358–59). Shortly thereafter she left London (*Thraliana* I.561).

James Barry[1]

SATURDAY 12 APRIL 1783

MS: Hyde Collection.

1. James Barry (1741–1806), R.A., painter (specializing in historical and mythological subjects) and Professor of Painting at the Royal Academy (1782–99). SJ, who admired Barry's "grasp of mind" (*Life* IV.224), had sat to him for his portrait (see frontispiece to Volume II). Later that year Barry was invited to join the Essex Head Club (*Post* To Joshua Reynolds, 4 Dec. 1783).

Sir: Apr. 12, 1783

Mr. Lowe's exclusion from the exhibition gives him more trouble than You and the other Gentlemen of the council could imagine or intend.[2] He considers disgrace and ruin as the inevitable consequences of your determination.

He says that some pictures have been received after rejection, and if there be any such precedent, I earnestly entreat that You will use your interest in his favour. Of his work I can say nothing; I pretend not to judge of painting, and this picture I never saw; but I conceive it extremely hard to shut out any man from the possibility of success, and therefore I repeat my request that you will propose the reconsideration of Mr. Lowe's case;[3] and if there be any among the council with whom my name can have any weight be pleased to communicate to them the desire of, Sir, Your most humble servant,

SAM. JOHNSON

2. Mauritius Lowe had submitted a large canvas, *The Deluge*, for possible inclusion in the Royal Academy's annual exhibition, but his effort, "execrable beyond belief," had been refused (James Northcote, *Life of Sir Joshua Reynolds*, 1818, II.142; *Life* IV.201).

3. SJ's appeals to Barry and to Reynolds (*Post* To Joshua Reynolds, 12 Apr. 1783) had the desired effect: Lowe's painting was admitted to the exhibition, where it was hung by itself in a room otherwise devoted to students' models of antique statuary (Northcote, *Reynolds*, II.141; M. R. Brownell, *Samuel Johnson's Attitude to the Arts*, 1989, p. 62).

Joshua Reynolds

SATURDAY 12 APRIL 1783

MS: Beinecke Library. The transcript (in JB's hand) used as copy for JB's *Life*.

HEADING: To Sir Joshua Reynolds.

Sir, April 12, 1783

Mr. Lowe considers himself as cut off from all credit and all hope by the rejection of his picture from the exhibition.[1]

1. *Ante* To James Barry, 12 Apr. 1783 and nn. 2, 3.

Upon this work he has exhausted all his powers and suspended all his expectations; and certainly, to be refused an opportunity of taking the opinion of the publick is in itself a very great hardship. It is to be condemned without a trial.

If you could procure the revocation of this incapacitating edict you would deliver an unhappy man from great affliction. The council has sometimes reversed its own determination and I hope that by your interposition this luckless picture may be got admitted.[2] I am Sir, your most humble servant,

SAM. JOHNSON

2. SJ intended Reynolds to read this letter at the meeting of the Council of the Royal Academy (C. R. Leslie and T. Taylor, *The Life and Times of Sir Joshua Reynolds*, 1865, II.396).

Lucy Porter

c. SATURDAY 12 APRIL 1783

PRINTED SOURCE: JB's *Life*, 1791, II.444.

It is with no great expectation of amendment that I make every year a journey into the country; but it is pleasant to visit those whose kindness has been often experienced.

Richard Paul Jodrell

TUESDAY 15 APRIL 1783

MS: Hyde Collection.

ADDRESS: To —— Jodrel, Esq., in Berners Street.

POSTMARK: PENY POST PAYD T TU.

Dear Sir: Apr. 15, —83

When I accepted your kind invitation at Mr. Paradise's I did not recollect that it was a week in which I do not much like to go abroad.[1] I will certainly pay my respects to You at another time, though I shall not easily pay as much respect as your Literature deserves.[2] I am, Sir, Your most humble servant,

SAM. JOHNSON

1. In 1783 Easter fell on 20 Apr. Cf. *Ante* To John Taylor, 17 Apr. 1772.
2. *Post* To Hester Thrale, 8 May 1783.

Thomas Cadell

WEDNESDAY 16 APRIL 1783

MS: Huntington Library.
ADDRESS: To Mr. Cadel.

Apr. 16

Mr. Johnson begs the favour of Mr. Cadel that he will order three sets of lives to be tied up separately with these directions.

To the Honourable Warren Hastings Esq. Governor general of Bengal.

To Sir Robert Chambers

To Joseph Fowke Esq.

and then let them all be put into one parcel, which Mr. Johnson will send for to morrow.[1]

1. The three sets of SJ's revised *Lives of the Poets* (*Ante* To John Nichols, 28 Oct. 1782, nn. 3, 5) were sent to Chambers for distribution (*Post* To Robert Chambers, 19 Apr. 1783; *Post* To Joseph Fowke, 19 Apr. 1783).

Thomas Lawrence

WEDNESDAY 16 APRIL 1783

PRINTED SOURCE: Maggs Catalogue 337, 1915, Lot No. 796, p. 74.

Since your departure I have often wanted your assistance as well as your conversation. I have been very ill, but am now better, and it would be a great comfort added to my recovery if I could hear that you are better too.

We can now do nothing more than pray for one another. God bless for Christ's sake.

Robert Chambers

SATURDAY 19 APRIL 1783

MS: Hyde Collection.

ENDORSEMENT: Doct. Sam. Johnson, Boltcourt, Fleetstreet, 19 Ap. 83.

Dear Sir: Bolt court, Fleetstreet, Apr. 19, 1783

Of the books which I now send You I sent you the first edition, but it fell by the chance of war into the hands of the French. I sent likewise to Mr. Hastings. Be[1] pleased to have these parcels properly delivered.[2]

Removed as We are with so much land and sea between us, We ought to compensate the difficulty of correspondence by the length of our letters, yet searching my memory, I do not [find] much to communicate. Of all publick transactions You have more exact accounts than I can give; You know our foreign miscarriages and our intestine[3] discontents, and do not want to be told that we have now neither power nor peace, neither influence in other nations nor quiet amongst ourselves. The state of the Publick, and the operations of government have little influence upon the private happiness of private men, nor can I pretend that much of the national calamities is felt by me; yet I cannot but suffer[4] some pain when I compare the state of this kingdom, with that in which we triumphed twenty years ago. I have at least endeavoured to preserve order and support Monarchy.

Having been thus allured to the mention of myself, I shall

1. MS: "B" superimposed upon "I"
2. *Ante* To Thomas Cadell, 16 Apr. 1783 and n. 1.
3. MS: "s" superimposed upon "r"
4. MS: "suffer" superimposed upon undeciphered erasure

give You a little of my story. That dreadful ilness which seized me at New inn Hall,[5] left consequences which have I think always hung upon me. I have never since cared much to walk. My mental abilities I do not perceive that it impaired. One great abatement of all miseries was the attention of Mr. Thrale, which from our first acquaintance was never intermitted. I passed far the greater part of many years in his house where I had all the pleasure of riches without the solicitude. He took me into France one year,[6] and into Wales another,[7] and if he had lived would have shown me Italy and perhaps many other countries, but he died in the Spring of eighty one,[8] and left me to write his epitaph.[9]

But for much of this time my constitutional maladies persued me. My thoughts were disturbed, my nights were insufferably restless, and by spasms in the breast I was condemned to the torture of sleepyness without the power to sleep. Those spasms after enduring them more than twenty years I eased by three powerful remedies, abstinence, opium, and mercury, but after a short time they were succeeded by a strange oppression of another kind which when I lay down disturbed me with a sensation like flatulence or intumescence which I cannot describe. To this supervened a difficulty of respiration, such as sometimes makes it painful to cross a street or climb to my chamber, which I have eased by venisection till the Physician forbids me to bleed, as my legs have begun to swel. Almost all the last year past in a succession of diseases ἐκ κακῶν κακά,[10] and this year till within these few days has heaped misery upon me. I have just now a lucid interval.

5. In all likelihood SJ refers to the unspecified illness that afflicted him in Apr. 1768, while he was working with Chambers on the Vinerian Lectures (*Ante* To Hester Thrale, 28 Apr. 1768).

6. *Ante* To Robert Levet, 18 Sept. 1775.

7. *Ante* To Bennet Langton, 5 July 1774.

8. *Ante* To Joshua Reynolds, 4 Apr. 1781.

9. For the monument to Henry Thrale in St. Leonard's, Streatham, SJ had composed a lengthy Latin epitaph (*Johns. Misc.* 1.238–39; *Thraliana* 1.542–43; H. W. Bromhead, *The Heritage of St. Leonard's Parish Church, Streatham*, 1932, pp. 24–25).

10. ἐκ κακῶν κακά: "evils upon evils" (perhaps a reminiscence of Sophocles, *Oedipus at Colonus*, l. 1238).

With these afflictions, I have the common accidents of life to suffer. He that lives long must outlive many, and I am now sometimes to seek for friends of easy conversation and familiar confidence. Mrs. Williams is much worn; Mr. Levet died suddenly in my house about a year ago.[11] Doctor Lawrence is totally di[s]abled by a palsy, and can neither speak nor write. He is removed to Canterbury.[12] Beauclerc died about two years ago and in his last sickness desired to be buried by the side of his Mother.[13] Langton has eight children by Lady Rothes. He lives very little in London, and is by no means at ease.[14] Goldsmith died partly of a fever and partly of anxiety, being immoderately and disgracefully in debt.[15] Dier lost his fortune by dealing in the East India Stock, and, I fear, languished into the grave.[16] Boswels father is lately dead, but has left the estate incumbered;[17] Boswel has, I think, five children. He is now paying us his annual visit, he is all that he was, and more. Doctor Scot prospers exceedingly in the commons, but I seldom see him; He is married and has a Daughter.[18]

Jones now Sir William, will give You the present state of the club, which is now very miscellaneous, and very heterogeneous,[19] it is therefore without confidence, and without pleasure. I go to it only as to a kind of publick dinner. Reynolds con-

11. *Ante* To Thomas Lawrence, 17 Jan. 1782.

12. *Ante* To Hester Thrale, 9 May 1782 and n. 3; *Ante* To John Taylor, 3 Aug. 1782.

13. *Ante* To JB, 8 Apr. 1780 and n. 5.

14. SJ refers to Langton's finances: see below and n. 31.

15. *Ante* To JB, 4 July 1774; *Ante* To Bennet Langton, 5 July 1774.

16. Samuel Dyer inherited £8,000 upon the deaths of his mother and brother. He then lost this sum—according to SJ and Sir John Hawkins, by investing unwisely in East India Company stock; according to Richard Gough, by taking SJ's advice "to sink his fortune in annuities on Lord Verney's estates" (Clifford, 1979, p. 37; Hawkins, p. 231; *Lit. Anec.* VI.266 n. *). "When Dyer died suddenly at the age of forty-seven in 1772, it was rumored that he had committed suicide, leaving insufficient money even to pay for his funeral" (Clifford, 1979, p. 37). SJ forgets that Chambers did not leave for India until 1774, and would therefore have heard of Dyer's death.

17. *Ante* To JB, 7 Sept. 1782 and n. 2.

18. In 1781 William Scott had married Anna Maria Bagnall, eldest daughter of John Bagnall, Earley Court, Berks. Their daughter's name was Mary Anne (*c.* 1783–1842).

19. *heterogeneous*: "not kindred; opposite or dissimilar in nature" (SJ's *Dictionary*).

tinues to rise in reputation and in riches, but his health has been shaken.[20] Dr. Percy is now Bishop of Dromore, but has I believe lost his only son.[21] Such are the deductions from human happiness.

I[22] have now reached an age which is to expect many diminutions of the good, whatever it be, that life affords; I have lost many friends, I am now either afflicted or threatened by many diseases, but perhaps not with more than are commonly incident to encrease of years, and I am afraid that I bear the weight of time with unseemly, if not with sinful impatience. I hope that God will enable me to correct this as well as my other faults, before he calls me to appear before him.

In return for this history of myself I shall expect some account of You, who by your Situation have much more to tell. I hope to hear that the Ladies and the Children are all well, and that your constitution accommodates itself easily to the climate. If You have health, You may study, and if You can study, You will surely not miss the opportunity which place and power give You, beyond what any Englishman qualified by previous knowledge, ever enjoyed before, of enquiring into Asiatick Literature. Buy manuscripts, consult the Scholars of the country, learn the languages, at least select one, and master it.[23] To the Malabarick Books Europe is, I think, yet a Stranger.[24] But my advice comes late; what You purpose to do, You have already begun, but in all your good purposes

20. *Ante* To Joshua Reynolds, 14 Nov. 1782 and n. 1.

21. *Ante* To JB, 13 Nov. 1779, n. 6.

22. MS: "I I"

23. In 1797 Chambers was elected President of the Asiatic Society of Bengal. In his presidential address, 18 Jan. 1798, he confessed: "I thought myself deficient in one attainment which might be expected in a President, in as much as I have but a slight and superficial knowledge of any *Asiatick* language. . . . If it is now too late, at the age of sixty, greatly to increase my own stock of Oriental literature, I will at least endeavour to promote the increase of it in others" (*Asiatick Researches*, 1801, VI.5). Nevertheless, "by the end of his life in 1803, Chambers had collected the largest private library of Sanskrit manuscripts in any European's possession" (T. M. Curley, "Samuel Johnson and India," in *Re-Viewing Samuel Johnson*, ed. Nalini Jain, 1991, p. 26).

24. SJ may refer to Tamil palm-leaf manuscripts, to books printed from the Tamil types introduced by the Portugese, or to Tamil literature in general.

persevere. Life is short, and You do not intend to pass all your life in India.

How long You will stay, I cannot conjecture.[25] The effects of English Judicature are not believed here to have added any thing to the happiness of the new dominions. Of You, Sir, I rejoice to say that I have heard no evil. There was a trifling charge produced in parliament, but it seems to be forgotten, nor did it appear to imply any thing very blamable.[26] This purity of character You will, I hope continue to retain. One of my last wishes for you, at a gay table was *ἀρετήν τε καὶ ὀλβόν*.[27] Let me now add in a more serious hour, and in more powerful words. *Keep innocency, and take heed to the thing that is right, for that shall bring a Man peace at the last.*[28]

I shall think myself favoured by any help that [you] shall give to Mr. Joseph Fowke, or Mr. Laurence.[29] Fowke was always friendly to me, and Laurence is the son of a Man, whom I have long placed in the first rank of my friends. Do not let my recommendation be without effect.

Let me now mention an occasion on which You may perhaps do great good without evil to yourself. Langton is much embarrassed by a mortgage made, I think, by his grandfather, and perhaps aggravated by his father. The Creditor calls for his money, and it is in the present general distress very difficult to make a *versura*.[30] If You could let him have six thousand pounds upon the security of the same land, you would save him from the necessity of selling part of his Estate under the great disadvantage produced by the present high price of money.[31] This proposal needs give You

25. Chambers returned to England in 1799.

26. *Ante* To Richard Chambers, 8 July 1782.

27. *ἀρετήν τε καὶ ὄλβον*: "success and prosperity" (Homeric Hymn xv, "To Heracles the Lion-Hearted," l. 9, trans. H. G. Evelyn-White, Loeb ed.).

28. "Keep innocency, and take heed unto the thing that is right: for that shall bring a man peace at the last" (Psalm 37:38, Book of Common Prayer).

29. *Ante* To Robert Chambers, 30 Sept. 1773 and n. 4.

30. *versura*: "the process of exchanging one creditor for another (by borrowing to pay a debt)" (*Oxford Latin Dictionary*).

31. The estate in question appears to have been a property of over one thousand

no pain, for Langton knows[32] nothing of it, and may perhaps have settled his affairs before the answer can be received. As the security is good, You should not take more than four per cent.

Nothing now, I think, remains but that I assure you, as I do, of my kindness, and good wishes, and express my hopes that You do not forget your old Friend and humble servant,

SAM. JOHNSON

Mr. Langton, who is just com[e] in, sends his best respects. But he knows still nothing.

---

acres in Oxcombe, Lincolnshire, which had been owned by the Langton family since *c.* 1641. It seems likely that in the early 1790s Langton was obliged to sell the estate (Fifer, p. 276 n. 2).

32. MS: "k" superimposed upon "n"

Joseph Fowke

SATURDAY 19 APRIL 1783

PRINTED SOURCE: *Original Letters*, ed. Rebecca Warner, 1817, pp. 207–9.

Dear Sir, April 19, 1783

To shew you, that neither length of time, nor distance of place, withdraws you from my memory, I have sent you a little present, which will be transmitted by Sir Rob. Chambers.[1]

To your former letters I made no answer, because I had none to make. Of the death of the unfortunate man,[2] I believe Europe thinks as you think;[3] but it was past prevention; and it

1. *Ante* To Thomas Cadell, 16 Apr. 1783 and n. 1.

2. Warner interpolates, "(meaning Nundocomar)" (p. 207).

3. Raja Nandakuma Bahadur, known to his English contemporaries as "Nundocomar," was "one of the most ambitious and unprincipled of the Indians connected with the Government of Bengal" (L. S. Sutherland, "New Evidence on the Nandakuma Trial," *English Historical Review* 72, 1957, pp. 438, 439). In 1775, the Raja had joined with opponents of Warren Hastings, including Joseph Fowke, to accuse the Governor-General of corruption. Key witnesses, however, charged Nandakuma with perjury and forgery. He was arrested, tried, and convicted by

was not fit for me to move a question in public, which I was not qualified to discuss; as the enquiry could then do no good, and I might have been silenced by a hardy denial of facts, which, if denied, I could not prove.[4]

Since we parted, I have suffered much sickness of body, and perturbation of mind. My mind, if I do not flatter myself, is unimpaired, except that sometimes my memory is less ready; but my body, though by nature very strong, has given way to repeated shocks.

Genua labant, vastos quatit æger anhelitus artus.[5] This line might have been written on purpose for me. You will see, however, that I have not totally forsaken literature. I can apply better to books than I could in some more vigorous parts of my life, at least than I *did*; and I have one more reason for reading; that time has, by taking away my companions, left me less opportunity of conversation. I have led an inactive and careless life; it is time at last to be diligent. There is yet provision to be made for eternity.

Let me know, dear Sir, what you are doing. Are you accumulating gold, or picking up diamonds? Or are you now sated with Indian wealth, and content with what you have? Have you vigour for bustle, or tranquillity for inaction? Whatever you do, I do not suspect you of pillaging or oppressing; and shall rejoice to see you return, with a body unbroken, and a mind uncorrupted.

You and I had hardly any common friends; and, therefore, I have few anecdotes to relate to you. Mr. Levet, who brought us into acquaintance, died suddenly at my house last year,[6] in his seventy-eighth year, or about that age. Mrs. Williams, the blind lady, is still with me, but much broken by a very weari-

---

the Supreme Court of Bengal, and executed 5 Aug. 1775 (Sutherland, "Nandakuma," pp. 439–41).

4. Cf. *Ante* To Francis Fowke, 11 July 1776.

5. *genua labant, vastos quatit aeger anhelitus artus*: "yet his slow knees totter and tremble and a painful gasping shakes his huge frame" (Virgil, *Aeneid* v.432, trans. H. R. Fairclough, Loeb ed.).

6. *Ante* To Thomas Lawrence, 17 Jan. 1782.

some and obstinate disease. She is, however, not likely to die; and it would delight me, if you would send her some *petty* token of your remembrance. You may send me one too.

Whether we shall ever meet again in this world, who can tell? Let us, however, wish well to each other. Prayers can pass the line, and the Tropics. I am, dear Sir, yours sincerely,

SAMUEL JOHNSON

The Mercers' Company

SATURDAY 19 APRIL 1783

PRINTED SOURCE: JB's *Life*, ed. Malone, 1811, IV.226.
ADDRESS: To the Worshipful Company of the Mercers.

Bolt-court,
Fleet-street, April 19, 1783

Gentlemen,

At the request of the Reverend Mr. James Compton, who now solicits your votes to be elected Under-Master of St. Paul's School,[1] I testify, with great sincerity, that he is in my opinion, a man of abilities sufficient, and more than sufficient, for the duties of the office for which he is a candidate.[2] I am, Gentlemen, Your most humble servant,

SAM. JOHNSON

1. St. Paul's School, St. Paul's Churchyard, was founded in 1512 by John Colet, Dean of the Cathedral. Boys "were to be admitted without restriction of kin, country, or station; to be taught, free of expense, by a master, sur-master, and chaplain; and the oversight of the school was committed by the founder to the Mercers' Company" (Wheatley and Cunningham III.63).

2. "Though this testimony in Mr. Compton's favour was not attended with immediate success . . . yet Johnson's kindness was not without effect . . . for his letter procured Mr. Compton so many well-wishers in the respectable company of Mercers, that he was honoured, by the favour of several of its members, with more applications to teach Latin and French, than he could find time to attend to" (JB's *Life*, ed. Edmond Malone, 1811, IV.226, Malone's note).

Elizabeth Way

WEDNESDAY 23 APRIL 1783

MS: Stowe School Library, Buckinghamshire.

Dear Madam: Apr. 23, 1783

I have been so long oppressed by ilness, that my Friends must forgive many omissions. I am now better, and am desirous of clearing myself from all appearance of incivility and ingratitude by returning thanks for the elegant pocket book, which You have been pleased to send me, and which I shall look and think on with emotions of tenderness. I am, Dear Madam, Your most obliged, humble Servant,

SAM. JOHNSON

Lord Dartmouth

FRIDAY 25 APRIL 1783

PRINTED SOURCE: *The Manuscripts of the Earl of Dartmouth* (HMC XI. App.v.), 1887, I.447.

My Lord, April 25, 1783

The bearer, Mr. Desmoulins,[1] has persuaded himself that some testimonial from me will be useful to him in his application to your Lordship, and I hope that what I yield merely to his importunity will not be imputed to any vain conceit of my own importance.

He desires indeed nothing to be said but what is true; that he is not in difficulties by his own fault; that he has a brother and sister in great distress, and that if he should by your Lordship's favour now obtain any little employment, he will, I hope, do the business faithfully, and use the income properly. I am, my Lord, Your Lordship's most obedient and most humble servant,

SAM. JOHNSON

1. SJ may refer to John Desmoulins.

Hester Maria Thrale

SATURDAY 26 APRIL 1783

MS: The Earl of Shelburne.

ADDRESS: To Miss Thrale at Bath.

POSTMARK: ⟨26⟩ AP.

My dearest Love: London, Apr. 26, 1783

You did very kindly in writing to me and I hope you will let me hear of you very often. You have done very wisely in taking a Master for arithmetick, a science of which I would not have you soon think that you have enough. It will seem at first difficult, but you will soon find its usefulness so great that you will disregard the difficulty; and the progress will be easier than the beginning. Do not be content with what a single master dictates, but procure books. Different authours exhibit the same thing in different views, and what is obscure in one, may be clear in another. When you can readily apply numbers on emergent occasions, you will find yourself to think with so much clearness and certainty that the pleasure of arithmetick will attract you almost as much as the use.

I am not quite well, but so much better that the sight of me raises wonder. The cough goes and comes, but is not violent, I breathe with tolerable freedom, and the pain in my foot is gone. I may perhaps, with a little caution, have an easy summer. In the winter I shall envy my friend Ramsay's residence.[1]

The storms of life have for some time beaten hard upon us. I hope, we are all now in port, and glad to find ourselves out of the tumult, *though sails and tackling torn*.[2] Make my compliments. I am, Madam, Your humble servant,

SAM. JOHNSON

1. Allan Ramsay had gone to Italy in an attempt to improve his failing health.

2. SJ appears to have conflated "of sails and tackling reft" (*Richard III* IV.iv.234) with "though Shrouds and Tackle torn" (*Paradise Lost* II.1044).

Hester Thrale

THURSDAY 1 MAY 1783

MS: Hyde Collection.

ADDRESS: To Mrs. Thrale at Bath.

POSTMARK: 1 MA.

Dear Madam: London, May day, 1783

I am glad that You went to Streatham, though You could not save the dear, pretty, little girl.[1] I loved her, for She was Thrale's and your's, and by her dear Father's appointment in some sort mine;[2] I love You all, and therefore cannot without regret see the phalanx broken, and reflect that You and my other dear Girls are deprived of one that was born your friend. To such friends every one that has them, has recourse at last, when it is discovered, and discovered it seldom fails to be, that the fortuitous friendships of inclination or vanity are at the mercy of a thousand accidents. But we must still our disquiet with remembring that, where there is no guilt, all is for the best. I am glad to hear that Cecily is so near recovery.[3]

For some days after your departure I was pretty well, but I have begun to languish again, and last night was very tedious and oppressive. I excused myself to day from dining with General Paoli, where I love to dine, but I was griped by the talons of necessity.[4]

On Saturday I dined, as is usual, at the opening of the exhibition. Our company was splendid, whether more numerous than at any former time, I know not.[5] Our Tables seem always

1. On 18 Apr. Hester Thrale was summoned from Bath by the news that Harriet had died (*Ante* To Hester Thrale, 23 Mar. 1783, n. 1; Hyde, 1977, p. 237).

2. SJ, as one of the four executors appointed by Henry Thrale's will, shared the guardianship of the children (Clifford, 1952, p. 200).

3. *Ante* To Hester Thrale, 31 Mar. 1783, n. 2.

4. "I therefore told her, that destiny had ordained us to part; and that nothing should have torn me from her but the talons of necessity" (*Rambler* No. 113; *Works*, Yale ed. IV.239).

5. Eighty people paid eight shillings apiece to attend the Royal Academy dinner as compared with fifty-seven in 1781 (C. R. Leslie and T. Taylor, *The Life and Times of Sir Joshua Reynolds*, 1865, II.397 n. 1).

full. On monday, if I am told truth, were received at the door one hundred and ninety pounds, for the admission of three thousand eight hundred Spectators.[6] Supposing the show open ten hours, and the Spectators staying one with another each an hour, the rooms never had fewer than three hundred and eighty justling each other. Poor Lowe met some discouragement, but I interposed for him, and p[r]evailed.[7]

Mr. Barry's exhibition was opened the same day, and a book is published to recommend it, which, if You read it, You will find decorated with some satirical pictures of Sir Joshua and others. I have not escaped. You must however think with some esteem of Barry for the comprehension of his design.[8] I am, Madam, Your most humble servant,

SAM. JOHNSON

6. SJ was misinformed: the takings at the door on 28 Apr. amounted to £95 7*s.*—representing a total of 1,907 paying visitors (information supplied by Mr. Nicholas Savage, Royal Academy of Arts).

7. *Ante* To James Barry, 12 Apr. 1783 and nn. 2, 3; *Ante* To Joshua Reynolds, 12 Apr. 1783.

8. Working from 1777 to 1783, James Barry decorated the new exhibition room in the Adelphi (designed by Robert Adam for the Society of Arts) with an ambitious cycle of canvases on the subject of human culture. To accompany his project, Barry also composed a pamphlet entitled *An Account of a Series of Pictures in the Great Room of the Society of Arts, Manufactures, and Commerce* (1783). In this pamphlet Barry continues the attack on Reynolds that had begun in his *Inquiry into the Arts in England* (1775). Though he praises SJ as a patron of the arts, Barry does include derogatory references to ignorant "book-makers" and "short-sighted literati" (James Barry, *An Account*, in Barry, *Works*, 1809, II.309). M. R. Brownell suggests that there may also be an implicit criticism of SJ's praise for Reynolds in *Idler* No. 45 (Brownell, *Samuel Johnson's Attitude to the Arts*, 1989, pp. 69–70).

Joshua Reynolds

FRIDAY 2 MAY 1783

PRINTED SOURCE: JB's *Life*, 1793, III.474.

Dear Sir, May 2, 1783

The gentleman who waits on you with this, is Mr. Cruikshanks, who wishes to succeed his friend Dr. Hunter as Professor of

Anatomy in the Royal Academy.[1] His qualifications are very generally known, and it adds dignity to the institution that such men are candidates.[2] I am, Sir, Your most humble servant,

SAM. JOHNSON

1. William Cumberland Cruikshank (1745–1800), anatomist and surgeon, first studied and then collaborated with William Hunter, whose death on 30 Mar. had created the vacancy in question.

2. On 17 July the post went to the other candidate, John Sheldon (*GM* 1783, p. 626).

Hester Thrale

THURSDAY 8 MAY 1783

MS: Hyde Collection.

ADDRESS: To Mrs. Thrale at Bath.

POSTMARK: ⟨8⟩ MA.

Dear Madam: London, May 8, 1783

I thought your letter long in coming. I suppose it is true that I looked but languid at the exhibition,[1] but I have been worse since. Last wednesday the wednesday of last week[2] I came home ill from Mr. Jodrels, and after a tedious oppressive impatient night, sent an excuse to General Paoli, and took on thursday, two brisk cathartícks, and a dose of calomel. Little things do me no good. At night I was much better. Next day cathartick again, and the third day opium for my cough. I lived without flesh, all the three days. The recovery was more than I expected. I went to church on Sunday quite at ease.

The exhibition prospers so much that Sir Joshua says it will maintain the academy, he estimates the probable amount at three thousand pounds.[3] Steevens is of opinion that Crofts's

1. *Ante* To Hester Thrale, 1 May 1783.

2. MS: "the wednesday of last week" inserted above line for clarification

3. *Ante* To Hester Thrale, 1 May 1783. The total takings from the exhibition amounted to £2,629 19*s*. ("Royal Academy Cash Book, 1769–95": information supplied by Mr. Nicholas Savage, Royal Academy of Arts).

books will sell for near three times as much as they cost,[4] which however is not more than might be expected.

⟨Mrs.⟩ ⟨*three words*⟩ I know, but whom did Sir Joshua offend, and what did he do or think, that could so much displease?[5]

Favour me with a direction to Musgrave of Ireland, I have a charitable office to propose to him. Is he Knight or Baronet?[6]

My present circle of enjoyment is as narrow for me as the circus for Mrs. Montague.[7] When I first settled in this neighbourhood I had Richardson, and Lawrence, and Mrs. Allen at hand, I had Mrs. Williams then no bad companion, and Levet for a long time always to be had. If I now go out I must go far for company, and at last come back to two sick and discontented women,[8] who can hardly talk, if they had any thing to say, and whose hatred of each other makes one great exercise of their faculties.

But, with all these evils positive and privative, my health in its present humour promises to mend, and I, in my present humour, promise to take care of it, and, if we both keep our words, we may yet have a brush at the cobwebs in the sky.[9]

Let my dear Loves write to me, and do You write often yourself to, Dear Madam, Your most obliged and most humble servant,

SAM. JOHNSON

4. SJ refers to Herbert Croft.

5. MS: entire sentence heavily del.

6. *Ante* To Hester Thrale, 18 May 1776, n. 7. It is possible that SJ meant to recommend Anna Maria Phillips (*Post* To William Windham, 31 May 1783 and n. 3).

7. SJ suggests that Elizabeth Montagu, who lived expansively in London, felt (or would feel) confined by the comparatively restricted scale of the Circus at Bath, whose elegant terrace houses were designed to evoke the Coliseum in miniature.

8. SJ refers to Anna Williams and Elizabeth Desmoulins.

9. *Ante* To Hester Thrale, 3 Nov. 1777, n. 5.

Hester Maria Thrale

THURSDAY 22 MAY 1783

MS: The Earl of Shelburne.

ADDRESS: To Miss Thrale at Bath.

POSTMARK: 22 MA.

My dearest Love: London, May 22, 1783

What a terrible accident![1] How easily might it have been yet more mischievous. I hope my Mistress's hurt is neither of any danger nor of much pain. It teaches however, what though every thing teaches, is yet always forgotten, that we are perpetually within the reach of death.

I am glad that you have settled your mind to arithmetick, a species of knowledge perpetually useful, and indubitably certain. Do not content yourself with your master's lessons, but buy the books which treat of numbers.[2] Such as, Cocker's,[3] Hodder's,[4] and Wingate's Arithmetick,[5] and any other which every shop or stall will put in your way. Every writer will show you something which you did not know, or did not recollect.

Last week I was on Monday night at Lady Rothes's conversation,[6] it was a heavy night, Mrs. Montague missed.[7] On Tuesday I was at club, and dined out, I think, two days more. This Week I have been driven to opium and abstinence and physick, but I have been much visited. I am not much better for my regimen, but yesterday I dined with Langton, to day I dine with Mr. Whitebread,[8] and to morrow with Sir Joseph Banks. I believe, I refused an invitation for Saturday.

1. No details of this accident, which caused Hester Thrale both "hurt" and "fright," have been recovered (Cf. *Post* To Hester Maria Thrale, 2 June 1783).

2. *Ante* To Hester Maria Thrale, 26 Apr. 1783.

3. *Ante* To Hester Thrale, 6 Sept. 1773, n. 30.

4. SJ refers to *Hodder's Arithmetick* (1661).

5. SJ refers to *Arithmetique Made Easie* (1630), a manual by Edmund Wingate (1596–1656).

6. *Ante* To Hester Thrale, 11 Oct. 1779, n. 4.

7. The context makes it likely that SJ refers not to Bennet Langton's wife but to Jane Elizabeth Leslie (1750–1810), Countess of Rothes *suo jure*, the wife of Lucas Pepys.

8. It is likely that SJ refers to Samuel Whitbread.

Mrs. Desmoulins left us last week, so that I have only one sick woman to fight or play with instead of two, and there is more peace in the house.[9]

Let me know, my dear Love, how my Mistress goes on, and tell Susy that I shall answer her short letter.[10]

I am writing over the little garden. The poplars, which I have just now watered, grow kindly; they may expect not to be neglected for they came from Streatham.

Crescent illæ, crescetis amores.[11] I am, dear Madam, your most humble Servant,

SAM. JOHNSON

9. Troubled relations with Anna Williams may have driven Elizabeth Desmoulins away (*Ante* To Hester Thrale, 8 May 1783 and n. 8). She had departed by 17 May, but returned to SJ's household by June 1784 (*Boswell: The Applause of the Jury, 1782–1785*, ed. I. S. Lustig and F. A. Pottle, 1981, pp. 143, 226).

10. *Post* To Susanna Thrale, Late Spring or Early Summer 1783.

11. *certum est in silvis, inter spelaea ferarum / malle pati tenerisque meos incidere amores / arboribus: crescent illae, crescetis, amores*: "Well I know that in the woods, amid wild beasts' dens, it is better to suffer and carve my love on the young trees. They will grow; thou, too, my love, wilt grow" (Virgil, *Eclogues* x.52–54, trans. H. R. Fairclough, Loeb ed.).

John Wilkes

SATURDAY 24 MAY 1783

MS: British Library.

May 24, 1783[1]

Mr. Johnson returns thanks to Mr. and Miss Wilkes[2] for their kind invitation, but he is engaged for tuesday to Sir Joshua Reynolds, and for wednesday to Mr. Paradise.[3]

1. MS: "1783" added in an unidentified hand

2. Mary Wilkes (1750–1802), John Wilkes's only child.

3. SJ's note is accompanied by several lines in JB's hand, dated "Sunday, 25 May": "Mr. Boswell presents his best compliments to Mr. and Miss Wilkes, encloses Dr. Johnson's answer; and regrets much that so agreable a meeting must be deferred till next year, as Mr. Boswell is to set out for Scotland in a few days. Hopes Mr. Wilkes will write to him there" (MS: British Library). JB had engineered the invitation from Wilkes to SJ (*Life* IV.224 n. 2).

William Windham[1]

SATURDAY 31 MAY 1783

MS: Hyde Collection.

ENDORSEMENT: Dr. Johnson recommd. Philips.—May (Qy. June) 21st 1783.

HEADING in JB's hand: To The Right Honourable William Windham.

Sir: London, May 31, 1783

The Bringer of this letter is the Father[2] of Miss Philips a singer who comes to try her voice on the Stage at Dublin.[3]

Mr. Philips is one of my old Friends, and, as I am of opinion that neither he nor his daughter will do any thing that can disgrace their benefactors, I take the liberty of entreating You to countenance and protect them so far as may be suitable to your station and character;[4] and shall consider myself as obliged by any favourable notice which they shall have the honour of receiving from You. I am, Sir, Your most humble Servant,

SAM. JOHNSON

1. William Windham (1750–1810), of Felbrigg Hall, Norfolk, scholar and mathematician, later (1784–1802) M.P. for Norwich, "whom, though a Whig, he [SJ] highly valued" (*Life* IV.200; Namier and Brooke III.648). Windham, a member of The Club since 1778, later (Dec. 1783) joined the Essex Head Club, and attended SJ faithfully during the last months of his life (Fifer, pp. xcviii–xcix).

2. Peregrine Phillips (d. 1801), attorney and official in the Wine License Office (*Life* IV.521).

3. Anna Maria Phillips (1763–1805), prominent singer and actress, later (m. 1785) wife of Lieut. Rawlings Edward Crouch, R.N. Phillips made her debut in 1780 at Drury Lane, with which she remained associated throughout her career. During the season of 1783–84, however, she performed at Smock Alley Theatre, Dublin (*A Biographical Dictionary of Actors, Actresses, Musicians, Dancers, Managers, and Other Stage Personnel in London, 1660–1800*, ed. P. H. Highfill et al., 1975, IV.80–84).

4. "Mr. Windham was at this time in Dublin, Secretary to the Earl of Northington, then Lord Lieutenant of Ireland" (JB's note: *Life* IV.227). Windham's stay was short: he left for Ireland on 29 May and returned to England on 8 July, thereafter resigning his post (R. W. Ketton-Cremer, *TLS*, 7 Aug. 1903, p. 641).

William Langley

MID-MAY 1783[1]

PRINTED SOURCE: Chapman III.27.

Dear Sir:

A long continuance of ill health with the evils that attend it, must be allowed as an excuse for many omissions, and you will not therefore much blame me for omitting hitherto those thanks which your honest diligence has deserved. I am compleatly satisfied with what you have done, and written, but could make out no case that I thought could help the girls,[2] if indeed, which dos not very plainly ⟨a line cut out⟩ wish that they should act by any advice of M⟨ine⟩ in opposition to any other. To require that they should give up their contingent claim is certainly a hardship, though that claim as they have a brother and sister[3] is worth very little. You, Sir, have been very friendly.

A new edition of the Lives of the Poets has been lately printed in 4 vol 8vo.[4] I shall send a set to morrow to Mr. Davenport, to be transmitted to you,[5] which I desire you to accept from, Sir, your most humble servant.

1. See below, n. 5.

2. *Ante* To John Taylor, 2 Mar. 1782 and n. 1.

3. Thomas Flint (b. 1769) and Martha Flint (b. 1767) (*Johns. Glean.* IX.29).

4. *Ante* To John Nichols, 12 Aug. 1782, n. 1; *Ante* To JB, 24 Aug. 1782; 7 Dec. 1782.

5. On 19 May 1783 Langley replied: "The favour which you have sent to W. Davenport for me, of which he has informed me by this day's post, I shall receive with peculiar pleasure. They will be a distinguished ornament in my small collection of books, and confer credit upon me from every person who shall be told that they are a present from Dr. Johnson" (*GM* 1878, pp. 700–1).

Joshua Reynolds

MONDAY 2 JUNE 1783

MS: Hyde Collection.

ADDRESS: To Sir Joshua Reynolds.

ENDORSEMENT: Dr. Johnson.

Dear Sir: June 2, 1783

I have sent You some of my Godson's performances of which I do not pretend to form any opinion.[1] When I took the liberty of mentioning him to you, I did not know, what I have been since told, that Mr. Moser had admitted him among the Students of the academy.[2] What more can be done for him I earnestly entreat You to consider, for I am very desirous that he should derive some advantage from my connexion with him. If You are inclined to see him I will bring him to wait on You at any time that You shall be pleased to appoint. I am, Sir, Your most humble Servant,

SAM. JOHNSON

1. SJ refers to Charles Paterson (*Life* IV.227 n. 3; *Ante* To Joshua Reynolds, 3 Aug. 1776 and n. 1).

2. *Ante* To Joshua Reynolds, 3 Aug. 1776 and n. 2. George Michael Moser (1704–83) had been first Keeper of the Royal Academy.

Hester Maria Thrale

MONDAY 2 JUNE 1783

MS: The Earl of Shelburne.

ADDRESS: To Miss Thrale at Bath.

POSTMARK: 2 IV.

My dear Love: London, June 2, 1783

In the beginning of your arithmetical studies suffer me to give you one important direction.[1]

1. *Ante* To Hester Maria Thrale, 26 Apr. 1783; 22 May 1783.

Accustom yourself to make all your figures with critical exactness. In writing a series of language some inattention may be allowed, because one word and one letter explains another, but in numbers every character has its own independent power, which, if by bad delineation it becomes doubtful, cannot be deduced or inferred from any of its concomitants. By a little negligence your own computations will become in a short time unintelligible to your self. Get an exact copy of all the figures, and do not either for haste or negligence deviate from it.

The same attention is to be preserved in words which connexion does not ascertain, such as names and numbers. Very few write their own names in such a manner as that if they stood alone they could be read. I have lately seen letters of which neither those to whom they were sent nor any to whom they have been shown are able to discover the abode of the writer, though he has spread it widely enough upon paper. This inconvenience is easily avoided by writing all such words in single letters without ligatures, for it is by joining them that they are made obscure, as *Thrale*, *T h r a l e*. This I mention the rather because you suffer your writing to grow very vagrant and irregular.

I have for some time past been much oppressed, but this [is] a very tolerable day.

I hope my Mistress is recovered from[2] her hurt and her fright.[3] Why do you write so seldom to, Dearest Love, Your most humble servant,

SAM. JOHNSON

2. MS: "from" altered from "for"

3. *Ante* To Hester Maria Thrale, 22 May 1783 and n. 1.

Unidentified Correspondent

MONDAY 2 JUNE 1783

MS: Hyde Collection.

Sir: June 2, 1783

Please to deliver to the Bearer a set of Ramblers, and put it to the account of, Sir, Your humble servant,

SAM. JOHNSON

Anthony Hamilton[1]

WEDNESDAY 4 JUNE 1783

PRINTED SOURCE: JB's *Life*, ed. Croker, 1835, x.282–83.

Reverend Sir, Bolt Court, June 4, 1783

Be pleased to excuse this application from a stranger in favour of one who has very little ability to speak for herself. The unhappy woman who waits on you with this, has been known to me many years.[2] She is the daughter of a clergyman of Leicestershire, who by an unhappy marriage is reduced to solicit a refuge in the workhouse of your parish, to which she has a claim by her husband's settlement.[3]

Her case admits of little deliberation; she is turned out of her lodging into the street. What my condition allows me to do for her I have already done, and having no friend, she can have recourse only to the parish. I am, reverend Sir, etc.

SAM. JOHNSON

1. Anthony Hamilton (1739–1812), D.D., F.S.A., Vicar of St. Martin's in the Fields (1776–1812), "noted for his preaching, his benevolence and his social popularity" (*Alum. Cant.* II.iii.211; *Scots Peerage* II.50).

2. SJ may refer to Mrs. Pellé (*Post* To Anthony Hamilton, 11 Feb. 1784; 17 Feb. 1784).

3. The law of settlement determined to which parish an indigent person belonged and therefore the parish from which he or she was entitled to public assistance. Settlement could be obtained through birth, through apprenticeship in a particular parish, or by marriage to a man who had settlement in the parish (R. K. Webb, *Modern England*, 1975, p. 31).

Hester Thrale

THURSDAY 5 JUNE 1783

MS: Hyde Collection.
ADDRESS: To Mrs. Thrale at Bath.
POSTMARK: 5 IV.

Dear Madam: London, June 5, 1783

Why do You write so seldom? I was very glad of your letter, You were used formerly to write more when I know not why You should have had much more to say. Do not please yourself with showing me that You can forget me, who do not forget You.

Mr. Desmoulins account of my health rather wants confirmation.[1] But complaints are useless.

I have by the migration of one of my Ladies more peace at home,[2] but I remember an old savage chief that says of the Romans with great indignation. Ubi solitudinem faciunt, pacem appellant.[3]

Mrs. Lewis was not Calamity, it was her sister, to whom I am afraid the term is now seriously applicable, for she seems to have fallen some way into obscurity.[4] I am afraid by a palsy.

Whence Your pity arises for the thief that has made the hangman idle, I cannot discover. I am sorry indeed for every suicide, but I suppose he would have gone to the gallows without being lamented.

You will soon see that Miss Hudson, if she finds countenance, and gets scholars, will conquer her vexations.[5] Is not

1. *Ante* To Lord Dartmouth, 25 Apr. 1783, n. 1.

2. *Ante* To Hester Maria Thrale, 22 May 1783 and n. 9.

3. *ubi solitudinem faciunt, pacem appellant*: "they make a desolation and they call it peace" (Tacitus, *Agricola* 30, trans. Maurice Hutton, Loeb. ed.).

4. "Miss [Frances] Cotterell was conceited, and lamented small Matters in large Words I suppose, so She got the Nick Name of Calamity Cotterell. She and Mrs. Lewis were Daughters of Adml. Cotterel" (Piozzi II.259). Cf. *Ante* To Hester Thrale, 25 Apr. 1780 and n. 6.

5. Miss Hudson, an embroiderer or seamstress at Bath, also taught needlework to Susanna Thrale. She suffered from delusions of persecution (*The Piozzi Letters*,

Susy likewise one of her pupils? I owe Susy a Letter, which I purpose to pay next time.[6]

I can tell You of no new thing in town, but Dr. Maxwel, whose Lady is by ill health detained with two little babies at Bath.[7]

You give a cheerful account of your way of life, I hope You will settle into tranquillity.

When I can repay You with a narrative of my felicity, You shall see Description. —I am, Madam, Your most humble servant,

SAM. JOHNSON

ed. E. A. Bloom and L. D. Bloom, 1989, I.69 n. 4). *Post* To Hester Thrale, 8 July 1783.

6. *Post* To Susanna Thrale, Late Spring or Early Summer 1783.

7. The Rev. William Maxwell (1732–1818), D.D., former Rector of Mount Temple, Co. Westmeath, moved to Bath *c.* 1780. SJ, who had known Maxwell since 1754, became well acquainted with him during the years that he was serving as Reader of the Temple Church (*Life* II.116). In 1777 Maxwell married Anne Massingberd (d. 1789) (*GM* 1789, p. 1053), daughter of William Burrell Massingberd (1719–1802), of Ormsby, Lincolnshire (Fifer, p. lv).

Hester Thrale

FRIDAY 13 JUNE 1783

MS: Hyde Collection.

ADDRESS: To Mrs. Thrale at Bath.

POSTMARK: 13 IV.

Dear Madam: London, June 13, 1783

Yesterday were brought hither two parcels directed *to Mrs. Thrale to the care of Dr. Johnson.* By what the touch can discover, they contain some thing of which cloaths are made; and I suspect them to be Musgrave's long expected present.[1] You will order them to be called for, or let me know whither I shall send them.

1. "so it was—a beautiful Irish Stuff" (Piozzi, *Letters* II.262, annotated copy at Trinity College, Cambridge).

Crutchley has[2] had the gout but is abroad again. Seward called on me yesterday. He is going only for a few weeks, first to Paris, and then to Flanders to contemplate the pictures of Claude Loraine and he asked me if that was not as[3] good a way as any of spending time.—That time which returns no more,—of which however a great part seems to be very foolishly spent, even by the wisest and the best.

That time at least is not lost in which the evils of life are relieved, and therefore the moments which You bestow on Miss Hudson, are properly employed.[4] She seems to make an uncommon impression upon You. What has she done or suffered out of the common course of things? I love a little secret history.

Poor Dr. Laurence and his youngest son died almost on the same day.[5]

Mrs. Dobson, the Directress of rational conversation, did not translate Petrarch; but epitomised a very bulky French life of Petrarch. She translated, I think, the Memoirs of D'Aubigné.[6]

Your last letter was very pleasing, it expressed ⟨such⟩ kindness to me, and some degree of placid acquiescence in your present mode of life, which is, I think, the best, which is at present within your reach.

2. MS: "has" altered from "had"

3. MS: "as" altered from "a"

4. *Ante* To Hester Thrale, 5 June 1783 and n. 5.

5. Thomas Lawrence died 6 June (*GM* 1787, p. 193; *Life* IV.230 n. 2). The date of his son John's death remains uncertain: the obituary notice in the *GM* is not to be trusted (1783, p. 542).

6. Susannah Dobson (d. 1795), wife of Matthew Dobson (d. 1784), M.D., F.R.S., Hester Thrale's physician in Bath (*Thraliana* I.580, 584). In 1775 she published a *Life of Petrarch* based on the *Mémoires pour la vie de Pétrarque* (1764) of J.F.P.A. de Sade (1705–78). Her next work (1778), also adapted from the French, was a *Literary History of the Troubadours*—not (pace SJ) the memoirs of Théodore Agrippa d'Aubigné. Hester Thrale, together with Frances Burney, had met Susannah Dobson in 1780; Burney described her at the time as "coarse, low-bred, forward, self-sufficient, and flaunting," yet also possessed of "a strong and masculine understanding, and parts that, had they been united with modesty, or fostered by education, might have made her a shining and agreeable woman" (*Diary and Letters of Madame D'Arblay*, ed. Austin Dobson, 1904, I.370).

My powers and attention have for a long time, been almost wholly employed upon my health, I hope, not wholly without success, but solitude is very tedious. I am, Madam, Your most humble servant,

SAM. JOHNSON

Edmund Allen

TUESDAY 17 JUNE 1783

PRINTED SOURCE: William Cooke, *The Life of Samuel Johnson, LL.D.*, 1785, pp. 68–69. Collated with texts in Hawkins (p. 557) and JB's *Life* (1793, III.481–82).

ADDRESS: To Mr. William Allen.[1]

Dear Sir,

It hath pleased Almighty God[2] this morning to deprive me of the powers of speech;[3] and as I do not know but that it might[4] be his further[5] good pleasure to deprive me soon of my senses, I request you will, on the receipt of this note, come to me, and act for me, as the exigencies of my case might[6] require. I am sincerely your's,

S. JOHNSON[7]

1. "To Mr. Edmund Allen" (JB)
2. "pleased God" (JB)
3. In his diary entry for 16 June, SJ recorded, "I went to bed, and, as I conceive, about 3 in the morning, I had a stroke of the palsy" (*Works*, Yale ed. I.359). For a detailed account, *Post* To Hester Thrale, 19 June 1783.
4. "may" (Hawkins, JB)
5. "farther" (Hawkins)
6. "may" (Hawkins, JB)
7. "SAM. JOHNSON" (JB)

John Taylor

TUESDAY 17 JUNE 1783

MS: Berg Collection, New York Public Library.[1]

1. The many corrections in this letter testify to the effect of SJ's stroke. In practice it has proved impossible at several points to distinguish slips of the pen from considered alterations in phrasing.

To JOHN TAYLOR, 17 *June* 1783

ADDRESS: To the Reverend Dr. Taylor.

ENDORSEMENTS: 1783, 17 July 83. On Loss of his Speech by a paralytic Stroke.

Dear Sir: June 17, 1783

It has pleased God by a paralytick stroke in the night to deprive me of speech.[2]

I am very desirous of Dr. Heborden['s] assistance as I think my case is not past remedy. Let me see You as soon as it is possible. Bring Dr. Heborden with you if you can, but come your self, at all events. I am glad you are so well, when[3] I am so dreadfully attacked.

I think that by a speedy application of stimulants much may be done. I question if a[4] vomit vigorous and rough would not rouse the organs of speech to action.

As it is too early to send I will try to recollect what I can that can be suspected to have brough[t] on this dreadful distress.

I have been accustomed to bleed frequently for an asthmatick complaint but have forborn for some time by Dr. Pepys's persuasion, who perceived my legs beginning to swell.

I sometimes alleviate a painful, or more properly an oppressive constriction of my[5] chest, by opiates, and have lately taken opium frequently but the last, or[6] two last times in smaller quantities. My largest dose is three grains, and last night I took but two.

You will suggest these thing[s], and they are all that I can call to mind, to Dr. Heborden. I am etc.

SAM. JOHNSON

Dr. Brockelsby will be with me to meet Dr. Heborden, and I shall have previously make master of the case, as well as I can.

2. *Ante* To Edmund Allen, 17 June 1783 and n. 4.

3. MS: "when when"

4. MS: "a a"

5. MS: "opiate the" del. before "my"

6. MS: "or" written above "but" del.

Thomas Davies

WEDNESDAY 18 JUNE 1783

PRINTED SOURCE: JB's *Life*, 1791, II.460.

Dear Sir, June 18, 1783

I have had, indeed, a very heavy blow; but God, who yet spares my life, I humbly hope will spare my understanding, and restore my speech.[1] As I am not at all helpless, I want no particular assistance, but am strongly affected by Mrs. Davies's tenderness; and when I think she can do me good, shall be very glad to call upon her. I had ordered friends to be shut out, but one or two have found the way in; and if you come you shall be admitted: for I know not whom I can see that will bring more amusement on his tongue, or more kindness in his heart. I am, etc.

SAM. JOHNSON

1. *Ante* To Edmund Allen, 17 June 1783 and n. 4.

Hester Thrale

THURSDAY 19 JUNE 1783

MS: Hyde Collection.

Dear Madam: Bolt Court, Fleetstreet, June 19, 1783

I am sitting down in no chearful solitude to write a narrative which would once have affected you with tenderness and sorrow, but which You will perhaps pass over now with the careless glance of frigid indifference. For this diminution of regard however, I know not whether I ought to blame You, who may have reasons which I cannot know, and I do not blame myself who have for a great part of human life done[1] You what good I could, and have never done you evil.

I had been disordered in the usual way,[2] and had been re-

1. MS: "have" del. before "done"
2. MS: comma and "and" del. before "way"

lieved by the usual methods, by opium and cathartick, but had rather lessened my dose of opium.

On Monday the 16 I sat for my picture,[3] and walked a considerable way with little inconvenience. In the afternoon and evening I felt myself light and easy, and began to plan schemes of life. Thus I went to bed, and in a short time waked and sat up as has been long my custom when I felt a confusion and indistinctness in my head[4] which lasted, I[5] suppose about half a minute. I was alarmed and prayed God, that however he might afflict my body he would spare my understanding. This prayer, that I might try the integrity of my faculties I made in Latin verse.[6] The lines were not very good, but I knew them not to be very good, I made them easily, and concluded myself to be unimpaired in my faculties.

Soon after I perceived that I had suffered a paralytick stroke, and that my speech was taken from me. I had no pain, and so little dejection in this dreadful state that I wondered at my own apathy, and considered[7] that perhaps death itself when it should come, would excite less horrour than seem[s] now to attend it.

In order to rouse the vocal organs I took two drams, Wine has been celebrated for the production of eloquence; I put myself into violent motion, and, I think, repeated it. But all was vain; I then went to bed, and, strange as it may seem, I think, slept. When I saw light, it was time to contrive what I should do. Though God stopped my speech he left me my

3. SJ could refer either to Frances Reynolds's long-term portrait (*Ante* To Frances Reynolds, 16 June 1780 and n. 1; *Post* To Hester Thrale, 20 Aug. 1783) or to the first sitting for his portrait by John Opie (*Post* To John Taylor, 3 Sept. 1783 and n. 1; K. K. Yung, *Samuel Johnson 1709–84*, 1984, p. 132).

4. MS: "my head" written above "which" del.

5. MS: "I" superimposed upon "a"

6. *Summe Pater, quodcunque tuum de corpore Numen / Hoc statuat, precibus Christus adesse velit: / Ingenio parcas, nec sit mihi culpa rogâsse, / Qua solum potero parte, placere tibi*: "Father Supreme, whatever be Thy care / Touching this body (Jesu, plead the prayer), / Spare me my mind, nor count it fault in me / If that I ask which most pertains to Thee" (*Poems*, p. 237; translated by Morris Bent, *Notes and Queries* 12, 1903, p. 389).

7. MS: "considered" written above "could not" del.

hand, I enjoyed a mercy which was not granted to my Dear Friend Laurence, who now perhaps overlooks me as I am writing and rejoices that I have what he wanted.[8] My first note was necessarily to my servant, who came in talking, and could not immediately comprehend why he should read what I put into his hands.

I then wrote a card to Mr. Allen,[9] that I might have a discreet friend at hand to act as occasion should require. In penning this note I had some difficulty, my hand, I know not how nor why, made wrong letters.[10] I then wrote to Dr. Taylor to come to me, and bring Dr. Heberden,[11] and I sent to Dr.[12] Brocklesby, who is my neighbour. My Physicians are very friendly and very disinterested; and give me great hopes, but You may imagine my situation. I have so far recovered my[13] vocal powers, as to repeat the Lord's Prayer with no very imperfect articulation. My memory, I hope, yet remains as it was. But such an attack produces solicitude[14] for the safety of every Faculty.

How this will be received by You, I know not, I hope You will sympathise with me, but perhaps

My Mistress gracious, mild, and good,
Cries, Is he dumb? 'tis time he shou'd.[15]

But can this be possible, I hope it cannot. I hope that[16] what, when I could speak, I spoke of You, and to You, will be in a sober and serious hour[17] remembred by You, and surely it cannot be remembred but with some degree of kindness. I

8. *Ante* To Hester Thrale, 13 June 1783, n. 5.

9. *Ante* To Edmund Allen, 17 June 1783.

10. "The available evidence . . . indicates an apoplectic disorder of speech not very severe, and comparatively short in duration: that the disability was not a mere articulatory disorder but a dysphasic one, is shown by defects in his written compositions" (Macdonald Critchley, "Dr. Samuel Johnson's Aphasia," *Medical History* 6, 1962, p. 35). *Ante* To John Taylor, 17 June 1783, n. 1.

11. *Ante* To John Taylor, 17 June 1783.

12. MS: "Br" del. before "Dr."

13. MS: "th" del. before "my"

14. MS: "s" superimposed upon "a"

15. "The Queen, so Gracious, Mild and Good, / Cries, 'Is he gone? 'Tis time he shou'd'" (Swift, *Verses on the Death of Dr. Swift*, ll. 181–82).

16. MS: "that" written above "You" del.

17. MS: "hours"

have loved you with virtuous affection, I have honoured You with sincere Esteem. Let not all our endearment be forgotten, but let me have in this great distress your pity and your prayers. You see I yet turn to You with my complaints as a settled and unalienable friend, do not, do not drive me from You, for I have not deserved either neglect or hatred.

To the Girls, who do not write often, for Susy has[18] written only once, and Miss Thrale owes me a letter, I earnestly recommend as their Guardian and Friend, that They remember their Creator in the days of their Youth.[19]

I suppose You may wish to know how my disease is treated by the physitians. They put a blister upon my back, and two from my ear[20] to my throat, one on a side. The blister on the back has done little, and those on the throat have not risen. I bullied, and bounced, (it sticks to our last sand)[21] and compelled the apothecary to make his salve according to the Edinburgh dispensatory that it might adhere better.[22] I have two on now of my own prescription. They likewise give me salt[23] of hartshorn, which I take with no great confidence, but am satisfied that what can be done, is done for me.[24]

O God, give me comfort and confidence in Thee, forgive my sins, and if it be thy good pleasure, relieve my diseases for Jesus Christs sake. Amen.

I am almost ashamed of this querulous letter, but now it is written, let it go. I am Madam, Your most humble servant,

SAM. JOHNSON

18. MS: "h" superimposed upon "w"

19. "Remember now thy Creator in the days of thy youth, while the evil days come not" (Ecclesiastes 12:1).

20. MS: "from my ear" written above "on each may" del.

21. "Time, that on all things lays his lenient hand, / Yet tames not this; it sticks to our last sand" (Pope, *Epistle to Cobham*, ll. 224–25).

22. It is likely that SJ refers to the *Pharmacopoeia Edinburgensis; or, the Dispensatory of the Royal College of Physicians in Edinburgh* (1st ed., 1746), which contains a recipe for "blistering ointment" composed of hog's lard, turpentine, wax, and cantharides.

23. MS: "of" del. before "salt"

24. MS: "me" written above "him" del.

Mauritius Lowe

FRIDAY 20 JUNE 1783

PRINTED SOURCE: JB's *Life*, ed. Croker, 1831, v.113.

Sir, Friday, 20th June, 1783

You know, I suppose, that a sudden illness makes it impracticable to me to wait on Mr. Barry, and the time is short. If it be your opinion that the end can be obtained by writing, I am very willing to write,[1] and, perhaps, it may do as well: it is, at least, all that can be expected at present from, sir, your most humble servant,

SAM. JOHNSON

If you would have me write, come to me: I order your admission.

1. Cf. *Ante* To James Barry, 12 Apr. 1783 and nn. 2, 3.

Hester Thrale

FRIDAY 20 JUNE 1783

MS: Current location unknown. Transcribed from photostat in the Hyde Collection.

ADDRESS: To Mrs. Thrale at Bath.

POSTMARK: 20 IV.

Dearest Lady: London, June 20, 1783

I think to send you for some time a regular diary. You will forgive the gross images which disease must necessarily present. Dr. Laurence said that medical treatises should be always in Latin.[1]

The two vesicatories[2] which I procured with so much

1. Thomas Lawrence practiced what he preached: all his published works, from *Oratio Harvaeana* (1748) onward, are written in Latin.

2. *vesicatory*: "a blistering medicine" (SJ's *Dictionary*). *Ante* To Hester Thrale, 19 June 1783.

trouble did not perform well, for being applied to the lower part of the fauces[3] a part always in motion their adhesion was continually broken. The back, I hear, is very properly flayed.

I have now healing application to the cheeks and have my head covered with one formidable diffusion of Cantharides,[4] from which Dr. Heberden assures me that experience promises great effects. He told me likewise that my utterance has been improved since Yesterday, of which however I was less certain. Though doubtless they who see me at interval can best judge.

I never had any distortion of the countenance, but what Dr. Brocclesby calld a little prolapsus which went away the second day.

I was this day directed to eat Flesh, and I dined very copiously upon roasted Lamb and boiled pease, I then went to sleep in a chair, and when I waked[5] I found Dr. Brocclesby sitting by me, and fell to talking to him in such a manner as made me glad, and, I hope, made me thankful. The Dr. fell to repeating Juvenal's tenth satire,[6] but I let him see that the province was mine.

I am to take wine to night, and hope it may do me good. I am, Madam, Your humble Servant,

SAM. JOHNSON

3. *fauces*: "the cavity at the back of the mouth, from which the larynx and pharynx open out" (*OED*).

4. *cantharides*: "Spanish flies; used to raise blisters" (SJ's *Dictionary*).

5. MS: "waked" repeated as catchword

6. On SJ's deathbed, "when talking on the subject of prayer, Dr. Brocklesby repeated from Juvenal, *Orandum est, ut sit mens sana in corpore sano*, and so on to the end of the tenth satire" (*Life* IV.401).

Hester Thrale

SATURDAY 21 JUNE 1783

MS: Hyde Collection.

ADDRESS: To Mrs. Thrale at Bath.

POSTMARK: 21 IV.

To HESTER THRALE, 21 *June* 1783

Dear Madam: London, June 21, 1783

I continue my Journal.[1] When I went to Bed last night I found the new covering of my[2] head uneasy, not painful, rather too warm.[3] I had however a comfortable and placid night. My Physicians this morning thought my amendment not inconsiderable, and my friends who visited me said that my look was spritely and cheerful. Nobody has shown more affection than Paradise. Langton and he were with me a long time to day. I was almost tired.

When my friends were gone, I took another liberal dinner such as my Physicians recommended and slept after it, but without such evident advantage as[4] was the effect of Yesterday's *siesta*. Perhaps the sleep was not quite so sound, for I am harrassed by a very disagreeable operation of the cantharides[5] which I am endeavouring to control by copious dilution.

My disorders are in other respects less than usual, my disease whatever it was seems collected into this one dreadful effect. My Breath is free, the constrictions of the chest are suspended, and my nights pass without oppression.

To day I received a letter of consolation and encouragement from an unknown hand without a name, kindly and piously, though not enthusiasti[c]ally[6] written.

I had just now from Mr. Pepys, a message enquiring in your name after my health,[7] of this I can give no account. I am, Madam, Your most humble Servant,

SAM. JOHNSON

1. *Ante* To Hester Thrale, 20 June 1783. 2. MS: "my my"

3. *Ante* To Hester Thrale, 20 June 1783.

4. MS: "advantage as" written above "and" del.

5. *Ante* To Hester Thrale, 20 June 1783 and n. 4.

6. *enthusiast*: "one who vainly imagines a private revelation; one who has a vain confidence of his intercourse with God" (SJ's *Dictionary*).

7. MS: initial "h" altered from "th"

Hester Thrale

MONDAY 23 JUNE 1783

MS: Hyde Collection.

Dear dear Madam: London, June 23, 1783

I thank you for your kind letter, and will continue my diary.[1] On the night of the 21st I had very little rest, being kept awake by an effect[2] of the cantharides[3] not indeed formidable, but very irksome and painful. On the 22 The Physicians released me from the salts of hartshorn. The Cantharides continued their persecution, but I was set free from it at night. I had however not much sleep but I hope for more to night. The vesications on my back and face are healing, and only that on my head continues to operate.[4]

My friends tell me that my power of utterance[5] improves daily, and Dr. Heberden declares that he hopes to find me almost well to morrow.

Palsies are more common than I thought. I have been visited by four friends who have had each a stroke, and one of them, two.

Your offer, dear Madam, of coming to me is charmingly kind,[6] but I will lay up for future use, and then let it not be considered as obsolete. A time of dereliction may come, when I may have hardly any other friend, but in the present exigency, I cannot name one who has been deficient in activity or attention. What man can do for man, has been done for me. Write to me very often. I am, Madam, Your most humble servant,

SAM. JOHNSON

1. *Ante* To Hester Thrale, 20 June 1783. 2. MS: "effects"

3. *Ante* To Hester Thrale, 20 June 1783 and n. 4.

4. *Ante* To Hester Thrale, 20 June 1783 and n. 2.

5. MS: "utterance" repeated as catchword

6. Hester Thrale's journal entry for 24 June suggests that this offer was meant to preempt a more onerous commitment: "I sincerely wish the Continuance of a Health so valuable; but have no Desire that he [SJ] should come to Bath" (*Thraliana* 1.568).

Hester Thrale

TUESDAY 24 JUNE 1783

MS: The Chequers Estate.

Dear Madam: London, June 24, 1783

The journal now like other journals grows very *dry*, as it is not diversified either by operations or events.[1] Less and less is done, and, I thank God, less and less is suffered every day. The Physicians seem to think that little[2] more needs to be done. I find that they consulted to day about sending me to Bath, and thought it needless. Dr. Heberden takes leave to morrow.

This day I watered the garden,[3] and did not find the watering pots more heavy than they have hitherto been, and my breath is more free.

Poor dear ⟨*one word*⟩[4] has just been here with a present. If it ever falls in your way to do him good, let him have your favour.

Both Queeny's letter and Yours gave me to day great pleasure. Think as well and as kindly of me as You can, but do not flatter me. Cool reciprocations of esteem are the great comforts of life, hyperbolical praise only corrupts the tongue of one, and the ear of another. I am, Dear Madam, Your most humble servant,

SAM. JOHNSON

Your letter has no date.

1. *Ante* To Hester Thrale, 20 June 1783.

2. MS: initial "l" superimposed upon "m"

3. *Ante* To Hester Maria Thrale, 22 May 1783.

4. H. L. Piozzi, who heavily deleted the name, restores it as "Sastres" in both annotated sets of her letters (Piozzi II.279; Trinity College Library, Cambridge). *Pace* Chapman (III.40 n. 2) the traces do not rule out this identification.

Lucy Porter

WEDNESDAY 25 JUNE 1783

MS: Hyde Collection.

Dear Madam: London, June 25, 1783

Since the papers have given an account of my ilness,[1] it is proper that I should give my Friends some account of it Myself.

Very early in the morning of the 16th of this month,[2] I perceived my speech taken from me. When it was light I sat down, and wrote such directions as appeared proper. Dr. Heberden and Dr. Brocklesby were called. Blisters were applied, and medicines given; before night I began to speak with some freedom, which has been encreasing[3] ever since, so that I now have very [little] impediment in my utterance. Dr. Heberden took his leave this morning.

Since I received this stroke I have in other respects been better than I was before, and hope yet to have a comfortable summer. Let me have your prayers.

If writing is not troublesome let me know whether You are pretty well, and how You have passed the Winter and Spring.

Make my compliments to all my Friends. I am, dear Madam, Your most humble servant,

SAM. JOHNSON

1. "Dr. Johnson had a Stroke of the Palsy on Tuesday, and recovers but slowly. From his great Strength of Constitution, his Physicians are in hopes of his longer Life" (*Public Advertiser*, 21 June 1783, p. 4).

2. The correct date was the 17th: *Ante* To Edmund Allen, 17 June 1783.

3. MS: "s" del. before "a"

Hester Thrale

SATURDAY 28 JUNE 1783

MS: Hyde Collection.

ADDRESS: To Mrs. Thrale at Bath.

POSTMARK: 28 IV.

Dear Madam: London, June 28, 1783

Your letter is just such as I desire, and as from You I hope always to deserve.

The black Dog I hope always to resist,[1] and in time to drive though I am deprived of almost all those that used to help me. The neighbourhood is impoverished. I had once Richardson and Laurence in my reach. Mrs. Allen is dead. My house has lost Levet, a man who took interest in every thing and therefore was very ready at conversation. Mrs. Williams is so weak that [she] can be a companion no longer. When I rise my breakfast is solitary, the black dog waits to share it, from breakfast to dinner he continues barking, except that Dr. Brocklesby for a little keeps him at a distance. Dinner with a sick woman You may venture to suppose not much better than solitary. After Dinner what remains but to count the clock, and hope for that sleep which I can scarce expect. Night comes at last, and some hours of restlessness and confusion, bring me again to a day of solitude. What shall exclude the black dog from a habitation like this? If I were a little richer I would perhaps take some cheerful Female into the House.

Your Bath news shows me new calamities.[2] I am afraid Mrs. Lewis is left with a numerous family very slenderly supplied.[3] Mrs. Sheward is an[4] old Friend, I am afraid, yet sur le pavé.

Welch, if he were well, would be well[5] enough liked, his Daughter has powers and knowledge, but no art of making them agreeable.[6]

I must touch my Journal.[7] Last night fresh flies were put to

1. *Ante* To Hester Thrale, 14 Nov. 1778 and n. 1.

2. *Ante* To Hester Thrale, 5 June 1783 and n. 4.

3. John Lewis had just died (*GM* 1783, p. 628). Both Hester Thrale and SJ erroneously assumed that his widow Charlotte was left scantily provided for. In fact, Mrs. Lewis's private income was more than sufficient for herself and her two children (*The Piozzi Letters*, ed. E. A. Bloom and L. D. Bloom, 1989, I.280 n. 9).

4. MS: "an" repeated as catchword

5. MS: "liked" partially erased before "well"

6. SJ refers to Saunders Welch and his daughter Anne ("Nancy").

7. *Ante* To Hester Thrale, 20 June 1783.

my head,[8] and hindred me from sleeping. To day I fancy myself incommoded by ⟨the⟩ heat.

I have however watered the garden both yesterday and to day, just as I watered the laurel in the Island.[9] I am, Madam, Your most humble servant,

SAM. JOHNSON

8. *Ante* To Hester Thrale, 20 June 1783 and n. 4.

9. The lake at Streatham Park included an island at its northwest end (*Ante* To Hester Thrale, 23 Aug. 1777, n. 4; H. W. Bromhead, *The Heritage of St. Leonard's Parish Church Streatham*, 1932, p. 43).

Hester Thrale

MONDAY 30 JUNE 1783[1]

MS: Berg Collection, New York Public Library.

ADDRESS: To Mrs. Thrale at Bath.

POSTMARK: 30 IV.

Dear Madam:

Among those that have enquired after me, Sir Philip is[2] one,[3] and Dr. Burney was one of those who came to see me. I have had no reason to complain of indifference or neglect. Dick Burney is come home, five inches taller.[4]

Yesterday in the Evening I went to Church and have been to day to see the great Burning glass, which does more than was ever done before by transmission of the Rays, but is not equal in power to those which reflect them.[5] It wastes a diamond placed in the focus, but causes no diminution of pure

1. MS: dateline torn away; dated by postmark, contents, and placement in Piozzi, *Letters*

2. MS: "is" superimposed upon "was" partially erased

3. SJ refers to Sir Philip Jennings Clerke.

4. Richard Thomas Burney (1768–1808), Charles Burney's son by his second marriage, had been studying at Winchester College, to which SJ had accompanied him when he was first enrolled (*Life* III.367). When Burney was eighteen or nineteen he emigrated to India, where he eventually became headmaster of the Orphan School of Kiddepore (*The Early Journals and Letters of Fanny Burney*, ed. Lars Troide, 1988, I.xliv).

5. At the end of the seventeenth century experiments began to be conducted

gold. Of two rubies exposed to its action one was made more vivid, the other, paler. To see the glass, I climbed up stairs to the garret, and then[6] up a ladder to the leads, and talked to the artist rather too long, for my voice though clear and distinct for a little while soon tires and falters. The organs of Speech are yet very feeble, but will I hope be by the mercy of God finally restored, at present like any other weak limb, they can endure but little labour at once. Would You not have been very [sorry] for me, when I could scarcely speak?

Fresh Cantharides were this morning applied to my head, and are to be continued some time longer.[7] If they play me no treacherous tricks they give me very little pain.

Let me have your kindness and your prayers and think on me, as on a man who for a very great portion of Your life, has done You all the good he could, and desires still to be considered as, Madam, Your most humble servant,

SAM. JOHNSON

---

with "burning glasses" and "burning mirrors"—large lenses and arrays of mirrors that focused the sun's rays so as to cause an object at the focal point to burn. In 1695 a large burning glass was employed to melt a diamond (Guy Benveniste, "Burning Glasses: From Archimedes to Lavoisier," *The Sun at Work* 1, 1956, p. 5). In 1718 a similar experiment was performed with "*a concave* [*mirrour*] *of forty-seven inches wide, and ground to a sphere of seventy-six inches radius*" (*GM* 1774, p. 220). SJ's description suggests that he observed a lens, not a mirror.

6. MS: "then" altered from "the"

7. *Ante* To Hester Thrale, 20 June 1783 and n. 4.

Hester Thrale

TUESDAY 1 JULY 1783

MS: Hyde Collection.

ADDRESS: To Mrs. Thrale at Bath.

POSTMARK: 1 IY.

Dear Madam: London, July 1, 1783

This morning I took the air by a ride to Hampstead, and this afternoon I dined with the Club. But fresh Cantharides were this day applied to my Head.[1]

Mr. Cator called on me to day, and told that he had invited You back to Streatham, I showed the unfitness of your return thither, till the neighbourhood should have lost its habits of depredation,[2] and he seemed to be satisfied. He invited me very kindly and cordially to try the air of Beckenham,[3] and pleased me very much by his affectionate attention to Miss Cecy.[4] There is much good in his character, and much usefulness in his knowledge.

Queeney seems now to have forgotten me.

Of the different appearance of the hills and vallies an account may perhaps be given, without the supposition of any prodigy. If the [day] had been hot and the Evening was breezy; the exhalations would rise from the low grounds very copiously; and the wind that swept and cleared the hills, would only by its cold condense the vapours of the sheltered vallies.[5]

Murphy is just gone from me; he visits me very kindly, and I have no unkindness to complain of.

I am sorry that Sir Philip's request was not treated with more respect, nor can I imagine what has put them so much out of humour; I hope their business is prosperous.[6]

I hope that I recover by degrees, but my nights are restless,

1. *Ante* To Hester Thrale, 20 June 1783 and n. 4.

2. At the Surrey Summer Assizes nine defendants were sentenced to death for theft of various kinds, including "foot-pad" and "highway" robbery (*GM* 1783, p. 710).

3. In 1773 Henry Cator had purchased the manor of Beckenham, in Kent, from the second Viscount Bolingbroke (*Life* IV.538). According to JB, SJ "found a cordial solace" there (*Life* IV.313).

4. Cecilia Thrale was boarding at Russell House, a school at Streatham (*Thraliana* I.563 and n. 1).

5. Presumably Hester Thrale had described as "prodigious" a day in Bath on which the city was enveloped by mist while the uplands were clear.

6. SJ refers to an incident involving John Perkins and Robert Barclay: "Mr. Perkins's gross Ingratitude deserves mentioning . . . he refused to put a poor Fellow into his Brewhouse the other Day, though strongly solicited by Sir Philip Jennings [Clerke] and myself" (*Thraliana* I.572).

and you will suppose the nervous system to be somewhat enfeebled. I am, Madam, Your most humble servant,

SAM. JOHNSON

James Boswell

THURSDAY 3 JULY 1783

PRINTED SOURCE: JB's *Life*, 1791, II.461.

Dear Sir, London, July 3, 1783

Your anxiety about my health is very friendly, and very agreeable with your general kindness.[1] I have, indeed, had a very frightful blow. On the 17th of last month, about three in the morning, as near as I can guess, I perceived myself almost totally deprived of speech.[2] I had no pain. My organs were so obstructed, that I could say *no*, but could scarcely say *yes*. I wrote the necessary directions, for it pleased God to spare my hand, and sent for Dr. Heberden and Dr. Brocklesby. Between the time in which I discovered my own disorder, and that in which I sent for the doctors, I had, I believe, in spite of my surprize and solicitude, a little sleep, and Nature began to renew its operations. They came, and gave the directions which the disease required, and from that time I have been continually improving in articulation. I can now speak, but the nerves are weak, and I cannot continue discourse long; but strength, I hope, will return. The physicians consider me as cured. I was last Sunday at church. On Tuesday I took an airing to Hampstead, and dined with the Club,[3] where Lord Palmerston was proposed, and, against my opinion, was rejected.[4]

1. On 27 June JB learned of SJ's stroke from his brother Thomas David; on the 28th he sent a letter of solicitous inquiry (*Boswell: The Applause of the Jury*, ed. I. S. Lustig and F. A. Pottle, 1981, p. 159).

2. *Ante* To Edmund Allen, 17 June 1783.

3. *Ante* To Hester Thrale, 1 July 1783.

4. Henry Temple (1739–1802), second Viscount Palmerston in the Irish peerage, of Broadlands, Hampshire, M.P. for a number of boroughs (1762–1802). Palmerston had occupied various government posts, serving most recently as a Lord

I design to go next week with Mr. Langton to Rochester, where I purpose to stay about ten days, and then try some other air.[5] I have many kind invitations. Your brother has very frequently enquired after me.[6] Most of my friends have, indeed, been very attentive. Thank dear Lord Hailes for his present.

I hope you found at your return every thing gay and prosperous, and your lady, in particular, quite recovered and confirmed.[7] Pay her my respects. I am, dear Sir, Your most humble servant,

SAM. JOHNSON

---

of the Treasury (1777–82) (Namier and Brooke III.519). In Dec. 1783 he was proposed again for membership in The Club, and was elected Feb. 1784 (Fifer, pp. 150–51 and n. 3).

5. SJ left for Rochester on 10 July and returned on the 23rd (*Post* To Hester Thrale, 23 July 1783; *Works*, Yale ed. I.360–61).

6. See above, n. 1.

7. JB had left London on 30 May and returned via Berwick-upon-Tweed to Auchinleck, where he found his son James recuperating from an illness (Lustig and Pottle, *Applause of the Jury*, pp. 158–59).

Hester Thrale

THURSDAY 3 JULY 1783

MS: Hyde Collection.

ADDRESS: To Mrs. Thrale at Bath.

POSTMARK: 3 IY.

Dear Madam: London, July 3, 1783

Dr. Brocklesby yesterday dismissed the Cantharides,[1] and I can now find a soft place upon my pillow. Last night was cool, and I rested well, and this morning I have been a friend at a poetical difficulty. Here is now a glimpse of daylight again. But how near is the Evening—None can tell, and I will not prognosticate; We all know that from none of us it can be far distant; may none of us know this in vain.

1. *Ante* To Hester Thrale, 20 June 1783 and n. 4.

I went, as I took care to boast, on Tuesday, to the Club,[2] and hear that I was thought to have performed as well as usual. I dined on Fish, with the wing of a small Turkey chick, and left roast Beef, Goose, and venison pye untouched. I live much on peas, and never had them so good, for so long a time, in any year that I can remember.

When do You go [to] Weymouth? and why do you go?[3] only I suppose to a new place, and the reason is sufficient to those who have no reason to withold them. Mrs. Lewis knows well enough how to live on four hundred a year, but whence is she to have it. Had the Dean any thing of his own unsettled?[4]

I am glad that Mrs. Sheward talks of me, and loves me, and have in this still scene of life great comfort in reflecting that I have given very few reason[s] to hate me; I hope scar[c]ely any man has known me closely but to his benefit, or cursorily, but to his innocent entertainment. Tell me You that know me best, whether this be true, that according to your answer I may continue my practice, or try to mend it.

Along with your kind letter yesterday, came a one likewise very kind from the Astons at Lichfield, but I do not know whether as the summer is so far advanced I shall travel so far, though I am not without hopes that frequent changes of air may fortify me against the winter, which has been, in modern phrase, of late years very *inimical*[5] to, Madam, Your affectionate, humble servant,

SAM. JOHNSON

2. *Ante* To Hester Thrale, 1 July 1783.

3. On 12 Aug. Hester Thrale recorded, "I am come here [Weymouth] chiefly on my own Account to repair my lost Health by Sea bathing" (*Thraliana* 1.569).

4. *Ante* To Hester Thrale, 28 June 1783 and n. 3. Most of John Lewis's estate was bequeathed to the children of his first marriage (*The Piozzi Letters*, ed. E. A. Bloom and L. D. Bloom, 1989, 1.280 n. 9).

5. Although *inimical* does not appear in SJ's *Dictionary*, it was in use at least as early as 1643 (*OED*).

Lucy Porter

SATURDAY 5 JULY 1783

MS: Hyde Collection.

Dear Madam: London, July 5th 1783

The account which You [give] of your health is but melancholy; May it please God to restore You.

My disease affected my speech, and still continues in some degree to obstruct my utterance, my voice is distinct enough for a while, but the organs being yet weak are quickly weary.[1] But in other respects I am, I think, rather better than I have lately been, and can let You know my state without the help of any other hand.

In the opinion of my friends, and in my own I am gradually mending. The Physicians consider[2] me as cured, and I had leave four days ago to wash the Cantharides from my head.[3] Last tuesday I dined at the Club.[4]

I am going next week into Kent,[5] and purpose to change the air frequently this summer; whether I shall wander so far as Staffordshire I cannot tell.[6] I should be glad to come.

Return my thanks to Mrs. Cobb, and Mr. Pearson, and all that have shown attention to me.

Let us, my Dear, pray for one another, and consider our sufferings as notices mercifully given us to prepare ourselves for another state.

I live now but in a melancholy way. My old Friend Mr. Levett is dead, who lived with me in the house, and was useful and compani[on]able, Mrs. Desmoulins is gone away,[7] and Mrs. Williams is so much decayed, that she can add little to anothers

1. *Ante* To Hester Thrale, 30 June 1783.

2. MS: "consider" repeated as catchword

3. *Ante* To Hester Thrale, 3 July 1783.

4. *Ante* To Hester Thrale, 1 July 1783.

5. *Ante* To JB, 3 July 1783 and n. 5.

6. SJ did not visit Lichfield again until the following summer (*Post* To Richard Brocklesby, 21 July 1784).

7. *Ante* To Hester Maria Thrale, 22 May 1783 and n. 9.

gratifications. The world passes away, and we are passing with it, but there is, doubtless, another world which will endure for ever; Let us all fit ourselves for it. I am, Dear Madam, Your humble servant,

SAM. JOHNSON

Hester Thrale

SATURDAY 5 JULY 1783

MS: Hyde Collection.

ADDRESS: To Mrs. Thrale at Bath.

POSTMARK: 5 IY.

Dear Madam: London, July 5, 1783

That Dr. Pepys is offended I am very sorry, but if the same state of things should recur, I could not do better.[1] Dr. Brocklesby is, you know, my neighbour and could be ready at call, he had for some time very diligently solicited my Friendship; I depended much upon the skill of Dr. Heberden, and him I had seen lately at Brocklesby's. Heberden I could not bear to miss, Brocklesby could not decently be missed, and to call three, had made me ridiculous by the appearance of self importance. Mine was one of those unhappy cases, in which something must be wrong. I can only be sorry.

I have now no doctor, but am left to shift for myself, as opportunity shall serve. I am going next week with Langton to Rochester where I expect not to stay long.[2] Eight children in a small house will probably make a chorus not very diverting. My purpose is to change the air frequently this Summer.

Of the imitation of my stile, in a criticism on Grays Churchyard, I forgot to make mention. The authour is, I believe, utterly unknown, for Mr. Steevens cannot hunt him out.[3] I know

1. Apparently Hester Thrale had reported that Lucas Pepys felt slighted by SJ's preference for other doctors in the aftermath of his stroke.

2. *Ante* To JB, 3 July 1783 and n. 5.

3. SJ refers to *A Criticism on the Elegy written in a Country Churchyard* (1783) by

little of it, for though it was sent me, I never [cut] the leaves open, I had a letter with [it] representing it to me, as my own work; in such an account to the publick, there[4] may be humour, but to myself it was neither serious nor comical. I suspect the writer to be wrongheaded; as to the noise which it makes, I have never heard it, and am inclined to believe that few attacks either of ridicule or invective make much noise, but by the help of those that they provoke.

I think Queeney's silence has something either of laziness or unkindness,[5] and I wish her free from both for both are very unamiable, and will both increase by indulgence. Susy is, I believe at a loss for matter. I shall be glad to see pretty Sophy's Production.

I hope I still continue mending. My organs are yet feeble. I am, Madam, Your most humble servant,

SAM. JOHNSON

John Young (*c.* 1746–1820), Professor of Greek (1774–1820) at Glasgow (*Life* IV.392 and n. 1, 551).

4. MS: "they"

5. Cf. *Ante* To Hester Thrale, 1 July 1783.

Susanna Thrale

LATE SPRING *or* EARLY SUMMER 1783[1]

MS: The Earl of Shelburne.

ADDRESS: To Miss Susanna Thrale at Bath.

Dearest Miss Susy:

When You favoured me with your letter, you seemed to be in want of materials to fill it,[2] having met with no great adven-

1. MS: mutilated; complimentary close, signature, and dateline missing. Placed by H. L. Piozzi between SJ's letters of 5 and 8 July, it could have been written as early as the final week of May (*Ante* To Hester Maria Thrale, 22 May 1783) or as late as 9 July (the eve of SJ's departure for Rochester)

2. *Ante* To Hester Maria Thrale, 22 May 1783; *Ante* To Hester Thrale, 5 July 1783.

tures either of peril or delight, nor done or suffered any thing out of the common course of life.

When You have lived longer and considered more, you will find the common course of life very fertile of observation and reflection. Upon the common course of life must our thoughts and our conversation be generally employed. Our general course of life must denominate us wise or foolish; happy or miserable; if it is well regulated we pass on prosperously and smoothly; as it is neglected we live in embarrasment, perplexity, and uneasiness.

Your time, my Love, passes, I suppose, in Devotion, reading, work, and Company. Of your Devotions, in which I earnestly advise You to be very punctual, you may not perhaps think it proper to give me ⟨an⟩ account; and of work, unless I understood it better, it will [be] of no great use to say much; but Books and Company will always supply You with materials for your letters to me, as I shall be always pleased to know what you are reading, and with what you are pleased; and shall take great delight in ⟨knowing⟩ what impression new modes or new characters make upon you, and to observe with what attention you distinguish the tempers, dispositions, and abilities of your companions.

A letter may be always made out of the books of the morning or talk of the evening, and any letters from you, my dearest, will be welcome to ⟨   ⟩

John Ryland

TUESDAY 8 JULY 1783

MS: Loren Rothschild.

ADDRESS: To Mr. Ryland in Cranbrook, Kent.

POSTMARK: 8 IY.

Dear Sir: London, July 8, 1783

I am gratified to a very high degree with your anxiety for my recovery. Health itself is made more valuable by an intercourse with friends like You. Most of our friends You and I have lost, let us therefore cling close to each other, and cherish our mutual kindness by conversation or letters as the state of life admits.

My recovery, I think, advances, but its progress is[1] not quick. My voice has its usual tone, and a stranger in the beginning of our conversation does not perceive any depravation or obstruction. But the organs of articulation are weak, and quickly tire. I question if I could read, without pausing, a single page of a small book. This feebleness however will not, I hope, last very long.

I have some expectation of help from change of air, and purpose to pass the next week, or ten days with my friend Langton at Rochester,[2] and afterwards to move to some other place. I have been favoured with many invitations, and all, I think, sincere.

Of your retreat I think with pleasure; there is to a busy man great happiness in an interval of life which he can spend as he pleases, but it is seldom long[3] that the mind is sufficient for its own amusement, it returns soon[4] with eagerness to external occupations. Do not forget in your hours of leisure or of hurry, that You have one who wishes you well, in, Sir, Your humble Servant,

SAM. JOHNSON

1. MS: "is is" 2. *Ante* To JB, 3 July 1783 and n. 5.
3. MS: "long" superimposed upon "that" partially erased
4. MS: "in" del. before "soon"

Hester Thrale

TUESDAY 8 JULY 1783

MS: Berg Collection, New York Public Library.
ADDRESS: To Mrs. Thrale at Bath.
POSTMARK: 8 IY.

Dear Madam: London, July 8, 1783

Time makes great changes of opinion. The Dean of Ossory ran perpetually after Charlotte Cotterel in the lifetime of that Lady,[1] to whom he so earnestly desired to be reunited in the grave. I am glad Charlotte is not left in poverty, her disease seems to threaten her with a full share of misery.[2]

Of Miss Hudson whom You charge me with forgetting, I know not why I should much foster the remembrance; for I can do her no good, but I honestly recommend to your pity, for nothing but the opportunity of emptying her bosom with confidence, can save her from madness. To know at least one mind so disordered is not with[out] its use, it shows the[3] danger[4] of admitting passively the first irruption of irregular imaginations.[5]

Langton and I have talked of passing a little time at Rochester together,[6] till neither knows well how to refuse, though I think he is not eager to take me, and I am not desirous to be taken. His family is numerous, and his house little. I have let him know, for his relief, that I do not mean to burden him more than a week. He is, however, among those who wish me well, and would exert what[7] power he has to do me good.

I think You will do well in going to Weymouth for though it be nothing, it is, at least to the young ones, a new nothing, and they will be able always to tell that they have seen Weymouth.[8] I am for the present willing enough to persuade myself that a short succession of trifles may contribute to my reestablishment, but hope[9] to return, for it is surely time, to something of importance. I am, dear Madam, Your most humble servant,

SAM. JOHNSON

1. SJ refers to John Lewis's first wife, Catherine Villiers (d. 1756).
2. *Ante* To Hester Thrale, 28 June 1783 and n. 3; 3 July 1783.
3. MS: "the" superimposed upon "of" partially erased
4. MS: "danger" superimposed upon undeciphered erasure
5. *Ante* To Hester Thrale, 5 June 1783 and n. 5.
6. *Ante* to JB, 3 July 1783 and n. 5.
7. MS: "w" superimposed upon "th"
8. *Ante* To Hester Thrale, 3 July 1783 and n. 3.
9. MS: "h" superimposed upon "I"

Charles, Elizabeth, & Frances Burney

EARLY JULY 1783

MS: Hyde Collection.

ADDRESS: Leicester Fields.

July 11, 1783[1]

Mr. Johnson returns sincere thanks to Dr. and Mrs. and Miss Burney for their kind visits and enquiries.[2]

1. The day of the month and the year have been added in an unidentified hand. In the same hand appears a note on an accompanying page: "This Card is the Hand Writing of Dr. Samuel Johnson and was given me by Mrs. Burney 22 Septr. 1783" (MS: Hyde Collection). Presumably Elizabeth Burney misremembered the day in July: on the 11th SJ was in Rochester (*Works*, Yale ed. I.360).

2. After SJ's stroke on 17 June the Burneys repeatedly asked after him and stopped by Bolt Court (*Diary and Letters of Madame D'Arblay*, ed. Austin Dobson, 1904, II.213, 215).

William Strahan

TUESDAY 15 JULY 1783

MS: Hyde Collection.

ADDRESS: To William Strahan, Esq., M.P., in London.

POSTMARKS: ROCHESTER, 16 IY, FREE.

Sir: Rochester, July 15, 1783

I have enclosed the receipt;[1] and a Letter to Mrs. Williams which You do me the favour of sending to her.

The house where I am,[2] is very airy, and pleasant, and overlooks the Medway where the channel is very broad, so that I hardly imagine a habitation more likely to promote health, nor have I much reason to complain; My general health is better

1. SJ had sent to Strahan, who was continuing to act as his banker, the receipt for the second quarter's payment of his pension (*Works*, Yale ed. I.361).

2. *Ante* To JB, 3 July 1783 and n. 5.

than it has been for some years. My breath is more[3] free, and my nights are less disturbed. But my utterance is still impeded, and my voice soon grows weary with long sentences. This, I hope, time will remedy. I hope dear Mrs. Strahan continues well. I am, Sir, Your humble servant,

SAM. JOHNSON

3. MS: "more" superimposed upon undeciphered erasure

Hester Thrale

WEDNESDAY 23 JULY 1783

MS: Rosenbach Museum and Library.
ADDRESS: To Mrs. Thrale at Bath.
POSTMARK: ⟨23⟩ IY.

Dear Madam: London, July 23, 1783

I have been thirteen days at Rochester and am just now returned.[1] I came back by water in a common boat, twenty miles for a shilling,[2] and when I landed at Billingsgate I carried my budget[3] myself to Cornhil before I could get a coach, and was not much incommoded.

I have had Miss Susy's and Miss Sophy's letters, and [now] I am come home can write and write. While I was with Mr. Langton, we took four little journies in a Chaise, and made one little voyage on the Medway with four misses[4] and their maid, but they were very quiet.

I am very well except that my voice soon falters, and I have

1. *Ante* To JB, 3 July 1783 and n. 5.

2. SJ had traveled via Gravesend, which was connected to Rochester by coach service; boats plied between Gravesend and Billingsgate "every Tide" (*Post* To John Taylor, 24 July 1783; *London and its Environs*, 1761, III.55, VI.266; *The New Complete Guide to all Persons who have any Trade or Concern with the City of London*, 1783, p. 101).

3. *budget*: "a bag, such as may be easily carried" (SJ's *Dictionary*).

4. Presumably SJ refers to Langton's four oldest daughters: Mary (b. 1773), Diana (b. 1774), Jane (b. 1776), and Elizabeth (b. 1777) (Fifer, p. lviii n. 29).

not slept well, which I imputed to the heat which has been such as I never felt before, for so long time.[5] Three days we had of very great heat about ten years ago. I infer nothing from it but a good Harvest.

Whether this short rustication has done me any good I cannot tell, I certainly am not worse and am very willing to think myself better. Are you better? Sophy gave but a poor account of You. Do not let your mind wear out your body.[6] I am, Madam, Your most humble servant,

SAM. JOHNSON

5. On 15 July Horace Walpole reported to Lady Ossory: "Indeed, as much as I love to have summer in summer, I am tired of this weather . . . it parches the leaves, makes the turf crisp, claps the doors, blows the papers about, and keeps one in a constant mist that gives no dew, but might as well be smoke. The sun sets like a pewter plate red hot" (*Walpole's Correspondence*, Yale ed. XXXIII.404).

6. On 27 July Hester Thrale recorded, "Six Months have this Day elapsed since I suffered the inexpressible Agony of telling my Piozzi that we must absolutely part—and here I am *alive* though greatly shaken in my health" (*Thraliana* 1.569).

Sophia Thrale

THURSDAY 24 JULY 1783

MS: Current location unknown. Transcribed from photostat in the Hyde Collection.

ADDRESS: To Miss Sophia Thrale at Bath.

POSTMARK: 24 IY.

Dearest Miss Sophy: London, July 24, 1783

By my absence from home, and for one reason and another I owe a great number of letters, and I assure you that I sit down to write yours first. Why You should think yourself not a favourite I cannot guess; my favour will, I am afraid never be worth much, but be its value more or less, You are never likely to lose it, and less likely if you continue your studies with the same diligence as You have begun[1] them.

Your proficience in arithmetick is not only to be com-

1. MS: "began"

mended but admired. Your master does not I suppose, come very often, nor stay very long, yet your advance in the science of numbers is greater, than is commonly made by those who for so many weeks as you have been learning, spend six hour[s] a day in the writing School.

Never think, my Sweet, that You have arithmetick enough; when You have exhausted your Master, buy Books. Nothing amuses more harmlesly than computation, and nothing is oftener applicable to real business or speculative enquiries. A thousand stories which the[2] ignorant tell, and believe, dye away at once, when the computist takes them in his gripe. I hope You will cultivate in yourself a disposition to numerical enquiries; they will give You entertainment in solitude by the practice, and reputation in publick by the effect.

If You can borrow *Wilkins's Real Character*,[3] a folio which the Bookseller can perhaps let You have, You will [find] there a very curious calculation, which You are qualified to consider, to show that Noah's Ark was capable of holding all the known animals of the world with provision for all the time, in which the earth was under water.[4] Let me hear from you soon again. I am, Madam, Your humble servant,

SAM. JOHNSON

2. MS: "the the"

3. SJ refers to *An Essay towards a Real Character and a Philosophical Language* (1668) by John Wilkins (1614–72), D.D., Warden of Wadham College, Oxford (1648–59), Bishop of Chester (1668–72), and a founder of the Royal Society.

4. This "curious calculation" occurs on pp. 162–66 of Wilkins's *Essay*.

William Bowles

THURSDAY 24 JULY 1783

MS: Hyde Collection.

ADDRESS: To W. Bowles, Esq., at Heale near Salisbury.

POSTMARK: 24 IY.

Dear Sir: London, July 24, 1783

You will easily believe that the first seizure was alarming.[1] I

1. *Ante* To Edmund Allen, 17 June 1783.

recollected three that had lost their voices, of whom two continued speechless for life, but I believe, no means were used for their recovery. When the Physicians came they seemed not to consider the attack as very formidable, I feel now no effects from it but in my voice, which I cannot sustain for more than a little time.

When I received your kind letter I was at Rochester with Captain Langton, from whom I returned hither last night, and I f[l]atter myself that I shall be able to obey your generous and friendly invitation.[2] I hope I am well enough not to give any extraordinary trouble. Will it be convenient that I should bring a servant? I can very well do without one.[3]

Which day I shall come, I cannot yet quite settle. You shall therefore have another letter when the time comes nearer.[4]

Be pleased to make my most respectful compliments to your Lady.[5] I am, Sir, Your most humble servant,

SAM. JOHNSON

2. Bowles had invited SJ to visit him at Heale House, Wiltshire.

3. Francis Barber did not accompany SJ (*Post* To Francis Barber, 16 Sept. 1783).

4. SJ arrived at Heale House 28 Aug. and left 17 Sept., returning to London the following day (*Works*, Yale ed. I.363, 366; *Post* To William Bowles, 25 Aug. 1783; *Post* To Charles Burney, 20 Sept. 1783).

5. In 1779 Bowles had married Dinah Frankland, daughter of Admiral Sir Thomas Frankland, Bt. (*Life* IV.235 n. 5; Waingrow, p. 108 n. 1).

John Ryland

THURSDAY 24 JULY 1783

MS: Hyde Collection.

ADDRESS: To Mr. Ryland at Cranbrook, Kent [*Readdressed in an unidentified hand*] in London.

POSTMARK: 24 IY.

Dear Sir: London, July 24, 1783

For omitting mention of the verses in your first letter I had no particular reason; I did not read them critically, but upon a second view, they seem to me rather to favour solitude too much. Retreat from the world is flight rather than conquest, and in those who have any power of benefiting others, may be consider[ed] as a kind of *moral suicide*. I never found any *sweets* in solitude,[1] and it certainly admits not many *virtues*.

In a state of imbecillity retirement is not [only] lawful but decent and proper, and at all times intervals of recess may afford useful opportunities of recollection and such meditation as every Christian ought to practice. But we recollect in order to improve, and meditate for the sake of acting.

I am not yet willing to forsake *towred cities* or to leave *the busy hum of men*[2] quite behind me, but how long I shall be able to sustain my part among them, He only knows whose supe[r]vision comprises the great drama of the world.

Of the Latin verses, the first distich was very sweet, the second was less elegant.

Yesterday I returned from Rochester. I came from Gravesend by water.[3] I have been kindly treated, often amused, and hope I am come back rather better than I went. I am very warmly invited into Wiltshire, and think to go in the beginning of the next mo[n]th.[4] I am, Sir, Your most humble servant,

SAM. JOHNSON

There was not very long ago a Clergyman of great eminence for learning at Cranbroke, whose name was Johnson; enquire what is remembred concerning him.[5]

1. "And Wisdom's self / Oft seeks to sweet retired solitude" (Milton, *Comus*, ll. 374–75).

2. "Towered cities please us then, / And the busy hum of men" (Milton, *L'Allegro*, ll. 117–18).

3. *Ante* To Hester Thrale, 23 July 1783 and n. 2.

4. *Ante* To William Bowles, 24 July 1783 and n. 2.

5. SJ may refer to John Johnson (1662–1725), "Johnson of Cranbrook," of which he was Vicar (1707–25). Author of a number of pamphlets and books on theological subjects, Johnson was "a very able writer in controversial divinity" (*DNB*). SJ's library included "Johnson's canons" (Greene, 1975, p. 72).

John Taylor

THURSDAY 24 JULY 1783

MS: Berg Collection, New York Public Library.

ADDRESS: To the Reverend Dr. Taylor in Ashbourne, Derbyshire.

POSTMARK: 24 IY.

ENDORSEMENTS: 1783, 24 July 83.

Dear Sir: July 24, 1783

When Your letter came to me I was with Mr. Langton at Rochester.[1] I was suspicious that You were ill. He that goes away, you know, is to write, and for some time I expected a letter every post.[2]

My general health is undoubtedly better than before the seizure.[3] Yesterday I came from Gravesend by water, and carried my portmanteau from Billingsgate to Cornhil, before I could get a coach, nor did I find any great inconvenience in doing it.[4]

My voice in the exchange of salutations, or an[y] other little occasions is as[5] it was, but in a continuance[6] of conversation it soon tires. I hope it grows stronger but it does not make very quick advances.

I hope You continue well, or grow every day better, yet the time will come when one of us shall lose the other. May it come upon neither of us unprepared. I am, Dear Sir, Yours affectionately,

SAM. JOHNSON

1. *Ante* To JB, 3 July 1783 and n. 5.
2. Taylor had returned to Ashbourne from London in late June or early July.
3. *Ante* To Edmund Allen, 17 June 1783 and n. 4.
4. Cf. *Ante* To Hester Thrale, 23 July 1783.
5. MS: "as" altered from "at"
6. MS: "ance" repeated as catchword

Hester Maria Thrale

THURSDAY 24 JULY 1783

MS: The Earl of Shelburne.

Dear Madam: London, July 24, 1783

It is long since I wrote to you,[1] and indeed it is long since I wrote to any body. Rochester was out of the way, and I sent no letters from that place that could be omitted. The heat was sufficient besides to produce laziness. The thermometer was, as I am told within four degrees of the greatest heat in Jamaica.[2]

Your account of your time gives me pleasure. Never lose the habit of reading, nor ever suffer yourself to acquiesce in total vacuity. Encourage in yourself[3] an implacable impatience of doing nothing. He that cannot be idle, and will not be wicked, must be useful and valuable, he must be always improving himself or benefiting others. If you cannot at any particular time reconcile yourself to any thing important, be busy upon trifles. Of trifles the mind grows tired, and turns for its own satisfaction[4] to something better, but if it learns to sooth itself with the opiate of musing idleness, if it can once be content with inactivity,[5] all the time to come is in danger of being lost. And, I believe, that life has been so dozed away by many whom[6] Nature had originally qualified not only to be esteemed but admired.

If ever therefore you catch[7] yourself contentedly and placidly[8] doing nothing, *sors de l'enchantement*,[9] break away

1. *Ante* To Hester Maria Thrale, 2 June 1783.
2. *Ante* To Hester Thrale, 23 July 1783 and n. 5.
3. MS: "self" repeated as catchword
4. MS: "satisfaction" superimposed upon undeciphered erasure
5. MS: semicolon
6. MS: "whom" altered from "whose"
7. MS: "catch" altered from "cong[ratulate]"
8. MS: "placidly" repeated as catchword
9. "Sors de l'enchantement, Milord, laisse au vulgaire / Le séduisant espoir d'un bien imaginaire" (Pope, *Essay on Man*, trans. Abbé Du Resnel, 1737, p. 67, ll. 1–2).

from the snare, find your book or your needle,[10] or snatch the broom from the Maid.⟨ ⟩[11]

10. Cf. *Post* To Jane Langton, 10 May 1784.
11. MS: mutilated; middle section of sheet cut out

Susanna Thrale

SATURDAY 26 JULY 1783

MS: The Earl of Shelburne.
ADDRESS: To Miss Susanna Thrale at Bath.
POSTMARK: 26 IY.

Dear Miss Susan: London, July 26, 1783

I answer your letter last, because it was received last, and when I have answered I am out of debt to your house.[1] A short negligence throws one behind hand; this maxim if you consider and improve it, will be equivalent to the [tale of] your Parson and Bird, which is however a very good story, as it shows how far gluttony may proceed, which where it prevails is I think more violent and certainly more despicable than avarice itself.

Gluttony is, I think, less common among women, than among men. Women commonly eat more sparingly, and are less curious in the choice of meat; but if once you [find] a woman gluttonous, expect from her very little virtue. Her mind is enslaved to the lowest and grossest temptation.

A friend of mine, who courted a Lady of whom he did not know much, was advised to see her eat, and if she was voluptuous at[2] table to forsake her. He married her however, and in a few weeks came to his adviser with this exclamation, "It is the disturbance of my life to see this woman eat." She was, as might be expected, selfish and brutal, and after some years of discord they parted, and I believe, came together no more.

Of men the examples are sufficiently common. I had a

1. *Ante* To Hester Thrale, 23 July 1783.
2. MS: "a" superimposed upon "t"

friend of great eminence in the learned and the witty[3] world,[4] who had hung up some pots on his wall, to furnish nests for sparrows. The poor sparrows not knowing his character, were seduced by the convenience, and I never [heard] any man speak of any future enjoyment with such contortions of delight as he exhibited when he talked of eating the young ones.[5]

When you do me the favour to write again, tell me something of your studies, your work, or your amusements. I am, Madam, Your humble servant,

SAM. JOHNSON

3. MS: "witty" superimposed upon undeciphered erasure

4. "Isaac Hawkins Browne" (Piozzi II.298; Piozzi, *Letters* II.298, annotated copy at Trinity College, Cambridge). Isaac Hawkins Browne (1705–60), poet and M.P. for Wenlock (1744–54), judged by SJ "of all conversers ... the most delightful with whom I ever was in company" (*Johns. Misc.* I.266).

5. Browne was a man of voracious appetites: he also, according to SJ, "drank freely for thirty years" (*Life* V.156).

William Bowles

WEDNESDAY 30 JULY 1783

MS: Hyde Collection.

ADDRESS: To W. Bowles, Esq., at Heale near Salisbury.

POSTMARK: 30 IY.

Dear Sir: London, July 30, 1783

Your invitation is so affectionately pressing,[1] that I think it necessary to tell You the reason of any appearance of delay. To neglect such kindness would be not only incivility but ingratitude.

I will come to You when I can, but I am now delayed by the[2] necessity of suffering a rough chirurgical operation, of which I cannot tell what will [be] the consequence.[3] I need not tell

1. *Ante* To William Bowles, 24 July 1783 and n. 2.

2. MS: "the the"

3. *Post* To William Cruikshank, 30 July 1783; *Post* To John Mudge, 9 Sept. 1783.

You, dear Sir, that this delay is involuntary. I am, Sir, Your most o[b]liged and most humble servant,

SAM. JOHNSON

William Cruikshank

WEDNESDAY 30 JULY 1783

MS: Hyde Collection.

ADDRESS: To Mr. Cruikshank.

Sir: Bolt court, Fleetstreet, July 30, 1783

Notwithstanding the imaginary diminution of your character, I am going to put myself into your hands.[1]

I have for twenty months had, if I judge rightly a Hydrocele.[2] For twelve months it was totally without pain, and almost without inconvenience, but it has lately encreased so much that the water, if water it be, must be discharged.[3] I beg to see You as soon as you can come, and hope your skill will be able to relieve me. I am, Sir, Your most humble servant,

SAM. JOHNSON

1. *Ante* To Joshua Reynolds, 2 May 1783 and n. 1.

2. *hydrocele*: "a watery rupture" (SJ's *Dictionary*); "a tumour with a collection of serous fluid . . . dropsy of the testicle or of the scrotum" (*OED*).

3. For a detailed medical history of SJ's tumor, *post* To John Mudge, 9 Sept. 1783.

William Bowles

MONDAY 4 AUGUST 1783

MS: Hyde Collection.

ADDRESS: To W. Bowles, Esq., at Heal near Salisbury.

POSTMARK: 4 AV.

Dear Sir: London, Aug. 4, 1783

As I sincerely think that You take some interest in my health,

I tell You, what I tell very few, that the operation is over with less pain than I feared, and without the benefit which I desired and hoped;[1] I have suffered little, and gained little.

I am ashamed to write so often about a visit, as if I thought my presence or absence of importance. Surely life and experience have taught me better. But convalescence is a[2] very capricious and delusive state. However there will be no more need of writing,[3] till a note is sent to let You know, when you may expect at Salisbury,[4] Dear Sir, Your most humble servant,

SAM. JOHNSON

1. *Ante* To William Bowles, 30 July 1783; *Ante* To William Cruikshank, 30 July 1783.

2. MS: "a" repeated as catchword

3. MS: "w" altered from "p"

4. *Post* To William Bowles, 25 Aug. 1783.

William Cruikshank

WEDNESDAY 6 AUGUST 1783

MS: Hyde Collection.

HEADING in JB's hand: To Mr. Cruikshank.

Sir: Bolt court, Aug. 6, 1783

I beg your acceptance of these volumes as an acknowledgement of the great favour,[1] which you have bestowed on, Sir, Your most obliged and most humble Servant,

SAM. JOHNSON

1. In thanks for Cruikshank's surgical attentions, SJ presented him with a set of his *Lives* (*Life* IV.240; *Ante* To William Cruikshank, 30 July 1783).

Hester Thrale

WEDNESDAY 13 AUGUST 1783

MS: Beinecke Library.

ADDRESS: To Mrs. Thrale at Weymouth.

POSTMARK: ⟨13⟩ AV.

To HESTER THRALE, 13 *August* 1783

Dear Madam: London, August 13, 1783

Your letter was brought just as I was complaining that You had forgotten me.

I am glad that the Ladies find so much novelty at Weymouth.[1] Ovid says that the sea is undelightfully uniform.[2] They had some expectation of shells, which both by their form and colours have a claim to human curiosity. Of all the wonders I have had no account, except that Miss Thrale seems pleased with your little voyages.

Sophy mentioned a story which her[3] sisters would not suffer her to tell, because the[y] would tell it themselves, but it has never yet been told me.[4]

Mrs. Ing is, I think, a Baronet's Daughter, of an ancient house in Staffordshire.[5] Of her husband's father mention is made in the life of Ambrose Philips.[6]

Of this world in [which] You represent me as delighting to live, I can say little. Since I came I have only been to Church, once to Burney's, once to Paradise's, and once to Reynolds's. With Burney I saw Dr. Rose his new relation, with whom I have been many years acquainted.[7] If I discovered no reliques of disease I am glad, but Fanny's trade is fiction.

1. *Ante* To Hester Thrale, 3 July 1783 and n. 3.

2. *una est iniusti caerula forma maris*: "there is only the deep-blue form of the unjust sea" (Ovid, *Amores* II.xi.12, trans. Grant Showerman, Loeb ed.).

3. MS: "his"

4. *Post* To Hester Maria Thrale, 23 Aug. 1783; 3 Sept. 1783 and n. 2.

5. Henrietta Wrottesley (1715–90), daughter of Sir John Wrottesley (1683–1726), fourth Bt., of Wrottesley Hall, Staffordshire, married Theodore William Inge (d. 1753), of Thorpe Constantine, Staffordshire (*Staffordshire Record Society* 6 [N.S.], Part 2, 1903, p. 345; *GM* 1790, p. 864).

6. "He [Ambrose Philips] had great sensibility of censure, if judgment may be made by a single story which I heard long ago from Mr. Ing, a gentleman of great eminence in Staffordshire" (*Lives of the Poets* III.323). SJ refers to William Inge (1669–1731), scholar and antiquarian; "Thorpe Constantine is only some nine miles due east of Lichfield; but whether Johnson had occasion to visit him [Inge] there, or whether the meeting took place, say, under Mr. Walmesley's hospitable roof, we can only surmise" (*Johns. Glean.* V.72).

7. On 24 June Charles Burney the younger (1757–1817) had married Sarah Rose (1759–1821), daughter of William Rose (1719–86), LL.D., a Chiswick school-

I have since partaken of an epidemical disorder, but common evils produce no dejection.

Paradise's company, I fancy, disappointed him, I remember nobody. With Reynolds was the Archbishop of Tuam, a man coarse of voice, and inelegant of language.[8]

I am now broken with disease, without the alleviation of familiar friendship, or domestick society; I have no middle state between clamour and silence, between general conversation and self tormenting solitude. Levet is dead, and poor Williams is making haste to dye.[9] I know not if She will ever more[10] come out of her Chamber.

I am now quite alone, but let me turn my thoughts another way. I am, Madam, Your most humble Servant,

SAM. JOHNSON

---

master and Burney's employer (*Life* IV.509; *The Early Journals and Letters of Fanny Burney*, ed. L. E. Troide, 1988, I.xliv; Waingrow, p. 587 and n. 4).

8. Joseph Dean Bourke (1736–94) D.D., Bishop of Leighlin and Ferns (1772–82), Archbishop of Tuam (1782–94) and later (1792) third Earl of Mayo.

9. *Post* To Hester Thrale, 20 Aug. 1783 and n. 1.

10. MS: "more" written above "leave" del.

Frances Reynolds

MONDAY 18 AUGUST 1783

MS: Houghton Library.
ADDRESS: To Mrs. Reynolds.
ENDORSEMENT: Dr. Johnson, Aug. 83.

My dearest Dear: Aug. 18, 1783

I wish all that You have heard of my health were true, but be it as it may, if you will be pleased to name the day and hour when You would see me, I will be as punctual as I can.[1] I am, Madam, Your most humble servant.

SAM. JOHNSON

1. *Ante* To Frances Reynolds, 16 June 1780 and n. 1; *Post* To Hester Thrale, 20 Aug. 1783.

Hester Thrale

WEDNESDAY 20 AUGUST 1783

MS: Hyde Collection.

ADDRESS: To Mrs. Thrale at Weymouth.

POSTMARK: 20 AV.

Madam: London, Aug. 20, 1783

This has been a day of great emotion. The Office of the Communion of the Sick, has been performed in poor Mrs. Williams's chamber.[1] She was too weak to rise from her bed, and is therefore to be supposed unlikely to live much longer. She has, I hope, little violent pain, but is wearing out, by torpid inappetence and wearisome decay; but all the powers of her mind are in their full vigour, and when she has spirit[2] enough for conversation, she possesses all the intellectual excellence that she ever had. Surely this is an instance of mercy much to be desired by a parting Soul.

At home I see almost all my companions dead or dying. At Oxford I have just lost Wheeler the man with whom I most delighted to converse.[3] The sense of my own diseases, and the sight of the[4] world sinking round me, oppresses me perhaps too much.[5] I hope that all these admonitions will not be vain, and that I shall learn to dye as dear Williams is dying, who was very chearful before and after this aweful solemnity, and seems to resign herself with calmness and hope upon eternal Mercy.

I read your last kind letter with great delight, but when I came to *love* and *honour*, what sprang in my Mind?—How lov'd, how honour'd once, avails thee not.[6]

1. Anna Williams died 6 Sept. (*Post* To Joshua Reynolds, 6 Sept. 1783; *Post* To Susanna Thrale, 9 Sept. 1783).

2. MS: "spirit" superimposed upon undeciphered erasure

3. SJ refers to Benjamin Wheeler.

4. MS: "sight of the" written above "of" del.

5. Cf. *Ante* To Hester Thrale, 13 Aug. 1783.

6. "How lov'd, how honour'd once, avails thee not" (Pope, *Elegy to the Memory of an Unfortunate Lady*, l. 71.).

I sat to Mrs. Reynolds yesterday for my picture, perhaps the tenth time,[7] and I sat near three hours, with the patience of *Mortal born to bear.* At last She declared it quite finished and seems to think it fine. I told her it was Johnson's *grimly ghost.*[8] It is to be engraved, and I think, *In glided* etc. will be a good inscription. I am, Madam, Your most humble servant,

SAM. JOHNSON

7. *Ante* To Frances Reynolds, 16 June 1780 and n. 1; 18 Aug. 1783.

8. "In glided MARGARET's grimly ghost, / And stood at WILLIAM's feet" (David Mallet, "William and Margaret," in *The Works of David Mallet*, 1759, I.[B2r], ll. 3–4).

William Bowles

THURSDAY 21 AUGUST 1783

MS: Hyde Collection.

ADDRESS: To —— Bowles, Esq., at Heale near Salisbury.

POSTMARK: 21 AV.

Dear Sir: London, Aug. 21, 1783

My purpose was to have waited on You about the Sixth of this Month, and now on the twenty second, I am writing to You, to tell You that if it be yet convenient, I will yet come. But if You are now otherwise engaged, I entreat You to tell me, for I had much rather defer my own pleasure than incommode You. I beg you to believe that negligence or inconstancy have had[1] no part in this delay, which has been the effect of irresistible and distresful necessity.[2] I am, Sir, Your most humble servant,

SAM. JOHNSON

1. MS: "had" superimposed upon "made"

2. *Ante* To William Bowles, 30 July 1783; *Ante* To William Cruikshank, 30 July 1783; *Post* To John Mudge, 9 Sept. 1783.

Hester Maria Thrale

SATURDAY 23 AUGUST 1783

MS: The Earl of Shelburne.

ADDRESS: To Miss Thrale at Weymouth.

POSTMARK: 23 AV.

My dearest Love: London, Aug. 23, 1783

The story which Sophy was hindered from telling me, has not yet been told, though I have now expected it a fortnight. Pray let me have it at last with all its circumstances.[1]

My Mistress lately told me of something said in the papers of Boswel and Me. I have heard nothing of it, and should be [glad] to know what it was. Cut it out and send it under a cover to Mr. Strahan. There has seldom been so long a time in which I have had so little to do with Boswel, as since he left London. He has written twice and I have written once.[2] I remember no more.

Barry, the painter, has just told me what I delight to tell again, that Ramsay is now walking the streets of Naples in full possession of his locomotive powers.[3]

Poor Mrs. Williams, I am afraid, can expect no such renovation.[4] I have just been to see her, and I doubt she gave perverse answer to my enquiries, because she saw that my tenderness put it in her power to give me pain. This is hateful and despicable, and yet must not be too much hated or despised, for strongly entwisted with human nature is the desire of exercising power, however that power be gained or given. Let us pity it in others, and despise it in ourselves. Write, my dearest, to, Your humble servant,

SAM. JOHNSON

1. *Ante* To Hester Thrale, 13 Aug. 1783; *Post* To Hester Maria Thrale, 3 Sept. 1783 and n. 2.

2. *Ante* To JB, 3 July 1783 and n. 7.

3. *Ante* To Hester Maria Thrale, 26 Apr. 1783 and n. 1.

4. *Ante* To Hester Thrale, 20 Aug. 1783 and n. 1.

Frances Reynolds

SUNDAY 24 AUGUST 1783

MS: Hyde Collection.

ADDRESS: To Mrs. Reynolds.

ENDORSEMENT: Dr. Johnson, Aug. 24, 83.

Dear Madam: Aug. 24

When Your letter came, I was so engaged that I could not conveniently write. Whether I shall go to Salisbury I know not,[1] for I have had no answer to my last letter, but I would not have You put off Your journey, for all my motions are uncertain. I wish You a happy journey. I am, Madam, your most humble servant,

SAM. JOHNSON

1. *Ante* To William Bowles, 24 July 1783 and n. 2.

William Bowles

MONDAY 25 AUGUST 1783

MS: Hyde Collection.

ADDRESS: To W. Bowles, Esq., at Heale near Salisbury.

POSTMARK: 25 AV.

Dear Sir: London, Aug. 25, —83

You are very kind in accepting my apology.[1] I have taken a place for Thursday in a Coach which comes to the white Hart in Stall street, in Salisbury,[2] and hope at last to have the pleasure of sharing your rural amusements.[3] I am, Sir, Your most humble servant,

SAM. JOHNSON

1. *Ante* To William Bowles, 21 Aug. 1783.

2. SJ appears to have confused the White Hart, Stall Street, Bath, with the White Hart in Salisbury, where there was no Stall Street (T. S. Cotterell, *Historic Map of Bath*, 1st ed., 1897; *The Torrington Diaries*, ed. C. B. Andrews, 1934, I.106).

3. *Ante* To William Bowles, 24 July 1783 and n. 2.

Hester Thrale

TUESDAY 26 AUGUST 1783

MS: Hyde Collection.

ADDRESS: To Mrs. Thrale at Weymouth.

POSTMARK: 26 AV.

Dear Madam: London, Aug. 26,[1] 1783

Things stand with me much as they have done for some time. Mrs. Williams fancies now and then that she grows better, but her vital powers appear to be slowly burning out.[2] Nobody thinks, however, that she will very soon be quite wasted, and, as she suffers me to be of very little use to her, I have determined to pass some time with Mr. Bowles near Salisbury, and have taken a place for Thursday.[3]

Some benefit may be perhaps received from change of air, some from change of company, and some from mere change of place; It is not easy to grow well in a chamber where one has long been sick, and where every thing seen, and every person speaking revives and impresses images of pain. Though it be that no man can run away from himself, he may yet escape from many causes of useless uneasiness. That the *mind is its own place* is the boast of a fallen angel, that had learned to lie.[4] External locality has great effects, at least upon all embodied Beings. I hope this little journey will afford me at least some suspense of melancholy.

You give but an unpleasing account of your performance at Portland.[5] Your scrambling days are then over. I remember when no Miss, and few Masters could have left You behind, or *thrown You out in the persuit of honour*[6] or of curiosity. But *Tem-*

1. MS: "6" altered from "7"

2. *Ante* To Hester Thrale, 20 Aug. 1783 and n. 1.

3. *Ante* To William Bowles, 25 Aug. 1783.

4. "The mind is its own place, and in it self, / Can make a Heav'n of Hell, a Hell of Heav'n" (Satan in *Paradise Lost* I.254–55).

5. "We go to the Island of Portland tomorrow [21 Aug.] in a Boat" (*Thraliana* I.572).

6. "A virtue that has cast me at a distance / And thrown me out in the pursuits of honour" (Addison, *Cato* I.i.94–95).

pus edax rerum,[7] and no way has been yet ⟨found⟩ to draw his teeth. I am, Dear Madam, Your most humble servant,

SAM. JOHNSON

If You write to me, Mr. Strahan will send the letters after me.

7. *tempus edax rerum, tuque, invidiosa vetustas*: "O Time, thou great devourer, and thou, envious Age" (Ovid, *Metamorphoses* xv.234, trans. F. J. Miller, Loeb ed.).

Richard Brocklesby

FRIDAY 29 AUGUST 1783

MS: Hyde Collection.

ADDRESS: To Dr. Brockelsby in London.

POSTMARKS: SALISBURY, 1 SE.

Dear Sir: Heale near Salisbury, Aug. 29, 1783

Without appearing to want a just sense of your kind attention, I cannot omit to give an account of the day which seemed to appear in some sort perillous. I rose at five, and went out at six, and having reached Salisbury about nine, went forward a few miles in my friend's chariot. I was no more wearied with the journey, though it was a highhung rough coach, than I should have been forty years ago. The peccant part I so disposed,[1] that I know not when it has suffered less.[2] We shall now see what air will do. The country is all a plain, and the house in which I am, so far as I can judge from my Window, for I write before I have left my chamber, is sufficiently pleasant.

Be so kind as to continue your attention to Mrs. Williams, it is great consolation to the well, and still greater to the sick, that they find themselves not neglected, and I know that You will be desirous of giving comfort, even where You have no great hope of giving help.

1. "Imagination plies her dang'rous art, / And pours it all upon the peccant part" (Pope, *Essay on Man* II.143–44).

2. SJ refers to his testicular sarcocele (*Ante* To William Cruikshank, 30 July 1783; *Post* To John Mudge, 9 Sept. 1783).

Since I wrote the former part of the letter, I find that by the course of the post I cannot send it before the thirty first. I am, Dear Sir, Your obliged, humble Servant,

SAM. JOHNSON

John Taylor

WEDNESDAY 3 SEPTEMBER 1783

MS: Berg Collection, New York Public Library.

ADDRESS: To the Reverend Dr. Taylor at Ashbourne, Derbyshire.

POSTMARKS: SALISBURY, 6 SE.

ENDORSEMENTS: 1783, 3 Septr. 83.

Dear Sir: Heale near Salisbury, Sept. 3, 1783

I sat to Opey as long as he desired, and I think the head is finished, but it [is] not much admired.[1] The rest he is to add when he comes again to town.

I did not understand that You expected me in Ashbourne, and have been for a few days with a Gentleman in Wiltshire.[2] If you write to me at London my letters will be sent, if they[3] should happen to[4] come before I return. I am, Sir, Your most humble servant,

SAM. JOHNSON

1. John Opie (1761–1807), R.A. (1788), later (1805–07) Professor of Painting at the Royal Academy, described by Horace Walpole in 1782 as "a new genius . . . a Cornish lad . . . who has taught himself to colour in a strong, bold, masterly style by studying nature and painting from beggars and poor children" (*Walpole's Correspondence*, Yale ed. XXIX.184–85). Opie painted two versions of SJ's portrait; one now hangs in the Houghton Library (see frontispiece to Volume III), the other in a private collection (K. K. Yung, *Samuel Johnson 1709–84*, 1984, p. 132).

2. *Ante* To William Bowles, 24 July 1783 and n. 2.

3. MS: "sh" del. before "they"

4. MS: "to" repeated as catchword

Hester Maria Thrale

WEDNESDAY 3 SEPTEMBER 1783

MS: The Earl of Shelburne.

ADDRESS: To Miss Thrale at Weymouth.

POSTMARK: SALISBURY.

My dear Love: Heale near Salisbury, Sept. 3, 1783[1]

Your story is a very pretty story and is very prettily related. I read it to the Gentlemen, and it was agreed that our Consul showed nothing of the Hero. It is still not very easy to say what he should have done.[2]

I am here in a place which might furnish without any help from fiction the scene of a romance. A good house is it, but rather too modern and too convenient to seize the imagination,[3] but the lawn and the hill, and the thickets, and the water, are almost equal to the fancy of a TROUBADOUR.

Every thing is done, that I can be supposed to want, for ease or accommodation, but life in a new house is a kind of restraint, bothe to the guest and to the master, and how long we shall bothe like it, I cannot tell. You may, I find, write to me from Weymouth or Bath.

I think my general health not impaired. I came from London in one day, in a very rough stage coach, without fatigue.[4]

1. MS: "1783" altered from "1784"

2. Queeney's anecdote, recounted to her mother at Bath, involved HM Consul at Aleppo, who had planted a garden in the English style that piqued the curiosity of the local inhabitants. In the Consul's absence the local Pasha and his harem came by appointment to view the garden. That evening, after the Consul had returned and gone to bed, he was surprised by the sudden appearance of one of the Pasha's wives, who had concealed herself in his closet. She begged him to help her escape, but the Consul immediately informed the Pasha, who had his errant wife executed the following day (Hester Maria Thrale to SJ, 26 Aug. 1783, MS: Hyde Collection).

3. The Heale House SJ visited was built between 1660 and 1690. It was "a small rectangular house of red brick. . . . Its entrance front faced west and it had three strictly symmetrical facades" (*A History of Wiltshire*, ed. Elizabeth Crittall, 1962, VI.224).

4. *Ante* To Richard Brocklesby, 29 Aug. 1783.

My days pass with ease, for the greater part, but my nights are not quiet.

I cannot hear nor guess what was said of Bozzy and me, if you can recover it send it me, my suspicion is, that Bozz inserted it.[5]

Mrs. Bowles, the Lady of this house, is so taken with[6] your story that she has asked leave to copy it.

My Mistress, I am afraid, forgets me, but if she is got well, she may entertain Mr. Burke and his Brother, who have just past by in their way to Weymouth.[7] I am, Dearest, Your most humble servant,

SAM. JOHNSON

5. *Ante* To Hester Maria Thrale, 23 Aug. 1783. JB had a habit of writing himself up in the newspapers (*Lit. Car.*, p. xxiii).

6. MS: "with" repeated as catchword

7. Edmund, Richard, and Jane Burke spent approximately a month on a tour of southwestern England; their itinerary included Devon, Bristol, and Bath (*Burke's Correspondence* v.113; *Post* To Joshua Reynolds, 6 Sept. 1783, n. 2; *Post* To Hester Thrale, 9 Oct. 1783).

Joshua Reynolds

SATURDAY 6 SEPTEMBER 1783

MS: Hyde Collection.

ADDRESS: To Sir Joshua Reynolds.

ENDORSEMENT: Dr. Johnson.

Dear Sir: Heale, Sept. 6, 1783

Your kind attention has done all for me that it could. My Loss is really great. She had been my domestick companion for more than thirty years, and when I come home I shall return to a desolate habitation. I hope all her miseries are past.[1]

Mr. Bowles desires me to tell You that he shall take a visit on your return, as a great favour.

1. SJ refers to the death of Anna Williams (*Ante* To Hester Thrale, 20 Aug. 1783 and n. 1).

Be pleased to assure Mr. Burke of my gratitude for his late favour. I am, Sir, Your most humble servant,

SAM. JOHNSON

I am not well. I wish You a pleasant journey.[2]

2. Reynolds was planning to rendezvous with the Burkes in Devon (C. R. Leslie and T. Taylor, *The Life and Times of Sir Joshua Reynolds*, 1865, II.418; *Ante* To Hester Maria Thrale, 3 Sept. 1783, n. 7).

John Mudge

TUESDAY 9 SEPTEMBER 1783

MS: Hyde Collection.

ADDRESS: To Mr. Mudge, Surgeon, in Plimouth.

POSTMARK: [Undeciphered].

Dear Sir: Heale near Salisbury, Sept. 9, 1783

My conviction of your Skill, and my belief of your friendship determine me to intreat your opinion and advice.

About the latter end of the year —81, I by some accident perceived that my left testicle was much larger than the right. It for some time encreased slowly but without pain or inconvenience, till at last its bulk made it troublesome. In the beginning of this year it a little incommoded my walk, and considering it as a Hydrocele,[1] I, as soon as more formidable disorders gave me leisure intended to discharge the water; But when I showed it to Cruikshank and Pot,[2] they both suspected, and piercing it at my request with a trocar,[3] they found it to be a sarcocele.[4]

This experiment was made about a month ago, since which

1. *Ante* To William Cruikshank, 30 July 1783, n. 2.

2. Percivall Pott (1714–88), F.R.S., noted London surgeon, who operated successfully on Goldsmith in 1772 (*Life* III.501).

3. *trocar*: "a surgical instrument consisting of a perforator . . . enclosed in a metal tube or cannula, used for withdrawing fluid from a cavity, as in dropsy" (*OED*).

4. *sarcocele*: "a fleshy excrescence of the testicles, which sometimes grows so large as to stretch the scrotum much beyond its natural size" (SJ's *Dictionary*).

time the tumour has encreased both in surface and in weight, and by tension of the skin is extremely tender, and impatient of pressure or friction. Its weight is such as to give great pain, when it is not suspended, and its bulk such as the[5] common dress does but ill conceal, nor is there any appearance that its growth will stop. It is so hot, that I am afraid it is in a state of perpetual inflammation.

In this state, I with great earnestness desire You to tell me, what is to be done. Excision is doubtless necessary, to the cure, and I know not any means of palliation. The operation is doubtless painful, but is it dangerous? The pain I hope to endure with decency, but I am loath to put life into much hazard.

Give me, dear Sir, your thoughts upon my case as soon as You can, I shall stay here till I may receive your letter.[6] If You[7] wish to see me, I will come to Plymouth.

My Godson called on me lately. He is weary, and rationally weary of a military life. If You can place him in some other state, I think you may encrease his happiness and secure his virtue.[8] A soldiers time is past in distress and danger, or in idleness and corruption. I am, Dear Sir, Your most humble servant,

SAM. JOHNSON

5. MS: "t" superimposed upon "a"

6. Mudge recommended an immediate operation, but SJ delayed in order to consult with Heberden and Pott (*Post* To Bennet Langton, 24 Sept. 1783; *Post* To William Bowles, 30 Sept. 1783). By the time Pott examined him for a second time, SJ's condition had improved; consequently, Pott decided "to wait the process of Nature" (*Post* To William Bowles, 7 Oct. 1783; *Post* To Hester Thrale, 9 Oct. 1783; *Post* To John Taylor, 20 Oct. 1783).

7. MS: "You You"

8. Despite his rational weariness, William Mudge remained in the army, rising to the rank of Major General (1819).

Susanna Thrale

TUESDAY 9 SEPTEMBER 1783

MS: The Earl of Shelburne.

Dear Miss: [Heale] Sept. 9, 1783

I am glad that you and your sisters have been at Portland.[1] You now can tell what is a quarry, and what is a cliff. Take all opportunities of filling your mind with genuine scenes of nature. Description is always fallacious, at least till you have seen realities, you can not know it to be true. This observation might be extended to Life, but Life cannot be surveyed with the same safety as Nature, and it is better to know vice and folly by report than by experience. A painter, says Sydney, mingled in the battle, that he might know how to paint it, but his knowledge was useless for some mischievous sword took away his hand.[2] They whose speculation upon characters leads them too far in to the world, may ease that nice sense of good and evil, by which characters are to be tried. Acquaint yourself therefore both with the pleasing and the terrible parts of nature; but in life wish to know only the good.

Pray shew Mamma this passage of a letter from DR. BROCKLESBY. "Mrs. Williams, from mere inanition, has at length paid the last debt to Nature about 3 o'clock this morning (Sept. 6). She died without a struggle, retaining her faculties intire to the very last and, [as] she expressed it, having set her house in order, was prepared to leave it at the last summons of Nature."

I do not now[3] say any thing more, than[4] that I am, my Dearest, Your most humble servant,

SAM. JOHNSON

1. *Ante* To Hester Thrale, 26 Aug. 1783 and n. 5.

2. "This painter was to counterfeit the skirmishing between the Centaurs and Lapiths and had been very desirous to see some notable wounds, to be able the more lively to express them; and this morning . . . the foolish fellow was even delighted to see the effect of blows—but this last happening near him so amazed him that he stood stock still, while Dorus with a turn of his sword strake off both his hands; and so, the painter returned well-skilled in wounds, but with never a hand to perform his skill" (Philip Sidney, *The Countess of Pembroke's Arcadia*, ed. Victor Skretkowicz, 1987, Book II, p. 282).

3. MS: "no" superimposed upon "sa"

4. MS: "that"

Francis Barber

TUESDAY 16 SEPTEMBER 1783

MS: Hyde Collection.

Dear Francis: Heale, Sept. 16, 1783

I rather wonder that You have never written, but that is now not necessary, for I purpose to be with [you] on Thursday before dinner.[1]

As Thursday is my Birthday, I would have a little dinner got, and would have You invite Mrs. Desmoulins, Mrs. Davis that was about Mrs. Williams,[2] and Mr. Allen, and Mrs. Gardiner. I am, Your etc.

SAM. JOHNSON

1. *Post* To Charles Burney, 20 Sept. 1783.
2. *Ante* To Sir James Caldwell, 12 Feb. 1767, n. 8.

Charles Burney

SATURDAY 20 SEPTEMBER 1783

MS: John Comyn.

ADDRESS: To Dr. Burney.

ENDORSEMENTS: Sept. 20, 1783, No. 7. From Dr. Johnson, Septr. 20th 1783, No. 9.

Dear Sir: Septr. 20, 1783

I came home on the 18th at noon to a very desolate house. You and I have lost our Friends,[1] but you have more friends at home. My domestick companion is taken from me.[2] She is much missed, for her acquisitions were many, and her curiosity universal, so that she partook of every conversation. I am not well enough to go much out, and to sit, and eat or fast

1. Two of Charles Burney's close friends had died in the past six months: Samuel ("Daddy") Crisp in April and William Bewley on 5 Sept. (*Life* IV.239 n. 3).
2. SJ refers to Anna Williams (*Ante* To Hester Thrale, 20 Aug. 1783, n. 1).

alone, is very wearisome. I always mean to send my compliments to all the Ladies. I am, Sir, Your most humble Servant,

SAM. JOHNSON

Bennet Langton

SATURDAY 20 SEPTEMBER 1783

MS: Hyde Collection.

ADDRESS: To Benet Langton, Esq., in Rochester, Kent.

POSTMARK: 20 SE.

Dear Sir: London, Sept. 20, 1783

You may very reasonably charge me [with] insensibility of your kindness, and that of Lady Rothes, since I have suffered so much time to pass without paying any acknowledgement. I now at last return my thanks,[1] and why I did it not sooner I ought to tell you. I went into Wiltshire as soon as I well could,[2] and was there much employed in palliating my own malady. Disease produces much selfishness; a man in pain is looking after ease, and lets most other things go, as chance shall dispose them. In the mean time I have lost a companion, to whom I have had recourse for domestick amusement for thirty years, and Whose variety of knowledge never was exhausted; and now return to a habitation vacant and desolate.[3] I[4] carry about a very troublesome and dangerous complaint, which admits no cure but by the Chirurgical knife.[5] Let me have your prayers. I am, Sir, Your most humble servant,

SAM. JOHNSON

1. SJ thanks Langton for his hospitality in Rochester. *Ante* To JB, 3 July 1783 and n. 5; *Ante* To Hester Thrale, 23 July 1783.

2. *Ante* To William Bowles, 24 July 1783 and n. 2.

3. *Ante* To Susanna Thrale, 9 Sept. 1783.

4. MS: "I" altered from "In"

5. *Ante* To John Mudge, 9 Sept. 1783 and nn. 4, 6.

John Taylor

SATURDAY 20 SEPTEMBER 1783

MS: Gerald M. Goldberg.

ADDRESS: To the Reverend Dr. Taylor in Ashbourne, Derbyshire.

POSTMARK: 20 SE.

ENDORSEMENT: 1783, 20 Septr. 83.

Dear Sir: London, Sept. 20, 1783

I sent you a letter perhaps improperly short from Heale in Wiltshire,[1] where I was entertained with great kindness, but where want of health did not allow [me] to receive, and perhaps did not enable me to give much pleasure. I went thither ill and I am afraid came back worse. I have a dreadful disease which nothing but Mr. Pott's knife can remove, and the operation is not without[2] danger, but I think it more prudent to venture, than to delay what must probably be done at last, and will be less safe, as it is procrastinated longer.[3] I commit myself to eternal and infinite Mercy.

I am in other respects better than for some years past, and hope that I shall be able to sustain the operation. Write soon and often to, Sir, Your affectionate etc.

SAM. JOHNSON

1. *Ante* To John Taylor, 3 Sept. 1783. 2. MS: "wi" altered from "wh"
3. *Ante* To John Mudge, 9 Sept. 1783 and nn. 4, 6.

William Bowles

MONDAY 22 SEPTEMBER 1783

MS: Hyde Collection.

ADDRESS: To William Bowles, Esq., at Heale near Salisbury.

POSTMARK: [Undeciphered].

Dear Sir: London, Sept. 22, 1783

You insisted with great kindness upon knowing the result of the consultation upon my disease. Mr. Pot inspected the tumour on Saturday, and thought excision necessary. The operation is intended to be in the beginning of next week. Mr. Pot being this week called into Lincolnshire.[1]

I am otherwise well, except that the Gout has a slight inclination to be troublesome. I believe it will be no fit, and, if it be, it is wholly unconnected with the great complaint.

You may suppose that I am not without anxiety, but I hope, God will grant a happy Issue. Let me have your prayers.

Hoole, I think, is well. I know not whom else I have seen of your acquaintance. You will easily believe that I go little out, but my friends do not neglect me.

Be please[d] to pay my respects to your dear Lady. I have now little milk, and little fruit. Do not let the young ones quite forget me. I am, Sir, Your affectionate etc.

SAM. JOHNSON

1. *Ante* To John Mudge, 9 Sept. 1783 and nn. 4, 6.

Jane Gastrell

MONDAY 22 SEPTEMBER 1783

MS: Pembroke College, Oxford.

Bolt court,
Fleetstreet, Sept. 22, 1783

Dear Madam:

Your kind enquiries after me, certainly deserve immediate acknowledgement. I would gladly have come to You this Summer, but few thing[s] that we wish are obtained. I have suffered much pain of body and am likely to suffer more; Yet I hope, we shall meet again.

The death of Mrs. Williams has left me a solitary house, and I am not well enough to go much out of it. Let me have your prayers and those of dear Mrs. Aston, of whom I am glad to hear that she grows no worse. I can not say that of myself since You saw me. I am, Dear Madam, Your most humble Servant,

SAM. JOHNSON

Elizabeth Montagu

MONDAY 22 SEPTEMBER 1783

MS: Hyde Collection.

Madam: Sept. 22, 1783

That respect which is always due to beneficence makes it fit that You should be informed otherwise than by the papers, that on the sixth of this month, died your Pensioner Anna Williams,[1] of whom it may be truly said that she received your bounty with gratitude, and enjoyed it with propriety. You perhaps have still her prayers.

You have, Madam, the satisfaction of having alleviated the sufferings of a Woman of great merit both intellectual and moral. Her curiosity was universal, her knowledge was very extensive, and she sustained forty years of misery with steady fortitude. Thirty years and more she had been my companion, and her death has left me very desolate.

That I have not written sooner, You may impute to absence, to ill health, to any thing rather than want of regard to the Benefactress of my departed Friend. I am, Madam, Your most humble Servant,

SAM. JOHNSON

1. In 1775 Anna Williams began receiving "a small annuity, which the charity of Mrs. Montagu had secured" her. The annuity doubled Williams's income (JB's *Life*, ed. J. W. Croker, 1831, III.256).

Hester Thrale

MONDAY 22 SEPTEMBER 1783

MS: Hyde Collection.

ADDRESS: To Mrs. Thrale at Bath.

POSTMARK: 22 SE.

Dear Madam: London, Sept. 22, 1783

Happy are You, that have ease and leisure to want intelligence of air ballons.[1] Their existence is, I believe, indubitable, but I know not that they can possibly be of any use. The construction is this. The chymical philosop[h]ers have discovered a body (which I have forgotten, but will enquire) which dissolved by an acid emits an vapour lighter than the atmosp[h]erical air.[2] This vapour is caught, among other means, by tying a bladder compressed upon the bottle in which the dissolution is performed; the vapour rising swels the bladder, and fills it. The bladder is then tied and removed, and another applied, till as much of this light air is collected, as is wanted. Then a large spherical case is made, and very large it must be, of the lightest matter that can be found, secured by some method like that of oiling silk against all passage of air. Into this are emptied all the bladders of light air, and if there [be] light air enough, it mounts into the clouds, upon the same principle as a bottle filled with water, will sink in water, but a bottle filled with æther would float. It rises till[3] it come to air of equal tenuity with its own, if wind or water does not spoil it on the way. Such, Madam is an air ballon.

Meteors have been this autumn very often seen, but I have never been in their way.[4]

Poor Williams has I hope seen the end of her afflictions.

1. The mania for balloons and ballooning had began in France with the launching of the first hot-air balloon by the Montgolfier brothers (June 1783) and the first inflammable-air balloon by J.-A.-C. Charles and the Robert brothers (August 1783). The craze rapidly spread to England: within months of the French experiments, according to Horace Walpole, "all our views are directed to the air. *Balloons* occupy senators, philosophers, ladies, everybody" (*Walpole's Correspondence*, Yale ed. xxv.449, 450 n. 8). England's interest in ballooning peaked in 1784–85, when Vincenzo Lunardi conducted manned flights in London and several other cities (J. E. Hodgson, *The History of Aeronautics in Great Britain*, 1924, pp. 14–15, 117–36). *Post* To Joshua Reynolds, 18 Sept. 1784.

2. Iron dissolved by sulphuric acid produces hydrogen, SJ's "light air." *Post* To Hester Thrale, 23 Sept. 1783.

3. MS: "till" written above "upon" del.

4. On 18 Aug. a giant meteor had been sighted all over the British Isles (*GM* 1783, pp. 711–12, 885). There were other "very respectable meteors" as well (*Walpole's Correspondence*, Yale ed. xxv.427).

She acted with prudence, and she bore with fortitude. She has left me.[5]

> Then thy weary task hast done,
> Home art gone, and ta'en thy wages.[6]

Had she had good humour, and prompt elocution, her universal curiosity, and comprehensive knowledge, would have made her the Delight of [all] that knew her. She left her little to your charity school.[7]

The complaint about which you enquire is a sarcocele.[8] I thought it a hydrocele,[9] and heeded it but little. Puncture has detected the mistake. It can be safely suffered no longer. Upon inspection two days ago, it was determined extrema tentare.[10] If excision should be delayed there is danger of a gangrene.[11] You would not have me for fear of pain perish in putrescence. I shall, I hope, with trust in Eternal Mercy, lay hold of the possibility of life, which yet remains. My health is not bad, the gout is now trying at my feet. My appetite and digestion are good, and my sleep better than formerly. I am not dejected, and I am not feeble. There is however danger enough in such operations at seventy four. Let me have your prayers, and those of the young dear people. I am Madam, Your humble servant,

SAM. JOHNSON

Write soon, and often.

5. *Ante* To Hester Thrale, 20 Aug. 1783, n. 1.

6. "Thou thy worldly task hast done, / Home art gone and ta'en thy wages" (*Cymbeline* IV.ii.260–61).

7. *Ante* To Thomas Percy, 5 Nov. 1769, n. 1. Shortly before she died, Anna Williams had given the school £200; in her will, she bequeathed it an additional £157 (Hill II.334 n. 3).

8. *Ante* To John Mudge, 9 Sept. 1783, n. 4.

9. *Ante* To William Cruikshank, 30 July 1783, n. 2.

10. *extrema tentare*: "to attempt the extreme measures" (of surgery).

11. *Ante* To John Mudge, 9 Sept. 1783 and n. 6.

John Mudge

TUESDAY 23 SEPTEMBER 1783

MS: Hyde Collection.

Boltcourt,
Dear Sir: Fleetstreet, Sept. 23, 1783

I thank You for the letter which I received this day. It is such as I expected clear, judicious, and decisive. I will give an account of my case as it is at this time. The tension and inflammation are abated, and the abatement I ascribe first to a discharge not of *pus* but of *sanies*,[1] and that in no great quantity from the puncture made a month ago, which till now appeared externally to be healed, but is lately opened;[2] and again the gout which has laid hold on both my feet, seems to have translated the inflammation thither. Of this You must judge. I can now suspend the tumour without a defensative.[3] But its weight makes suspension necessary. I have not nor ever have had the least pain in my back, nor any other[4] pain but mere soreness, and the tension of the cord when the load is too long unsupported.

Mr. Pot and Mr. Cruikshank are both of opinion, I think, that the spermatick cord is yet unaffected; Pot felt it very accurately.

I felt very little inconvenience in travelling, though I came to Salisbury in a rough Stagecoach in one day.[5] I am, Sir, your obliged, humble servant,

SAM. JOHNSON

If any thing more occurs to you, I desire you to write again.

1. *sanies*: "thin matter; serous excretion" (SJ's *Dictionary*).

2. *Ante* To John Mudge, 9 Sept. 1783.

3. *defensative*: "a bandage, plaster, or the like, used to secure a wound from outward violence" (SJ's *Dictionary*).

4. MS: "o" superimposed upon "p"

5. Cf. *Ante* To Richard Brocklesby, 29 Aug. 1783.

Hester Thrale

TUESDAY 23 SEPTEMBER 1783

MS: Rylands Library.

Madam: London, Sept. 23, 1783

You will not much wonder that my own state of body is much in my thoughts, or that since You enquired about it, I should [write] what intelligence I obtain.

Having, with all that know him, a very high opinion of the chirurgical experience and skill of Mr. Mudge, I laid my case before him, and inclose his answer, which You may return as you can.[1]

When You have this opinion You will acquit[2] me of impatience or temerity, and perhaps encourage me by your suffrage.

I have written likewise to Dr. Heberden, who is now in his retreat at Windsor, and doubt not of his concurrence in the general opinion.

Consider [me] as one that has loved You much, and loved you long, and let me have your good wishes and your prayers.

Write as often as You can to, Madam, Your most humble servant,

SAM. JOHNSON

I am told that the *light air* is obtained from iron dissolved by the vitriolick, or sulphur acid.[3]—But I am not sure.

1. *Ante* To John Mudge, 9 Sept. 1783; 23 Sept. 1783.

2. MS: "ac" repeated as catchword

3. *Ante* To Hester Thrale, 22 Sept. 1783 and n. 2; *Post* To Hester Thrale, 1 Nov. 1783.

William Cruikshank

WEDNESDAY 24 SEPTEMBER 1783

MS: Hyde Collection.

ADDRESS: To Mr. Cruikshank.

To WILLIAM CRUIKSHANK, 24 *September* 1783

Sir: Sept. 24, 1783

The orifice of the puncture discharges so much as, in my opinion, to deserve[1] attention.[2] It has taken away the tension of the integuments, and much abated the general inflammation. I must entreat the favour of a visit this Evening, and wish You would bring with [You] some sticking plaster. I am, Sir, Your obliged, humble Servant,

SAM. JOHNSON

1. MS: "d" superimposed upon "s"
2. *Ante* To John Mudge, 9 Sept. 1783.

Bennet Langton

WEDNESDAY 24 SEPTEMBER 1783

MS: Hyde Collection.

ADDRESS: To Benet Langton, Esq., at Rochester.

POSTMARK: 24 SE.

Dear Sir: London, Sept. 24, 1783

My case, which you guessed at not amiss, is a Sarcocele;[1] a dreadful disorder which however, I hope, God will not suffer to destroy me. Let me have your prayers. I have consulted Mr. Mudge of Plymouth who strongly presses an immediate operation.[2] I expect Dr. Heberdens advice to morrow.[3] Make my compliments to your dear Lady, to my Jenny,[4] and to all the little ones.

The Gout has with[in] these four days come upon me with violence, which I never experienced before. It has made [me] helpless as an infant. It is no great evil in itself but the [fit] delays the Chirurgeon. I am, Sir, Your most etc.

SAM. JOHNSON

1. *Ante* To John Mudge, 9 Sept. 1783, n. 4.
2. *Ante* To John Mudge, 9 Sept. 1783, n. 6.
3. *Ante* To Hester Thrale, 23 Sept. 1783.
4. SJ refers to his goddaughter, Jane Langton.

John Taylor

WEDNESDAY 24 SEPTEMBER 1783

MS: Hyde Collection.

ADDRESS: To the Reverend Dr. Taylor in Ashbourne, Derbyshire.

POSTMARKS: 24 SE, 25 SE.

ENDORSEMENTS: 1783, 24 Sept. 83.

Dear Sir, London, Sept. 24, 1783

My case is what you think it, of the worst kind, a sarcocele.[1] There is I suppose nothing to be done but by the Knife.[2] I have within these four days been violently attacked by the gout, which if [it] should continue in its first [fury] would retard the other business; but I hope it will abate. I am, Dear Sir, Your[3] humble servant,

SAM. JOHNSON

1. *Ante* To John Mudge, 9 Sept. 1783, n. 4.
2. *Ante* To John Mudge, 9 Sept. 1783, n. 6.
3. MS: "Yours"

James Boswell

TUESDAY 30 SEPTEMBER 1783

PRINTED SOURCE: JB's *Life*, 1791, II.467.

You should not make your letters such rarities, when you know, or might know, the uniform state of my health. It is very long since I heard from you; and that I have not answered is a very insufficient reason for the silence of a friend.—Your *Anacreon* is a very uncommon book;[1] neither London nor Cambridge can supply a copy of that edition. Whether it should be reprinted, you cannot do better than consult Lord Hailes.[2]—

1. *Ante* To JB, *c.* 4 Feb. 1783 and n. 3.

2. "I wrote to him [SJ] . . . and mentioned that 'Baxter's Anacreon, which is in the library at Auchinleck, was, I find, collated by my father in 1727, with the MS. belonging to the University of Leyden, and he has made a number of Notes upon it. Would you advise me to publish a new edition of it?'" (*Life* IV.241). JB never

Besides my constant and radical disease,[3] I have been for these ten days much harassed with the gout, but that has now remitted. I hope God will yet grant me a little longer life, and make me less unfit to appear before him.

undertook this project, but an updated edition of Baxter did appear ten years later (Leipzig, 1793) (*Life* IV.525).

3. *Ante* To John Mudge, 9 Sept. 1783.

William Bowles

TUESDAY 30 SEPTEMBER 1783

MS: Houghton Library.

ADDRESS: To William Bowles, Esq., at Heale near Salisbury.

POSTMARK: 30 SE.

Dear Sir: London, Sept. 30, 1783

The letter which You sent me was from Mudge who had been from home, and was such as might be expected from a very skilful Man. It has raised more hope than fear.

By an unexpected discharge at the puncture, the tension is lessened, the bulk of the tumour diminished, and the inflammation abated,[1] I should have been for some time past almost without pain had not the gout attacked me with great violence. It has been very troublesome for about ten days but has now very much remitted.

Mr. Pot has been for some time in Lincolnshire, I expect to see him in a day or two, and then the resolution will be taken, and You shall be informed of the event.[2]

If ever I omit[3] my respects to your Lady you always suppose them intended. I am, Dear sir, Your obliged, humble Servant,

SAM. JOHNSON

1. *Ante* To John Mudge, 23 Sept. 1783.

2. *Ante* To John Mudge, 9 Sept. 1783, n. 6; *Post* To William Bowles, 7 Oct. 1783.

3. MS: "omit" altered from "omits"

Hester Maria Thrale

TUESDAY 30 SEPTEMBER 1783

MS: The Earl of Shelburne.
ADDRESS: To Miss Thrale at Bath.
POSTMARK: 30 SE.

Dear Madam: London, Sept. 30, 1783

I am in a state, I think, to be pitied, if pity be a passion ever to come in use. I have a radical disease of a formidable kind and of long continuance, for a great while uneasy, and at last very painful.[1] On sunday sev'nnight I was seized with the gout, with which in my present state, I did not care to play tricks, and which encreased upon me till I could not without many expedients and repeated efforts raise myself in bed; not without much pain [and] difficulty by the help of two sticks convey myself to a chair. Dr. Brocklesby allowed large doses of opium which naturally eased the pain. It then withdrew in part from the right foot, but fell furiously on the left. But one foot was a great acquisition. I now walk alone.

To crown my other comforts a tooth tormented me, I was weary of being diseased from top to bottom; I therefore sent for a Dentist, and pulled it out.

I am this day not in great pain, nor much dejected. I am not neglected by mankind, but he who lives by himself has many hours of unwelcome solitude, especially when his mind is battered by external evils. These two last years have pressed very hard upon me, and this has yet a severe stroke in store. I pray God for support and deliverance, and think that the symptoms are favourable, and hope that You, my dear Love, join your prayers with mine.

Mrs. Cholmondely came to me yesterday, and talked of retiring into Wales. I was not well enough to show the folly of her scheme, by explaining how she whose whole felicity is conversation, must fall into a state of languor and vacancy, where she found no community of knowledge, could expect no recip-

1. *Ante* To John Mudge, 9 Sept. 1783.

rocation of sentiments, nor any mind or manners congenial to her own.

Sheward was with me this morning, just such as Sheward uses to be.[2] I am, Dear Madam, your affectionate, humble servant,

SAM. JOHNSON

2. SJ may refer to William Seward or to Mrs. Sheward (*Ante* To Hester Thrale, 28 June 1783; 3 July 1783).

John Hoole

AUTUMN 1783[1]

PRINTED SOURCE: Sotheby's Catalogue, 12 Apr. 1875, Lot No. 653, p. 62.

ADDRESS: To Mr. Hoole in Queen's Street.

[Thanks him for his affectionate letter, and hopes] we shall both be the better for each other's friendship, [hoping that] we shall not very quickly be parted. [He then speaks of his state of health and says,] I am now grown somewhat easier in my body, but my mind is sometimes depressed. [He touchingly mentions the death of poor Williams, who] is gone I hope to Heaven, [adding] may we when we are called, be called to happiness.

1. Dated with reference to the death of Anna Williams, 6 Sept. 1783, and to the comparative improvement in SJ's health (cf. *Post* To John Taylor, 20 Oct. 1783).

Frances Reynolds

WEDNESDAY 1 OCTOBER 1783

MS: Yale Center for British Art.

ADDRESS: To Mrs. Reynolds.

To FRANCES REYNOLDS, 1 *October* 1783

Dear Madam: Oct. 1, 1783

I am very ill indeed, and to my former ilness is superadded the Gout.[1] I am now without Shoes, and have lately been almost motionless.

To my other afflictions is added solitude. Mrs. Williams, a companion of thirty years is gone.[2] It is a comfort to me, to have You near me. I am, Madam, your most etc.

SAM. JOHNSON

1. *Ante* To Bennet Langton, 24 Sept. 1783.

2. *Ante* To Susanna Thrale, 9 Sept. 1783.

Mr. Tomkison

WEDNESDAY 1 OCTOBER 1783

MS: Current location unknown. Transcribed from photostat in the Hyde Collection.

ADDRESS: To Mr. Tomkison in Southampton Street, Covent Garden.

POSTMARKS: 7 O'CLOCK T, PENY POST PAYD T WE.

Sir: Oct. 1, —83, Mr. Tomkison

I have known Mr. Lowe very familiarly a great while. I consider him as a man of very clear and vigorous understanding, and conceive his principles to be such, that whatever You transact with him, You have nothing to expect from him unbecoming a Gentleman. I am, Sir, Your humble servant,

SAM. JOHNSON

William Cruikshank

THURSDAY 2 OCTOBER 1783

PRINTED SOURCE: Chapman III.80.

ADDRESS: To Mr. Cruickshank.

Sir: Oct. 2, 1783

The critical night is now over. Let me see You as soon as You can, and tell me the success, that I may congratulate or console you. I am, Sir, Your obliged humble servant,

SAM. JOHNSON

My pain and lameness abate, and I am not very uneasy.

Robert Chambers

SATURDAY 4 OCTOBER 1783

MS: Loren Rothschild.

Dear Sir: London, Oct. 4, 1783

Perhaps You may be glad to receive another Letter from your old Friend. Yet what have I to tell you that you can wish to know? My paper will I am afraid, be covered with complaints and calamities. The two last years have lain very heavy upon me. One disease has with very short intervals succeeded to another. About four months ago I felt the stroke of a palsy,[1] which still in some degree impedes[2] my utterance, but has not shaken my general health, nor, I hope, weakened my intellectual powers. I have for some time had a sarcocele, of which the Surgeon's knife perhaps, is the only cure.[3]

Such is my state in my seventy fifth year. In the mean[time] my friends are summoned from me. Dr. Laurence is dead.[4] If I go to Oxford, Wheeler and Edwards are now in the grave.[5] Dear Mrs. Williams who had been my domestick companion for more than thirty years, died of lingering languour not many days ago.[6] She retained her full powers of reason, I believe to her last hour, and has now surely seen an end of misery. I now live alone, but not neglected by the world. But to be

1. *Ante* To Edmund Allen, 17 June 1783.

2. MS: "impedes" altered from "impeded"

3. *Ante* To John Mudge, 9 Sept. 1783 and nn. 4, 6.

4. *Ante* To Hester Thrale, 9 May 1782, n. 3; 13 June 1783, n. 5.

5. *Ante* To Hester Thrale, 20 Aug. 1783 and n. 3; *Post* To William Adams, 30 Mar. 1784.

6. *Ante* To Susanna Thrale, 9 Sept. 1783.

sick in solitude is a cheerless State. Superadded to other complaints I have now the gout, but in a manner very supportable.

You, dear Sir, have likewise your calamity in which may you and your Lady find that support which Christianity affords.[7] Let us not take too much delight in pleasures which we cannot long enjoy, nor grieve with too much dejection for evils which cannot long be felt.

I would write often to You if I had any thing to tell; You have much to tell, yet you never write. What leisure You have, I cannot know; You are in a part of the world that affords much employment for Speculation and curiosity, whether it be considered in its ancient or present state.[8] A System of life totally different from European manners, a country of vast extent, with great variety of productions, would easily furnish a few letters, though letters from you will be welcome, when[9] they bring nothing more than a proof that You remember me, and I hope You do not think that I have ever deserved to be forgotten.

If my name has yet any operation on your mind, I hope you show what countenance You can to Mr. Fowke who was formerly my friend,[10] and to Mr. Laurence who is my Friend's Son.[11] To the prosperity of either of them I should rejoice if my recommendation could contribute. Be pleased to do what favours you can to the Bearer of this letter; he comes from a house in the Hebrides where I was very kindly entertained.[12]

Make my compliments to Lady Chambers, and tell her I

7. Chambers's eldest son, Thomas Fitzmaurice (b. 1776), died somewhere along the coast of South Africa after the *Grosvenor*, the ship carrying him to England, was wrecked 4 Aug. 1782 (Russell Miller, *The East Indiamen*, 1980, pp. 137, 140; Alexander Dalrymple, *An Account of the Loss of the Grosvenor, Indiaman*, 1783, p. 20). Although Frances Chambers suffered a nervous breakdown after hearing the news, she eventually recovered (information supplied by Professor T. M. Curley).

8. Cf. *Ante* To Robert Chambers, 19 Apr. 1783.

9. MS: "tho" del. before "when"

10. *Ante* To Robert Chambers, 19 Apr. 1783.

11. *Ante* To Robert Chambers, 30 Sept. 1773 and n. 4; 19 Apr. 1783.

12. SJ may refer to the "young gentleman from Coriatachat" whom he had entertained the previous year (*Ante* To JB, 7 Sept. 1782 and n. 6).

wish for more of her journals.[13] I am, Dear Sir, Yours affectionately,

SAM. JOHNSON

13. *Ante* To Robert Chambers, 31 Oct. 1779.

Hester Thrale

MONDAY 6 OCTOBER 1783

MS: Houghton Library.
ADDRESS: To Mrs. Thrale at Bath.
POSTMARK: 7 OC.

Madam: London, Oct. 6, 1783

When I shall give a good and settled account of my health, I cannot venture to say, some account I am ready to give, because I am pleased to find that you desire it.[1]

I yet sit without shoes with my feet upon a pillow, but my pain and weakness are much abated; and I am no[2] longer crawling upon two sticks. To the Gout my mind is reconciled by another letter from Mr. Mudge,[3] in which he vehemently urges the excision, but tells me that the gout will secure me from every thing paralytick, if this[4] be true I am ready to say to the arthritick pains—Deh! venite ogni di, durate un anno.[5]

My Physician in ordinary is Dr. Brocklesby who comes almost every day, my Surgeon in Mr. Pott's absence is Mr. Cruikshank, the present reader in Dr. Hunter's school. Neither of them however do much more than look and talk. The general health of my body is as good as you have ever known it, almost as good as I can remember.

The carriage which you supposed made rough by my weak-

1. *Post* To Hester Thrale, 9 Oct. 1783.
2. MS: "no" altered from "not"
3. *Ante* To William Bowles, 30 Sept. 1783.
4. MS: "this" altered from "the"
5. SJ adapts part of his translation of a distich "spoken when the Duke of Modena ran away for Fear of the Comet": *Se al venir vostro i Principi sen' vanno, / Deh venga ogni Di,—durate un Anno*: "If at your coming princes disappear, / Comets! come every day—and stay a year" (*Thraliana* 1.209; *Poems*, p. 204).

ness, was the common Salisbury Stage, high hung, and driven to Salisbury in a day.[6] I was not fatigued.

Mr. Pott has been out of town, but I expect to see him soon, and will then tell you something of the the main affair, of which there seems now to be a better prospect.

This afternoon I have given to Mrs. Cholmondely, Mrs. Way, Lady Sheffields relation, Mr[s]. Kindersley the Describer of Indian manners,[7] and another anonymous Lady.

As Mrs. Williams received a pension from Mrs. Montague, it was fit to notify her death,[8] the account has brought me a letter not only civil but tender. So I hope, peace is proclaimed.[9]

The state of the Stocks I take to be this. When in the late exigencies,[10] the Ministry gave so high a price for money, all the money that could be disengaged from trade, was lent to the publick. The stocks sunk because nobody bought them. They have not risen since, because the money being already lent out, nobody has money to lay out upon them, till commerce shall by the help of peace bring a new supply. If they cannot rise they will sometimes fall, for their essence seems to be fluctuation, but the present sudden [decline] is[11] occasioned by the report of some new disturbances and demands, which the Irish are machinating.[12] I am, Madam, Your most etc.

SAM. JOHNSON

6. "Somebody tells me that you went in a rough Carriage from Salisbury to London, but you probably found any Carriage rough" (Hester Thrale to SJ, 25 Sept. 1783, MS: Houghton Library).

7. SJ refers to Jemima Kindersley (1741–1809), author of *Letters from the Island of Teneriffe . . . and the East Indies* (1777).

8. *Ante* To Elizabeth Montagu, 22 Sept. 1783 and n. 1.

9. *Ante* To Lord Westcote, 28 July 1780, n. 2.

10. SJ refers to the economic consequences of prosecuting the American War.

11. MS: "is" written above "prices" del.

12. In early September five hundred delegates from Ulster had met at Dungannon to discuss reformation of the Irish Parliament. The delegates called for annual parliaments, a widened franchise, a more equitable distribution of seats, the exclusion of placeholders, and a national convention on the issue of reform. Moreover, widespread unemployment in the Irish textile trades had led to demands for protection in the form of tariffs and nonimportation agreements; these

demands were directed in part against Great Britain (R. B. McDowell, *Ireland in the Age of Imperialism and Revolution*, 1979, pp. 302–5, 311–13).

William Bowles

TUESDAY 7 OCTOBER 1783

MS: Houghton Library.

ADDRESS: To William Bowles, Esq., at Heale near Salisbury.

POSTMARK: 7 OC.

Dear Sir: London, Oct. 7, 1783

In the account which I now send you, there will be something which your tenderness will dispose you to read with pleasure.

I told you that the tumour had been pierced for experiment.[1] That wound which seemed to close superficially, has since opened, and by a very copious [discharge] has so lessened the bulk, and so abated the inflammation of the morbid part, that Mr. Pot who ten days ago seemed to think excision indispensable has now determined to wait the process of Nature.[2]

I have had since I left you, a very sharp fit of the Gout, but it has now remitted, the pain is almost gone and weakness only remains. The tumour now is much less tender, and less cumbrous.

I do not recollect how the five airs were produced by Dr. Saul,[3] be so kind as to tell me, particularly how light air for the flying bubble is generated.[4]

1. *Ante* To William Bowles, 4 Aug. 1783.

2. *Ante* To William Bowles, 30 Sept. 1783; *Ante* To John Mudge, 9 Sept. 1783, n. 6.

3. It is probable that SJ mistakenly attributed to Edward Saul (1677–1754), author of *An Historical and Philosophical Account of the Barometer* (1730), the "five airs" described by Joseph Priestley in his *Experiments and Observations on Different Kinds of Air* (1774). Priestley's categories are "fixed air" (carbon dioxide), "nitrous air" (nitrous oxide), "acid air" (hydrochloric acid), "alkaline air" (ammonia), and "inflammable air" (hydrogen) (Priestley, *Experiments*, I.25–43, 55–69, 108–28, 143–54, 165–77, 203–51).

4. *Ante* To Hester Thrale, 22 Sept. 1783 and n. 2. While visiting Bowles, SJ had

I am now easy, but solitary. My Companion is gone,[5] and at seventy four it is very late to adopt another.

Make my compliments to Mrs. Bowles. I am, Dear Sir, Your most humble servant,

SAM. JOHNSON

"attended some experiments that were made by a physician at Salisbury, on the new kinds of air" (*Life* IV.237). *Post* To Hester Thrale, 9 Oct. 1783.

5. SJ refers to Anna Williams.

Hester Thrale

THURSDAY 9 OCTOBER 1783

MS: Rylands Library (first sheet, "Madam . . . at home"); Hyde Collection (second sheet, including signature and date).

Madam: London, Oct. 9, 1783

Many reasons hinder me from believing that opium had any part in my late disorder. I had a long time forborn it. I never used it in any quantity comparable to what is taken by those that habitually indulge themselves with it. It never produces palsies by the utmost excess. My Physicians had so little suspicion of it, though they know my practice, that they made use of it to obviate some effects of the blisters.

It was the paralytick affection which I mentioned sixteen year[s] ago to Dr. Laurence, when he allowed my fears to be reasonable. It appeared afterward as an asthma, from which since its invasion of another part I have been almost wholly free, and which in its paroxysms was relieved by opium.

The state of the tumour is now changed. When the Surgeons visited me, they thought it upon examination a sarcocele,[1] but I was willing to hope something better, and was likewise desirous of knowledge rather than conjecture; I therefore proposed an exploration by puncture; the operation was performed, and the unwelcome opinion was confirmed.

1. *Ante* To John Mudge, 9 Sept. 1783, n. 4.

The breach made in the integuments closed, but the internal wound never healed. The tumour increased with great encumbrance and very frequent pain, so tender as scarcely to endure any bandage, and so much inflamed as to threaten great mischief.

Such was my misery when I consulted Mr. Mudge, and was driven back to town. Mr. Pot found the danger not immediate but seemed to think excision unavoidable; but being to take a journey delayed it. While he was away the external wound burst open, and by very frequent effusions the tension is eased, the inflammation abated, and the protuberance so diminished as to incommode me very little, and scarcely to remind me of my disease by any pain.

Mr. Pot upon re-examination think[s] it best, since Nature has done so much, to look quietly on, and see what it will do more. I proposed another orifice, which I think Mr. Cruikshank seems to approve, but Mr. Pot thinks not proper. The operation is therefore at least suspended, but[2] the tumour is found not scirrous,[3] and therefore not likely to corrupt any other part; and, say[s] Pot, "one would not carry fire and sword further than is necessary."

I shall consult Mr. Mudge, whose eagerness You know, and of whose judgement I think with great esteem, and enquire whether this new view of the case reconciles him to delay.[4]

I cannot, Madam, yet give an account of settled health, or a cure either perfected or indeed attempted, but I hope, You will be glad to hear that from such a complication[5] of miseries I am now at ease. The Gout, which was for a while very oppressive, is now daily remitting, so that I walk easily enough without shoes between two rooms on the same floor.

I have thus *ended* for the present *joy and woe* and we may now *talk a little like folks of this world*.[6]

2. MS: "but" superimposed upon "?yet"

3. *scirrhous*: "indurated; covered with hard excrescences" (*OED*).

4. *Post* To John Mudge, 9 Oct. 1783.

5. MS: "compli" repeated as catchword

6. "Pr'ythee quit this Caprice; and (as OLD FALSTAF says) / Let Us e'en talk a

⟨*one or two words*⟩ always was a magnifier of herself, but by your description she seems to have improved in her inflations. She was one of ⟨*one or two words*⟩ first Scholars. She liked him at first, disliked him afterwards, and seems now to have resuscitated her original kindness.—Sit tibi exemplo—.[7]

When You write Latin to any body but me, take care to spell it right.—*It reflects upon me, as I know not my trade.*[8]

If Mr. Shepherd brings me a letter from You,[9] he will have much ado to miss a kind reception, and as my condition is at present he will not be told that I am not at home.

Two nights ago Mr. Burke sat with me a long time; he seems much pleased with his Journey.[10] We had both seen Stonehenge this summer for the first time.[11] I told him that the view had enabled me to confute two opinions which have been advanced about it.[12] One that the materials are not natural stones, but an artificial composition hardened by time. This notion is as old as Camdens time,[13] and has this strong argument to support it that stone of that species is no where to be found. The other opinion, advanced by Dr. Charlton, is that [it] was erected by the Danes.[14]

---

little like Folks of This World" (Matthew Prior, "A Better Answer (To Chloe Jealous)," ll. 3–4).

7. *sit tibi exemplo*: "may she be an example to you."

8. *Ante* To Hester Thrale, 21 Oct. 1779, n. 7.

9. The Rev. Thomas Shephard the younger (1757–1843), clergyman and schoolmaster (*Alum. Oxon.* II.iv.1286; *GM* 1843, p. 663; *The Piozzi Letters*, ed. E. A. Bloom and L. D. Bloom, 1989, I.138 n. 27). *Post* To Hester Maria Thrale, 20 Oct. 1783.

10. *Ante* To Hester Maria Thrale, 3 Sept. 1783, n. 7.

11. Writing to JB in 1787, William Bowles reported, "Whilst Dr. Johnson was in Wiltshire he viewed Stonehenge which he declared surpassed his ideas and was more curious than he expected to have found it" (Waingrow, p. 254).

12. MS: "one" del. before "it"

13. "Yet it is the opinion of some, that these stones are not natural or such as are dug out of the Quarries, but artificial, of fine sand cemented together, by a glewy sort of matter" (William Camden, *Britannia* [1586], trans. Edmund Gibson, 2d ed., 1722, I.121).

14. SJ refers to the theory advanced by Walter Charleton (1619–1707), M.D., royal physician (to Charles I and Charles II) and antiquarian: "I now at length conceive it [Stonehenge] to have been Erected by the DANES . . . and principally, if

Mr. Bowles made me observe that the transverse stones were fixed on the perpendicular supporters, by a knob formed on the top of the upright[15] stone, which entered into a hollow cut in the crossing stone. This is a proof, that the enormous Edifice was raised by a people who [had] not yet the knowledge of mortar, which cannot be supposed of the Danes who came hither in Ships, and were not ignorant certainly of the arts of life. This proves likewise the stones not to be factitious,[16] for they that could mould such durrable masses, could do much more than make mortar, and could have continued the transverse from the upright parts with the same paste.

You have doubtless seen Stonehenge, and if You have not, I should think it a hard task to make an adequate description.[17]

It is, in my opinion to be refered to the earliest habitation of the Island, as a Druidical monument of at least two thousand years, probably the most ancient work of Man upon the Island. Salisbury Cathedral[18] and its Neighbour Stonehenge, are two eminent monuments of art and rudeness, and may show the first essays and the last perfection of[19] architecture.

I have not yet settled my thoughts about the generation of light air, which I indeed once saw produced, but I was at the height of my great complaint.[20] I have made enquiry and [shall] soon be able to tell You how to fill a ballon.[21] I am, Madam, Your most humble Servant,

SAM. JOHNSON

---

not wholly Design'd to be a *Court Royal* or a place for the *Election* and *Inauguration* of their *Kings*" (*Chorea Gigantum; or, The most Famous Antiquity of Great-Britain, Vulgarly called STONE-HENG . . . Restored to the DANES*, 1663, p. [5]).

15. MS: "per" del. before "upright"

16. *factitious*: "made by art, in opposition to what is made by nature" (SJ's *Dictionary*).

17. "I saw Stonehenge once before this Letter was written in Company of my Father who said it was Druidical" (Piozzi II.316).

18. MS: "Catherdral"

19. MS: "or"

20. *Ante* To William Bowles, 7 Oct. 1783 and n. 4.

21. *Ante* To Hester Thrale, 22 Sept. 1783 and n. 2; *Post* To Hester Thrale, 1 Nov. 1783.

John Mudge

THURSDAY 9 OCTOBER 1783

MS: Hyde Collection.

Dear Sir: London, Oct. 9, 1783

By representing the Gout as an antagonist to the palsy, you have said enough to make it welcome.[1] This is not strictly the first fit, but I hope it is as good as the first,[2] for it is the second that ever confined me, and the first was ten years ago, much less fierce and firy than this.

Of the Sarcocele I will try to give a clear accou[n]t.[3] The bulk, and soreness of the tumour drove me [to] town, where I showed it to Mr. Pot, who seemed to think excision necessary, and I saw no reason for any other opinion. He was however to take a journey, and the operation was delayed to his return. In the mean[time] the puncture made experimentally by the trocar,[4] which though the skin perhaps united, never healed internally, again broke open, and by its discharge reduced the tumour to half its bulk, and by abating the inflammation took away the soreness. I now no longer feel its weight; and the skin of the scrotum which glistened with tension is now lax and corrugated.

Mr. Pot, seeing at his return, so great an alteration, thought it proper to suspend all violence, and as Nature has so far favoured us, to[5] wait the process.[6]

This he thinks more reasonable, if I understand him rightly, because the diseased part is totally free from all scirrosity, and he therefore thinks the spermatick cord in no danger.[7] The

1. *Ante* To Hester Thrale, 6 Oct. 1783.

2. *Ante* To Hester Thrale, 3 June 1776.

3. *Ante* To John Mudge, 9 Sept. 1783 and n. 4.

4. *Ante* To John Mudge, 9 Sept. 1783, n. 3.

5. MS: "o" superimposed upon "h"

6. *Ante* To William Bowles, 7 Oct. 1783.

7. *Ante* To John Mudge, 23 Sept. 1783; *Ante* To Hester Thrale, 9 Oct. 1783 and n. 3.

disorder, he says, is purely local, and indicates no depravity of the constitution.

I have now no pain from the tumour, and very little inconvenience, but I wish it was quite away. The running has now ceased for forty eight hours, and what hope I had, was of its continuance. I shall try if Mr. Pot will not open the orifice.

I write thus particularly because, as I trust much to your judgement, I would give a full state of the case. I can scarcely believe that the[8] diseased part will thus cure itself; yet if there be any such hope, as the Surgeon thinks, and, as he thinks likewise, no danger in delay, it were madness to demand or solicite the excision.

Write, dear Sir, what you can to inform or encourage me. The operation is not delayed by any fears or objections of mine.

I believe the spermatick cord is uninjured, as well because I find the Surgeons of that opinion, as because I never had any dorsal pains, nor any other pain than that of soreness, and of weight, when at its full size, the tumour[9] was sometimes suspended by the cord without support. It is[10] now so much diminished, that the truss is more troublesome than the weight. How long this will be its state I dare not conjecture. You must help me. I am, Sir, Your obliged, humble Servant,

SAM. JOHNSON

8. MS: "t" superimposed upon "i"

9. MS: "the tumour" written above "it" del.

10. MS: "is is"

Bennet Langton

SATURDAY 11 OCTOBER 1783

MS: Hyde Collection.

ADDRESS: To Benet Langton, Esq., in Rochester.

POSTMARK: [Undeciphered].

Dear Sir: London, Oct. 11, 1783

Your solicitude for my recovery by the safest means is very

kind. My disease is a Sarcocele,[1] a malady very formidable and when it is cured, to be cured commonly only by the excision of the morbid part.

When I was in Wiltshire I spent much of my time in pain, and was at last driven home by my distress. There was for some time little hope but from the knife, but as Mr. Pot was to take a journey the operation was delayed, and while he was away, by an unexpected change in the state of the tumour, the necessity of violence is at least suspended, and Mr. Pot seems to hope that it may be totally escaped.[2]

In the mean time I have had a very fierce fit of the gout, which however has now remitted, and yesterday I put on my Shoes.

You know, I suppose, that I have[3] lost dear Mr[s]. Williams who had been my domestick companion for thirty years, and whose death following that of Levet,[4] has now made my house a solitude. She left her little substance to a Charity School.[5] She is, I hope, where there is neither want, nor darkness, nor sorrow.

You will be kind enough to make my compliments to Lady Rothes, and all the young ones. I am, Sir, Your most humble Servant,

SAM. JOHNSON

1. *Ante* To John Mudge, 9 Sept. 1783, n. 4.
2. *Ante* To Hester Thrale, 9 Oct. 1783.
3. MS: undeciphered deletion before "have"
4. *Ante* To Thomas Lawrence, 17 Jan. 1782.
5. *Ante* To Hester Thrale, 22 Sept. 1783 and n. 7.

John Taylor

MONDAY 20 OCTOBER 1783

MS: Hyde Collection.

ADDRESS: To the Reverend Dr. Taylor in Ashbourne, Derbyshire.

POSTMARK: 21 OC.

ENDORSEMENTS: 1783, 20 Octr. 1783.

Sir: London, Oct. 20, 1783

Your prohibition to write till the operation is performed is[1] likely, if I observed it, to interrupt our correspondence for a long time.

When Mr. Pot and Mr. Cruikshank examined the tumid testicle, they thought it a Sarcocele, or flesh swelling, I had flattered myself that it was only a hydrocele or Waterswelling. This could be determined with certainty only by puncture, which at my request was made by Mr. Pot, and which confirmed their opinion. They advised some palliative, and I went to a Friend in Wiltshire, from whom the bulk and pain of the encreasing tumour drove me home for help. Mr. Pot seemed to think that there was no help but from the knife, and only postponed the operation to his return from a journey of a week. In that week the puncture burst open, and by its discharge, abated the inflammation, relaxed the tension, and lessened the tumor by at least half. Mr. Pot at his return found so much amendment, that he has left the disease for a time to nature. Mr. Cruikshank would cut another orifice, but Mr. Pot is not yet willing. In the mean time I have no pain, and little inconvenience.

When all was at the worst I consulted Mudge of Plimouth,[2] a very skilful man, and Dr. Heberden[3] who both vehemently pressed the excision, which perhaps would at last be the safer way, but Mr. Cruikshank is afraid of it. We must at present sit still.

I have for some weeks past had a sharp fit of the gout, to which I am reconciled by Mr. Mudge, who think[s] it a security against the palsy;[4] and indeed I recollect none that ever had both. I have now nothing of the gout, but feet a little tender, and ankles somewhat weak. I am in my general health better than for some years past. I am, Sir, Your most humble servant,

SAM. JOHNSON

1. MS: "performed is" superimposed upon undeciphered erasure
2. *Ante* To John Mudge, 9 Sept. 1783; 23 Sept. 1783; 9 Oct. 1783.
3. *Ante* To Hester Thrale, 23 Sept. 1783.
4. *Ante* To Hester Thrale, 6 Oct. 1783.

As it is too early to send I will try to recollect what I can that can be suspected to have brought on this dreadful distress.

I have been accustomed to bleed frequently for an asthmatick complaint, but have forborn for some time by Dr Pepys's persuasion, who perceived my legs beginning to swell.

I sometimes alleviate a painful, or more properly an oppressive constriction of my chest, by opiates, and have lately taken opium frequently but the last, or two last times in smaller quantities. My largest dose is three grains, and last night I took but two.

You will suggest these things, and they are all that I can call to mind, to Dr Heberden.

June 17. 1783 I am &c Sam: Johnson

TO JOHN TAYLOR, 17 JUNE 1783

written within hours of Johnson's "paralytick stroke"

(Berg Collection, New York Public Library)

My dearest Miss Jenny

I am sorry that your pretty Letter has been so long without being answered; but when I am not pretty well, I do not always write plain enough for young Ladies. I am glad, my Dear, to see that You write so well, and hope that You mind your pen, your book, and your needle, for they are all necessary. Your books will give you knowledge, and make You respected, and your needle will find You useful employment when You do not care to read. When You are a little older, I hope You will be very diligent in learning arithmetick; and above all, that through your whole life

TO JANE LANGTON, 10 MAY 1784

(Hyde Collection)

35 4

To Mrs Piozzi.

78

Dear Madam

What you have done, however I may lament it, I have no pretence to resent, as it has not been injurious to me. I therefore breathe out one sigh more of tenderness perhaps useless, but at least sincere.

I wish that God may grant you every blessing, that you may be happy in this world for its short continuance, and eternally happy in a better State. and whatever I can contribute to your happiness, I am very ready to repay for that kindness which soothed twenty years of a life radically wretched.

Do not think slightly of the advice which

I

TO HESTER THRALE, 8 JULY 1784

(Hyde Collection)

Dear Sir

Why you should desire to hear your own reasons for your own action I cannot find.

I remember, and entreat you to remember that virtus est vitium fugere, the first approach to riches is security from poverty. The condition upon which you have my consent to settle in London, is that your expence never exceeds your annual income. Fixing this basis of security, you cannot be hurt, and you may be very much advanced. The loss of your Scottish business which is all that you can lose, is not to be reckoned as any equivalen-

TO JAMES BOSWELL, 11 JULY 1784
(National Library of Scotland)

Hester Maria Thrale

MONDAY 20 OCTOBER 1783

MS: The Earl of Shelburne.

ADDRESS: To Miss Thrale at Bath.

POSTMARK: 20 OC.

My dearest Love: London, Oct. 20, 1783

The letter which I received from my Mistress last monday was very kind, but so short, that I considered it only as a prelude to a longer, which I have expected from post to post, but having been so often disappointed, begin to fear that the toothach, which at that time contracted her letter, has been succeeded by some more formidable malady. Dear Madam write immediately and free me from suspense.

Young Mr. Shepherd's commendatory letter dated the 8th of October, was not delivered by him till the 15th.[1] He was therefore in no great haste to pay his visit. He came just at di[n]ner time, if I had had any diner time. His unseasonableness did not much affect me, and I entertained him for about an hour, as civilly as I could and invited him to tea another day. I have seen no[2] more of him, and do not wonder nor complain that he find stronger attractions in other places, but let him not tell his father,[3] at his return, that he was coldly received.

You may get a Narrative of the loss of the Grosvenor India Ship, which I would have you read.[4] You will take the more interest in it, because Sir Robert Chambers, whom I think you must remember, and whose [portrait] is in the Library,[5] sent

1. *Ante* To Hester Thrale, 9 Oct. 1783 and n. 9.

2. MS: "hi" del. before "no"

3. The Rev. Thomas Shephard the elder (1716–96), Rector of Woodhay and Vicar of Speen, Berkshire (*Alum. Oxon.* II.iv.1286; *GM* 1796, p. 881; *The Piozzi Letters*, ed. E. A. Bloom and L. D. Bloom, 1986, I.138 n. 27).

4. It is likely that SJ refers to Alexander Dalrymple's *An Account of the Loss of the Grosvenor, Indiaman*, 1783.

5. SJ refers to one of fourteen Reynolds portraits of the Streatham Park circle that were commissioned by Henry Thrale and hung in the new library; the por-

in that ship to England his young Son for education. He was one of those who staid with the captain, of whom no account has yet been received, and[6] who probably have all perished. Consider the distress of his parents, to whom it be now a comfort to be sure that he is dead.[7]

I go on as I did when I wrote last, in all parts out of pain, but in one, I think, not out of danger. I have no very heavy pressure to sustain, my chief complaint is of sleepless nights, and sleepless without any assignable cause.

I am however not neglected. Yesterday I gave tea to Mrs. Siddons,[8] and to day Mr. Selwin sent me two partridges.[9] Let me know immediately how is your Mamma. I am, my dearest, your most humble servant,

SAM. JOHNSON

---

trait of Chambers (now in a private collection) was painted in 1773 (C. R. Leslie and T. Taylor, *The Life and Times of Sir Joshua Reynolds*, 1865, II.48; Mary Hyde, "The Library Portraits at Streatham Park," *The New Rambler*, 1979, pp. 10–24). See frontispiece to *A Course of Lectures on the English Law . . . by Sir Robert Chambers*, ed. T. M. Curley, 1986.

6. MS: "a" superimposed upon "wh"

7. *Ante* To Robert Chambers, 4 Oct. 1783, n. 7.

8. *Post* To Hester Thrale, 27 Oct. 1783. Sarah Siddons's brother, John Philip Kemble (1757–1823), provided JB with a further account of the meeting (*Life* IV.242–43).

9. In all likelihood SJ refers to Charles Selwyn (1715–94), of Down Hall, Essex, a retired banker whom SJ had met through the Thrales (*Life* IV.488; *Thraliana* II.1165; *Boswell, Laird of Auchinleck*, ed. J. W. Reed and F. A. Pottle, 1977, p. 302).

Hester Thrale

TUESDAY 21 OCTOBER 1783

PRINTED SOURCE: Piozzi, *Letters* II.318–20.

Dear Madam, London, October 21, 1783

I have formerly heard, what you perhaps have heard too, that—

The wheel of life is daily turning round,
And nothing in this world of certainty is found.

When in your letter of the eleventh, you told me that my two letters had obliged, consoled, and delighted you, I was much elevated, and longed for a larger answer;[1] but when the answer of the nineteenth came, I found that the obliging, consolatory, and delightful paragraphs had made so little impression, that you want again to be told what those papers were written to tell you, and of what I can now tell you nothing new. I am as I was; with no pain and little inconvenience from the great complaint, and feeling nothing from the gout but a little tenderness and weakness.

Physiognomy, as it is a Greek word, ought to sound the G: but the French and Italians, I think, spell it without the G; and from them perhaps we learned to pronounce it. G, I think, is sounded in formal, and sunk in familiar language.

Mr. Pott was with me this morning, and still continues his disinclination to *fire and sword*.[2] The operation is therefore still suspended; not without hopes of relief from some easier and more natural way.

Mrs. Porter the tragedian, with whom —— ——[3] spent part of his[4] earlier life, was so much the favourite of her time, that she was welcomed on the stage when she trod it by the help of a stick. She taught her pupils no violent graces; for she was a woman of very gentle and ladylike manners, though without much extent of knowledge, or activity of understanding.

You are now retired, and have nothing to impede self-examination or self-improvement. Endeavour to reform that instability of attention which your last letter has happened to betray. Perhaps it is natural for those that have much within to think little on things without; but whoever lives heedlessly lives but in a mist, perpetually deceived by false appearances of the

1. *Ante* To Hester Thrale, 6 Oct. 1783; 9 Oct. 1783.

2. *Ante* To Hester Thrale, 9 Oct. 1783.

3. "Mrs. [Frances] Cotterell" (Piozzi II.319; Piozzi, *Letters*, 1788, annotated copy at Trinity College, Cambridge). *Ante* To Frances Cotterell, 19 July 1755, n. 3.

4. "her" (Piozzi II.319; Piozzi, *Letters*, 1788, annotated copy at Trinity College, Cambridge).

past, without any certain reliance on recollection. Perhaps this begins to be my state; but I have not done my part very sluggishly, if it now begins.

The hour of solitude is now come, and Williams is gone.[5] But I am not, I hope, improperly dejected. A little I read, and a little I think. I am, etc.

5. *Ante* To Susanna Thrale, 9 Sept. 1783.

William Bowles

THURSDAY 23 OCTOBER 1783

MS: Houghton Library.

ADDRESS: To William Bowles, Esq., at Heale near Salisbury [*added in an unidentified hand*] Missent to Shaston.

POSTMARKS: 23 OC, 27 OC.

Dear Sir: London, Oct. 23, 1783

As I have no reason to doubt of your friendship and tenderness, I think [you] entitled to an account of my state from time to time.

The Gout has treated me with more severity than any former time, it however never climbed higher than my ankles, in which it [has] now left a weakness, as well as tenderness in my feet, but when I do not walk or stand too long I have no longer any pain.

The puncture by which the tumour discharged itself is now so far healed as to emit nothing. The tumour is so far reduced as to have no pain, or deformity, and very little inconvenience. Nor do I perceive it yet to grow bigger, though of that I am very much afraid.

I had neither pain nor sickness to hinder the enjoyment of Mrs. Bowles's kind present and yours. I called in two friends and dined on it last Sunday. You will both think, I hope, so well of me, as to suppose me thankful.

I still keep the house, except that I have once walked a very little way, and have been twice taken out by my friends in their carriages. I am, Sir, Your most obliged, humble Servant,

SAM. JOHNSON

Frances Reynolds

THURSDAY 23 OCTOBER 1783

MS: Hyde Collection.

ADDRESS: To Mrs. Reynolds.

ENDORSEMENT: Dr. Johnson, Octr. 83.

Dear Madam: Oct. 23, 1783

Instead of having me at your table which cannot, I fear, quickly happen, come, if You can, to dine this day with me. It will give pleasure to a sick friend.

Let me know whether you can come. I am, Madam, Yours affectionately,

SAM. JOHNSON

Frances Reynolds

MONDAY 27 OCTOBER 1783

MS: Hyde Collection. Collated with copy in the hand of Frances Reynolds (Hyde Collection).

My dearest Dear: London, Oct. 27, 1783

I am able enough to write, for I have now neither sickness nor pain, only the Gout has left my ankles some what weak.

While the Weather favours You, and the air does you good, stay in the country, when you come home, I hope we shall often see one another, and enjoy that friendship to which no time is likely to put an end, on the part of, Madam, Your most humble servant,

SAM. JOHNSON

Hester Thrale

MONDAY 27 OCTOBER 1783

PRINTED SOURCE: Piozzi, *Letters* II.320–22.[1]

Madam, London, October 27, 1783

You may be very reasonably weary of sickness; it is neither pleasant to talk nor to hear of it. I hope soon to lose the disgusting topick; for I have now neither pain nor sickness. My ancles are weak, and my feet tender. I have not tried to walk much above a hundred yards, and was glad to come back upon wheels. The Doctor[2] and Mr. Metcalf have taken me out. I sleep uncertainly and unseasonably. This is the sum of my complaint. I have not been so well for two years past. The great malady is neither heard, seen, felt, nor—understood. But I am very solitary.

Semperque relinqui
Sola sibi, semper longam incomitata videtur
Ire viam.[3]

But I have begun to look among my books, and hope that I am all, whatever that was, which I have ever been.

Mrs. Siddons in her visit to me behaved with great modesty and propriety, and left nothing behind her to be censured or despised.[4] Neither praise nor money, the two powerful corrupters of mankind, seem to have depraved her. I shall be glad[5] to see her again. Her brother Kemble[6] calls on me, and

1. Printed text collated with excerpts in Sotheby's Catalogue (5–6 Dec. 1904, Lot No. 339, p. 34), Quaritch Catalogue (Nov. 1906, No. 253, p. 15), and Anderson Galleries Catalogue (1919, No. 1424, Lot No. 537, p. 56).

2. SJ refers to John Taylor.

3. *semperque relinqui / sola sibi, semper longam incomitata videtur / ire viam et Tyrios deserta quaerere terra:* "and ever she seems to be left lonely, ever wending, companionless, an endless way, and seeking her Tyrians in a land forlorn" (Virgil, *Aeneid* IV.466–68, trans. H. R. Fairclough, Loeb ed.).

4. *Ante* To Hester Maria Thrale, 20 Oct. 1783 and n. 8.

5. "pleased" (Sotheby's, Quaritch)

6. *Ante* To Hester Maria Thrale, 20 Oct. 1783, n. 8. Kemble made his London debut this season at Drury Lane (*The Biographical Dictionary of Actors, Actresses,*

pleases me very well. Mrs. Siddons and I talked of plays; and she told me her intention of exhibiting this winter the characters of Constance, Catherine, and Isabella in Shakespeare.[7]

I have this day a letter from Mr. Mudge; who, with all his earnestness for operation, thinks it better to wait the effects of time, and, as he says, to let well alone.[8] To this the patient naturally inclines, though I am afraid of having the knife yet to endure when I can bear it less. Cruickshank was even now in doubt of the event; but Pott, though never eager, had, or discovered, less fear.

If I was a little cross, would it not have made patient Grisel cross, to find that you had forgotten the letter that you was answering?[9] But what did I care, if I did not love you? You need not fear that another should get my[10] kindness from you; that kindness which you could not throw away if you tried, you surely cannot lose while you desire to keep it. I am, Madam, Your, etc.

I have a letter signed S. A. Thrale; I take S. A. to be Miss Sophy:[11] but who is bound to recollect initials? A name should be written, if not fully, yet so that it cannot be mistaken.

Dancers, Managers, and Other Stage Personnel in London, 1660–1800, ed. P. H. Highfill et al., 1982, VIII.335, 340).

7. Sarah Siddons played the part of Isabella (*Measure for Measure*) in Nov. 1783 and again in Feb. 1784, and the part of Constance (*King John*) in Dec. 1783. These performances marked her London debut in both parts (*Lond. Stage*, Part v, ii.655–56, 658, 664–66, 678). There is no evidence that during this season she played Queen Katherine (*Henry VIII*).

8. *Ante* To John Mudge, 9 Sept. 1783, n. 6.

9. *Ante* To Hester Thrale, 21 Oct. 1783.

10. "any" (Anderson Galleries)

11. SJ was mistaken: "S. A." stands for "Susanna Arabella."

Sarah Wesley[1]

TUESDAY 28 OCTOBER 1783

MS: Hyde Collection.

1. Sarah Wesley (1759–1828), only surviving daughter of Charles and Sarah Wesley.

To SARAH WESLEY, 28 *October* 1783

Madam: Oct. 28, 1783

I will have the first day that You mention, come, my Dear, on Saturday next, and, if You can, bring Your Aunt[2] with you, to, Your most humble servant,

SAM. JOHNSON

2. Martha Hall (1707–91), the sister of Charles and John Wesley and the widow of the Rev. Wesley Hall (1771–76), a dissenting preacher. According to John Telford, SJ "greatly admired Mrs. Hall . . . and wished her to reside under his roof, but she feared that this step would arouse the jealousy of Johnson's other lady friends" (Telford, *The Life of the Rev. Charles Wesley, M.A.*, 1900, p. 279).

John Perkins

LATE OCTOBER 1783[1]

MS: Hyde Collection.

Mr. Johnson return[s] his sincere thanks to Mr. Perkins.

There is in the papers a wild account of a robbery of Mr. Perkins's house, which Mr. Johnson hopes is either totally false, or of no great or affecting consequence.[2]

1. See below, n. 2.

2. "The house of Mrs. Thrale, in the Borough, was robbed on Monday night, of plate, and other valuables, to the amount of one thousand pound" (*Morning Herald and Daily Advertiser*, 24 Oct. 1783, p. 3).

Hester Thrale

SATURDAY 1 NOVEMBER 1783

MS: Hyde Collection.

ADDRESS: To Mrs. Thrale at Bath.

POSTMARK: 1 NO.

Madam: London, Nov. 1, 1783

You will naturally wish to know what was done by the Robbers at the Brewhouse.[1] They climbed by the help of the lamp iron

1. *Ante* To John Perkins, Late Oct. 1783.

to the covering of the door, and there opening the window, which was never fastened, entered and went down to the parlour, and took the plate off the sideboard, but being in haste and probably without light, they did not take it all. They then unlocked the street door, and locking it again, carried away the key. The whole loss, as Mr. Perkins told me, amounts to near fifty pounds.

Mr. Pott bad me this day take no more care about the tumour. The Gout too is almost well in spite of all the luxury to which my Friends have tempted me by a succession of Pheasants, Partridges, and other delicacies. But Nature has got the better. I hope to walk to Church to morrow.

An air ballon has been lately procured by our Virtuosi, but it performed very little to their[2] expectation.

The air with [which] these balls are filled is procured by dissol[ving] iron filings in the vitriolick (or I suppose sulphureous) acid but the Smoke of burnt straw may be used, though its levity is not so great.[3]

If a case could be found at once light and strong a man might mount with his ball, and go whither the winds would carry him. The case of the ball which came hither was of gold beaters Skin.[4] The cases which have hitherto been used are apparently defective, for the ball[s] come to the ground, which they could never do, unless there were some breach made.

How old is the boy that likes Rambler better than apples and pears?

I shall be glad of Miss Sophy's letter, and will soon write to S.A. who since she is not Sophy must be Susy.[5] Methinks it is long since I heard from Q[u]eeny. I am, Madam, Your most humble servant,

SAM. JOHNSON

2. MS: "their" altered from "the"

3. *Ante* To Hester Thrale, 9 Oct. 1783.

4. *goldbeater's skin*: "the intestinum rectum of an ox, which goldbeaters lay between the leaves of their metal while they beat it, whereby the membrane is reduced thin, and made fit to apply to cuts or small fresh wounds" (SJ's *Dictionary*).

5. *Ante* To Hester Thrale, 27 Oct. 1783 and n. 11.

Lucy Porter

MONDAY 10 NOVEMBER 1783

PRINTED SOURCE: JB's *Life*, ed. Malone, 1804, IV.259–60.
ADDRESS: To Mrs. Lucy Porter, in Lichfield.

Dear Madam, Bolt-court, Fleet-street, Nov. 10, 1783

The death of poor Mr. Porter, of which your maid has sent an account, must have very much surprised you.[1] The death of a friend is almost always unexpected: we do not love to think of it, and therefore are not prepared for its coming. He was, I think, a religious man, and therefore that his end was happy.

Death has likewise visited my mournful habitation. Last month died Mrs. Williams,[2] who had been to me for thirty years in the place of a sister: her knowledge was great, and her conversation pleasing. I now live in cheerless solitude.

My two last years have passed under the pressure of successive diseases. I have lately had the gout with some severity. But I wonderfully escaped the operation which I mentioned,[3] and am upon the whole restored to health beyond my own expectation.

As we daily see our friends die round us, we that are left must cling closer, and, if we can do nothing more, at least pray for one another; and remember, that as others die we must die too, and prepare ourselves diligently for the last great trial. I am, Madam, Yours affectionately,

SAM. JOHNSON

1. Joseph Porter died 19 Oct. 1783 at Leghorn (*Johns. Glean.* VII.96).
2. *Ante* To Hester Thrale, 20 Aug. 1783, n. 1.
3. *Ante* To John Mudge, 9 Sept. 1783, n. 6.

John Taylor

MONDAY 10 NOVEMBER 1783

PRINTED SOURCE: Maggs Catalogue 396, Autumn 1920, Lot No. 2294A, p. 125; address supplied by Sotheby's Catalogue, 4 Dec. 1916, Lot No. 150, p. 15.

ADDRESS: To the Reverend Dr. Taylor, in Ashbourne, Derbyshire.

London, 10th November 1783

What there was in my letter that you could think peevish or unkind, I cannot imagine. When I wrote it, I had nothing in my mind that could dispose me to ill humour. My letter contained as I remember only an account of the process of my distemper. . . .[1]

My health has been in general wonderfully restored, God grant that I may use it well.

I am now enough at ease to enquire after my friends, and wish to know whether you went to Bosworth, and how you bore the journey. . . . .

I now live in great and melancholy solitude. But what is best, we do not know.

1. *Ante* To John Taylor, 20 Oct. 1783.

Richard Jackson[1]

TUESDAY 11 NOVEMBER 1783

MS: Current location unknown. Transcribed from photostat in the Rylands Library.

1. Richard Jackson (?1721–87), of Weasenham, Norfolk, M.P. for Weymouth and Melcombe Regis (1762–68) and New Romney (1768–84). A Bencher of the Inner Temple (1770), Jackson also had held various governmental posts, most recently that of Lord of the Treasury during the Shelburne Administration (July 1782–Apr. 1783) (Namier and Brooke II.669). He was known as "Omniscient" Jackson, because of "his extraordinary stores of knowledge"; SJ, however, preferred the term "all-knowing," reserving "omniscient" for God (*Life* III.19 and n. 1).

Dear Sir: Boltcour[t] Fleetstreet, Nov. 11, 1783

The Readership of the Temple being vacant,[2] I take the liberty of entreating your Countenance and vote for Mr. Hoole a young Clergyman,[3] whom I have known for a great part of his life, and whom I can confidently offer to your notice, as a Man of uncommon parts, and blameless character. I am, Sir, Your most humble Servant,

SAM. JOHNSON

2. The post of Reader at the Temple Church, whose function it was to read the divine service twice a day, was filled alternately by the Inner and Middle Temples. The incumbent, William Jeffs, had died 4 Nov. Because it was the turn of the Inner Temple to appoint a Reader, SJ had solicited Jackson, as Bencher, on Hoole's behalf. SJ's efforts were unsuccessful: on 27 Jan. 1784 the post went to the Rev. Haddon Smith (Charles Lamb, *The Old Benchers of the Inner Temple*, ed. F. D. Mackinnon, 1927, p. 24; *Alum. Oxon.* II.ii.746).

3. The Rev. Samuel Hoole (*c.* 1758–1839), son of John Hoole, later (1803–39) Rector of Poplar, Middlesex (*Alum. Oxon.* II.ii.686).

Hester Thrale

THURSDAY 13 NOVEMBER 1783

MS: Hyde Collection.

ADDRESS: To Mrs. Thrale at Bath.

POSTMARK: 13 NO.

Dear Madam: London, Nov. 13, 1783

Since You have written to me with the attention and tenderness of ancient time, your letters give me a great part of the pleasure which a life of Solitude admits. You will never bestow any share[1] of your good will on one who deserves better. Those that have loved longest, love best. A sudden blaze of kindness, may by a single blast of coldness be extinguished, but that fondness which length of time has connected with[2] many circumstances and occasions, though it may for a while [be] suppressed by disgust or resentment with or without a

1. MS: "sh" altered from "pa" 2. MS: "with with"

cause, is hourly revived by accidental[3] recollection. To those that have lived long together every thing heard and every thing seen recals some pleasure communicated, or some benefit confered, some petty quarrel or some slight endearment. Esteem of great powers or amiable qualities newly discovered may embroider a day or a week, but a friendship of twenty years is interwoven with the texture of life. A friend may be often found and lost, but an *old Friend* never can be found, and Nature has provided that he cannot easily be lost.

I have not forgotten the Davenants, though they seem to have forgotten me. I began very early to tell them what they have commonly found to be true. I am sorry to hear of their building. I always have warned those whom I loved, against that mode of ostentatious waste.

You seem to mention Lord Kilmurrey as a[4] stranger. We were at his house in Cheshire,[5] and he one day dined with Sir Lynch.[6] What he tells of the Epigram is not true, but perhaps he do[e]s not know it to be false.[7] Do not You remember how he rejoiced in having *no* park;[8] He could not disoblige his neighbours by sending them *no* venison.

The frequency of death to those who look upon it in the leisure of Arcadia is very dreadful.[9] We all know what it

3. MS: "dental" repeated as catchword

4. MS: "I"

5. John Needham (1711–91), tenth Viscount Kilmorey, of Shavington Hall, Shropshire (*Life* v.433 and n. 2, 584). SJ and the Thrales had visited him on their trip to Wales in 1774 (*Life* v.433).

6. SJ refers to Sir Lynch Cotton.

7. "I will endeavour to divert Care and Thought by writing out some stuff which Lord Killmorey says is written on the Window of a House in the common road to Naples—I forget where: 'In questa Casa trovarete / Tout ce que vous pouvez souhaiter; / Bonum Vinum, Lectos, Carnes, / Coaches, Chaises, Horses, Harness'" (*Thraliana* I.574–75, 23 Oct. 1783).

8. After visiting Shavington Hall, 23 July 1774, SJ recorded in his diary, "Lord K. showd the place with too much exultation. He has no park, and little water" (*Life* v.433).

9. SJ appears to have in mind a phrase attributed to Pope Clement IX, *Et in Arcadia ego*: "Even in Arcadia, there am I [Death]." The phrase had been explained to SJ by Joshua Reynolds, who incorporated it (as part of a visual quotation from Guercino's picture titled "Et in Arcadia ego") in his double portrait of Harriet Bouverie and Frances Anne Crewe (C. R. Leslie and T. Taylor, *The Life and Times of Sir Joshua Reynolds*, 1865, I.325; Erwin Panofsky, "Et in Arcadia Ego," in

should teach us, let us all be diligent to learn. Lucy Porter has lost her Brother.[10] But whom I have lost—let me not now remember. Let not your loss be added to the mournful catalogue. Write soon again to, Madam, Your most humble servant,

SAM. JOHNSON

Philosophy and History, ed. Raymond Klibansky and H. J. Paton, 1936, pp. 223–24, 233 n. 1, 254). Hester Thrale knew of the phrase and of Reynolds's portrait (*Thraliana* I.41–42).

10. *Ante* To Lucy Porter, 10 Nov. 1783 and n. 1.

John Hoole

c. NOVEMBER 1783[1]

MS: Hyde Collection.

Mr. Johnson has heard from Mr. Barrington,[2] and has seen Mr. Jackson, and begs to see Mr. Hoole as soon as he can.

1. Dated in relation to To Richard Jackson, 11 Nov. 1783.

2. The Hon. Daines Barrington (1727–1800), F.S.A., lawyer, antiquarian, and naturalist, the son of John Shute Barrington (1678–1734), first Viscount Barrington. The friendship between SJ and Barrington began when SJ sought him out after the publication of Barrington's *Observations on the Statutes* (1766); in Dec. 1783 he became a member of SJ's Essex Head Club (*Life* III.314, IV.254). Because Barrington was also a Bencher of the Inner Temple (1777), he could have been of use in supporting Samuel Hoole's appointment (*Calendar of the Inner Temple Records*, ed. R. A. Roberts, 1936, V.333; *Ante* To Richard Jackson, 11 Nov. 1783 and n. 2).

Susanna Thrale

TUESDAY 18 NOVEMBER 1783

MS: The Earl of Shelburne.

ADDRESS: To Miss S. A. Thrale at Bath.

POSTMARK: 18 NO.

Dear Miss: Novr. 18, 1783

Here is a whole week and nothing heard from your house. Baretti said what a wicked house it would be, and a wicked house it is. Of you however I have no complaint to make, for I owe you a letter. Still I live here by my own self, and have had of late very bad nights, but then I have had a pig to dinner which Mr. Perkins gave me. Thus life is checquered.[1]

I cannot tell you much news because I see nobody that you know. Do you read the Tatlers? They are part of the books which every body should read, because they are the Sources of conversation,[2] therefore make them part of your library. Bickerstaff in the Tatler gives as a specimen of familiar letters, an account of his Cat.[3] I could tell you as good things of Lily the white kitling, who is now at full growth, and very well behaved, but I do not see why we should descend below human Beings, and of one human Being I can tell something that you will like to hear.

A Friend whose name I will tell when your Mamma has tried to guess it, sent to My Physician to enquire whether this long train of ilness had brought me into any difficulties for want of money, with an invitation to send to him for what occasion required. I shall write this night to thank him, having no need to borrow.[4]

I have seen Mr. Seward since his return only once, he gave no florid account of my Mistress's health.[5] Tell her that I

1. *Ante* To Hester Thrale, 20 July 1771, n. 7.

2. "It is said by Addison, in a subsequent work [*The Freeholder*, No. 45] that they [*The Tatler* and *The Spectator*] had a perceptible influence upon the conversation of that time . . . an effect which they can never wholly lose, while they continue to be among the first books by which both sexes are initiated in the elegances of knowledge" (*Lives of the Poets* II.94–95).

3. "For my own Part, I am excluded all Conversation with Animals that delight only in a Country Life, and am therefore forced to entertain my self as well as I can with my little Dog and Cat" (*The Tatler*, ed. D. F. Bond, 1987, II.177, No. 112).

4. SJ refers to William Gerard Hamilton, who had applied to Richard Brocklesby (*Post* To William Gerard Hamilton, 19 Nov. 1783).

5. On 23 Oct. Hester Thrale recorded, "[William] Seward is come to Bath; by compassionate Attention to my Illness, and serious anxiety for my Recovery; by

hearken every day after a letter from her, and do not be long before you write yourself to, My dear, Your most humble servant,

SAM. JOHNSON

---

repeated Offers of Service proceeding from cordial Friendship, he has at length persuaded me to trust him with the Secret of my Love for Piozzi" (*Thraliana* I.574).

Frances Burney

WEDNESDAY 19 NOVEMBER 1783

MS: Houghton Library.
ADDRESS: To Miss Burney.

Madam: Bolt court, Nov. 19, 1783

You have been at home a long time and I have never seen you nor heard from You.[1] Have we quarreled?

I have sent a book which I have found lately, and imagine to be Dr. Burney's.[2] Miss Charlotte[3] will please to examine.

Pray write me a direction to Mrs. Chapone,[4] and pray let me sometime have the honour of telling You, how much I am, Madam, Your most humble servant,

SAM. JOHNSON

1. Frances Burney blamed her absence on "bad weather alone" and invited herself for tea that afternoon (*Diary and Letters of Madame D'Arblay*, ed. Austin Dobson, 1904, II.228). On the bottom margin of SJ's letter she noted, "F. B. flew to him instantly and most gratefully."

2. Frances Burney describes the book as "a volume of the *Philosophical Transactions*" (Dobson, *D'Arblay* II.227).

3. Charlotte Ann Burney (1761–1838), Charles Burney's youngest daughter by his first marriage (*The Early Journals and Letters of Fanny Burney*, ed. L. E. Troide, 1988, I.xliv).

4. Frances Burney replied, "Mrs. Chapone lives at either No. 7 or 8 in Dean Street, Soho" (Dobson, *D'Arblay* II.228). *Post* To Hester Chapone, 20 Nov. 1783.

William Gerard Hamilton

WEDNESDAY 19 NOVEMBER 1783

MS: Hyde Collection.

HEADING in JB's hand: To The Right Honourable William Gerrard Hamilton.

Dear Sir, Boltcourt, Fleetstreet, Nov. 19, 1783[1]

Your kind enquiries after my affairs, and your generous offers have been communicated to me by Dr. Brockelsby.[2] I return thanks with great sincerity, having lived long enough to know what gratitude is due to such Friendship; and entreat that my refusal may not be imputed to sullenness or pride. I am indeed in no want. Sickness is by the generosity of my Phisicians, of little expence to me. But if any unexpected exigence should press me, You shall see, dear Sir, how cheerfully I can be obliged to so much liberality. I am, Sir, your most obedient and most humble servant,

SAM. JOHNSON

1. MS: "Boltcourt, Fleetstreet, Nov. 1783" written above complete dateline
2. *Ante* To Susanna Thrale, 18 Nov. 1783.

John Taylor

WEDNESDAY 19 NOVEMBER 1783

MS: Pierpont Morgan Library.

ADDRESS: To the Reverend Dr. Taylor in Ashbourne, Derbyshire.

POSTMARKS: 19 NO, 20 NO.

ENDORSEMENTS: 1783, 9 Novr. 83.

Dear Sir: London, Nov. 19, 1783

You desire me to write often, and I write the same day, and should be sorry to miss any thing that might give you ease or pleasure.

From the fatigue of your journey no harm, I hope, will

ensue.[1] Exercise short of great fatigue, must be your great medicine, but painful weariness I would wish You to avoid. You will do well, if You have recourse again to Milk, which once restored you beyond expectation,[2] and will now perhaps help you again.

It does not appear from your Doctors prescription that he sees to the bottom of your distemper. What he gives You strikes at no cause, and is only intended for an occasional exciter of the stomach.

Exercise yourself every morning, and when you can catch a momentary appetite, have always something ready. Toast and hot wine will be good, or a jelly, or potted meat, or any thing that can be eaten without trouble, and dissolves of itself by warmth and moisture. Let nothing fret you; Care is to all a slow, and may now be to you a quick poison. No worldly thing but your health is now worth your thought, if any thing troublesome[3] occurs, drive it away without a parley. If I was[4] with you, perhaps I might help to keep you easy, but we are at a great distance.

I do not think that you have so much to hope for from physick as from regimen. Keep a constant attention to petty conveniences. Suffer neither heat nor cold in a disagreeable degree. Beware of costiveness. Take the air every morning, and very often let me know how You do, and what You eat or drink and how You rest.

My nights are restless, but my sarcocele gives me no trouble,[5] and the gout is gone, and my respiration when I am up is not uneasy.

Let us pray for one another. I am, Dear Sir, Yours affectionately,

SAM. JOHNSON

1. *Ante* To John Taylor, 10 Nov. 1783.
2. *Ante* To Hester Thrale, 10 Nov. 1781.
3. MS: "troubbesome"
4. MS: "wish" del. before "was"
5. *Ante* To John Mudge, 9 Sept. 1783 and nn. 4, 6.

Hester Chapone

THURSDAY 20 NOVEMBER 1783

MS: Castle Howard.

Madam: Bolt Court, Fleetstreet, Nov. 20, 1783

Though my paper is thus tardy, my compliance was quicker. Having some way put your letter out of sight, I was forced to ask Miss Burney for your direction.[1] But she knows no more, and You may with great confidence assure Lord Carlisle, that I have never once shown or mentioned his work,[2] which I return because I did not understand that I have a right to keep it. When it is more freely communicated, I hope not to be forgotten. I am, Madam, Your most obedient and most humble servant,

SAM. JOHNSON

1. *Ante* To Frances Burney, 19 Nov. 1783.
2. *Ante* To Hester Chapone, 9 Feb. 1782 and n. 1.

Hester Thrale

THURSDAY 20 NOVEMBER 1783

PRINTED SOURCE: Piozzi, *Letters* II.329–30.

Dear Madam, London, Nov. 20, 1783

I began to grieve and wonder that I had no letter, but not being much accustomed to fetch in evil by circumspection or anticipation, did not suspect that the omission had so dreadful a cause as the sickness of one of my dears. As her physician thought so well of her when you wrote, I hope she is now out of danger. You do not tell me her disease; and perhaps have not been able yourself fully to understand it.[1] I hope it is not of the cephalick race.

1. Sophia Thrale had suffered "sudden, unaccountable, unprovoked" attacks, apoplectic in nature (*Thraliana* 1.580). The doctors diagnosed her condition as "Attonitus"—a loss of muscle tone. "Sophy's fits, followed by loss of consciousness,

That frigid stillness with which my pretty Sophy melts away, exhibits a temper very incommodious in sickness, and by no means amiable in the tenour of life. Incommunicative taciturnity neither imparts nor invites friendship, but reposes on a stubborn sufficiency self-centered, and neglects the interchange of that social officiousness by which we are habitually endeared to one another. They that mean to make no use of friends, will be at little trouble to gain them; and to be without friendship, is to be without one of the first comforts of our present state. To have no assistance from other minds, in resolving doubts, in appeasing scruples, in balancing deliberations, is a very wretched destitution. If therefore my loves have this silence by temper, do not let them have it by principle; show them that it is a perverse and inordinate disposition, which must be counteracted and reformed. Have I said enough?

Poor Dr. Taylor represents himself as ill; and I am afraid is worse than in the summer.[2] My nights are very bad; but of the sarcocele I have now little but the memory.[3] I am, Madam, Your, etc.

---

suggest a cerebral irritation, a virus brain fever or a bacterial abscess of the middle ear" (Hyde, 1977, p. 239). By the end of the month she was on the slow road to recovery (*Thraliana* 1.581; *Post* To Hester Thrale, 29 Nov. 1783).

2. *Ante* To John Taylor, 19 Nov. 1783.

3. *Ante* To John Mudge, 9 Sept. 1783 and nn. 4, 6.

John Hawkins

SATURDAY 22 NOVEMBER 1783

PRINTED SOURCE: Hawkins, p. 562.

Dear Sir, Bolt court, Nov. 22, 1783

As Mr. Ryland was talking with me of old friends and past times, we warmed ourselves into a wish, that all who remained of the club should meet and dine at the house which once was

Horseman's, in Ivy lane.[1] I have undertaken to solicit you, and therefore desire you to tell on what day next week you can conveniently meet your old friends.[2] I am, Sir, Your most humble servant,

SAM. JOHNSON

1. In 1749 SJ and nine others—including Hawkins, John Ryland, and John Hawkesworth—began meeting every Tuesday evening for supper and conversation at the King's Head, "Horseman's well-known beefsteak house in Ivy Lane, between Paternoster Row and Newgate Street near St. Paul's" (Clifford, 1979, pp. 29, 32). The Ivy Lane Club, as it came to be known, gradually dissolved in the middle 1750s (Clifford, 1979, p. 163). In 1783 the remaining members, apart from SJ and Hawkins, were Ryland and John Payne (d. 1787), bookseller and banker (Hawkins, p. 563).

2. *Post* To John Hawkins, 3 Dec. 1783.

John Taylor

SATURDAY 22 NOVEMBER 1783

MS: Berg Collection, New York Public Library.

ADDRESS: To the Reverend Dr. Taylor in Ashbourne, Derbyshire.

POSTMARK: 22 NO.

ENDORSEMENTS: 1783, 22 Novr. 82, good.

Dear Sir: London, Nov. 22, 1783

You desired me to write often, and I now write though I have nothing new to tell You, for I know that in the tediousness of ill health a letter always give[s] some diversion to the mind, and I am afraid that You live too much in solitude.

I feel the weight of solitude very pressing, after a night of broken and uncomfortable slumber I rise to a solitary breakfast, and sit down in the evening with no companion. Sometimes however I try to read, and hope to read more and more.

You must likewise write to me and tell me how you live, and with what diet. Your Milk kept You so well that I know not why You forsook it,[1] and think it very reasonable to try it again.[2] Do not omit air and gentle exercise.

1. MS: "i" superimposed upon "a"

2. *Ante* To Hester Thrale, 10 Nov. 1781.

The Ministry talk of laying violent hands on the East India company, even to the abolition or at least suspension of their charter. I believe corruption and oppression are in India at an enormous height, but it has never appeared that they were promoted by the Directors, who, I believe see themselves defrauded, while the country is plundred, but the distance puts their officers out of reach, and I doubt whether the Government in its present state of diminished credit, will do more than give another evidence of its own imbecillity.[3]

You and I however have more urgent cares, than for the East India Company. We are old and unhealthy. Let us do what we can to comfort one another. I am, Dear Sir, etc.

SAM. JOHNSON

3. By 1783 the need for reform of the East India Company had become a major political issue. The Company was in serious administrative and financial difficulties; moreover, it was felt that the interests of the native Indian population had been unjustly sacrificed to commercial gain. Charles James Fox's East India Bill, introduced in November, proposed the transfer of power from the Company's directors to a board of seven commissioners, to be named initially by Parliament and later by the King. Nine assistant commissioners, chosen from shareholders holding £2,000 of East Indian stock, would manage the Company's commercial interests. Subsequent assistant commissioners would be elected by the shareholders (J. S. Watson, *The Reign of George III*, 1960, pp. 261, 263). Although Fox's Bill passed the House of Commons, it was voted down in the Lords, a move that paved the way for the dissolution on 18 Dec. of the Fox-North Coalition (Watson, *George III*, pp. 266–67).

Hester Thrale

MONDAY 24 NOVEMBER 1783

MS: Hyde Collection.

ADDRESS: To Mrs. Thrale at Bath.

POSTMARK: 24 NO.

Dear Madam: London, Nov. 24, 1783

The Post came in late to day, and I had lost hopes. If the Distress of my dear little Girl keep me anxious,[1] I have much consolation from the maternal and domestick character of your dear letters.

I do not much fear her pretty life, because scarcely any body dies of her disorder, but it is an unpromising entry upon a new period of life, and there is, I suspect, danger lest she should have to struggle for some years with a tender, irritable, and as it is not very properly called a nervous constitution. But we will hope better, and please ourselves with thinking that nature, or physick, will gain a complete victory, that dear Sophy will quite recover, and that She and her Sisters will love one another one degree more for having felt and excited pity, for having wanted and given help.

I received yesterday from your Physicians a note from which I received no information, they put their heads together to tell me nothing.[2] Be pleased to write punctually yourself, and leave them to their trade. Let me have something every post till my dear Sophy is better.

My nights are often very troublesome, so that I try to sleep in the day. The old convulsions of the chest have a mind to fasten their fangs again upon me. I am afraid that winter will pinch me. But I will struggle[3] with it, and hope to hold out yet against heat and cold. I am, Madam, Your most humble servant,

SAM. JOHNSON

1. *Ante* To Hester Thrale, 20 Nov. 1783 and n. 1.

2. When Sophia was taken ill, Hester Thrale called in Francis Woodward and Matthew Dobson (*c.* 1732–84), M.D. (*Thraliana* 1.580; *The Piozzi Letters*, ed. E. A. Bloom and L. D. Bloom, 1989, 1.61 n. 5).

3. MS: "gle" repeated as catchword

Frances Reynolds

THURSDAY 27 NOVEMBER 1783

MS: Hyde Collection.

ADDRESS: To Mrs. Reynolds.

ENDORSEMENT: Dr. Johnson, Nov. 27th 83.

Dear Madam: Bolt court, Nov. 27, 1783

I beg that you will let me know by this Messenger, whether You will do me the honour of dining with me, and if You will, whether we shall eat our dinner by our own selves, or call Mrs. Desmoulins. I am, Dearest Dear, Your most humble servant,

SAM. JOHNSON

Hester Thrale

THURSDAY 27 NOVEMBER 1783

MS: Hyde Collection.

ADDRESS: To Mrs. Thrale at Bath.

POSTMARK: 27 NO.

Dear Madam: London, Nov. 27, 1783

I had to day another trifling letter from the Physicians.[1] Do not let them fill your mind with terrours which perhaps they have not in their own, neither suffer yourself to sit forming comparisons between Sophy and her dear Father, between whom there can be no other resemblance than that of sickness to sickness.[2] Hystericks and apoplexies have no relation. Hystericks commonly cease at[3] the time, when apoplexies attack, and very rarely can be said to shorten life. They are the bug bears of disease of great terrour but little danger.

Mrs. Byron has been with me to day to enquire after Sophy, I sent her away free from the anxiety which she brought with her.

Do however what the Doctors order, they know well enough what is to be done. My pretty Sophy will be well, and Bath will ring with the great cure. I am, Dear Madam, Your most humble servant,

SAM. JOHNSON

1. *Ante* To Hester Thrale, 24 Nov. 1783 and n. 2.

2. Hester Thrale had described Sophia's fits as "Apoplectic, lethargic like her Father" (*Thraliana* I.580). *Ante* To Hester Thrale, 12 June 1779 and nn. 1, 2.

3. MS: "at" written above "in" del.

Hester Chapone

FRIDAY 28 NOVEMBER 1783[1]

MS: Castle Howard.

Madam: Nov. 1783

By sending the Tragedy to me a second time I think that a very honourable distinction has been shown me, and I did not delay the perusal, of which I am now to tell the effect.[2]

The construction of the play is not completely regular, the stage is too often vacant, and the scene[s] are not sufficiently connected. This however would be called by Dryden only a mechanical defect,[3] which takes away little from the power of the poem, and which is seen rather than felt.

A rigid examiner of the diction might perhaps wish some words changed, and some lines more vigorously terminated.[4] But from such petty imperfections what writer was ever free?

The general form and force of the dialogue is of more importance. It seems to want that quickness of reciprocation which characterises the English drama, and is not always sufficiently fervid or animated.

Of the sentiments I remember not one that I wished omitted. In the imagery I cannot forbear to distinguish the comparison of joy succeeding grief, to light rushing on the eye accustomed to darkness.[5] It seems to have all that can be desired to make it please. It is new, just, and delightful.

1. JB (*Life* IV.248) dated this letter 28 Nov. after receiving a letter from Hester Chapone, 27 Feb. 1791, in which she informed him that Lord Carlisle had responded to SJ's critique on 29 Nov. (Waingrow, p. 388 and n. 3).

2. *Ante* To Hester Chapone, 9 Feb. 1782 and n. 1; 20 Nov. 1783.

3. "I must farther declare freely that I have not exactly kept to the three mechanic rules of unity" (Dryden, Preface to *Don Sebastian*, in *"Of Dramatic Poesy" and Other Critical Essays*, ed. George Watson, 1962, II.49).

4. MS: "nated" repeated as catchword

5. "O Gods! / I could have borne my woes; that stranger Joy / Wounds while it smiles. The long-imprison'd wretch / Emerging from the night of his damp cell, / Shrinks from the sun's bright beams, and that which flings / Gladness o'er all, to him is agony" (*The Father's Revenge* III.iv, in *The Tragedies and Poems of Frederick Earl of Carlisle*, 1801, p. 66).

With the characters either as conceived or preserved, I have no fault to find; but was much inclined to congratulate a Writer who in defiance of prejudice and Fashion, made the Archbishop a good man, and scorned all thoughtless applause which a vicious Churchman would have brought him.[6]

The catastrophe is affecting. The Father and Daughter both culpable, both wretched, and both penitent, divide between them our pity and our sorrow.[7]

Thus, Madam, I have performed what I did not willingly undertake, and could not decently refuse. The noble Writer will be pleased to remember, that sincere criticism ought to raise no resentment, because judgement is not under the control of will, but involuntary criticism as it has still less of choice ought [to] be more remote from possibility of offence. I am, Madam, Your most humble Servant,

SAM. JOHNSON

6. SJ refers to the Archbishop of Salerno, who tries to restrain the tyrannical designs of his brother Tancred, ruler of Sicily.

7. The heroine Sigismonda disobeys her father, Tancred, by marrying Guiscard. Tancred orders Guiscard killed, and then presents his heart in a vase to Sigismonda, who dies of grief. At the end of the play Tancred falls, stricken with remorse, on his daughter's body.

Lucy Porter

SATURDAY 29 NOVEMBER 1783

MS: Hyde Collection.

ADDRESS: To Mrs. Lucy Porter in Lichfield.

POSTMARK: 29 NO.

Dear Madam: London, Nov. 29, 1783

You may perhaps think me negligent that I have not written to You again upon the loss of your Brother,[1] but condolences and consolations are such common and such useless things, that the omission of them is no great crime, and my own dis-

1. *Ante* To Lucy Porter, 10 Nov. 1783 and n. 1.

eases occupy my mind and engage my care. My nights are miserably restless, and my days therefore are heavy. I try however, to hold up my head as high as I can.

I am sorry that your hearing is impaired, perhaps the spring and the[2] summer may in some degree restore it,[3] but if not, we must submit to the inconveniences of[4] time, as to the other dispensations of eternal Goodness. Pray for me, and write to me, or let Mr. Pearson write for You. I am, my dear, Your most humble Servant,

SAM. JOHNSON

2. MS: "the the"

3. MS: "it" repeated as catchword

4. MS: "of of"

John Taylor

SATURDAY 29 NOVEMBER 1783

PRINTED SOURCE: Hill II.362.

ADDRESS: To the Reverend Dr. Taylor in Ashbourne, Derbyshire.

Dear Sir, London, Nov. 29, 1783

Your Doctor's fixed air recommends him but little to my esteem;[1] I like Doxy's prescription better, and your own regimen better than either. By persevering in the use of milk, I doubt not but you will gain health enough to keep your residence,[2] and that we can consult at leisure what may be best for both. This is but at two months distance. If your health or safety could be much promoted by any attention of mine, I would come down, but my own sickliness makes me unwilling to be far from my Physicians, and unless I were sure of some considerable good, such a journey is not to be undertaken. If I come to you, I must go to Lichfield.

1. "Fixed air" or carbon dioxide was commonly used to treat "many diseases in which a tendency to putridity is suspected" (William Lewis, *Materia Medica*, 3d ed., 1784, p. 21).

2. *Ante* To John Taylor, 23 Mar. 1775, n. 1.

While milk agrees with you, do not be persuaded to forsake it. Go to bed, and rise, as Nature dictates, not by rule but according to convenience. Make your mind easy, and trust God.

My time passes uncomfortably, my nights have been of late spasmodick without opium and sleepless with it. I hope that when we meet we shall both be better. I am, Sir, Your most humble servant,

SAM. JOHNSON

Hester Thrale

SATURDAY 29 NOVEMBER 1783

MS: Hyde Collection.

Dear Madam: London, Nov. 29, 1783

The life of my dear, sweet, pretty, lovely, delicious Miss Sophy is safe, let us return thanks to the great Giver of existence, and pray that her continuance amongst us may be a blessing to herself and to those that love her.[1] Multos et felices,[2] my dear Girl.

Now she is recovered, she must write me a little history of her sufferings. And impart her schemes of study and improvement. Life to be worthy of a rational Being must be always in progression; we must always purpose to do more or better than in time past. The Mind is enlarged and elevated by mere purposes, though they end as they begin by airy contemplation. We compare and judge though we do not practice.

She will go back to her arithmetick again,[3] a science which[4] will always delight her more, as by advancing further she discovers more of its use, and a science suited to Sophy's ease of mind, for You told in the last winter that she loved metaphysicks more than Romances. Her choice is certainly as laudable

1. *Ante* To Hester Thrale, 20 Nov. 1783 and n. 1.

2. *Ante* To Hester Thrale, 28 Oct. 1779 and n. 4.

3. *Ante* To Sophia Thrale, 24 July 1783.

4. MS: "which which"

as it is uncommon, but I would have her like what is good in Both.

God bless You and your Children, so says, Dear Madam, Your old friend,

SAM. JOHNSON

Hester Thrale

MONDAY 1 DECEMBER 1783

MS: Rylands Library.

ADDRESS: To Mrs. Thrale at Bath.

POSTMARK: 1 DE.

Dear Madam: Dec. 1, 1783

If you can be short, I can be as short as you, but though I had less inclination to write I would not forbear an immediate answer to your letter which I have just received, because I think you should lose no time before you go into the warm bath, which in my opinion, promises more help for the whole complication of your disorders, than any thing else.[1] It is at least safe, it can do no sudden mischief, and if any thing[2] forbids its use, you have it wholly in your power. Stay in the bath, each time, till you find some little relaxation, and go in twice a day. I think you will in a week have reason to praise your Physicians.[3]

Please to tell all my young Friends, that I love them, and wish them well. I am, Madam, Your most humble Servant,

SAM. JOHNSON

1. Hester Thrale, exhausted from nursing Sophia (*Ante* To Hester Thrale, 20 Nov. 1783 and n. 1) and worn down by her family's steadfast opposition to Gabriel Piozzi, had suffered "a complete nervous breakdown" (Hyde, 1977, p. 239).

2. MS: "things"

3. *Ante* To Hester Thrale, 24 Nov. 1783, n. 2.

William Cruikshank

WEDNESDAY 3 DECEMBER 1783

MS: Hyde Collection.

ADDRESS: To Mr. Cruikshank.

Dec. 3

Dr. Johnson earnestly desires to see Mr. Cruikshanks as soon as is possible.

John Hawkins

WEDNESDAY 3 DECEMBER 1783

PRINTED SOURCE: Hawkins, p. 563.

Dear Sir, Dec. 3

In perambulating Ivy lane, Mr. Ryland found neither our landlord Horseman, nor his successor. The old house is shut up, and he liked not the appearance of any near it: he, therefore, bespoke our dinner at the Queen's Arms, in St. Paul's church yard, where, at half an hour after three, your company will be desired to-day, by those who remain of our former society.[1] Your humble servant,

SAM. JOHNSON

1. *Ante* To John Hawkins, 22 Nov. 1783 and n. 1.

Joshua Reynolds

THURSDAY 4 DECEMBER 1783

MS: Hyde Collection.

ADDRESS: To Sir Joshua Reynolds.

ENDORSEMENT: D. Johnson.

Dear Sir: Dec. 4, 1783

It is inconvenient to me to come out, I should else have waited on You with an account of [a] little evening club which we [are] establishing in Essex Street in the Strand, and of which you may be sure that You are desired to be one. It will be held at the Essex head now kept by an old Servant of Thrale's.[1] The Company is numerous, and as You will be [able to] see by the list miscellaneous.[2] The terms are lax, and the expences light. Mr. Barry was adopted by Dr. Brocklesby who joined with [me] in forming the plan. We meet thrice a week,[3] and he [who] misses, forfeits two pence.

If You are willing to become a Member, draw a line under your name.[4] Return the list. We meet for the first time on Monday at eight. I am, Sir, Your most humble servant,

SAM. JOHNSON

1. SJ refers to Samuel Greaves, former footman of Henry Thrale (Madame D'Arblay, *Memoirs of Dr. Burney*, 1832, II.261).

2. The membership of the Essex Head Club included JB, Richard Clark, Richard Paul Jodrell, Arthur Murphy, John Nichols, John Paradise, and William Windham (*Life* IV.254 and n. 2; *Lit. Anec.* II.553).

3. The Club met on Mondays, Thursdays, and Saturdays (William Cooke, *The Life of Samuel Johnson*, 1785, p. 70).

4. Reynolds chose not to join; one plausible explanation is the hostile relationship between him and James Barry (*Life* IV.436–37; M. R. Brownell, *Samuel Johnson's Attitude to the Arts*, 1989, pp. 69–70).

John Perkins

FRIDAY 5 DECEMBER 1783

MS: Hyde Collection.

ADDRESS: To Mr. Perkins.

Friday, Decem. 5, —83

Mr. Johnson's compliments to Mr. and Mrs. Perkins.

If Mr. Perkins is to be at home to day Mr. Johnson will wait on him about six to tea, and to do a little business.

Frances Reynolds

MONDAY 8 DECEMBER 1783

MS: Yale Center for British Art.

ADDRESS: To Mrs. Reynolds.

ENDORSEMENT: Dr. Johnson, Decr. 8, 83.

Dear Madam: Dec. 8, —83

Be so kind as to dine to day with your humble servant,

SAM. JOHNSON

Richard Clark[1]

SATURDAY 13 DECEMBER 1783

MS: Houghton Library.

ENDORSEMENT: 13 Decr. 1783, Dr. Johnson.

Sir: Dec. 13, 1783

The Club to which [you] seemed willing to give your name, met last Monday, and Wednesday, and will meet again to day at the Essex Head, in Essex Street in the Strand,[2] and your company will be desired as soon as You can conveniently give it us. I am, Sir, Your most humble servant,

SAM. JOHNSON

1. The endorsement in Clark's hand, his membership in the Essex Head Club, and the fact that this letter was preserved among his papers—all establish the identity of the addressee beyond reasonable doubt.

2. *Ante* To Joshua Reynolds, 4 Dec. 1783; *Post* To Richard Clark, 27 Jan. 1784.

Hester Thrale

SATURDAY 13 DECEMBER 1783

MS: Hyde Collection.

ADDRESS: To Mrs. Thrale at Bath.

POSTMARK: 13 DE.

To HESTER THRALE, 13 *December* 1783

Dear Madam: London, Dec. 13, 1783

I think it long since I wrote, and sometimes venture to hope that You think it long too. The Intermission has been filled with spasms, opiates, sleepless nights, and heavy days. These vellications[1] of my breast shorten my breath, whether they will much shorten my life I know not; but I have been for some time past very comfortless. My friends however continue kind, and much notice is taken of me.

I had two pretty letters from Susy and Sophy to which I will send answers, for they are two dear girls. You must all guess again at my Friend.[2]

I dined about a fortnight ago with three[3] old Friends,[4] we[5] had not met together for thirty years, and one of us thought the other grown very old. In the thirty years two of our set have died.[6] Our meeting may be supposed to be somewhat tender.[7] I boasted that I had passed the day with three friends, and that no mention had been made among[8] us of the air ballon, which has taken full possession, with a very good claim of every philosophical mind and mouth.[9] Do you not wish for the flying coach?

Take care of your own health,[10] compose your mind, and you have yet strength of body to be well. I am, Madam, Your most humble Servant,

SAM. JOHNSON

1. *vellication*: "twitching; stimulation" (SJ's *Dictionary*).

2. *Ante* To Susanna Thrale, 18 Nov. 1783; *Ante* To William Gerard Hamilton, 19 Nov. 1783.

3. MS: "three" written above "four" del.

4. *Ante* To John Hawkins, 22 Nov. 1783; 3 Dec. 1783.

5. MS: "?of four" del. before "we"

6. SJ has John Hawkesworth and Samuel Dyer in mind (*Post* To Hester Thrale, 19 Apr. 1784). In fact four other members had died: Richard Bathurst, William McGhie, Edmund Barker, and Samuel Salter (Clifford, 1979, pp. 33–34).

7. "When we were collected, the thought that we were so few, occasioned some melancholy reflections. . . . We dined, and in the evening regaled with coffee. At ten, we broke up, much to the regret of Johnson, who proposed staying; but finding us inclined to separate, he left us with a sigh that seemed to come from his heart" (Hawkins, p. 563).

8. MS: "among of"

9. *Ante* To Hester Thrale, 22 Sept. 1783 and n. 1.

10. *Ante* To Hester Thrale, 1 Dec. 1783 and n. 1.

John Taylor

SATURDAY 20 DECEMBER 1783

MS: Historical Society of Pennsylvania.

ADDRESS: To the Reverend Dr. Taylor in Ashbourne, Derbyshire.

POSTMARK: 20 DE.

ENDORSEMENT: 1783, 20 Decr. 83.

Dear Sir: London, Dec. 20, 1783

Perhaps You wonder that I do not write. I am very severely crushed by my old spasms which suffering me to get no sleep in the night,[1] necessarily condemn the day to sluggishness and uselessness. I am indeed exceedingly distressed.

I think you have chosen well, in taking a later month for Yourself,[2] but I was sorry to miss you so long a time. I am indeed heavily loaded with distempers. Sometimes I fancy that exercise would help me, but exercise I know not how to get; sometimes I think that a warmer climate would relieve me, but the removal requires a great deal of money. At present I subsist by opiates, and with them shall try to fight through the winter, and try something efficacious, if Life be granted me, in the spring. The testicle continues well.[3] Write to [me] what comfort you can. We are almost left alone. I am, Sir, Your affectionate etc.

SAM. JOHNSON

1. MS: "day" del. before "night"
2. *Ante* To John Taylor, 23 Mar. 1775 and n. 1.
3. *Ante* To John Mudge, 9 Sept. 1783 and nn. 4, 6.

Hester Maria Thrale

SATURDAY 20 DECEMBER 1783

MS: The Earl of Shelburne.

ADDRESS: To Miss Thrale at Bath.

POSTMARK: 20 DE.

Dearest Love: London, Dec. 20, 1783

My Breast was so much obstructed a week ago, that Dr. Brocklesby who came with me to my door, came, as he said, next day to see if I were alive. An opiate however relieved the paroxysm, and the Dr. next day, when he saw me so much better made this observation. "I was afraid last night that your disease was an Hydrops pectoris,[1] but I have[2] reason now to think it only nervous and spasmodick, for if any of the great organs of life were obstructed, you could [not] obtain so much relief by such slight means in so short a time." This is so comfortable that I am very willing to think it right.

But I am very heavily crushed. As I have little sleep in the night, I have little spirit in the day; and though I have for some time before [my] last Attack written letters for amusement, I have for several days now shrunk from writing. I have now begun again.

You are suffering your hand, my Dearest, to grow negligent and indistinct, I found your last letter hard to be read. The name of CORBETS if I had not known it I should never have disentangled.[3] Names and numbers must always be written plainly. Now I write again, I will take you all round,[4] for I am, with great kindness, your humble servant,

SAM. JOHNSON

1. *hydrops pectoris*: "dropsy of the chest."

2. MS: "h" superimposed upon "n"

3. Queeney may have referred to her cousin Hester Cotton D'Avenant's relations by marriage: Mrs. D'Avenant's husband, Corbet D'Avenant, took his mother's family name, becoming Sir Corbet Corbet, Bt. (*Thraliana* II.721 n. 3).

4. SJ wrote to Hester Thrale on 27 Dec., but letters to her daughters from this period (assuming that SJ fulfilled his promise) have not been recovered.

Frances Reynolds

TUESDAY 23 DECEMBER 1783

MS: Hyde Collection. A copy in the hand of Frances Reynolds.

Dearest Madam: Dec. 23, —83

You shall doubtless be very welcome to me on christmas Day. I shall not dine alone, but the company will all be people whom we can stay with or leave. I will expect You at three if I hear no more.

I am this day a little better. I am, dear Madam, your most humble Servant,

SAM. JOHNSON

I mean, do not be later than three, for as I am afraid, I shall not be at Church, you cannot come too soon.

James Boswell

WEDNESDAY 24 DECEMBER 1783

PRINTED SOURCE: JB's *Life*, 1791, II.471–72.

Dear Sir, London, Dec. 24, 1783

Like all other men who have great friends, you begin to feel the pangs of neglected merit, and all the comfort that I can give you is, by telling you that you have probably more pangs to feel, and more neglect to suffer. You have, indeed, begun to complain too soon; and I hope I am the only confidant of your discontent. Your friends have not yet had leisure to gratify personal kindness; they have hitherto been busy in strengthening their ministerial interest.[1] If a vacancy happens in Scotland, give them early intelligence; and as you can serve Government as powerfully as any of your probable competitors, you make in some sort a warrantable claim.

Of the exaltations and depressions of your mind you delight to talk, and I hate to hear. Drive all such fancies from you.

1. As SJ notes in the third paragraph, he began this letter before the fall of the Fox-North Coalition (18 Dec.) put an end to JB's hopes of preferment—hopes that centered on Edmund Burke, who held the office of Paymaster of the Forces. Since taking office in Apr. 1783 Burke had evaded or ignored all of JB's overtures (*Later Years*, pp. 247–48; Baker, pp. 87–90).

On the day when I received your letter, I think, the foregoing page was written;[2] to which, one disease or another has hindered me from making any additions. I am now a little better. But sickness and solitude press me very heavily. I could bear sickness better, if I were relieved from solitude.

The present dreadful confusion of the publick ought to make you wrap yourself up in your hereditary possessions,[3] which, though less than you may wish, are more than you can want; and in an hour of religious retirement return thanks to God, who has exempted you from any strong temptation to faction, treachery, plunder, and disloyalty.

As your neighbours distinguish you by such honours as they can bestow,[4] content yourself with your station, without neglecting your profession. Your estate and the Courts will find you full employment; and your mind well occupied will be quiet.

The usurpation of the nobility, for they apparently usurp all the influence they gain by fraud, and misrepresentation, I think it certainly lawful, perhaps your duty to resist. What is not their own they have only by robbery.[5]

2. JB's letter, dated 22 Nov., ought to have arrived in London *c.* 26 Nov. (JB's Register of Letters, MS: Beinecke Library).

3. *Ante* To John Taylor, 22 Nov. 1783 and n. 3. On 18 Dec. George III dismissed the Coalition and appointed William Pitt the younger as First Lord of the Treasury. Pitt's was the fourth administration in eighteen months. Despite the King's support of Pitt, Fox continued to hold a majority in the House of Commons well into Feb. 1784 (J. S. Watson, *The Reign of George III*, 1960, pp. 265–72).

4. In his letter of 22 Nov. JB had given SJ "some account of my life at Auchinleck; and expressed my satisfaction that the gentlemen of the county had, at two publick meetings, elected me their *Præses*, or Chairman" (*Life* IV.248). JB had been elected præses of the Quarter Sessions for Ayrshire, and then of a general meeting of Ayrshire landowners (*Later Years*, p. 248).

5. JB had asked SJ "whether the unconstitutional influence exercised by the Peers of Scotland in the election of the representatives of the Commons, by means of fictitious qualifications, ought not to be resisted" (*Life* IV.248). Because the franchise in Scotland was determined by property qualifications, electoral power could be multiplied by distributing land to suitably loyal relatives and dependents, whose votes were controlled by the donor. The creation of such nominally independent votes was widespread during the second half of the eighteenth century, despite attempts to curb the practice by requiring potential voters to have held the

Your question about the horses gives me more perplexity.[6] I know not well what advice to give you. I can only recommend a rule which you do not want—give as little pain as you can. I suppose that we have a right to their service while their strength lasts; what we can do with them afterwards I cannot so easily determine. But let us consider. Nobody denies that man has a right first to milk the cow, and to sheer the sheep, and then to kill them for his table. May he not, by parity of reason, first work a horse, and then kill him the easiest way, that he may have the means of another horse, or food for cows and sheep? Man is influenced in both cases by different motives of self-interest. He that rejects the one must reject the other. I am, etc.

SAM. JOHNSON

A happy and pious Christmas; and many happy years to you, your lady, and children.

---

franchise-conferring property for at least a year and a day before an election, and by obliging them to swear that they were the true owners of their property. The result was an extremely corrupt electoral system, in which the power of choosing representatives to the House of Commons was concentrated in the hands of a small number of powerful men (Namier and Brooke I.38–39).

6. JB had asked SJ "what, in propriety and humanity, should be done with old horses unable to labour" (*Life* IV.248).

Hester Thrale

SATURDAY 27 DECEMBER 1783

MS: Houghton Library.

ADDRESS: To Mrs. Thrale at Bath.

POSTMARK: 27 DE.

Dear Madam: London, Dec. 27, 1783

The wearisome solitude of the long evenings did indeed suggest to me the convenience of a club in my neighbourhood, but I have been hindred from attending it, by want of breath.

If I can complete the scheme, you shall have the names and the regulations.[1]

The time of the year, for I hope the fault is rather in the weather than in me, has been very hard upon me. The muscles of my breast are much convulsed. Dr. Heberden recommends opiates, of which I have such horrour that I do not think of them but *in extremis.* I was however driven to them last night for refuge, and having taken the usual quantity durst not go to bed, for fear of that uneasiness to which a supine posture exposes me, but rested all night in a chair, with much relief, and have been to day more warm, active and cheerful.

You have more than once wondered at my complaint of solitude, when you hear that I am crowded with visits. Inopem me copia fecit.[2] Visitors are no proper companions in the chamber of sickness. They come when I could sleep, or read, they stay till I am weary, they force me to attend, when my mind calls for relaxation, and to speak when my powers will hardly actuate my tongue. The amusements and consolations of languor and depression are conferred by familiar and domestick companions, which can be visited or called at will, and can occasionally be quitted or dismissed, who do not obstruct accommodation by ceremony, or destroy indolence by awakening effort.

Such society I had with Levet and Williams, such I had where—I am never likely to have it more.

I wish, dear Lady, to you and my dear Girls, many a cheerful and pious Christmas. I am, your most etc.

SAM. JOHNSON

1. *Ante* To Joshua Reynolds, 4 Dec. 1783 and n. 2.

2. *quod cupio mecum est: inopem me copia fecit*: "what I desire, I have; the very abundance of my riches beggars me" (Ovid, *Metamorphoses* III.466, trans. F. J. Miller, Loeb ed.).

Hester Thrale

WEDNESDAY 31 DECEMBER 1783

MS: Pembroke College, Oxford.

ADDRESS: To Mrs. Thrale at Bath.

POSTMARK: 1 IA.

Dear Madam: London, Dec. 31, 1783[1]

Since You cannot guess, I will tell You that the generous Man was Gerard Hamilton.[2] Why one of the young ⟨dears should show him an⟩ ⟨*five or six words*⟩ ⟨send⟩,[3] I returned him a very thankful and respectful letter.

Your enquiry about Lady Carlisle I cannot answer,[4] for I never saw her, unless perhaps without knowing her, at a conversation.

Sir Joshua has just been here, and knows nothing of Miss Bingham, if One of Lord Lucan['s] daughters be meant, the eldest is now Lady Spencer, the [second] is languishing in France with a diseased leg, and the third is a child.[5]

Pray send the letter which You think will divert me, for I have much need of entertainment, spiritless, infirm, sleepless, and solitary, looking back with sorrow and forward with terrour. But I will stop.

Barry of Ireland had a notion that a Man's pulse wore ⟨him⟩ out;[6] my beating breast wears out me. The Physicians yesterday covered it with a blister, of which the effect cannot yet be

1. MS: "8" superimposed upon "4"

2. *Ante* To Susanna Thrale, 18 Nov. 1783; *Ante* To William Gerard Hamilton, 19 Nov. 1783; *Ante* To Hester Thrale, 13 Dec. 1783.

3. MS: entire sentence ("Why . . . ⟨send⟩") heavily del.

4. Margaret Leveson-Gower (1753–1824), daughter of the first Marquess of Stafford, married Frederick Howard, fifth Earl of Carlisle, in 1770.

5. SJ is confused: Lord Lucan had four daughters, and the youngest was sixteen years old (*Ante* To Hester Thrale, 2 Nov. 1779, n. 3).

6. "Johnson mentioned Dr. Barry's System of Physick. . . . His notion was, that pulsation occasions death by attrition; and that, therefore, the way to preserve life is to retard pulsation" (*Life* III.34). The "notion" in question is found in *A Treatise on a Consumption of the Lungs . . . and of the Structure and Use of the Lungs* (1727) by Sir Edward Barry (1698–1776), Bt., M.D., F.R.S. (*Life* III.476).

known. Good God, prosper their endeavours. Heberden is of opinion that while the weather is so oppressive we must palliate.

In the mean time I am well fed, I have now in the house, Pheasant, Venison, Turkey, and Ham, all unbought. Attention and respect give pleasure, however late, or however useless. But they are not[7] useless, when they are late, it is reasonable to rejoice as the day declines, to find that [it] has been spent with the approbation of mankind.

The ministry is again broken, and to any man who extends his thoughts to national considerations the times are dismal and gloomy.[8] But to a sick man what is the publick?[9]

The new year is at hand, may God make it happy to Me, to You, to us all for Jesus Christ's sake. Amen. I am, Madam, Your most humble servant,

SAM. JOHNSON

7. MS: "not" superimposed upon undeciphered erasure

8. *Ante* To John Taylor, 22 Nov. 1783 and n. 3; *Ante* To JB, 24 Dec. 1783 and n. 3.

9. MS: three letters del. after "publick"

William Bowles

SATURDAY 3 JANUARY 1784

MS: Hyde Collection.

ADDRESS: To W. Bowles, Esq., at Heale near Salisbury.

POSTMARK: 3 ⟨IA⟩.

Dear Sir: London, Jan. 3, 1783[1]

A dreadful interruption of my health, the effect, in some part at least, of the hard weather, as my Physicians flatter me, and as I am very willing to flatter myself, has hindred me not only from accepting but from acknowledging your kind invi[ta]tion. My experience of the general course of life at Heal, presents to my Mind a very delightful image of a Heal Christmas,

1. The contents (particularly the references to Heale, which SJ had not visited before Aug. 1783) make it clear that SJ misdated the letter.

but I have from some time been too ill for pleasure. I have been too troublesome for any house but my own. The state of a sick man is to want much, and enjoy little. Your attention and that of your dear Lady would be fatigued by perpetuity of distress.

My pleasure in my former sickness was to write to my friends, but even this employment has been now less attractive, and even your letter has lain unanswered.

I have not forgotten Dr. Talbot's book,[2] when I go up into my study I will try to pick it up,[3] and send it, and any thing else that You desire, I shall be glad to do.

The time is, I hope, yet to come when change of air shall be recommended; and if you will then receive me, I know not any air like the air of Heale, a place where the elements and the inhabitants concur to procure health or preserve it.

You live in a very happy region, yet I suppose you have frost and snow. I should like to see their effect upon my little friends to whom they are new. I hope they starve their little fingers and feet, and cry, and wonder what it is that ails them. Is your River frozen over?[4]

Have you made a Ballon? Your plain would be a good place for mounting. The effects already produced are wonderful, but hitherto of no use, but perhaps use will come hereafter.[5] I am, Sir, Your most humble Servant,

SAM. JOHNSON

2. SJ may refer to the reprint of Thomas Talbot's three essays relating to the Hereford Infirmary (E. L. McAdam and A. T. Hazen, "Dr. Johnson and the Hereford Infirmary," *Huntington Library Quarterly* 3, 1940, pp. 360–61; *Ante* To Hester Thrale, 22 May 1775, n. 16).

3. In addition to the respiratory difficulties that made climbing stairs painful, SJ was suffering from dropsy (*Ante* To Robert Chambers, 19 Apr. 1783; *Post* To Hester Thrale, 12 Jan. 1784).

4. Heale House fronts on the Avon (*Life* IV.522).

5. *Ante* To Hester Thrale, 22 Sept. 1783 and n. 1.

John Taylor

SATURDAY 3 JANUARY 1784

MS: Houghton Library.

ADDRESS: To the Reverend Dr. Taylor in Ashbourne, Derbyshire.

POSTMARK: 3 IA.

ENDORSEMENT: 1784, 3 Jany. 84.

Dear Sir: London, Jan. 3, 1784

I was intending to write to you, to quarrel with your silence, when waking after a short sleep in my chair, I found your kind letter lying on the table.

Since your Milk has restored you, let it preserve you, do not forsake it again for any length of time.[1] As for me, I know not on which side to turn me, I am irregular in nothing. My breast is now covered with a blister, which is, I believe, to be kept open; it gives no pain, and perhaps has hitherto produced no benefit, for though I have not since its application, suffered any thing from Spasms, I have never been without opium, and therefore know not, which has helped me; nor am I helped much, for in bed I scarce get any sleep; what I have is in a chair. Dr. Heberden tells me that I must be content to support myself by opiates in the winter, and try to get better help in hotter weather.

In Spring I have a desire of trying milk somewhere in the country. My lower parts begin to swell. May we all be received to Mercy.

—There is likely to be a vacancy soon in[2] Wicher's Almshouses in Chappel street,[3] which it will [be] your Dean's turn to fill up.[4] A poor relation of mine wants a habitation. His

1. *Ante* To John Taylor, 29 Nov. 1783.

2. MS: "in in"

3. "George Witchers' Almshouses for 6 poor people" in the City of Westminster supplied its inhabitants with free housing and a weekly allowance of half a crown (Walter Besant, *London in the Eighteenth Century*, 1903, p. 630; Hawkins, p. 603).

4. SJ refers to John Thomas (1712–93), Dean of Westminster (1768) and Bishop of Rochester (1774).

name is Heely, I intend to ask Dr. Bell's interest,[5] and if you [think] it proper, wish you would write to the Dean in Heely's favour.[6]

I wish us both a happy year. I am, Sir, affectionately yours,

SAM. JOHNSON

Write soon, and often.

5. William Bell's "interest" derived from his position as prebendary of Westminster.

6. Responding to SJ's request, Thomas awarded the vacancy to Humphrey Heeley (Hawkins, p. 599).

John Perkins

MONDAY 5 JANUARY 1784

MS: Hyde Collection.

ADDRESS: To Mr. Perkins.

Dear Sir: Jan. 5 —84

I have kept the house under great oppression of ilness, for several weeks, and dare not yet [think] of going out, as soon as my Physicians allow to go abroad, I will send you word. I am, Sir, your obliged, humble servant,

SAM. JOHNSON

Many happy years to you all.

Charles Dilly

TUESDAY 6 JANUARY 1784

MS: Hyde Collection.

ADDRESS: To Mr. Dilly, Bookseller in the Poultry, Jan. 7, morning.

POSTMARKS: PENY POST PAYD, [Undeciphered].

ENDORSEMENT: Jan. 7, morning.

Sir: Bolt court, Jan. 6, 1784

There is in the world a set of Books, which used to be sold by the Booksellers on the bridge,[1] and which I must entreat You to procure me. They are called *Burton's Books*,[2] the title of one is, *Admirable Curiosities, Rarities and Wonders in England*.[3] I believe there [are] about 5 or 6 of them they seem very proper to allure backward Readers, be so kind as to get them for me, and send me [them] with the best printed edition of Baxter's call to the unconverted.[4] I am, Sir, Your humble servant,

SAM. JOHNSON

1. Houses and shops, many of them booksellers' premises, occupied both sides of London Bridge; these were demolished between 1758 and 1762 (Wheatley and Cunningham II.422; John Pudney, *Crossing London's River*, 1972, p. 31).

2. Nathaniel Crouch (?1632–?1725), writer and publisher, assumed the name of Richard or Robert Burton. He compiled over forty chapbooks (chiefly devoted to historical topics) that originally sold at a shilling apiece and achieved widespread popularity.

3. *Wonderful Curiosities, Rarities, and Wonders in England, Scotland, and Ireland* appeared in 1682 and was frequently reprinted.

4. *A Call to the Unconverted to Turn and Live* by Richard Baxter (1615–91), "one of Johnson's favorite religious writers," was first published in 1658; it went through numerous editions thereafter, the "best" of which may have been that issued in London in 1782 (Greene, 1975, p. 34; *Life* IV.527; D. J. Greene, "Dr. Johnson's 'Late Conversion': A Reconsideration," in *Johnsonian Studies*, ed. Magdi Wahba, 1962, pp. 76–77).

John & Amelia Perkins

SUNDAY 11 JANUARY 1784

PRINTED SOURCE: John Grant Catalogue, 1931, p. 1.

Jan. 11 —84

Mr. Johnson's compliments to Mr. and Mrs. Perkins. Mr. Johnson had a sleepless night, but is better to day.

Hester Thrale

MONDAY 12 JANUARY 1784

MS: Houghton Library.

ADDRESS: To Mrs. Thrale at Bath.

POSTMARK: 12 IA.

Dear Madam: London, Jan. 12, 1784

If, as You observe my former letter was written with trepidation,[1] there is little reason, except the habit of enduring, why this should show more steadiness. I am confined to the house; I do not know that any things grow better; my Physicians direct me to combat the hard weather with opium; I cannot well support its turbulence, and yet cannot forbear it, for its immediate effect is ease; Having kept me waking all the night, it forces sleep upon me in the day, and recompenses a night of tediousness, with a day of uselessness. My legs and my thighs grow very tumid. In the mean time my appetite is good, and if my Physicians do not flatter me, death is [not] rushing upon me. But this is in the hand of God.

The first talk of the Sick is commonly of themselves, but if they talk of nothing else, they cannot complain if they are soon left without an audience.

You observe, Madam, that the Ballon engages all Mankind, and it is indeed a wonderful and unexpected addition to human knowledge;[2] but we have a daring projector who disdaining the help of fumes and vapours is making better than Dædalean wings, with which he will master the ballon and its companions, as an Eagle master[s] a goose. It is very seriously true, that a subscription of eight hundred pounds has been raised, for the wire and workmanship of iron wings; one pair of which and, I think, a tail, are now shown in the hay market, and they are making another pair at Birmingham.[3] The whole

1. *Ante* To Hester Thrale, 31 Dec. 1783.

2. *Ante* To Hester Thrale, 22 Sept. 1783, n. 1.

3. SJ appears to have conflated two aeronautical schemes. The first involved a balloon with wings attached; this project was directed by "a Scotch artist, who is

is said to weigh two hundred pounds, no specious preparation for flying, but there are those who expect to see him in the sky. When I can leave the house I will tell you more.

I had the same old friends to dine with me on Wednesday,[4] and may say that since I lost sight of you, I have had one pleasant day. I am, Madam, Your most humble servant,

SAM. JOHNSON

Pray send me a direction to Sir—Musgrave in Ireland.[5]

---

already supported by a subscription of seven hundred guineas to complete it. The machine is to be in the form of a bird; the body is to contain the inflammable air, the shaft of the wings to be nine feet long, and nine inches wide; both to be made of the purest elastic steel" (*The Air Balloon: Or a Treatise on The Aerostatic Globe*, 1st ed., 1783, pp. 26–27). The second project consisted of "a machine in the form of a canoe, to which are to be attached a pair of artificial wings and a tail. . . . These the artist works with great facility, spreading and contracting both at pleasure" (*The Air Balloon*, 3d ed., 1783, pp. 34–35). As precedent, John Wilkins's idea for a "flying Chariot" is cited (from Wilkins's *Mathematical Magick*, 1648). SJ had drawn upon Wilkins for chapter 6 of *Rasselas* (G. J. Kolb, "Johnson's 'Dissertation on Flying,'" in *New Light on Dr. Johnson*, ed. F. W. Hilles, 1959, pp. 91–106).

4. *Ante* To John Hawkins, 22 Nov. 1783 and n. 1.

5. SJ refers to Sir Richard Musgrave, Bt.

William Bowles

WEDNESDAY 14 JANUARY 1784

MS: Hyde Collection.

ADDRESS: To W. Bowles, Esq., at Heale near Salisbury.

POSTMARK: 14 IA.

Dear Sir: London, Jan. 14, 1784

What can be the reason that You do not write to me? A Friends letter is always comfortable, and I, who have now been many weeks confined to the house, have much need of comfort. My nights are sleepless; I sat in a[1] chair till six this morning, to avoid the miseries of bed. My Physicians, who are zealous to

1. MS: "a" superimposed upon "t"

help me, can give nothing but opium, with which they fortify me against the violence of the winter. Opium dismisses pain but does not always bring quiet, and never disposes me to sleep, till a long time after it has been taken;[2] Thus I am harrassed between sickness, and a palliative remedy which is still to be repeated, for I need not tell You that opium cures nothing, though by setting the powers of life at ease, I sometimes flatter myself that it may give them time to rectify themselves.

In this state You may suppose I think sometimes of Heale, which I hope to see again when I can enjoy it more. Do not forget me, nor suppose that I can forget You, or your Lady or your young ones. I wish You all many and many happy years, and am, Dear Sir, Your most obedient servant,

SAM. JOHNSON

2. MS: "taken" repeated as catchword

John Perkins

WEDNESDAY 21 JANUARY 1784

MS: Hyde Collection.
ADDRESS: To Mr. Perkins.
ENDORSEMENT: 21 Janry. 1784.

Dear Sir: Jan. 21, 1784

I was very sorry not to see You, when you were so kind as to call on me, but to disappoint friends and if they are not very good natured, to disoblige them, is one of the evils of Sickness. If You will please to let me know which of the afternoons in this week, I shall be favoured with another visit by You and Mrs. Perkins, and the pretty young people I will take all the measures that I can to be pretty well at that time. I am, Dear Sir, Your most humble Servant,

SAM. JOHNSON

Hester Thrale

WEDNESDAY 21 JANUARY 1784

MS: Hyde Collection.
ADDRESS: To Mrs. Thrale at Bath.
POSTMARK: 21 IA.

Dear Madam: London, Jan. 21, 1784

Dr. Heberden this day favoured me with a visit, and after hearing what I had to tell him of miseries and pains, and comparing my present with my past state, declared me well. That his opinion is erroneous I know with too much certainty, and yet was glad to hear it, as it set extremities at a greater distance; he who is by his physician thought well, is at least not thought in immediate danger. They therefore whose attention to me makes them talk of my health, will, I hope, soon not drop, but lose their subject. But, alas, I had no sleep last night, and sit now panting over my paper. Dabit Deus his quoque finem.[1] I have really hope from Spring, and am ready like Almanzor to bid the Sun *fly swiftly* and *leave weeks and months behind him.*[2] The Sun has looked for five thousand years upon the world to little purpose, if he does not know that a Sick man is almost as impatient as a lover.

Mr. Cator gives such an account of Miss Cecy as you and all of us must delight to hear; Cator has a rough, manly, independent understanding, and does not spoil it by complaisance, he never speaks merely to please, and seldom is mistaken in things which he has any right to know. I think well of her for pleasing him, and of him for being pleased; and at the close am delighted to find him delighted with her excellence.[3] Let

1. *o passi graviora, dabit deus his quoque finem*: "O ye who have borne a heavier lot, to this, too, God will grant an end" (*Aeneid* I.199, trans. H. R. Fairclough, Loeb ed.).

2. "Move swiftly, Sun; and fly a lovers pace; / Leave weeks and months behind thee in thy race!" (Dryden, *The Conquest of Granada*, Part II, v.iii.339–40).

3. MS: "cellence" repeated as catchword

your Children, dear Madam, be *his*[4] care, and *your* pleasure;[5] close your thoughts upon them, and when sad[6] fancies are excluded, health and peace will return together. I am, Dear Madam, Your old Friend,

SAM. JOHNSON

4. MS: "his" superimposed upon undeciphered partial erasure

5. Cator was one of the executors of Henry Thrale's will and a guardian of the children.

6. MS: "sad" superimposed upon undeciphered partial erasure

John & Amelia Perkins

FRIDAY 23 JANUARY 1784

MS: Hyde Collection.

Jan. 23 —84[1]

Dr. Johnson sends compliments to Mr. and Mrs. Perkins, and the young Gentlemen, and begs to know when they will favour him with their company.

1. MS: "—84" added in an unidentified hand

John Taylor

SATURDAY 24 JANUARY 1784

MS: Huntington Library.

ADDRESS: To the Revd. Dr. Taylor in Ashbourne, Derbyshire.

POSTMARK: 24 IA.

ENDORSEMENTS: 1784, 24 Jany. 84.

Dear Sir: London, Jan. 24, 1784

I am still confined to the house, and one of my amusements is to write letters to my friends, though they being busy in the common scenes of life, are not equally diligent in writing to me.

Dr. Heberden was with me two or three days ago, and told

me that nothing ailed me, which I was glad to hear though I know it not to be true. My nights are restless, my breath is difficult, and my lower parts continue tumid.

The struggle, You see, still continues between the two sets of ministry; those that are *out* and *in* one can scarce call them, for who is *out* or *in* is perhaps four times a day a new question.[1] The tumult in government is, I believe, excessive, and the efforts of each party outrageously violent, with very little thought on any national interest, at a time when we have all the world for our enemies, when the King and parliament have lost even the titular dominion of America,[2] and the real power of Government every where else. Thus Empires are broken down when the profits of administration are so great, that ambition is satisfied with obtaining them, and he that aspires to greatness needs do nothing more than[3] talk himself into importance. He has then all the power which danger and conquest used formerly to give. He can raise a family and reward his followers.

Mr. Burke has just sent me his speech upon the affairs of India, a volume of above one hundred pages closely printed.[4] I will look into it; but my thoughts now seldom travel to great distances.

I would gladly know when You think to come hither, and whether this year You will come or no. If my life be continued, I know not well how I shall bestow myself. I am, Sir, Your affectionate etc.

SAM. JOHNSON

1. *Ante* To JB, 24 Dec. 1783, n. 1. Although Fox and his colleagues had been dismissed as ministers, Fox maintained his majority in the House of Commons and blocked any action on the part of the new ministry (J. S. Watson, *The Reign of George III*, 1960, pp. 268–69).

2. All claims had been relinquished in the Treaty of Paris, Sept. 1783.

3. MS: "than" altered from "that"

4. Burke's speech in the House of Commons on behalf of Fox's East India Bill (1 Dec. 1783) had been published 22 Jan. as a separate pamphlet by James Dodsley (W. B. Todd, *A Bibliography of Edmund Burke*, 1982, p. 123).

Richard Clark

TUESDAY 27 JANUARY 1784

MS: Hyde Collection.

ADDRESS: To Richard Clark, Esq.

ENDORSEMENTS: 27 Jan. 1784, Dr. Johnson.

Dear Sir: Bolt court, Fleetstreet, Jan. 27, —84

You will receive a requisition, according to the rules of the club,[1] to be at the house as President of the night. This turn comes once a month, and the Member is obliged to attend, or send another in his place. You were enrolled in the club by my invitation and I ought to introduce you, but as I am hindered by sickness, Mr. Hoole will very properly supply my place as introductor, or yours, as President. I hope in milder weather to [be] a very constant attendant. I am, Sir, Your most humble Servant,

SAM. JOHNSON

You ought [to be informed][2] that the forfeits began with the year, and that every night of nonattendance, incurs the mulct of three pence, that is nine pence a week.

1. *Ante* To Joshua Reynolds, 4 Dec. 1783 and n. 2; *Ante* To Richard Clark, 13 Dec. 1783. 2. "to be informed" supplied by JB (*Life*, 1791, II.478)

Hester Maria Thrale

SATURDAY 31 JANUARY 1784

MS: The Earl of Shelburne.

ADDRESS: To Miss Thrale at Bath.

POSTMARK: 31 IA.

Dear Madam: London, Jan. 31, 1784

It is indeed a long time since I wrote to Bath, I may [be] allowed to be weary of telling that I am sick, and sick, and you may well be weary of hearing, but having now kept the house for seven weeks, and not being likely soon to come out, I have my want of health much in my mind, and am indeed very deeply dejected.

I have however continued my connection with the world so far as to subscribe to a new ballon which is [to] sustain five hundred weight, and[1] by which, I suppose, some Americo Vespucci, for a new Columbus he cannot now be, will bring us what intelligence he can gather in the clouds.[2] Sure as I am by reason and by example that there is no great danger in the expedition, I could not see the earth a mile below me, without a stronger impression on my brain than I should like to feel. The King of Prussia taught his soldiers to load marching, because they would not think of the enemy when they had something to do.[3] The aerial[4] adventurers have their globe to ballance, and glass tubes to watch,[5] and therefore look less often down.

My friends call on me much oftener, than my feebleness allows me to admit them. I am afraid some of them will be angry. This is among the other evils of Sickness.

My inability to attend the Essex head makes the club droop,[6] but if it does languish quite away, I hope my return to it will invigorate and establish it, and then I will transmit to you our

1. MS: "and" repeated as catchword

2. SJ refers either to the Chevalier de Moret's scheme for a giant balloon in the shape of a Chinese temple or to the oblong balloon projected by John Sheldon and Allen Keegan. On 10 Aug. 1784 Moret attempted an ascent from Chelsea that ended in disaster: the balloon never rose and at last caught fire. On 16 Aug. 1784 Sheldon and Keegan also failed: their balloon was damaged before the ascent could begin. During a second attempt, 29 Sept. 1784, the balloon caught fire and was completely destroyed (J. E. Hodgson, *A History of Aeronautics in Great Britain*, 1924, pp. 111–16; *Post* To Richard Brocklesby, 21 Aug. 1784).

3. SJ may be referring to Frederick William of Prussia (1688–1740), who promulgated in 1714 the first comprehensive set of infantry regulations for the Prussian army (Gordon Craig, *The Politics of the Prussian Army*, 1955, p. 12). Included among these regulations were instructions for loading and firing while advancing (*Regulations for the Prussian Infantry translated from the German Original*, 1759, p. 59).

4. MS: "aeririal"

5. SJ refers to the barometers carried by balloonists.

6. *Ante* To Joshua Reynolds, 4 Dec. 1783.

number, our names, and our laws.[7] I am, Dear Madam, Your most humble Servant,

SAM. JOHNSON

7. The rules of the Essex Head Club specified that membership was limited to twenty-four; that the Club would meet three times every week, except during the week before Easter; and that absent members would be fined threepence (*Life* IV.254 n. 5).

William Bowles

TUESDAY 3 FEBRUARY 1784

MS: Hyde Collection.

ADDRESS: To W. Bowles, Esq., at Heale near Salisbury.

POSTMARK: 3 FE.

Dear Sir: London, Feb. 3, 1784

I am still confined to the house, this is the eighth week of my incarceration. I am utterly unable to sustain the violence of the weather. I am willing to be persuaded, and a sick man never wants flatterers, that I am rather oppressed without than weak within, and that I shall find ease and comfort return, when Winter raises the siege.

Confinement I should not much lament, if confinement were my whole restraint.[1] If I could employ my time at will, I could perhaps procure to myself instruction or amusement, but so it is, that my nights passing without sleep, drag days after them of little use. Few states are more uncomfortable, and few more unprofitable than[2] that of drowsiness without sleep.

Opiates, without any encrease of quantity, are still efficacious in quelling any irregular concussions of the body, but I dread their effects upon the mind more than those of wine or distilled spirits.

The encrease of warmth I have tried, and am compelled to practice in all the instances which You so kindly recommended.

1. MS: undeciphered erasure before "restraint"

2. MS: "that"

I have fits of great dejection and cheerlesness: I take delight in recollecting our evening worship; let me have a place in your devotions.

—I subscribed a few days ago to a new ballon, which is to carry five hundred weight, and with which some daring adventurer is expected to mount, and bring down the state of regions yet unexplored.[3] This power of mounting and descending is a strange thing, but I am afraid we shall never be able to give so wide a surface any horizontal direction. We can ⟨not⟩ row it. And to make the discoveries which it really puts in our power, the rise ought to be taken from the summit of Teneriffe,[4] for so far we know the atmosphere without its help. The summits of the Alps may be sufficient, and thither[5] the philosophers of Geneva are not unlikely to carry[6] it. I wish well to such soaring curiosity.

Be pleased to [make] my compliments to your dear Lady, to your Father, and to my little friends.—and to all friends. I am, dear Sir, etc.

SAM. JOHNSON

3. *Ante* To Hester Maria Thrale, 31 Jan. 1784, n. 2.

4. The volcanic peak of Teneriffe, Canary Islands, rises to 12,180 feet. In *The Vision of Theodore* and *Rambler* No. 117, SJ had drawn on the traditional association of the mountain with great height (*Works*, Yale ed. XVI.187).

5. MS: "thither" altered from "thence"

6. MS: undeciphered deletion before "carry"

John Nichols

WEDNESDAY 4 FEBRUARY 1784

PRINTED SOURCE: Chapman III.130.[1]

Feb. 4

Mr. Johnson having been for many ⟨weeks⟩ confined, is very cheerless, and wishes that when (*sic*) Mr. Nichols would now and then bestow an hour upon him.

1. Though Chapman's citation ("Sotheby 18 Nov. 1929") is inaccurate, the correct source has not been traced.

William Heberden

FRIDAY 6 FEBRUARY 1784

MS: Hyde Collection.

HEADING in an unidentified hand: To Dr. Heberden.

Dear Sir: Bolt court, Fleetstreet, Febr. 6, 1784

When you favoured me with your last visit, you left me full of cheerfulness and hope. But my Distemper prevails, and my hopes sink, and dejection oppresses me. I entreat You to come again to me, and tell me if any hope of amend[m]ent remains and by what medicines or methods it may be promoted. Let me see You, dear Sir, as soon as You can. I am, Sir, Your most obliged and most humble Servant,

SAM. JOHNSON

John Nichols

SATURDAY 7 FEBRUARY 1784

MS: British Library.

ADDRESS: To Mr. Nichols.

Febr. 7

Mr. Johnson desires the favour of Mr. Nichols's company, to meet Mr. Allen, at din[n]er on Monday the 9th.

Frances Reynolds

MONDAY 9 FEBRUARY 1784

MS: Hyde Collection.

ADDRESS: To Mrs. Reynolds.

ENDORSEMENT: Dr. Johnson, Feb. 84.

Dear Madam: Febr. 9

I think very well of your dinner, and intend soon to have

something like it. If I could as easily get good nights as good dinners, I should perhaps soon be well—but I am yet very ill. I am, Madam, your most etc.

SAM. JOHNSON

Hester Thrale

MONDAY 9 FEBRUARY 1784

MS: Hyde Collection.

ADDRESS: To Mrs. Thrale at Bath.

POSTMARK: 9 FE.

Dear Madam: London, Febr. 9, 1784

The remission of the cold did not continue long enough to afford me much relief. You are, as I perceive afraid of the opium. I had the same terrour, and admitted its assistance only under the pressure of insupportable distress, as of an auxiliary too powerful and too dangerous. But in this pinching season I cannot live without it, and the quantity which I take is less than it once was.

My Phisicians flatter me, that the season is a great part of my disease, and that when warm weather restores perspiration, this watery disease will evaporate.[1] I am at least, willing to flatter my self.

I have been forced to sit up many nights by an obstinate sleeplesness, which makes the time in bed intolerably tedious, and which continues my drowsy [lethargy] the following day. Besides I can sometimes sleep erect, when I cannot close my eyes in a recumbent posture. I have just bespoke a flannel dress which I can easily slip off and on, as I go into bed, or get out of it. Thus pass my days and nights in morbid wakefulness, in unseasonable sleepiness, in gloomy solitude with unwel-

1. SJ refers to the dropsy in his legs and thighs (*Ante* To Hester Thrale, 12 Jan. 1784).

come visitors, or ungrateful exclusions, in variety of wretchedness. But I snatch every lucid interval, and animate my self with such amusements as the time offers.

One thing which I have just heard, You will think to surpass expectation. The Chaplain of the factory at Petersburg[2] relates that the Rambler is now by the command of the Empress translating into Russian,[3] and has promised when it is printed to send me a copy.

Grant, O Lord that all who shall read my pages, may become more obedient to thy Laws, and when the wretched writer shall appear before Thee, extend thy mercy to him, for the sake of Jesus Christ. Amen. I am, Madam, your most etc.

SAM. JOHNSON

2. William Tooke (1744–1820), historian of Russia and chaplain to the English Factory at St. Petersburg (1774–92). The first of his several histories of Russia appeared 1780–83.

3. No Russian translation of SJ's *Rambler* has been traced (information supplied by Dr. J. D. Fleeman). A Russian *Rasselas* had appeared in 1764 (*Ante* To William White, 4 Mar. 1773, n. 7).

James Boswell

WEDNESDAY 11 FEBRUARY 1784

PRINTED SOURCE: JB's *Life*, 1791, II.478–79.

Dear Sir, Feb. 11, 1784

I hear of many inquiries which your kindness has disposed you to make after me.[1] I have long intended you a long letter, which perhaps the imagination of its length hindered me from beginning. I will, therefore, content myself with a shorter.

Having promoted the institution of a new Club in the neigh-

1. JB had written to SJ on 8 Jan., "anxiously inquiring as to his health" (*Life* IV.258). Hearing nothing, JB wrote on 6 Feb. to Sir Joshua Reynolds, asking for a report on SJ's condition (Fifer, p. 149).

bourhood, at the house of an old servant of Thrale's,[2] I went thither to meet the company, and was seized with a spasmodick asthma so violent, that with difficulty I got to my own house, in which I have been confined eight or nine weeks, and from which I know not when I shall be able to go even to church. The asthma, however, is not the worst. A dropsy gains ground upon me; my legs and thighs are very much swollen with water, which I should be content if I could keep there, but I am afraid that it will soon be higher. My nights are very sleepless and very tedious. And yet I am extremely afraid of dying.

My physicians try to make me hope, that much of my malady is the effect of cold, and that some degree at least of recovery is to be expected from vernal breezes and summer suns. If my life is prolonged to autumn, I should be glad to try a warmer climate; though how to travel with a diseased body, without a companion to conduct me, and with very little money, I do not well see. Ramsay has recovered his limbs in Italy;[3] and Fielding was sent to Lisbon, where, indeed, he died; but he was, I believe, past hope when he went.[4] Think for me what I can do.

I received your pamphlet, and when I write again may perhaps tell you some opinion about it;[5] but you will forgive a man struggling with disease his neglect of disputes, politicks, and pamphlets. Let me have your prayers. My compliments to your lady, and young ones. Ask your physicians about my

2. *Ante* To Joshua Reynolds, 4 Dec. 1783.

3. *Ante* To Hester Maria Thrale, 23 Aug. 1783.

4. Henry Fielding (1707–54), playwright, novelist, and magistrate, suffered in the last two years of his life from gout, asthma, and cirrhosis of the liver (the contemporary diagnosis of which was dropsy); among the physicians who treated him was William Heberden (M. C. Battestin with R. R. Battestin, *Henry Fielding*, 1989, pp. 577, 580, 584). In June of 1754 Fielding set sail for Lisbon on the advice of his doctors, who "concurred that his only chance of life was having a proper summer in which to gain strength enough to support the rigors of another winter" (Battestin and Battestin, *Fielding*, p. 584). He died in Lisbon on 8 Oct.

5. Along with his letter of 8 Jan., JB had sent a copy of his *Letter to the People of Scotland, On the Present State of the Nation*, which had appeared in May 1783 (*Life* IV.258; *Lit. Car.*, p. 105 and n. 1). *Post* To JB, 27 Feb. 1784.

case;[6] and desire Sir Alexander Dick to write me his opinion.[7] I am, dear Sir, etc.

SAM. JOHNSON

6. JB responded energetically to SJ's request, consulting first with Thomas Gillespie (d. 1804), M.D., who had been Lord Auchinleck's physician (*Life* IV.262, 527; *Post* To JB, 2 Mar. 1784 and n. 1). On 7 Mar. he wrote to three physicians, all members of the medical faculty of the University of Edinburgh: William Cullen (1710–90), M.D.; John Hope (1725–86), M.D.; and Alexander Monro (1733–1817), M.D. (*Boswell: The Applause of the Jury*, ed. I. S. Lustig and F. A. Pottle, 1981, p. 191). "All of them paid the most polite attention to my letter, and its venerable object. . . . Dr. Hope corresponded with his friend Dr. Brocklesby. Doctors Cullen and Monro wrote their opinions and prescriptions to me, which I afterwards . . . communicated to Johnson" (*Life* IV.264).

7. SJ remembered that Dick had once practiced as a physician. *Post* To JB, 2 Mar. 1784 and n. 1.

Anthony Hamilton

WEDNESDAY 11 FEBRUARY 1784

PRINTED SOURCE: JB's *Life*, ed. Croker, 1835, x.283.

Sir, Bolt Court, Feb. 11, 1784

My physicians endeavour to make me believe that I shall sometime be better qualified to receive visits from men of elegance and civility like yours.

Mrs. Pellè shall wait upon you, and you will judge what will be proper for you to do.[1] I once more return you my thanks, and am, Sir, etc.

SAM. JOHNSON

1. *Ante* To Anthony Hamilton, 4 June 1783 and n. 2; *Post* To Anthony Hamilton, 17 Feb. 1784.

William Cruikshank

FRIDAY 13 FEBRUARY 1784

MS: Hyde Collection.

ADDRESS: To Mr. Cruikshank.

Sir: Febr. 13, 1784

I beg that you would send me a large adhesive plaster spread upon thick leather; it should be about fourteen inches long, and about eight broad; it is for a defensative[1] for my breast. The salve I leave to You; perhaps Pix Burgundica[2] may be as good as any thing. If You are at home let this messenger bring it, if not, send it to night by any body, and I will pay him. I am, Sir, Your humble servant,

SAM. JOHNSON

1. *defensative*: "a bandage, plaster, or the like, used to secure a wound from outward violence" (SJ's *Dictionary*).

2. *Pix Burgundica*, also known as "Burgundy pitch": "the resinous juice of the Spruce-fir" (*OED*).

William Cruikshank

TUESDAY 17 FEBRUARY 1784

MS: Hyde Collection.

ADDRESS: To Mr. Cruikshank in Leicester Fields.

Dear Sir: Febr. 17, 1784

An issue is to be made in my thigh, to drain away the water. As You called Mr. Pott before I beg You to do the same again, and come as soon as You can together to the Assistance of, Sir, Your most humble Servant,

SAM. JOHNSON

Anthony Hamilton

TUESDAY 17 FEBRUARY 1784

PRINTED SOURCE: JB's *Life*, ed. Croker, 1835, x.283.

Sir, Feb. 17, 1784

I am so much disordered that I can only say that this is the person whom I recommend to your kindness and favour.[1] I am, Sir, etc.

SAM. JOHNSON

1. *Ante* To Anthony Hamilton, 11 Feb. 1784.

Mary Rogers[1]

TUESDAY 17 FEBRUARY 1784

MS: Hyde Collection.

Madam: Bolt court, Fleetstreet, Febr. 17, 1784

A very dangerous and enervaiting distemper admonishes me to make my will. One of my cares is for poor Phebe Herne to whom your worthy Mother left so kind a legacy.[2] When I am gone who shall pay the rest of her maintenance? I have not much to leave, but if You, Madam, will be pleased to undertake it, I can leave You an hundred pounds.[3] But I am afraid that is hardly an equivalent, for my part has commonly amounted to twelve pounds or more. The payment to the house is eight shilling a week, and some cloaths must be had however few or coarse.

Be pleased, Madam, to let me know your resolution on my proposal, and write soon, for the time may be very short.[4] I am, Madam, your most humble Servant,

SAM. JOHNSON

1. *Ante* To Mary Prowse, 14 Aug. 1780, n. 1.
2. *Ante* To Mary Prowse, 14 Aug. 1780 and n. 3.
3. *Ante* To Mary Prowse, 14 Aug. 1780, n. 3.
4. Mary Rogers promptly replied: "Mr. Rogers desires me to inform you that he will accept of the hundred pounds and will so far be answerable for Mrs. Hearnes Maintenance as to secure to her an annuitty of 23£" (Holograph copy, MS: Hyde Collection).

William Bowles

MONDAY 23 FEBRUARY 1784

MS: Hyde Collection.

ADDRESS: To W. Bowles, Esq., at Heale near Salisbury.

POSTMARK: 23 FE.

Dear Sir: London, Febr. 23, 1784

I was too well pleased with your name not to send it immediately to the club;[1] You will have I suppose this night notice of your reception.[2]

Whether I shall ever see the Club again is yet a doubt. But I trust in God's mercy, who has already granted me great relief. Last week I emitted in about twenty hours, full twenty pints of[3] urine, and the tumour of my body is very much lessened, but whether water will not gather again, He only knows by whom we live and move.

My dejection has never been more than was suitable to my condition. A Sinner approaching the grave, is not likely to be very cheerful.

My present thoughts do not allow me to take pleasure in the expectation[4] of seeing a mind so pure as yours, exposed to the contagion of publick life, and contending with the corrupt, and contaminated atmos[p]here of the house of commons.[5] If half of them were like you, I should wish You among them. Consider well, and God direct You. I am, Sir, Your most humble servant,

SAM. JOHNSON

1. *Ante* To Joshua Reynolds, 4 Dec. 1783.

2. Bowles was duly elected, but does not seem to have attended before SJ's death (*Post* To William Bowles, 3 May 1784).

3. MS: "of of"

4. MS: "thought" del. before "expectation"

5. Presumably Bowles had mentioned the possibility of offering himself as a candidate for Salisbury in the spring election. If so, he was persuaded not to run: William Henry Bouverie and William Hussey were both returned without a contest (Namier and Brooke I.419).

Lucy Porter

MONDAY 23 FEBRUARY 1784

MS: Hyde Collection.

ADDRESS: To Mrs. Lucy Porter in Lichfield.

POSTMARK: 23 FE.

My dearest Love: Febr. 23, 1784

I have been extremely ill of an Asthma and dropsy, but received by the mercy of God sudden and unexpected relief last thursday by the discharge of twenty pints of water.[1] Whether I shall continue free, or shall fill again, cannot be told. Pray for me.

Death, my dear, is very dreadful, let us think nothing worth our care but how to prepare for it, what we know amiss in ourselves let us make haste to amend, and put our trust in the mercy of God, and the intercession of our Saviour. I am, Dear Madam, your most humble Servant,

SAM. JOHNSON

1. For a thorough investigation of possible medical explanations for this sudden diuresis, see W. W. Fee, "Samuel Johnson's 'Wonderful' Remission of Dropsy," *Harvard Library Bulletin* 23, 1975, pp. 271–88. SJ interpreted his recovery—marked not only by the diuresis itself but also by a new "serenity"—as a divine response to prayer and fasting (Hawkins, pp. 565–66; *Life* IV.271–72). This dramatic improvement marked the beginning of what SJ described in a deathbed prayer as "my late conversion" (*Works*, Yale ed. I.417–18; D. J. Greene, "Dr. Johnson's 'Late Conversion': A Reconsideration," in *Johnsonian Studies*, ed. Magdi Wahba, 1962, pp. 61–92).

James Boswell

FRIDAY 27 FEBRUARY 1784

PRINTED SOURCE: JB's *Life*, 1791, II.480.

Dear Sir, London, Feb. 27, 1784

I have just advanced so far towards recovery as to read a pamphlet; and you may reasonably suppose that the first pamphlet which I read was yours.[1] I am very much of your opinion, and, like you, feel great indignation at the indecency with which the King is every day treated. Your paper contains very considerable knowledge of the history and of the constitution, very properly produced and applied.[2] It will certainly raise your character, though perhaps it may not make you a Minister of State.

* * * * * *

I desire you to see Mrs. Stewart once again, and tell her, that in the letter-case was a letter relating to me, for which I will give her, if she is willing to give it me, another guinea.[3] The letter is of consequence only to me. I am, dear Sir, etc.

SAM. JOHNSON

1. *Ante* To JB, 11 Feb. 1784 and n. 5.

2. *A Letter to the People of Scotland* condemned Fox's East India Bill for violating the property rights of the East India Company and for diminishing the royal prerogative. JB also urged the people of Scotland to express their support, through public addresses, for the King's dismissal of the Coalition Ministry and his appointment of Pitt as Prime Minister (*Later Years*, p. 249; *Lit. Car.* p. 108).

3. *Ante* To JB, 8 Apr. 1780 and n. 12; *Post* To JB, 18 Mar. 1784.

James Boswell

TUESDAY 2 MARCH 1784

PRINTED SOURCE: JB's *Life*, 1791, II.481.

Dear Sir, London, March 2, 1784

Presently after I had sent away my last letter, I received your kind medical packet.[1] I am very much obliged both to you and your physicians for your kind attention to my disease. Dr. Gillespie has sent an excellent *consilium medicum*, all solid practical experimental knowledge. I am at present, in the opinion of my physicians (Dr. Heberden and Dr. Brocklesby) as well as

1. On 23 Feb. JB had sent SJ a letter from Sir Alexander Dick and a "full opinion upon his case by Dr. Gillespie" (*Life* IV.262; JB's Register of Letters, MS: Beinecke Library). *Ante* To JB, 11 Feb. 1784 and nn. 6, 7.

my own, going on very hopefully. I have just begun to take vinegar of squills.[2] The powder hurt my stomach so much, that it could not be continued.

Return Sir Alexander Dick my sincere thanks for his kind letter; and bring with you the rhubarb which he so tenderly offers me.[3]

I hope dear Mrs. Boswell is now quite well, and that no evil, either real or imaginary, now disturbs you.[4] I am, etc.

SAM. JOHNSON

2. "One of the principal diuretic medicines used in the eighteenth century was derived from the white squill, a plant that grows along the Mediterranean Sea. The bulb was dried and taken as a powder, or steeped in vinegar or wine until its chemical agents had been extracted, after which it was strained out and the liquid was taken. . . . Squill, like digitalis, by improving heart function, has a diuretic effect on cardiac patients with edema" (W. W. Fee, "Samuel Johnson's 'Wonderful' Remission of Dropsy," *Harvard Library Bulletin* 23, 1975, pp. 283–84).

3. "From his [Dick's] garden at Prestonfield, where he cultivated that plant with such success, that he was presented with a gold medal by the Society of London for the Encouragement of Arts, Manufactures, and Commerce" (JB's note: *Life* IV.263 n. 1).

4. Chapman (III.136) hypothesizes that the passage excised from To JB, 27 Feb. 1784, "dealt with 'imaginary evil.'"

Hester Thrale

TUESDAY 2 MARCH 1784

MS: Gerald M. Goldberg.
ADDRESS: To Mrs. Thrale at Bath.
POSTMARK: 2 MR.

Madam: London, March 20, 1784[1]

Your last letter had something of tenderness. The accounts which You have had of my danger and distress were, I suppose, not aggravated. I have been confined ten weeks with an Asthma and Dropsy. But I am now better. God has in his

1. SJ misdated this letter; see postmark.

mercy granted me a reprieve, for how much time his mercy must determine.

On the 19th of last Month I evacuated twenty pints of water, and I think I reckon exactly, from that time the tumour has subsided, and I now begin to move with some freedom. You will easily believe that I am still at a great distance from health,[2] but I am as my Chirurgeon expressed it amazingly better. Heberden seems to have great hopes.

Write to me no more about *dying with a grace*. When You feel what I have felt in approaching Eternity—in fear of soon hearing the sentence of which there is no revocation, you will know the folly, my wish is that you may know it sooner. The distance between the grave and the remotest point of human longevity is but a very little, and of that little no part is certain. You know all this, and I thought that I knew it too, but I know it now with a new conviction. May that new conviction not be vain.

I am now cheerful, I hope this approach to recovery is a token of Divine Mercy.[3] My Friends continue their kindness. I give a din[n]er to morrow.

Pray let me know how my dear Sophy goes on.[4] I still hope that there is in her fits more terrour than danger. But I hope, however it be, that she will speedily recover. I will take care to pay Miss Susy her letter. God bless You all. I am, Madam, Your most humble servant,

SAM. JOHNSON

2. MS: "health" repeated as catchword

3. *Ante* To Lucy Porter, 23 Feb. 1784, n. 1.

4. *Ante* To Hester Thrale, 20 Nov. 1783, n. 1.

Lucy Porter

WEDNESDAY 10 MARCH 1784

MS: Hyde Collection.

Bolt court,
My Dearest Love: Fleetstreet, March 10, 1784

I will not suppose that it is for want of kindness that You did not answer my last letter,[1] and I therefore write again to tell You, that I have, by Gods great mercy, still continued to grow better. My Asthma is seldom troublesome, and my Dropsy has ran itself almost away, in a manner which my Physician says is very uncommon. I have been confined from the fourteen of December, and shall not soon venture abroad, but I have this day dressed my self as I was before my sickness.

If it be inconvenient to You to write, desire Mr. Pearson to let me know how You do and how You have passed this long Winter. I am now not without hopes that we shall once more see one another.

God bless You. Pray for me.

Make my compliments to Mrs. Cobb, and Miss Adey, and to all my friends, particularly to Mr. Pearson. I am, My dear, Your most humble servant,

SAM. JOHNSON

1. *Ante* To Lucy Porter, 23 Feb. 1784.

Hester Thrale

WEDNESDAY 10 MARCH 1784

MS: Hyde Collection.

ADDRESS: To Mrs. Thrale in Bath.

POSTMARK: 10 MR.

Madam: London, March 10, 1784

You know I never thought confidence with respect to futurity any part of the character of a brave, a wise, or a good man.[1] Bravery has no place where it can avail nothing, Wisdom impresses strongly the consciousness of those faults, of which it is itself perhaps an aggravation; and Goodness always wishing

1. *Ante* To Hester Thrale, 2 Mar. 1784.

to be better, and imputing every deficience to criminal negligence, and every fault to voluntary corruption, never dares to suppose the conditions of forgiveness fulfilled, nor what is wanting in the virtue supplied by Penitence.

This is the state[2] of the best, but what must be the condition of him whose heart will not suffer him to rank himself among the best, or among the good, such must be his dread of the approaching trial, as will[3] leave him little attention to the opinion of those whom he is leaving for ever, and the serenity that is not felt, it can be no virtue to feign.

The sarcocele ran off long ago, at an orifice made for mere experiment.[4]

The water passed naturally by God's mercy in a manner of which Dr. Heberden has seen but four examples.[5] The Chirurgeon has been employ[ed] to heal some excoriations, and four out of five are no longer under his care.[6] The Physicians laid on a blister,[7] and I ordered, by their consent, a salve,[8] but neither succeeded and neither was very easily healed.

I have been confined from the fourteenth of December, and know not when I shall get out, but I have this day dressed me, as I was dressed in health.

Your kind expressions gave me great pleasure, [do not] eject me from your thoughts. Shall we ever exchange confidence by the fireside again?

I hope dear Sophy is better,[9] and intend quickly to pay my debt to Susy.[10] I am, Madam, Your most humble servant,

SAM. JOHNSON

2. MS: "s" superimposed upon "c"
3. MS: "must" del. before "will"
4. *Ante* To John Mudge, 9 Sept. 1783, nn. 4, 6.
5. *Ante* To Lucy Porter, 23 Feb. 1784 and n. 1.
6. SJ refers to William Cruikshank.
7. MS: "a blister" altered from "blisters"
8. *Ante* To William Cruikshank, 13 Feb. 1784.
9. *Ante* To Hester Thrale, 20 Nov. 1783 and n. 1; 2 Mar. 1784.
10. *Ante* To Hester Thrale, 2 Mar. 1784.

Elizabeth Aston & Jane Gastrell

THURSDAY 11 MARCH 1784

MS: Pembroke College, Oxford.

Bolt court,
Dear Ladies: Fleetstreet, London, March 11, 1784

The kind and speedy answer with which you favoured me to my last letter, encourages me to hope, that You will be glad to hear again that my recovery advances. My Disorders are an Asthma and Dropsy. The Asthma gives me no great trouble when I am not in motion, and the water of the dropsy has passed away in so happy a manner, by the Goodness of God, as Dr. Heberden declares himself not to have known more than four times in all his practice. I have been confined to the house from December the fourteenth, and shall not venture out till the weather is settled, but I have this day dressed myself as before I became ill. Join with me[1] in returning thanks, and pray for me that the time now granted me, may not be ill spent.

Let me now, dear Ladies, have some account of you. Tell[2] me how You[3] have endured this long and sharp Winter, and give me hopes that we may all meet again with kindness and cheerfulness. I am, Dear Ladies, Your most humble Servant,

SAM. JOHNSON

1. MS: "me altered from "my"
2. MS: "L" partially erased before "T"
3. MS: "how the You"

Eva Maria Garrick & Hannah More

MONDAY 15 MARCH 1784

MS: Folger Shakespeare Library.

March 15

Mr. Johnson sends his respects to Mrs. Garrick and Miss Moor.

He has been confined to the house by diseases from Dec. 13 but is now much better, and hopes to wait on Mrs. Garrick in a few weeks, and to tell Miss Moor all that *envy* will suffer him to say of her last poem,[1] which Mrs. Reynolds showed him.

1. "I had a very civil note from Johnson about a week since. . . . He tells me he longs to see me, to praise the Bas Bleu as much as envy can praise" (William Roberts, *Memoirs of the Life and Correspondence of Mrs. Hannah More*, 1834, I.319). Although it was not published until 1786, *The Bas Bleu* was circulating in manuscript (*Post* To Hester Thrale, 19 Apr. 1784).

Hester Thrale

TUESDAY 16 MARCH 1784

MS: Hyde Collection.
ADDRESS: To Mrs. Thrale at Bath.
POSTMARK: 16 MR.

Dear Madam: London, March 16, 1784

I am so near to health as a mo[n]th ago I despaired of being. The dropsy is almost wholly run away, and the Asthma unless irritated by cold seldom attacks me. How I shall bear motion I do not yet know. But though I have little of pain, I am wonderfully weak. My muscles have almost lost all their spring, but I hope that warm weather when it comes will restore me. More than three months have I now been confined. But my deliverance has been very extraordinary.

Of one thing very remarkable I will tell you. For the Asthma and perhaps other disorders, my Physicians have advised the frequent use of opiates. I resisted them as much as I could, and complained that it made me almost delirious. This Dr. Heberden seemed not much to heed, but I was so weary of it that I tried when I could not wholly omit it, to diminish the dose, in which contrarily to the know[n] custom of the takers of opium, and beyond what it seemed reasonable to expect, I have so far succeeded, that having begun with three grains, a large quantity, I now appease the paroxysm, with a quarter of an ounce of diacodium estimated as equivalent only to half a grain, and this quantity it is now eight days since I took.

That I may send to Mrs. Lewis,[1] for when I shall venture out I do not know, you must let me know where she may be found, which you omitted to tell me.

I hope my dear Sophy will go on recovering.[2] But methinks Miss Thrale rather neglects me, suppose she should try to write me a little Latin Letter.

Do you however write to me often, and write kindly, perhaps we may sometime see each other. I am, Madam, Your most humble servant,

SAM. JOHNSON

1. SJ refers to Charlotte Cotterell Lewis.

2. *Ante* To Hester Thrale, 20 Nov. 1783, n. 1; 2 Mar. 1784.

James Boswell

THURSDAY 18 MARCH 1784

PRINTED SOURCE: JB's *Life*, 1791, II.482–83.

Dear Sir, London, March 18, 1784

I am too much pleased with the attention which you and your dear lady show to my welfare,[1] not to be diligent in letting you know the progress which I make towards health. The dropsy, by God's blessing, has now run almost totally away by natural evacuation; and the asthma, if not irritated by cold, gives me little trouble. While I am writing this, I have not any sensation of debility or disease. But I do not yet venture out, having been confined to the house from the thirteenth of December, now a quarter of a year.

When it will be fit for me to travel as far as Auchinleck, I am not able to guess; but such a letter as Mrs. Boswell's might draw any man, not wholly motionless, a great way. Pray tell

1. Margaret Boswell "had written him [SJ] a very kind letter" (JB's note: *Life* IV.264 n. 1).

the dear lady how much her civility and kindness have touched and gratified me.

Our parliamentary tumults have now begun to subside, and the King's authority is in some measure re-established.[2] Mr. Pitt will have great power; but you must remember, that what he has to give must, at least for some time, be given to those who gave, and those who preserve his power.[3] A new minister can sacrifice little to esteem or friendship; he must, till he is settled, think only of extending his interest.

* * * * * *

If you come hither through Edinburgh, send for Mrs. Stewart, and give from me another guinea for the letter in the old case, to which I shall not be satisfied with my claim, till she gives it me.[4]

Please to bring with you Baxter's Anacreon;[5] and if you procure heads of Hector Boece, the historian, and Arthur Johnston, the poet, I will put them in my room, or any other of the fathers of Scottish literature.

I wish you an easy and happy journey,[6] and hope I need not tell you that you will be welcome to, dear Sir, Your most affectionate humble servant,

SAM. JOHNSON

2. After the dismissal of the Coalition ministry, Dec. 1783, Charles James Fox's control of the House of Commons gradually declined. By early March William Pitt had garnered enough support to reduce Fox's majority to one vote. On 25 Mar. 1784 Parliament was dissolved and a general election called (J. S. Watson, *The Reign of George III*, 1960, pp. 268–70).

3. JB had sent Pitt a copy of his *Letter to the People of Scotland*, with a letter expressing his support for the new Ministry; Pitt replied with a warm acknowledgment. As a consequence, JB's hopes for political preferment were revived (*Life* IV.261 n. 3; *Later Years*, pp. 250–51).

4. *Ante* To JB, 27 Feb. 1784.

5. *Ante* To JB, *c.* 4 Feb. 1783 and n. 3.

6. JB left for London 22 Mar. In York, however, he learned of the dissolution of Parliament, and returned to Edinburgh on the 29th (*Boswell: The Applause of the Jury*, ed. I. S. Lustig and F. A. Pottle, 1981, pp. 196, 200; *Later Years*, p. 251). *Post* To JB, 30 Mar. 1784.

John Taylor

MONDAY 22 MARCH 1784

MS: Hyde Collection.

ADDRESS: To the Reverend Dr. Taylor in Ashbourne, Derbyshire.

POSTMARKS: 22 MR, 23 MR.

ENDORSEMENTS: 1784, 22 March 84.

Dear Sir: London, March 22, 1784

A Gentleman with a message from You called on me to day. You are, I find, not well, and I never hear of any disorder, but I hear of your bleeding. I am afraid lest you should bleed too often for a man that has ⟨*three or four words*⟩[1] year. I know not indeed the exigences nor the quantity taken away, but I can earnestly advise you to be very cautious.

I have, by such a blessing as I hope never to forget, been recovering now for several weeks; my [body] is in my opinion, and Dr. Heberden's entirely disburthened of the dropsical water; such a relief, which he dos not suppose to be at all owing to medecine, he has known, he says in all his practice to have happened [no] more than four times. I have now nothing of the dropsy remaining except that one leg is still a little tumid. My Asthma is certainly not cured but it is in my present course of life very rarely troublesome. How I shall bear exercise is yet to be tried; I have not been out of the house since the 13th of December. A ⟨*two words*⟩ confinement, but terminating, as my health now stands, more happily than I ever ventured to hope, for though the Physicians pertinaciously told me that I was not very near death, yet they did not think that I ever should recover, but imagined that my Soul would for some time, more or less inhabit an unwieldy, bloated half drowned body.

I have now by accident got a cold and cough, but am otherwise without any morbid sensation, except that I am very weak; but if no disease crosses the course of nature, my

1. MS: mutilated by heavy erasure

strength will return in the warm weather, from which, I suppose You may expect the same benefit.

I am sorry to hear that You are in doubt whether you can come to your residence.[2] Come, if You can. I am, Sir, yours affectionately,

SAM. JOHNSON

2. *Ante* To John Taylor, 23 Mar. 1775 and n. 1.

Susanna Thrale

THURSDAY 25 MARCH 1784

MS: The Earl of Shelburne.[1]

ADDRESS: ⟨To Miss S. A.⟩ Thrale ⟨at⟩ Bath.

POSTMARK: 25 MR.

My dearest Miss Susy:

Since You are resolved to stand it out, and keep *Mum* till you have,[2] I must at last comply, and indeed compliance costs me now no trouble, but as it irritates a cough, which I got, as You might ⟨have⟩ done, by standing at an open window, and w⟨hich has now harassed me many days, and is too strong for diacodium, nor has yet given much way to opium itself. However, having been so long used to so many worse things, I mind it but little. I have not bad nights; and my stomach has never failed me. But when I shall go abroad again, I know not.⟩

With Mr. Herschil it will certainly be very right to cultivate an acquaintance, for he can show You in the sky what no man before him has ever seen, by some wonderful improvements which he has made in the telescope.[3] What he has to show is

1. MS: badly mutilated; except for address, text in angle brackets from Piozzi, *Letters* II.356–57

2. H. L. Piozzi supplements this elliptical construction with "heard from me" (*Letters* II.356).

3. William Herschel (1738–1822), musician and astronomer, had constructed a telescope by which he had discovered the planet Uranus in 1781. "This famous astronomer, whose discoveries, or whose hope of future discoveries begin to fill

indeed a long way off, and perhaps concerns us but little, but all truth is valuable and all knowledge is pleasing in its first effects, and may be subsequently useful. Of whatever we see we always wish to know⟨; alway⟩s congratulate our selves when we know that of which ⟨we perceive another to be ignorant. Take therefore all opportunities of learning that offer themselves, however remote the matter may be from common life or common conversation. Look in Herschel's telescope; go into a chymist's laboratory; if you see a manufacturer at work, remark his operations. By this activity of attention, you will find in every place diversion and improvement.

Now dear Sophy is got well, what is it that ails my mistress? She complains, and complains, I am afraid, with too much cause; but I know not distinctly what is her disorder.[4] I hope that time and a quiet mind will restore her. I am, my dearest, Your, etc.⟩

---

the mouths of our Bath talkers, and I fancy my friend Mrs. Lewis could introduce me" (Piozzi, *Letters* II.336–37).

4. *Ante* To Susanna Thrale, 18 Nov. 1783 and n. 5.

Bennet Langton

SATURDAY 27 MARCH 1784

MS: Hyde Collection.

ADDRESS: To Benet Langton, Esq., in Rochester, Kent.

POSTMARK: 27 MR.

Dear Sir: London, March 27, 1784

Since You left me, I have continued in my own opinion and in Dr. Brocklesby's, to grow better[1] with respect to all my formidable and dangerous distempers, though to a body battered and shaken as mine has lately been, it is to be feared that weak attacks may be sometimes[2] mischievous. I have indeed by

1. MS: "better better" 2. MS: "sometimes sometimes"

standing carelessly at an open window, got a very troublesome cough, which it has been necessary to appease by[3] opium, in larger quantities, than I like to take and I have not found it give way so readily as I expected, its obstinacy however seems at[4] last disposed to submit to the remedy, and I know not,[5] whether I shall then have a right to complain of any morbid sensation. My Asthma is, I am afraid, constitutional, and incurable, but it is only occasional, and unless it be excited by labour or by cold, gives me no molestation, nor does it lay very close siege to life, for Sir John Floyer, whom the physical race consider, as authour of one of the best books upon it,[6] panted on to ninety, as was supposed; and why were we content with supposing a fact so interesting of a man so conspicuous, because he corrupted, at perhaps seventy or eighty, the register, that he might pass for younger than he was.[7] He was not much less than eighty, when to a man of rank who modestly asked him his age. He answered—Go, look, though he[8] was in general a man of civility and elegance.

The Ladies I find are at your house all well, except Miss Langton,[9] who will probably soon recover her health, by light suppers. Let her eat at dinner as she will, but not take a full stomach to bed. Pay my sincere respects to the two principal Ladies in your house, and when you write to[10] dear Miss Langton in Lincolnshire let her know that I mean not to break our league of friendship, and that I have a set of lives for her, when I have the means of sending it.[11] I am, Sir, Your most humble servant,

SAM. JOHNSON

3. MS: "appease by appease by"

4. MS: "at" repeated as catchword 5. MS: "not not"

6. John Floyer (1649–1734), Kt., Lichfield physician, author of *Treatise on the Asthma* (1698). It was Floyer who recommended that the two and one-half-year-old SJ be touched by Queen Anne for scrofula (*Life* I.42; Clifford, 1955, pp. 9–12).

7. The parish register entry for Floyer's birth had been corrected, giving rise to the story that Floyer had tampered with it (*Life* IV.528).

8. MS: "he" repeated as catchword

9. SJ refers to Bennet Langton's eldest daughter, Mary.

10. MS: "write to write to"

11. SJ refers to Bennet Langton's eldest sister, Elizabeth.

William Adams

TUESDAY 30 MARCH 1784

MS: Chapman III.147–48.

ADDRESS: To the Reverend Dr. Adams at Pembroke College, Oxford.

POSTMARK: 30 MR.

Sir: London, Bolt c⟨ourt⟩, March 30, 1784

In my letter to you of the miscarriage of which I can no⟨t⟩ account, was inclosed a letter from the Prior of the Benedictines,[1] informing me, that the collation of the manuscripts in the King's library at Paris for the use of Dr. Edwards is finished,[2] and that of the manuscripts two had never been collated before, and to desire directions how to transmit the papers.

The letter came to me when I was very hard beset with an As[t]hma and a Dropsy, from both which the Goodness of God has very much relieved me. Of the Dropsy my Physicians seem to think ⟨me⟩ quite recovered, and the Ashma is not very troublesome. I did not however neglect the latter, though my attention has happened to be useless.

The Prior ought to have an answer. The book being printed, almost all the expence is already incurred, and the addition of so many various readings will of itself make it valuable. Thus we shall complete the desire and preserve the memory of our friend, of a man whom I never found deficient in any offices of civility. The collators must, I suppose, be paid. My Guinea is ready.

You, Sir, must, I think write to Dr. Owen to send me the necessary intelligence.[3] I cannot wait on him, having never

1. SJ refers to Father William Cowley.

2. Edward Edwards had requested such a collation for his edition of Xenophon's *Memorabilia*, then in press (*Life* III.529). Three manuscripts out of the eleven examined for the edition came from the King's Library in Paris (*Memorabilia*, 1785, pp. iii–v).

3. Henry Owen (1716–95), M.D., Rector of St. Olave, London (1760–94), and of Edmonton, Middlesex (1775–95), was revising Edwards's edition as it went

been beyond the door from the 13th of December. I have however not suffered any sharp pain.

Younger Men die daily about me. I much regret the loss of Dr. Wheeler.[4] O God when thou shalt call me, receive me to thy mercy for Jesus Christ's sake.

I have not forgotten the kindness with which Miss Adams invited me to Oxford. I hope to see you in the Summer for a few days.[5] But a sick Man is a very perverse being, he gives much trouble, he receives many favours, yet is never pleased and not often thankful. I wil try however when I come to leave both the miseries and vices of disease behind me. I am, Sir, Your most humble Serva⟨nt⟩,

SAM. JOHNSON

---

through the press (*Life* III.529; *GM* 1795, p. 884; *Ante* To Edward Edwards, 2 Nov. 1778, n. 5).

4. *Ante* To Hester Thrale, 20 Aug. 1783.

5. SJ spent 3–16 June with Adams in Oxford (*Life* IV.283, 285, 311; *Post* To Hester Thrale, 17 June 1784).

James Boswell

TUESDAY 30 MARCH 1784

PRINTED SOURCE: JB's *Life*, 1791, II.483–84.

Dear Sir, London, March 30, 1784

You could do nothing so proper as to haste back when you found the Parliament dissolved.[1] With the influence which your address must have gained you, it may reasonably be expected that your presence will be of importance, and your activity of effect.[2]

Your solicitude for me gives me that pleasure which every

---

1. *Ante* To JB, 18 Mar. 1784, n. 6.

2. JB had been the driving force behind Ayrshire's loyal address to George III, which supported the King's dismissal of the Coalition and his appointment of William Pitt as Prime Minister (*Life* IV.265; *Boswell: The Applause of the Jury*, ed. I. S. Lustig and F. A. Pottle, 1981, pp. 193–94).

man feels from the kindness of such a friend; and it is with delight I relieve it by telling, that Dr. Brocklesby's account is true, and that I am, by the blessing of God, wonderfully relieved.

You are entering upon a transaction which requires much prudence.[3] You must endeavour to oppose without exasperating; to practise temporary hostility, without producing enemies for life. This is, perhaps, hard to be done; yet it has been done by many, and seems most likely to be effected by opposing merely upon general principles, without descending to personal or particular censures or objections. One thing I must enjoin you, which is seldom observed in the conduct of elections; —I must entreat you to be scrupulous in the use of strong liquors. One night's drunkenness may defeat the labours of forty days well employed. Be firm, but not clamorous; be active, but not malicious; and you may form such an interest, as may not only exalt yourself, but dignify your family.

We are, as you may suppose, all busy here. Mr. Fox resolutely stands for Westminster, and his friends say will carry the election. However that be, he will certainly have a seat.[4] Mr. Hoole has just told me, that the city leans towards the King.

Let me hear, from time to time, how you are employed, and what progress you make.

Make dear Mrs. Boswell, and all the young Boswells, the sincere compliments of, Sir, your affectionate humble servant,

SAM. JOHNSON

3. JB "had some intention" of standing for Parliament (*Life* IV.265), but in the event decided against doing so (*Later Years*, p. 253).

4. Opposing Fox at Westminster were Sir Cecil Wray (1734–1805), Bt., of Fillingham, Lincolnshire, and Admiral Lord Samuel Hood (1724–1806), the celebrated naval hero (Namier and Brooke II.636, III.663). Because Hood's popularity guaranteed him election, the contest centered on Fox and Wray, who had the backing of the Ministry. When the poll closed on 17 May, after an inflammatory campaign, Fox and Hood had won pluralities; however, Wray called for a scrutiny of the vote. In the interim, Fox sat for Kirkwall, Tain Burghs, Scotland. In Feb. 1785 he and Hood were declared the winners, and took their seats for Westminster (Loren Reid, *Charles James Fox*, 1969, pp. 199–205, 212).

Charlotte Lewis

SUNDAY 4 APRIL 1784

MS: Hyde Collection.

ADDRESS: To Mrs. Lewis.

Dear Madam: Bolt court, Fleetstreet, Apr. 4, 1784

That You had left Bath, and were gone[1] to town, I had heard from Mrs. Thrale; but She did not tell me where I might find You.

I hope You do not think that I have forgotten, or can forget Miss Charlotte Cotterel. But as we are both ill, the first visit must be paid by him or her who goes first abroad. I have been confined longer than a quarter of a year, and my Physicians on this day have forbidden me to go out for some time to come.

If You can dine with me, name your day. I will invite Mr. Sastres to meet You, and we will be as cheerful as we can, together, and as soon as I can, I will come to You. I am, Madam, Your most humble Servant,

SAM. JOHNSON

1. MS: "gone gone"

William Bowles

MONDAY 5 APRIL 1784

MS: Hyde Collection.

ADDRESS: To W. Bowles, Esq., at Heale near Salisbury.

POSTMARK: 6 AP.

Dear Sir: London, Apr. 5, 1784[1]

My Health appears both to my Physicians and my self to grow in the main every day better and better notwithstanding the unusual length and ruggedness of the winter. I have known Winters that had greater cold than we have felt in this; such

1. MS: "1748"

as those in which the great rivers and æstuaries have frozen, and in which very deep snows have lain very long upon the ground; but I remember no Winter that has encroached so much upon the Spring, or continued such severity so long beyound the Equinox. Here will be a season lost. The physical, though not the astronomical, Summer begins in May, *a Geminis æstas* says Manilius,[2] and Winter yet keeps fast hold of April. But the Sun will prevail at last.

Relating to the club leave the business to me.[3] The basis of our constitution is commodiousness. You may come for sixpence, and stay away for threepence. This week the club does not meet.[4]

I am pleased with Collins's project.[5] My friend Sir John Hawkins, a man of very diligent enquiry and very wide intelligence, has been collecting materials for the completion of Walton's lives, of which one is the life of Herbert.[6] I will tell him of the edition intended and he will probably suggest some improvements.

It does not occur to me how I can write a preface to which it can be proper to put my name, and I am not to sink my own value without raising at least proportionally that of the book. This is therefore to be considered. I am, Dear Sir, Your most humble Servant,

SAM. JOHNSON

You will make my compliments to Mrs. Bowles; to your Father who is, I hope, recovered; to your Young people; and to all, and when I leave out services and compliment, you must suppose them.

2. *aestas a Geminis, autumnus Virgine surgit*: "summer comes with the Twins, autumn with the Virgin" (Manilius, *Astronomica* II.266, trans. G. P. Goold, Loeb ed.).

3. *Ante* To Joshua Reynolds, 4 Dec. 1783; *Ante* To William Bowles, 23 Feb. 1784.

4. *Ante* To Hester Maria Thrale, 31 Jan. 1784, n. 7.

5. The Rev. John Collins (1741–97), impecunious Shakespearean commentator, appears to have been planning an edition of George Herbert's poetry. There is no record of the publication of such a project.

6. According to B. H. Davis, these "materials were never brought together in a published volume" (*A Proof of Eminence: The Life of Sir John Hawkins*, 1973, p. 321).

Ozias Humphry[1]

MONDAY 5 APRIL 1784

MS: Houghton Library.

ADDRESS: To Mr. Humphrey in Newman Street, Oxford Road.

Sir: Bolt court, Fleet street, Ap. 5, 1784

Mr. Hoole has told me with what benevolence You listened to a request which I was almost afraid to make, of leave to a young Painter to attend you from time to time in your painting room, to see your operations, and receive your instructions.

The young Man has perhaps good parts, but has been without any regular education; He is my Godson,[2] and therefore I interest my self in his progress and success, and shall think my self much favoured, if I receive from You a permission to send him.[3]

My health is, by Gods blessing, much restored, but I am not yet allowed by the Physicians to go abroad, nor indeed do I think myself yet able to endure the weather. I am, Sir, your most humble servant,

SAM. JOHNSON

1. Ozias Humphry (1743–1810), later (1791) R.A., portrait painter. Humphry, who had known SJ since 1764 (*Johns. Misc.* II.400), "executed a beautiful miniature in enamel" based on Reynolds's portrait of 1769 (*Life* IV.421 n. 2, 449).

2. SJ refers to Charles Paterson.

3. *Post* To Ozias Humphry, 13 Apr. 1784; 31 May 1784.

Bennet Langton

THURSDAY 8 APRIL 1784

MS: Hyde Collection.

ADDRESS: To Benet Langton, Esq., in Rochester, Kent.

POSTMARK: 8 AP.

Dear Sir: London, Apr. 8, 1784

I am still disturbed by my cough, but what thanks have I not [to] pay, when my cough is the most painful sensation that I feel, and from that I expect hardly to be released, while winter continues to gripe us with so much pertinacity.[1] The year has[2] now advanced eighteen days beyond the equinox, and still there is very little remission of the cold. When warm weather comes, which surely must come at last, I hope it will help both me and your young Lady.

The Man so busy about addresses is neither more nor less than our own Boswel, who had come as far as York towards London, but turned back on the dissolution, and is said now to stand for some place.[3] Whether they wish him success, his best Friends hesitate.

Let me have your prayers for the completion of my recovery, I am now better than I ever expected to have been. May God add to his mercies the Grace that may enable me to use them according to his will.

My Compliments to All. I am, Sir, Your most affectionate, humble servant,

SAM. JOHNSON

1. MS: "pertinacity" superimposed upon undeciphered erasure

2. MS: "has has"

3. *Ante* To JB, 18 Mar. 1784, n. 6; 30 Mar. 1784 and nn. 2, 3.

John Nichols

MONDAY 12 APRIL 1784

MS: Hyde Collection.

ENDORSEMENT: Dr. Johnson, April 12, 1784 (with Plan of Ignoramus).

Sir: Apr. 12, 1784

I have sent You inclosed a very curious proposal from Mr. Hawkins, the son of Sir John Hawkins,[1] who, I believe, will

1. John Sidney Hawkins (1757–1842), elder son of Sir John, was preparing an edition of *Ignoramus*, a Latin comedy by George Ruggle (1575–1622). In his proposals (which were corrected by SJ) Hawkins discussed the advantages of a careful collation of manuscripts and printed texts, and explained the need for copious annotation (MS: Hyde Collection). Hawkins's edition appeared in 1787, published

take [care] that whatever his son promises shall be performed.[2]

If you are inclined to publish this compilation the Editor will agree for an Edition on the follow[ing] terms which I think liberal enough.

That You shall print the Book at your own charge.

That the sale shall be wholly for your benefit till your expences be repaid; except that at the time of publication You shall put into the hands of the Editor without price . . . copies, for his Friends.

That when You have been repaid, the profit arising from the sale of the remaining copies shall be divided equally between You and the Editor.

That the Edition shall not comprise fewer than five hundred. I am, Sir, Your most humble Servant,

SAM. JOHNSON

---

by Nichols (*Lit. Anec.* IX.35–36; B. H. Davis, *A Proof of Eminence: The Life of Sir John Hawkins*, 1973, pp. 62, 366).

2. Nichols noted, "It is but justice to declare that every part of the engagement was punctually fulfilled" (*Lit. Anec.* IX.36).

Frances Reynolds

MONDAY 12 APRIL 1784

MS: Hyde Collection.

ENDORSEMENT: Dr. Johnson, Apr. 12, 84.

Dear Madam: Apr. 12

I am not yet able to wait on You, but I can do your business commodiously enough. You must send me the copy to show the printer.[1] If You will come to tea this afternoon, we will talk together about it. Pray send me word whether You will come. I am, Madam, Your most humble servant,

SAM. JOHNSON

1. It is likely that SJ refers to Reynolds's "Enquiry Concerning the Principles of Taste" (*Ante* To Frances Reynolds, 21 July 1781 and nn. 1, 2).

John Taylor

MONDAY 12 APRIL 1784

MS: Berg Collection, New York Public Library.

ADDRESS: To the Revd. Dr. Taylor in Ashbourn, Derbyshire.

POSTMARKS: 12 AP, 13 AP.

ENDORSEMENTS: 1784, 12 April 84, very fine.

Dear Sir: London, Easter Monday, April 12, 1784

What can be the reason that I hear nothing from You? I hope nothing disables You from writing. What I have seen, and what I have felt, gives me reason to fear every thing. Do not omit giving me the comfort of knowing that after all my losses I have yet a friend left.

I want every comfort. My Life is very solitary and very cheerless. Though it has pleased [God] wonderfully to deliver me from the Dropsy,[1] I am yet very weak, and have not passed the door since the 13th of December. I hope for some help from warm weather, which will surely come in time.

I could not have the consent of the Physicians to go to Church yesterday; I therefore received the holy Sacrament at home, in the room where I communicated with dear Mrs. Williams a little before her death.[2] O, my Friend, the approach of Death is very dreadful. I am afraid to think on that which I know, I cannot avoid. It is vain to look round and round, for that help which cannot be had. Yet we hope and hope, and fancy that he who has lived to day may live tomorrow. But let us learn to derive our hope only from God.

In the mean time let us be kind to one another. I have no Friend now living but You and Mr. Hector that was the friend of my youth. Do not neglect, Dear Sir, yours affectionately,

SAM. JOHNSON

1. "Almighty God, my Creator and my Judge, who givest life and takest it away, enable me to return sincere and humble thanks for my late deliverance from imminent death" (SJ's Easter prayer, 11 Apr. 1784, *Works* 1.368). *Ante* To Lucy Porter, 23 Feb. 1784, n. 1.

2. *Ante* To Hester Thrale, 20 Aug. 1783.

Ozias Humphry

TUESDAY 13 APRIL 1784

MS: Hyde Collection.

ADDRESS: To Mr. Humphry.

Sir: Bolt court, Apr. 13, 1784

The Bearer is my Godson whom[1] I take the liberty of recommending to your kindness, which I hope he will deserve by his respect to your excellence, and his gratitude for your favours.[2] I am, Sir, Your most humble servant,

SAM. JOHNSON

1. MS: "w" superimposed upon "t"
2. *Ante* To Ozias Humphry, 5 Apr. 1784.

Lord Portmore[1]

TUESDAY 13 APRIL 1784

MS: Hyde Collection.

ADDRESS: To the Right Honourable Earl of Portmore.

Bolt court, Fleetstreet, Apr. 13, 1784

Dr. Johnson acknowledges with great respect the honour of Lord Portmore's notice. He is better than he was; and will as his Lordship directs, write to Mr. Langton.[2]

1. Charles Colyear (1700–1785), second Earl of Portmore, M.P. for Andover (1727–30) (G.E.C., *Complete Peerage*, 1926, x.605). Lord Portmore and Bennet Langton knew each other through business dealings (the Wey Navigation scheme) and through family alliances (Portmore's son had married Lady Rothes's stepdaughter) (Fifer, pp. lix–lx).
2. *Post* To Bennet Langton, 13 Apr. 1784.

Bennet Langton

TUESDAY 13 APRIL 1784

MS: Hyde Collection.

ADDRESS: To Benet Langton, Esq., in Rochester, Kent.

POSTMARK: 13 AP.

Dear Sir: Easter Tuesday, Apr. 13, 1784

I had this evening a note from Lord Portmore, desiring that I would give You an account of my health.[1] You might have had it with less circumduction.[2] I am, by God's Blessing, I think, free from all morbid sensations, except a cough, which is only troublesome. But I am still weak, and can have no great hope of strength till the weather shall be softer. The summer, if it be kindly, will, I hope, enable me to support the winter. God, who has so wonderfully restored me, can preserve me in all seasons.

Let me enquire in my turn after the state of your family, great and little. I hope Lady Rothes and Miss Langton are both well.[3] That is a good basis of content. Then how goes George on with his Studies? How does Miss Mary?[4] and how does my own Jenny? I think, I owe Jenny a Letter, which I will take care to pay.[5] In the mean time tell her that I acknowledge the debt.

Be pleased to make my compliments to the Ladies.[6] If Mrs. Langton comes to London, she will favour me with a visit, for I am not well enough to go out. I am, Sir, your most humble servant,

SAM. JOHNSON

1. *Ante* To Lord Portmore, 13 Apr. 1784.

2. *circumduction*: "a leading about" (SJ's *Dictionary*).

3. *Ante* To Bennet Langton, 27 Mar. 1784 and n. 9.

4. *Ante* To Bennet Langton, 27 Mar. 1784 and n. 9.

5. *Post* To Jane Langton, 10 May 1784.

6. SJ refers to Langton's mother (Diana) and his eldest sister (Elizabeth), who lived in Lincolnshire. *Ante* To Bennet Langton, 27 Mar. 1784.

John Perkins

TUESDAY 13 APRIL 1784

MS: Hyde Collection.
ADDRESS: To Mr. Perkins.

Dear Sir: Apr. 13, 1784

The kindness which [you] and Mrs. Perkins, I hope, have for me, will dispose You to hear with pleasure, that, though not yet able to go abroad, I am totally, I think, recovered by God's Blessing from the dropsy, and find all my complaints very much alleviated.

I have now fifteen pounds due to me, from which must be deducted, what you paid for me of the tax on Servants,[1] and what I owe You for two chaldrons of coals, I think they were two, if they were more deduct the difference.

I hope that Mr. Barclay is recovered from his late disorder,[2] and that Mrs. Perkins and yourself, and all your young people are well. I am, Sir, Your most humble Servant,

SAM. JOHNSON

1. According to the provisions of 17 George III, *c.* 39 (1777), an employer was required to pay an annual assessment of 21*s.* for each male servant (*Statutes at Large*, ed. Owen Ruffhead, 1763–1800, XIII.103).

2. SJ refers to Robert Barclay.

Bolt court, April 13, 1784

You will be pleased to send me what you find due to me any day this week, unless you can be so kind as to call, and bring it.

Hester Thrale

THURSDAY 15 APRIL 1784

MS: Hyde Collection.
ADDRESS: To Mrs. Thrale at Bath.
POSTMARK: 15 AP.

Dear Madam: London, Apr. 15, 1784

Yesterday I had the pleasure of giving another din[n]er to the remainder of the old Club.[1] We used to meet weekly about the year fifty, and we were as cheerful as in former times; only I could not make quite so much noise, for since the paralytick affliction my voice is sometimes weak.[2]

Metcalf and Cruchley without knowing each other are both members of parliament for Horsham in Sussex. Mr. Cator is chosen for Ipswich.[3]

But a sick man's thoughts soon turn back upon himself. I am still very weak, though my appetite is keen, and my digestion potent, and I gratify myself more at table than ever I did at my own cost before. I have now an inclination to luxury which even your table did not excite, for till now my talk was more about the dishes than my thoughts. I remember You commended me for seeming pleased with my din[n]ers, when You had reduced, your table; I am able to tell You with great veracity, that I never knew when the reduction began, nor should have known that it was made, had not you told me. I now think and consult to day what I shall eat to morrow. This disease likewise will, I hope be cured. For there are other things, how different! which ought to predominate in the mind of such a man as I, but in this world the body will [have] its part, and my hope is that it shall have no more, my hope but not my confidence. I have only the timidity of a Christian[4] to deter me, not the wisdom of a Stoick to secure me.[5]

I hope all my Dears are well. They should not be too nice in requiring letters. If my Sweet Queeney writes more Letters

1. *Ante* To John Hawkins, 22 Nov. 1783 and n. 1; 3 Dec. 1783.

2. *Ante* To Edmund Allen, 17 June 1783; *Ante* To Hester Thrale, 30 June 1783; *Ante* To Lucy Porter, 5 July 1783.

3. John Cator's election was declared void 18 June 1784 (Namier and Brooke I.380).

4. MS: "an" repeated as catchword

5. SJ viewed Stoic "wisdom" with marked skepticism; see *Rambler* No. 32 for his caustic comments on the "wild enthusiastick virtue" of the "scholars of Zeno" (*Works*, Yale ed. III.174).

like her last,[6] when Franks come in again I will correct them and return them.[7] I am, Madam, your most humble Servant,

SAM. JOHNSON

6. Queeney Thrale may well have acted on SJ's suggestion to write him in Latin (*Ante* To Hester Thrale, 16 Mar. 1784).

7. The franking privilege accorded M.P.s was in abeyance until the new Parliament opened 18 May 1784. During the last years of his life SJ turned regularly to William Strahan for franked covers.

Hester Thrale

MONDAY 19 APRIL 1784

MS: National Portrait Gallery, London.
ADDRESS: To Mrs. Thrale at Bath.

Dear Madam: London, Apr. 19, 1784

I received in the Morning your magnificent Fish, and in the afternoon your apology for not sending it.[1] I have invited the Hooles and Miss Burney to dine upon it to-morrow.[2]

The Club which has been lately instituted is at Sam's, and there was I when I was last out of the house.[3] But the people whom I mentioned in my letter are the remnant of a little Club that used to meet in Ivy Lane about three and thirty years ago,[4] out of which we have lost Ha[w]kesworth and Dyer, the rest are yet on this side the grave.[5] Our meetings now are serious and, I think, on all parts tender.

Miss Moore has written a poem called Le Bas blue which is in my opinion, a very great performance.[6] It wanders about in manuscript, and surely will soon find its way to Bath.

1. "Your comical Account of your own Voracity reached me just as the Salmons came in today, pray accept this very fine one till Pipers and Dorees come in" (Hester Thrale to SJ, 17 Apr. 1784, MS: Rylands Library).

2. *Post* To Hester Thrale, 21 Apr. 1784.

3. *Ante* To Joshua Reynolds, 4 Dec. 1783 and n. 1.

4. *Ante* To John Hawkins, 22 Nov. 1783 and n. 1; *Ante* To Hester Thrale, 15 Apr. 1784.

5. *Ante* To Hester Thrale, 13 Dec. 1783 and n. 6.

6. *Ante* To Eva Maria Garrick and Hannah More, 15 Mar. 1784 and n. 1.

I shall be glad of another Letter from my dear Queeny, the former was not much to be censured.[7] The reckoning between me and Miss Sophy is out of my head. She must write to tell me how it stands.

I am sensible of the ease that your repayment of Mr. Crutchley has given,[8] you felt yourself *genée* by that debt, is there an English word for it?

As you do not[9] now use your books, be pleased to let Mr. Cator know that I may borrow what I want. I think at present to take only Calmet,[10] and the Greek Anthology. When I lay sleepless, I used to drive the night along, by turning Greek Epigrams into Latin. I know not if I have not turned a hundred.[11]

It is now time to return you thanks for your present. Since I was sick I know not if I have not had more delicacies sent me, than[12] I had ever seen, till I saw your table.

It was ⟨always⟩ Dr. Heberden's enquiry whether my appetite for food continued. It indeed never failed me, for he considered the cessation of appetite, as the despair of Nature yielding up her power to the force of the disease. I am, Madam, your most humble servant,

SAM. JOHNSON

7. Hester Thrale had informed SJ, "Your Pupil says She will soon hatch up another Letter at least as good as the last" (17 Apr. 1784, MS: Rylands Library). *Ante* To Hester Thrale, 15 Apr. 1784 and n. 6.

8. Hester Thrale had borrowed £300 from Jeremiah Crutchley to help arrive at the financial settlement with Lady Salusbury (*Ante* To Hester Thrale, 30 Nov. 1782, n. 1; *Thraliana* 1.562).

9. MS: "not not"

10. *Ante* To Frederick Barnard, 28 May 1768, n. 33.

11. The posthumous edition of SJ's Latin poems prepared by Bennet Langton includes translations of ninety-eight epigrams; for most of these it is clear that SJ used Brodaeus's edition of the *Anthology* (Basle, 1549) (*Poems*, pp. 241–59).

12. MS: "than" altered from "that"

Hester Thrale

WEDNESDAY 21 APRIL 1784

MS: Hyde Collection.

ADDRESS: To Mrs. Thrale at Bath.

POSTMARK: 21 AP.

Dear Madam: London, Apr. 21, 1784

I make hast[e] to send you intelligence which if I do not still flatter myself, you will not receive without some degree of pleasure. After a confinement of one hundred twenty nine days, more than the third part of a year, and no inconsiderable part of human life, I this day returned thanks to God in St. Clement's Church, for my recovery, a recovery in my seventy fifth year from a distemper which few in the vigour of youth are known to surmount; a recovery of which neither myself, my friends, nor my physicians had any hope, for though the[y] flattered me[1] [with] some continuance of life, they never supposed[2] that I could cease to be dropsical. The Dropsy however, is quite vanished, and the Asthma so much mitigated, that I walked to day with a more easy respiration than I have known, I think, for perhaps two years past. I hope the Mercy that lengthens my days, will assist me to use them well.[3]

The Hooles, Miss Burney, and Mrs. Hall (Wesly's sister) feasted yesterday with me very cheerfully on your noble salmon.[4] Mr. Allen could not come, and I sent him a piece, and a great tail is still left.

Dr. Brocklesby forbids the club at present, not caring to venture the chilness of the evening, but I purpose to show myself

1. MS: "my"

2. MS: "sup" repeated as catchword

3. The following month SJ "communicated" to JB, "with solemn earnestness, a very remarkable circumstance which had happened in the course of his illness, when he was much distressed by the dropsy. He had shut himself up, and employed a day in particular exercises of religion,—fasting, humiliation, and prayer. On a sudden he obtained extraordinary relief, for which he looked up to Heaven with grateful devotion" (*Life* IV.271–72).

4. *Ante* To Hester Thrale, 19 Apr. 1784 and n. 1.

on Saturday at [the] Academy's feast;[5] I cannot publish my return to the world more effectually, for, as the Frenchman says, *tout le monde s'y trouvera.*

For this occasion I ordered some cloaths, and was told by the taylor, that when he brough[t] me a sick dress,[6] he never expected to make me any thing of any other kind. My recovery is indeed wonderful. I am, Dear Madam, Your most humble servant,

SAM. JOHNSON

5. *Ante* To Mauritius Lowe, 28 Apr. 1778, n. 3; *Post* To Hester Thrale, 26 Apr. 1784.

6. *Ante* To Hester Thrale, 9 Feb. 1784.

Lucy Porter

MONDAY 26 APRIL 1784

PRINTED SOURCE: JB's *Life*, ed. Malone, 1804, IV.291.

My Dear, London, April 26, 1784

I write to you now, to tell you that I am so far recovered that on the 21st I went to church, to return thanks, after a confinement of more than four long months.[1]

My recovery is such as neither myself nor the physicians at all expected, and its such as that very few examples have been known of the like. Join with me, my dear love, in returning thanks to God.

Dr. Vyse has been with [me] this evening; he tells me that you likewise have been much disordered, but that you are now better. I hope that we shall sometime have a cheerful interview. In the mean time let us pray for one another. I am, Madam, Your humble servant,

SAM. JOHNSON

1. Cf. *Ante* To Hester Thrale, 21 Apr. 1784.

Hester Thrale

MONDAY 26 APRIL 1784

MS: Hyde Collection; dateline, complimentary close, and signature supplied from H. G. Commin Catalogue No. 549, p. 17.

ADDRESS: ⟨To⟩ Mrs. Thrale at Bath.

POSTMARK: 26 AP.

Madam: London, Apr. 26, 1784

On saturday I showed myself again to the living world at the exhibition, much and splendid was the Company;[1] But like the Doge of Genoa at Paris I admired nothing but myself.[2] I went up all the stairs to the Pictures without stopping to rest or to breathe, "In[3] all the madness of superfluous Health."[4]

The Prince of Wales had promised to be there, but when we had waited an hour and half, sent us word that He could not come.

My cough still torments me, but it is only a cough and much less oppressive than some of former times, but it disturbs my nights.

Mrs. Davenant called to pay me a Guinea, but I gave two for You. Whatever reasons You have for frugality, it[5] is not worth while to save a Guinea a year by withdrawing it from a publick charity.

I know not whether I told You that my old Friend Mrs. Cotterel, now no longer Miss, has called to see me.[6] Mrs. Lewis is not well.

Mrs. Davenant says that You regain your Health. That You regain your health, is more than a common recovery, because I infer that you regain your peace of mind. Settle your thoughts, and control your imagination, and think no more of

1. *Ante* To Hester Thrale, 21 Apr. 1784.

2. *Ante* To Hester Thrale, 30 Sept. 1773 and n. 41.

3. MS: "I" superimposed upon "i"

4. "In all the madness of superfluous health" (Pope, *Essay on Man* III.3).

5. MS: "it" altered from "is"

6. Frances Cotterell had never married, but having reached middle age, she was entitled to be addressed as "Mrs." (cf. "Mrs." Lucy Porter).

Hesperian felicity.[7] Gather yourself and your Children into a little system, in which each may promote the ease, the safety, and the pleasure of the rest.

Mr. Howard called on Me a few days ago, and gave the new Edition much enlarged of his account of prisons.[8] He has been to survey the prisons on the continent, and in Spain tried to penetrate the dungeons of the Inquisition, but his curiosity was very imperfectly gratified. At Madrid, they shut him quite out; at Villadolid, they showed him some publick rooms.[9]

While I am writing the post has brought your kind letter. Do not think with dejection of your own condition; a little patience will probably give You health, it will certainly give you riches, and all the accommodations that riches can procure. I am, Madam, Your most humble Servant,

SAM. JOHNSON

7. It cannot be established conclusively how much SJ knew, or suspected, of the details of Hester Thrale's involvement with Gabriel Piozzi. Speaking to JB on 16 May, SJ showed concern about what he considered a misguided attachment, but spoke as if the episode were over—"there was an Italian singer" (*Boswell: The Applause of the Jury*, ed. I. S. Lustig and F. A. Pottle, 1981, p. 213). However, according to Frances Burney, writing to Queeney on 24 May, "he [SJ] knows the whole affair" (*The Queeney Letters*, ed. The Marquis of Lansdowne, 1934, p. 97). As J. C. Riely observes, this statement "can only be interpreted as meaning that Johnson now knew of Mrs. Thrale's unabated passion for Piozzi and probably also of his returning to England" ("Johnson's Last Years with Mrs. Thrale: Facts and Problems," *Bulletin of the John Rylands University Library* 57, 1974, p. 208). Yet SJ's "anguish and astonishment" at the news of the marriage suggest that he had not anticipated (or allowed himself to anticipate) the probable outcome of events (*Post* To Hester Maria Thrale, 1 July 1784; *Post* To Hester Thrale, 2 July 1784).

8. John Howard (?1726–90), philanthropist and reformer of hospitals and prisons. The third edition of his *The State of the Prisons of England and Wales* (1777) appeared in 1784 (Greene, 1975, p. 70).

9. In 1783 Howard had attempted unsuccessfully to examine the cells used by the Inquisition in Portugal and Spain. In Lisbon he saw nothing, in Madrid he was shown the tribunal room but not the prison, and in Valladolid he managed to view various parts of the prison itself (D. L. Howard, *John Howard: Prison Reformer*, 1958, pp. 102–3).

Frances Reynolds

FRIDAY 30 APRIL 1784

MS: Hyde Collection.

ADDRESS: To Mrs. Reynolds.

ENDORSEMENT: Dr. Johnson, Ap. 30, 84.

Dear Madam: Bolt court, Apr. 30, 1784

Mr. Allen has looked over the papers and thinks that one hundred copies will come to five pounds.[1]

Fifty will cost 4£ 10s. and five and twenty will cost 4£ 5s. It seems therefore scarcely worth while to print fewer than a hundred.

Suppose You printed 250 at 6£ 10. and without any name tried the sale, which may be secretly done. You would then see the opinion of the publick without hazard, if nobody knows but I. If any body else is in the secret, you shall not have my consent to venture. I am, Dear Madam, Your most affectionate, and most humble Servant,

SAM. JOHNSON

1. *Ante* To Frances Reynolds, 12 Apr. 1784 and n. 1. Apparently publication was delayed for another year (*Ante* To Frances Reynolds, 21 July 1781, n. 2; *Post* To Frances Reynolds, 28 May 1784).

William Bowles

MONDAY 3 MAY 1784

MS: Houghton Library.

ADDRESS: To W. Bowles, Esq., at Heale near Salisbury.

POSTMARK: 3 MA.

Dear Sir: London, May 3, 1784

Your attention to me in my acquaintance with you, gives you a right to be told that after a confinement of more than four months I was at Church on the 21st, to present myself before God after my recovery, such a recovery as my Physicians have very rarely seen.[1] I have since been a little abroad, and was again at the Club, a few days ago.

I suppose you had a copy[2] of the Statutes,[3] and therefore know that every Absentee forfeits threepence a night.[4] The forfeit is so small that no excuse is ever made. I paid regularly during my long ilness. Your forfeits now amount to six shillings, which I purpose to pay for you, and to continue to pay as they rise, for it is better not to suffer those ludicrous expences ever to amount to much at a time.

I am, I think, and so think the Physicians, quite free from the dropsy, and the Asthma, though not cured, troubles me but little. But I am very weak in my limbs, from a false step I do not easily recover. I walked however a few days ago to the picture room in the Academy without stopping to rest or breathe.[5] I hope we shall meet again more cheerfully than we parted.

Be pleased to make my compliments to dear Mrs. Bowles, to your Father, and all our friends, and to the young ones, if they yet have any traces of me. When any occasion brings you to town, I will introduce you to the Club. I am, Dear sir, Your most humble servant,

SAM. JOHNSON

1. Cf. *Ante* To Hester Thrale, 21 Apr. 1784.
2. MS: "c" superimposed upon "p"
3. *Ante* To Hester Maria Thrale, 31 Jan. 1784, n. 7.
4. *Ante* To William Bowles, 23 Feb. 1784 and n. 2.
5. *Ante* To Hester Thrale, 26 Apr. 1784.

Jane Langton

MONDAY 10 MAY 1784

MS: Hyde Collection.

Bolt court,
Fleetstreet, May 10, 1784

My dearest Miss Jenny:

I am sorry that your pretty Letter has been so long without

being answered; but when I am not pretty well, I do not always write plain enough for young Ladies.

I am glad, my Dear, to see that You write so well, and hope that You mind your pen, your book, and your needle, for they are all necessary. Your books will give you knowledge, and make You respected, and your needle will find You useful employment when You do not care to read. When You are a little older, I hope You will be very diligent in learning arithmetick;[1] and above all, that through your wholl life,[2] You will carefully say your prayers, and read your Bible. I am, my Dear, Your most humble Servant,

SAM. JOHNSON

1. Cf. *Ante* To Sophia Thrale, 24 July 1783.
2. MS: "life" repeated as catchword

Hester Thrale

THURSDAY 13 MAY 1784

MS: Hyde Collection.

Madam: London, Thursday, May 13, 1784

Now I am broken loose, my friends seem willing enough to see me. On Monday I dined with Paradise, Tuesday, Hoole; Wednesday, Dr. Taylor; to day with Jodrel; Friday, Mrs. Garrick; Saturday, Dr. Brocklesby. Next monday, Dilly.

But I do not now drive the World about; the world drives or draws me.[1] I am very weak, the old distress of sleeplessness comes again upon me. I have however one very strong basis of Health, an eager appetite, and strong digestion.

Queeney's letter I expected before now. Susy is likewise in debt. I believe I am in debt to Sophy, but the dear Loves ought [not] to be too rigorous.

Dr. Taylor has taken St. Margaret's in Westminster vacant

1. "He taught the Gospel rather than the Law: / And forc'd himself to drive; but lov'd to draw" (Dryden, "The Character of a Good Parson," ll. 30–31).

by Dr. Wilson's death.[2] How long he will keep it I cannot guess. It is of no great value, and its income consists much of voluntary contributions. I am, Madam, Your most humble servant,

SAM. JOHNSON

You never date fully.

2. *Ante* To Hester Thrale, 23 May 1780, n. 9; 6 June 1780.

Unidentified Correspondent

TUESDAY 25 MAY 1784

MS: Pierpont Morgan Library.

Sir: May 25, 1784

I have spoken to Mr. Davies more than once to settle with Mr. Evans, as I rather think I have paid him, the reason why I think it, is inclosed, and I will do just as You would have me, for I am not sure. I am, Sir, Your most humble servant,

SAM. JOHNSON

Frances Reynolds

FRIDAY 28 MAY 1784

MS: Hyde Collection.

ADDRESS: To Mrs. Reynolds.

ENDORSEMENT: Dr. Johnson believe in 84, May 28th.

Madam: May 28th

You do me wrong by imputing my omission to any captious punctiliousness. I have not yet seen Sir Joshua, and when I do see him, know not how to serve You. When I spoke upon your affair to him at Christmas, I received no encouragement to speak again.[1]

1. *Ante* To Frances Reynolds, 15 Feb. 1779 and n. 1.

But We shall never do business by letters, We must see one another.

I have returned Your papers, and am glad that You laid aside the thought of printing them.[2] I am, Madam, your most humble Servant,

SAM. JOHNSON

2. *Ante* To Frances Reynolds, 12 Apr. 1784 and n. 1; 30 Apr. 1784.

William Adams

MONDAY 31 MAY 1784

MS: Hyde Collection.

Sir: Bolt court, Fleetstreet, May 31, 1784

Let me not be thought insensible of your kind invitations, if I have hitherto delayed to accept them. I have been confined to the house one hundred and twenty nine days, and it may be easily supposed that I am yet languid with the debility of so long an ilness, from only part of which I have recovered.

I hope however, that I have strength yet remaining sufficient to carry me to Oxford, and with Mr. Boswel, my old fellow traveller, I hope to see You on Thursday the 3d of June.[1]

Our wish is, if it can [be] easily allowed us, to lodge and live in the college.

A sick Man is a very troublesome visitant. I bring my servant with me, who must be some way or other provided for.

I return dear Miss Adams my sincere thanks for her two kind visits, and for her imperturbab[l]e and irresistible tenderness and civility. I am, Sir, your most humble Servant,

SAM. JOHNSON

1. *Ante* To William Adams, 30 Mar. 1784, n. 5.

Ozias Humphry

MONDAY 31 MAY 1784

MS: Beinecke Library. The transcript (in JB's hand) used as copy for the *Life*.

HEADING: To Mr. Ozias Humphry.

Sir: May 31, 1784

I am very much obliged by your civilities to my Godson,[1] but must beg of you to add to them the favour of permitting him to see you paint, that he may know how a picture is begun, advanced, and completed.

If he may attend you in a few of your operations I hope he will shew that the benefit has been properly conferred, both by his proficiency and his gratitude. At least I shall consider you as enlarging your kindness to, Sir, your humble servant,

SAM. JOHNSON

1. *Ante* To Ozias Humphry, 5 Apr. 1784; 13 Apr. 1784.

Hester Thrale

MONDAY 31 MAY 1784

PRINTED SOURCE: Chapman III.165.

Dear Madam: London, May 31, 1784

Why you expected me to be better than I am I cannot imagine; I am better than any that saw me in my ilness ever expected to have seen me again.[1] I am however at a great distance from

1. Hester Thrale had spent approximately a week in London (*c.* 11–*c.* 17 May), visiting Frances Burney and making arrangements for her marriage (*The Piozzi Letters*, ed. E. A. Bloom and L. D. Bloom, 1989, I.60 n. 1). K. C. Balderston suggests that during this time "she probably did see Johnson, fleetingly, either at his own house or at hers" (*Thraliana* I.593 n. 3). According to Balderston, SJ's first sentence "is hard to explain without assuming a personal interview, and an expression of concern from Mrs. Thrale at his appearance" (*Thraliana* I.593 n. 3). Chapman is "disposed to agree with Miss Balderston" (III.165). However, the evidence

health, very weak and very asthmatick, and troubled with my old nocturnal distresses. So that I am little asleep in the night, and in the day too little awake.

I have one way or other been disappointed hitherto of that change of air from which I think some relief may possibly be obtained; but Boswel and I have settled our resolution to go to Oxford on Thursday.[2] But since I was at Oxford, my convivial friend, Dr Edwards, and my learned friend, Dr Wheeler, are both dead, and my proba⟨bi⟩lities of pleasure are very much diminished. Why, when so many are taken away, have I been yet spared? I hope that I may be fitter to die.

How long we shall stay at Oxford, or what we shall do when we leave it, neither Bozzy nor I have yet settled; he is for his part resolved to remove his family to London, and try his fortune at the English Bar. Let us all wish him success.[3]

Think of me, if You can, with tenderness. ⟨. . .⟩[4] I am, Madam, Your most humble servant,

SAM. JOHNSON

---

remains equivocal: Frances Burney claims that Hester Thrale "saw nobody else," and SJ might well have been responding to a comment in a letter, not a face-to-face meeting (*Diary and Letters of Madame D'Arblay*, ed. Austin Dobson, 1904, II.258). Moreover, it seems questionable whether, with her secret marriage plans so far advanced, Hester Thrale would have chosen to call on SJ and dissimulate.

2. *Ante* To William Adams, 30 Mar. 1784, n. 5.

3. *Post* To JB, 11 July 1784.

4. "A line follows, so heavily erased that I could make out nothing" (Chapman III.165 n. 1).

Joshua Reynolds

TUESDAY 1 JUNE 1784

MS: Hyde Collection.

ADDRESS: To Sir Joshua Reynolds.

Dear Sir: June 1, 1784

I am ashamed to ask for some relief for a poor man to whom, I hope, I have given what I can be expected to spare. The man importunes me and the blow goes round. I am going to try another air on Thursday.[1] I am, Sir your most etc.

SAM. JOHNSON

1. SJ refers to his impending trip to Oxford (*Ante* To William Adams, 31 May 1784).

Anthony Hamilton

WEDNESDAY 2 JUNE 1784

PRINTED SOURCE: JB's *Life*, ed. Croker, 1835, x.283–84.

Sir, June 2, 1784

You do every thing that is liberal and kind. Mrs. Pellè is a bad manager for herself, but I will employ a more skilful agent, one Mrs. Gardiner,[1] who will wait on you and employ Pellè's money to the best advantage. Mrs. Gardiner will wait on you.

I return you, Sir, sincere thanks for your attention to me. I am ill, but hope to come back better,[2] and to be made better still by your conversation. I am, Sir, etc.

SAM. JOHNSON

1. Presumably SJ refers to Ann Gardiner.
2. *Ante* To Joshua Reynolds, 1 June 1784 and n. 1.

Hester Maria Thrale

THURSDAY 3 JUNE 1784

MS: The Earl of Shelburne.
ADDRESS: To Miss Thrale at Bath.
POSTMARK: 3 IV.

My dear Love: London, June 3, 1784

I am going to Oxford,[1] and perhaps further and hear that

1. *Ante* To William Adams, 31 May 1784.

you are going to Brighthelmston.[2] I hope we shall receive help from our excursions. My nights are very tedious, and my As[t]hma of late is very troublesome, and as the King has for near a year paid me nothing, I am very poor.

The Speaking Image, about which you enquire, is a very subtle and wonderful deception.[3] The answer to the question is doubtless made by ventriloquy, or the art of directing the voice in what the speaker wills, but [how] the question is conveyed to the speaker,[4] wherever he is, has not yet been discovered. The statue is of wax, and incapable of any mechanical operation. Besides, that no mechanism can provide answers to arbitrary questions. No chimes can be set to play any tune that may be called. The artifice is according to all accounts astonishing, yet it will sometime [be] resolved into some petty trick.

That I love you, and wish you all wise and good, and happy, I hope needs not be told by, Dearest Love, your most humble servant,

SAM. JOHNSON

2. Queeney, Susanna, and Sophia Thrale, all opposed to their mother's impending marriage, had decided to remove themselves to Brighton as soon as Gabriel Piozzi returned to England. Accordingly, they left Bath on 25 June (Clifford, 1952, p. 226; Hester Thrale to the executors, 30 June 1784, MS: Hyde Collection).

3. In 1784 exhibitors charged half a crown to see "*a Speaking Figure,*" an automaton "about the size of a very young child," which would answer any question put to it in English, French, German, or Italian ([Philip Thicknesse], *The Speaking Figure and the Automaton Chess-Player, Exposed and Detected*, 1784, pp. 3, 6). Later that year, on her honeymoon in Paris, H. L. Piozzi "saw the Speaking Figure again," and reported that "She eats Sugar Plums now d'une très bonne grace" (*The French Journals of Mrs. Thrale and Doctor Johnson*, ed. Moses Tyson and Henry Guppy, 1932, p. 207).

4. MS: "spea" repeated as catchword

Edmund Allen

MONDAY 7 JUNE 1784

MS: Hyde Collection.

ADDRESS: To Mr. Allen in Bolt court, Fleet street, London.

POSTMARKS: OXFORD, 8 IV.

Dear Sir: Pembroke College, Oxford, June 7, 1784

I came hither on Thursday without the least trouble or fatigue, but I do not yet perceive any improvement of my health. My Breath is very much obstructed, my legs are very soon tired, and my Nights are very restless.

Boswel went back next day, and is not yet returned,[1] Miss Adams, and Miss Moore are not yet come.[2] How long I shall stay, or whither I shall go, I cannot yet guess; While I am away I beg that You will sit for me at the club,[3] and that You will pay Betsy Barber five shilling a week. I hope I shall by degrees be better. I am, Sir, your most humble Servant,

SAM. JOHNSON

1. JB accompanied SJ to Oxford on 3 June, but returned to London the following day in order to attend the Handel Commemoration on 5 June at Westminster Abbey. He came back to Oxford on 9 June (*Boswell: The Applause of the Jury*, ed. I. S. Lustig and F. A. Pottle, 1981, pp. 220–21, 228, 231).

2. Sarah Adams was in Oxford by 10 June (*Life* IV.291–92), but Hannah More did not arrive until the day of SJ's departure. "They [the Adamses] told me he did me the honour to be very angry and out of humour, that I did not come so soon as I had promised" (William Roberts, *Memoirs of the Life and Correspondence of Mrs. Hannah More*, 1834, I.188–89).

3. SJ refers to the Essex Head Club.

George Nicol[1]

TUESDAY 8 JUNE 1784

MS: Johnson House, London.

ADDRESS: To Mr. Nicol, Bookseller in the Strand, London.

POSTMARKS: OXFORD, 9 IV.

Sir: [Pembroke College, Oxford] June 8, 1784

You were pleased to promise me that when the great Voyage should be published, you would send it to me.[2] I am now at

1. George Nicol (1741–1829), bookseller, and Bookseller to the King (1781–1820) (Ian Maxted, *The London Book Trades, 1775–1800*, 1977, p. 162).

2. The third and last of James Cook's voyages, *A Voyage to the Pacific Ocean* (3 vols.), had been published posthumously on 4 June by Thomas Cadell and George Nicol (*London Chronicle* 22–25 May 1784, LV.499).

Pembroke College, Oxford, and if you can conveniently enclose it in a parcel, or send it any other way, I shall think the perusal of it a great favour. I am, Sir, Your most humble Servant,

SAM. JOHNSON

John Taylor

TUESDAY 8 JUNE 1784

MS: Berg Collection, New York Public Library.

ADDRESS: To the Reverend Dr. Taylor in Westminster.

POSTMARKS: OXFORD, 9 IV.

ENDORSEMENTS: 1784, 8 June 1784.

Dear Sir: Pembroke College, Oxford, June 8, 1784

I came hither on Thursday without any sense of fatigue, but cannot perceive that change of place does me any good. I am very weak in my legs, and suspicious that the[y] swell again, but of that I am not sure. My breath is very laborious, and my nights restless and tedious. I am very kindly treated here.

Let me know how You go on. In the first place think on your health. Let nothing vex you, for what is there that can desire the sacrifice of your quiet? Then tell me what is your determination about the bill;[1] and when You expect to be restored to your house in Ashbourne.[2] I am, Sir, your most humble servant,

SAM. JOHNSON

1. MS: "bill" repeated as catchword
2. *Post* To John Taylor, 23 June 1784.

John & Amelia Perkins

SATURDAY 12 JUNE 1784

PRINTED SOURCE: Sotheby's Catalogue, 21 Jan. 1899, Lot No. 342, p. 27.

Mr. Johnson spent a sleepless night, but is better to-day.

Hester Thrale

THURSDAY 17 JUNE 1784

MS: Hyde Collection.

Dear Madam: London, June 17, 1784

I returned last night from Oxford, after a fortnight's abode with Dr. Adams, who treated me as well as I could expect or wish; and he that contents a sick man, a man whom it is impossible to please, has surely done his part well. I went in the common vehicle with very little fatigue, and came back, I think, with less. My stomach continues good, and according to your advice, I spare neither asparagus nor[1] pease; and hope to do good execution upon all the summer fruits. But my nights are bad, very bad; The Asthma attacks me often, and the Dropsy is watching an opportunity to return. I hope, I have checked [it], but great caution must be used, and indeed great caution is not a high price for health or ease.

What I shall do next I[2] know not, all my scheme[s] of rural pleasure have been some way or other disappointed. I have now some thought of Lichfield, and Ashbourne. Let me know, dear Madam, your destination. I am, Madam, Your most humble servant,

SAM. JOHNSON

1. MS: "nor" altered from "ne"
2. MS: "a"

John Taylor

SATURDAY 19 JUNE 1784

MS: Hyde Collection.
ADDRESS: To the Reverend Dr. Taylor.
ENDORSEMENTS: 1784, 19 June 84.

Sir: Bolt court, June 19, 1784

When we parted last night, I thought worse of your case, than I think since I have thought longer upon it. Your general distemper is, I think, a hectic fever, for which the bark is proper, and which quietness of mind, and gentle exercise, and fresh air may cure. Your present weakness is the effect of such waste of blood, as would weaken a young man in his highest vigour. It might be necessary, but it must sink both your courage and strength.

Dr. Nichols hurt himself extremely in his old age by lavish phlebotomy.[1] Do not bleed again very soon and when you can delay no longer, be more moderate.

I think You do right in going home, and hope you will have an easy and pleasant Journey. I am, dear Sir, yours affectionately,

SAM. JOHNSON

1. Frank Nicholls (1699–1778), M.D., F.R.S., physician to George II (1753–60) and author of *De Anima Medica* (1750). Nicholls died of "a catarrh, and an inveterate asthmatic cough" (*GM* 1785, p. 14), for which bloodletting had been prescribed (Thomas Lawrence, *Franci Nichollsii . . . Vita*, 1780, p. 103).

John Taylor

WEDNESDAY 23 JUNE 1784

MS: Huntington Library.

ADDRESS: To the Reverend Dr. Taylor in Ashbourne, Derbyshire.

POSTMARKS: 23 IV, 24 IV.

ENDORSEMENTS: 1784, 23 June 84.

Dear Sir: June 23, 1784

It is now Wednesday Evening. I hope You are lodged easily and safely in Ashbourne. Since we parted I have not been well. I dined on Saturday with Dr. Brocklesby, and was taken ill at his house, but went to the club.[1] On Monday I was so uneasy that I staid at home. On Tuesday I dined at the club,[2] but was not well at night, nor am well to day but hope the fit is abating. Boswel has a great mind to draw me to Lichfield, and as I love

1. SJ refers to the Essex Head Club (*Ante* To Joshua Reynolds, 4 Dec. 1783, n. 3).

2. SJ refers to The Literary Club (*Life* IV.326).

to travel with him, I have a mind to be drawn if I could hope in any short time to come to your house, for Lichfield will I am afraid, not be a place for long continuance, and, to tell the truth, I am afraid of seeing myself so far from home, as I must return alone.

Sir John Hawkins has just told me that You preached on Sunday with great vigour. You have therefore a great fund of Strength left, which I entreat You not to bleed away.[3] I am, Sir, yours affectionately,

SAM. JOHNSON

3. *Ante* To John Taylor, 19 June 1784.

Hester Thrale

SATURDAY 26 JUNE 1784

MS: Hyde Collection.

Dear Madam: London, June 26, 1784

This Morning I saw Mr. Lysons.[1] He is an agreeable young Man, and likely enough to do all that he designs. I received him, as one sent by You has a right to be received, and I hope, he will tell you that he was satisfied, but the initiatory conversation of two strangers is seldom pleasing or instructive to any great degree, and ours was such as other occasions of the same kind produce.

A message came to me yesterday, to tell me that Macbean, after three days of illness, is dead of a suppression of urine. He was one of those who, as Swift says, *stood as a Screen between me and death.*[2] He has, I hope, made a good exchange. He was

1. Samuel Lysons (1763–1819), lawyer, antiquarian, and artist; later, F.S.A. (1786), F.R.S. (1797), and Keeper of the Records of the Tower of London (1803–19) (*The Piozzi Letters*, ed. E. A. Bloom and L. D. Bloom, 1989, I.78 n. 10). Hester Thrale, who had met Lysons at Bath in January, found him "a Young Man . . . of very uncommon parts" (*Thraliana* I.586). Lysons was to assist in the compilation of H. L. Piozzi's *Anecdotes of the Late Samuel Johnson, LL.D.* (1786) and *Letters to and from the Late Samuel Johnson, LL.D.* (1788) (Clifford, 1952, pp. 241–45, 296).

2. "The Fools, my Juniors by a Year, / Are tortur'd with Suspence and Fear. /

very pious. He was very innocent. He did no ill, and of doing good a continual tenour of distress allowed him few opportunities. He was very highly esteemed in the house.[3]

Write to me, if you can, some words of comfort. My dear Girls seem all to forget me. I am, Madam, Your most humble servant,

SAM. JOHNSON

Who wisely thought my Age a Screen, / When Death approach'd, to stand between" (Swift, *Verses on the Death of Dr. Swift*, ll. 219–22).

3. *Ante* To William Vyse, 10 Apr. 1781 and n. 1.

Hester Maria Thrale

THURSDAY 1 JULY 1784

MS: The Earl of Shelburne.

ADDRESS: To Miss Thrale at Brighthelmston, Sussex.

POSTMARK: 1 IY.

My Dearest: London, July 1, 1784

I read your letter with anguish and astonishment, such as I never felt before. I had fondly flattered myself that time had produced better thoughts.[1] I can only give You this consolation that, in my opinion, You have hitherto done rightly. You have not left your Mother, but your Mother has left You.[2]

You must now be to your Sisters what your Mother ought to have been, and if I can give You any help, I hope never to desert You. I will write to the other Guardians.[3]

I send my kindest respects to your Sisters, and exhort them to attend to your counsels, and recommend You all to the care

1. *Ante* To Hester Thrale, 26 Apr. 1784, n. 7.

2. Determined to marry Gabriel Piozzi, Hester Thrale awaited his arrival at Bath. Her daughters, condemning their mother's choice, moved to the family house in Brighton with a chaperone/companion, Jane Nicholson (1755–1831) (*The Piozzi Letters*, ed. E. A. Bloom and L. D. Bloom, 1989, 1.62 n. 2, 73 n. 3). *Post* To Hester Thrale, 2 July 1784 and n. 1.

3. SJ refers to John Cator, Jeremiah Crutchley, and Henry Smith (*Ante* To Hester Thrale, 5 Apr. 1781, n. 6).

of Him who is the Father of the fatherless. I am, Dear Madam, your most humble servant,

SAM. JOHNSON

Hester Thrale

FRIDAY 2 JULY 1784

MS: Hyde Collection.
ADDRESS: To Mrs. Thrale at Bath.
POSTMARK: 2 IY.

Madam: July 2, 1784

If I interpret your letter right, You are ignominiously married, if it is yet undone, let us once talk together.[1] If You have abandoned your children and your religion, God forgive your wickedness; if you have forfeited your Fame, and your country, may your folly do no further mischief.

If the last act is yet to do, I, who have loved you, esteemed you, reverenced you, and served you, I who long[2] thought you the first of humankind, entreat that before your fate is irrevocable, I may once more see You. I was, I once was, Madam, most truly yours,

SAM. JOHNSON

I will come down if you permit it.[3]

1. On 30 June Hester Thrale sent SJ (along with her daughters' three other guardians) an official announcement of her impending marriage to Gabriel Piozzi (MS: Hyde Collection). With this "circular Letter" she included a note in which she begged SJ's "pardon for concealing from you a Connection which you must have heard of by many, but I suppose never believed. . . . I could not have borne to reject that Counsel it would have killed me to take, and I only tell it you now, because all is *irrevocably settled*" (Hester Thrale's holograph copy, MS: Hyde Collection). The Roman Catholic ceremony took place in London on 23 July, the Anglican ceremony on the 25th in Bath (Clifford, 1952, p. 229).

2. MS: "who" del. before "long"

3. *Post* To Hester Thrale, 8 July 1784, n. 1.

Hester Maria Thrale

SATURDAY 3 JULY 1784

MS: The Earl of Shelburne.

ADDRESS: To Miss Thrale at Brighthelmston, Sussex.

POSTMARK: 3 IY.

Dear Madam: London, July 3, 1784

In telling You that I sincerely pity You, and that I approve your Conduct I tell You only what will be said by all Mankind.[1] What I think of your Mothers conduct I cannot express, but by words which I cannot prevail upon myself to use.

Your Guardians, I suppose, have been now with You; I am sorry that I am not with You too. But they have more power to help you than I, and not less inclination. We all compassionate and love You and your Sisters, and I hope by our Friendship, and Your own Virtue, Prudence, and Piety, You may, though thus unworthily deserted, pass a life of security, Happiness, and honour. I am, Dearest Love, your most humble servant,

SAM. JOHNSON

1. *Ante* To Hester Maria Thrale, 1 July 1784 and n. 2.

Hester Maria Thrale

TUESDAY 6 JULY 1784

MS: The Earl of Shelburne.

ADDRESS: To Miss Thrale at Brighthelmston.

POSTMARK: 6 IY.

Dear Madam: London, July 6, 1784

Mr. Cruchley gave me an account of your interview, and of the plan which is for the present exigence settled between You and your Friends.[1] But I either misunderstood him or you, for the two accounts seem very different.

1. Jeremiah Crutchley and John Cator, who distrusted the Thrales' companion

If you comply for the time with proposals not very agreeable, You know that any necessity of compliance can be but short. You will soon be mistress of Yourself.[2] Do your best; and be not discouraged. Serve God; read, and pray. You have in your hand all that the world considers as materials of happiness. You have riches, Youth, and Hea[l]th, all which I shall delight to see You enjoy. But believe a Man whose experience has been long, and who can have no wish to deceive you and who now tells you that the highest honour, and most constant pleasure this life can afford, must be obtained by passing it with attention fixed upon Eternity. The longest life soon passes away. You that are blooming in all the gayety of youth, will be, before You are aware, as old as he that has now the honour of being, Madam, your most humble servant,

SAM. JOHNSON

Jane Nicholson, were making plans to dismiss her in August. Thereafter Cator took Queeney to live with him and his wife, while Susanna, Sophia, and Cecilia were sent to boarding school (Hester Thrale to Hester Maria Thrale, 15 July 1784, *The Piozzi Letters*, ed. E. A. Bloom and L. D. Bloom, 1989, I.90, 91 n. 3; *Thraliana* II.612 n. 1).

2. Queeney's twenty-first birthday was fourteen months away.

John Taylor

WEDNESDAY 7 JULY 1784

MS: Hyde Collection.

ADDRESS: To the Reverend Dr. Taylor in Ashbourne, Derbyshire.

POSTMARKS: 7 IY, 8 IY.

ENDORSEMENTS: 1784, 7 July 84.

Dear Sir: July 7, 1784

Your letter written in a hot day has been received by me in a day when the heat scarcely supportable by a weakly man, made it doubly welcome. My Engagements do not allow me to set out this week, but I intend to lose no time. I think of coming first to Lichfield, and hope that from thence You will fetch me to Ashbourn,[1] where I hope by fresh air and your kindness to grow better. I am, Sir, etc.

SAM. JOHNSON

1. SJ left for Lichfield 12 July, arrived on the 14th, and departed for Ashbourne on the 20th (*Post* To JB, 11 July 1784; 26 July 1784).

Lucy Porter

THURSDAY 8 JULY 1784

MS: Hyde Collection.

ADDRESS: To Mrs. Lucy Porter in Lichfield.

POSTMARK: 8 IY.

ENDORSEMENT in an unidentified hand: 1784.

Dear Madam: London, July 8, 1784

I am coming down to Ashbourne, and, as You may believe, shall visit You in my way.

I shall bring a poor, broken, unweildy body, but I shall not trouble You long, for Dr. Taylor will in a few days send for me.[1] I hope to find You better than You will find me. I hear that poor Mrs. Aston is very ill. I am, Dear Madam, Your most humble Servant,

SAM. JOHNSON

1. *Ante* To John Taylor, 7 July 1784, n. 1.

Joshua Reynolds

THURSDAY 8 JULY 1784

MS: Hyde Collection.

ENDORSEMENT: Dr. Johnson.

Dear Sir: Bolt court, July 8, 1784

I am going, I hope, in a few days to try the air of Derbyshire,[1]

1. *Ante* To John Taylor, 7 July 1784, n. 1.

but hope to see You before I go. Let me however mention to You what I have much at heart.

If the Chancellor should continue his attention to Mr. Boswel's request, and confer with You upon the means of relieving my languid state,[2] I am very desirous to avoid the appearance of asking money upon false pretences.[3] I[4] desire You to represent to his Lordship what as soon as it is suggested he will perceive to be[5] reasonable.

That, if I grow much worse, I shall be afraid to leave my Physicians, to suffer the inconveniences of travel, and pine in the solitude of a foreign country.

That, if I grew much better, of which indeed there is now little appearance, I shall not wish to leave my friends, and my domestick comforts. For I do not travel for pleasure or curiosity. Yet if I should recover curiosity would revive.

In my present State, I am desirous to make a struggle for a little longer life, and hope to obtain some help from a softer climate.

Do for me what You can. I am, Dear Sir, Your most humble Servant,

SAM. JOHNSON

2. MS: period

3. Alarmed by SJ's deteriorating health, his friends wished to make it possible for him to "retreat from the severity of a British winter, to the mild climate of Italy" (*Life* IV.326). This they could accomplish only by appealing to the King to augment SJ's pension. After consulting with Sir Joshua Reynolds, JB wrote to the Lord Chancellor, Edward Thurlow, who replied that he would support the application to the best of his ability. On 30 June JB, Reynolds, and SJ met to discuss the proposed trip. "He himself catched so much of our enthusiasm, as to allow himself to suppose it not impossible that our hopes might in one way or other be realised" (*Life* IV.337). Because JB was about to leave for Scotland, Reynolds agreed to act as liaison with Thurlow (*Life* IV.327–28). *Post* To Joshua Reynolds, 9 Sept. 1784; *Post* To Edward Thurlow, 9 Sept. 1784.

4. MS: "Before I receive the King's bounty to enable me to breath the softer air of the continent" del. before "I"

5. MS: "be" repeated as catchword

Hester Thrale

THURSDAY 8 JULY 1784

MS: Hyde Collection.
ADDRESS: To Mrs. Thrale at Bath.
POSTMARK: 8 IY.

Dear Madam: London, July 8, 1784

What You have done, however I may lament it, I have no pretence to resent, as it has not been injurious to me. I therefore breathe out one sigh more of tenderness perhaps useless, but at least sincere.[1]

I wish that God may grant you every blessing, that You may be happy in this world for its short continuance, and eternally happy in a better State. And whatever I can contribute to your happiness, I am very ready to repay for that kindness which soothed twenty years of a life radically wretched.

Do not think slightly of the advice which I[2] now presume to offer. Prevail upon Mr. Piozzi to settle in England.[3] You may live here with more dignity than in Italy, and with more security. Your rank will be higher, and your fortune more under your own eye. I desire not to detail all my reasons; but every argument of prudence and interest is for England, and only s⟨ome⟩ phantoms of imagination seduce you to Italy.

I am afraid, however, that my counsel is vain, yet I have eased my heart by giving it.

When Queen Mary took the resolution of sheltering herself in England, the Archbishop of St. Andrew's attempting to dissuade her, attended on her journey and when they came to

1. Responding to SJ's denunciation of 2 July, Hester Thrale had sent a dignified reproof, dated 4 July, in which she defended her conduct and Gabriel Piozzi's character, social standing, and professional achievement. She concluded, "Till you have changed your Opinion of Mr. Piozzi—let us converse no more" (MS: Hyde Collection).

2. MS: "I" repeated as catchword

3. In her reply, dated 15 July, Hester Thrale told SJ: "Have no Fears for me however; no *real* Fears. My Piozzi will need few Perswasions to settle in a Country where he has succeeded so well" (MS: Rylands Library). After an extended trip to Italy, the Piozzis returned to England in 1787.

the irremeable Stream[4] that separated the two kingdoms, walked by her side into the water, in the middle of which he seized her bridle, and with earnestness proportioned to her danger and his own affection, pressed her to return. The Queen went forward.[5] —If the parallel reaches thus far; may it go no further. The tears stand in my eyes.

I am going into Derbyshire,[6] and hope to be followed by your good wishes, for I am with great affection, Your most humble servant,

SAM. JOHNSON

Any letters that come for me hither, will be sent me.[7]

4. *Ante* To Hester Thrale, 3 Oct. 1767 and n. 2.

5. As SJ well knew from his readings in Scots history, Mary Stuart crossed from Scotland to England by ship, embarking at Kirkcudbright and landing at Workington, Cumberland. However, as Mary Lascelles argues, SJ in his distraught state drew here upon a more apposite fictionalized account, one that derives ultimately from Boisguillebert's *Marie Stuart Reyne d'Escosse, Nouvelle Historique* (1674). In this version John Hamilton (?1511–71), Archbishop of St. Andrews (1546–71), attempts passionately to dissuade the Queen from taking refuge in England, and even follows her into "un ruisseau qui separe les deux Royaumes" (Lascelles, "Johnson's Last Allusion to Mary Queen of Scots," *RES* 8 [N.S.], 1957, pp. 32–37).

6. *Ante* To John Taylor, 7 July 1784, n. 1.

7. SJ did not respond to Hester Thrale's conciliatory letter of 15 July (see above, n. 3). On 25 Nov. he told Frances Burney: "I drive her quite from my mind. If I meet with one of her letters, I burn it instantly" (*Diary and Letters of Madame D'Arblay*, ed. Austin Dobson, 1904, II.271).

William Bowles

SATURDAY 10 JULY 1784

MS: Hyde Collection.

ADDRESS: To W. Bowles, Esq., at Heale near Salisbury.

POSTMARK: 10 IY.

Dear Sir: Bolt court, July 10, 1784

Your kind invitation came two or three days after an engagement to pay a visit to a friend in Derbyshire, towards whom I shall, I hope, set out to morrow.[1] When I come back, your kindness can do again what it[2] has already done, and, I hope, may be enjoyed, more than I have been yet able to enjoy it.

Be pleased in the mean time to accept my thanks, and pay my respects to your amiable Lady, and your worthy Father, and all my friends, great and little.

The Club flourishes;[3] We fill the table. Mr. Strahan has resigned, and my fellowtraveller Mr. Boswel is put in his place.[4] This is all the change that has happened in our State. I am, Dear Sir, Your most humble Servant,

SAM. JOHNSON

1. *Ante* To John Taylor, 7 July 1784, n. 1.   2. MS: "is"

3. SJ refers to the Essex Head Club (*Ante* To Joshua Reynolds, 4 Dec. 1783; *Ante* To Hester Maria Thrale, 31 Jan. 1784, n. 7).

4. William Strahan had resigned on 26 June (*Lit. Anec.* II.553).

William Adams

SUNDAY 11 JULY 1784

MS: Pierpont Morgan Library.

ENDORSEMENT: Dr. Johnson, June 11, 1784.

Dear Sir: London, June 11,[1] 1784

I am going into Staffordshire and Derbyshire in quest of some relief,[2] of which my need is not less than when I was treated at your house with so much tenderness.

I have now received the collations for Xenophon,[3] which I have sent You with the letters that relate to them. I cannot at present take any part in the work; but I would rather pay for a collation of Oppian, than see it neglected; for the Frenchmen act with great liberality.[4] Let us not fall below them.

1. "June" is a slip for "July": on 11 June SJ was in Oxford, staying with Adams, and with no immediate plans for visiting the Midlands.

2. *Ante* To John Taylor, 7 July 1784, n. 1.

3. *Ante* To William Adams, 30 Mar. 1784 and n. 2.

4. The Bodleian did not acquire an Oppian MS until 1785. However, SJ may

I know not in what state Dr. Edwards left his book. Some of his Emendations seemed to me to [be] irrefragably certain, and such therefore as ought not to be lost. His rule was not [to] change the text, and therefore, I suppose he has left notes to be subjoined. As the book is posthumous some account of the Editor ought to be given.[5]

You have now the whole process of the correspondence before you. When the Prior is answered,[6] let some apology be made for me.

I was forced to devide the Collation, but as it is paged, you will easily put every part in its proper place.[7]

Be pleased to[8] convey my respects to Mrs.[9] and Miss[10] Adams. I am Sir, Your most humble servant,

SAM. JOHNSON

---

have been asked to arrange for a collation of the scholia on the ἁλιευτικά, part of MS Barocci 38, which came to the Library in 1629 (information supplied by Dr. Richard Sharpe).

5. *Ante* To William Adams, 30 Mar. 1784, n. 3. In his preface, dated 20 Jan. 1785, Henry Owen says that, by the time of Edwards's death, the Greek text and the Latin translation were complete, but that notes and variant readings had to be supplied posthumously (*Memorabilia*, 1785, p. iii). Owen does not provide a biographical account of Edwards.

6. SJ refers to Father William Cowley.

7. Postal regulations obliged SJ "to devide" the manuscript: a franked packet could not exceed two ounces (R. M. Willcocks, *England's Postal History*, 1975, p. 56). Cf. *Ante* To JB, 14 Jan. 1775, n. 1.

8. MS: "to" superimposed upon "my"

9. Sarah Hunt (d. 1785) married William Adams in 1742.

10. MS: "Miss" repeated as catchword

James Boswell

SUNDAY 11 JULY 1784

MS: National Library of Scotland.

ADDRESS: To James Boswel, Esq., in Edinburgh.

POSTMARK: 12 IY.

To JAMES BOSWELL, 11 *July* 1784

Dear Sir: London, July 11, 1784

Why You should desire to hear your own reasons for your own actions I cannot find.[1]

I remember, and entreat You to remember that virtus est vitium fugere,[2] the first approach to riches is security from poverty. The condition upon which You have my consent to settle in London, is that your expence never exceeds your annual income. Fixing this basis of security, You cannot be hurt, and You may be very much advanced.[3] The loss of your Scottish business which is all that you can lose, is not to be reckoned as any equivalent[4] to the hopes and possibilities that open here upon you. If You succeed, all question of prudence is at an end, every body will [think][5] that done rightly which ends happily, and though your expectations, of which I would not advise you to talk too much, should not be wholly answered, you can hardly [fail][6] to get friends who[7] will do for you, all that your present Situation allows You to hope; and if after a few years You should return to Scotland, You will return with a mind supplied by various conversation, and many opportunities of enquiry, with much knowledge and materials for reflexion and instruction.

I am setting out to morrow for Lichfield and Ashbourne; my health has not mended since You left me, but I am yet in hope of benefit from the country. Of your kind negotiation I have yet found no consequence, but I shall leave it in the hands of Sir Joshua, and try to go down with hope and tranquillity.[8]

1. "Having after repeated reasonings, brought Dr. Johnson to agree to my removing to London, and even to furnish me with arguments in favour of what he had opposed; I wrote to him requesting he would write them for me; he was so good as to comply" (*Life* IV.351). For SJ's own account of his conditional willingness to support JB's projected move, *post* To William Forbes, 7 Aug. 1784.

2. *virtus est vitium fugere*: "To flee vice is the beginning of virtue" (Horace, *Epistles* I.i.41, trans. H. R. Fairclough, Loeb ed.).

3. MS: comma del. before period

4. MS: "equiva" repeated as catchword

5. MS: "think" inserted in JB's hand

6. MS: "fail" inserted in JB's hand

7. MS: "who" altered from "which"

8. *Ante* To Joshua Reynolds, 8 July 1784 and n. 3.

The Asthma is very oppressive, but the water does not much rise above the leg. I take Squills in powder often three grains a day, or at least forty drops of vinegar of Squills. I have observed a phænomenon which I did not expect. Forty drops of vinegar of Squills (I suppose of any vinegar) fills not more than half the Space occupied by forty drops of water, so much greater is the cohesion or mutual attraction of water than of vinegar. Let me know how much of the vinegar your Physicians generally consider as a powerful dose.

If You direct to me hither, the letters will be sent to me, but when I come to Ashbourne if I find myself disposed to stay, I will write to you [from] there. Convey my respects to Mrs. Boswel. I am, Dear Sir, etc.

SAM. JOHNSON

Thomas Bagshaw

MONDAY 12 JULY 1784

MS: Sarah Markham.

Sir: Bolt court, Fleetstreet, July 12, 1784

Perhaps You may remember that in the year 1753, You committed to the ground my dear Wife;[1] I now entreat your permission to lay a stone upon her, and have sent the inscription, that if You find it proper, You may signify your allowance.[2]

You will do me a great favour by showing the place where she lies, that the stone may protect her remains.

Mr. Ryland will wait on You for the inscription, and procure it to be engraved.[3] You will easily believe that I shrink from

1. In fact Elizabeth Johnson had died in 1752 (*Ante* To John Taylor, 18 Mar. 1752 and n. 1; *Post* To John Ryland, 4 Nov. 1784). SJ was correct, however, in remembering that Bagshaw had performed the burial service (*Ante* To Thomas Bagshaw, 8 May 1773, n. 1).

2. For SJ's own translation of the Latin inscription (*Life* 1.241 n. 2), *post* To Lucy Porter, 2 Dec. 1784.

3. John Ryland oversaw the engraving and placement of the gravestone (*Post* To John Ryland, 12 July 1784; 30 Oct. 1784; 4 Nov. 1784).

this mournful[4] office. When it is done, if I have strength remaining, I will visit Bromley once again, and pay you part of the respect to which You have a right from, Reverend Sir, Your most humble Servant,

SAM. JOHNSON

4. MS: "ful" repeated as catchword

Bennet Langton

MONDAY 12 JULY 1784

MS: Hyde Collection.

ADDRESS: To Benet Langton, Esq., in Rochester, Kent.

POSTMARK: 12 IY.

Dear Sir: London, July 12, 1784

I cannot but think that in my languid and a[n]xious state I have some reason to complain that I receive from You neither enquiry nor consolation. You know how much I value your friendship, and with what confidence I expect your kindness, if I wanted any act of tenderness that You could perform, at least if you do not know it, I think your ignorance is your own fault. Yet how long is it that I have lived almost in your neighbourhood, without the least notice.

I do not however consider this neglect, as[1] particularly[2] shown to me, I have two of your most valuable friends make the same complaint. But why are all these overlooked, you are not oppressed by sickness, you are not distracted by business; if you are sick you[3] are sick of leisure, and allow your self to be told that no disease is more to be dreaded or avoided. Rather to do nothing, than do good is the lowest state of a degraded mind. Boileau says to his pupil.

> Que les vers ne soient pas vôtre eternel emploi,
> Cultivez vos amis.—[4]

1. MS: "as" altered from "at"
2. MS: "par" repeated as catchword
3. MS: "you" altered from "your"
4. "Que les vers ne soient pas vostre éternel employ. / Cultivez vos amis, soyez

That voluntary debility, which modern language is content to term indolence, will, if it is not counteracted by resolution, render in[5] time the strongest faculties, useless, and turn the flames to the smoke of virtue.

I do not expect nor desire to see You, because I am much pleased to find that You[r] Mother stays so long with You, and I should think you neither elegant nor grateful if you did not study her gratification. You will pay my respects to both the Ladies, and to all the young people.

I am going northward for a while to try what help the country can give me,[6] but if you write, the letter will come after me. I[7] am, Sir, Your affectionate, humble servant,

SAM. JOHNSON

---

homme de foy" (Nicholas Boileau, *L'Art poétique* IV.121–22, Boileau, *Épîtres, Art poétique, Lutrin*, ed. C.-H. Boudhors, 1952, p. 113).

5. MS: "the" del. before "in"

6. *Ante* To John Taylor, 7 July 1784, n. 1.

7. MS: "Mr. Wright gets a rule and called on me lately. He looked well" del. before "I"

John Ryland

MONDAY 12 JULY 1784

MS: Hyde Collection.

ADDRESS: To Mr. Ryland in Muscovy Court, Towerhill.

POSTMARKS: [Undeciphered].

Dear Sir: July 12, 1784

Mr. Payne[1] will pay you fifteen pounds towards the stone of which You have kindly undertaken the care. The Inscription is in the hands of Mr. Bagshaw, who has a right to inspect it, before he admits it into his Church.[2]

Be pleased to let the whole be done with privacy, that I may elude the vigilance of the papers.

1. SJ refers to John Payne.

2. *Ante* To Thomas Bagshaw, 12 July 1784 and n. 3.

I am going for a while into Derbyshire in hope of help from the air of the country.[3] I hope your journey has benefited You. The Club prospers;[4] we meet by ten at a time.

God send that You and I may enjoy and improve each other. I am, Dear Sir, you most humble Servant,

SAM. JOHNSON

3. *Ante* To John Taylor, 7 July 1784, n. 1.
4. SJ refers to the Essex Head Club.

John Hawkins

SUMMER 1784

PRINTED SOURCE: Hawkins, p. 571.

[In a letter . . . written from Ashbourn, [SJ] thus delivered his sentiments:] Poor Thrale! I thought that either her virtue or her vice would have restrained her from such a marriage. She is now become a subject for her enemies to exult over, and for her friends, if she has any left, to forget or pity.[1]

1. Hester Thrale's marriage to Gabriel Piozzi alienated most of her friends, especially those in the Bluestocking circle; it also provoked widespread hostile comment in the newspapers (Clifford, 1952, pp. 229–31; *The Piozzi Letters*, ed. E. A. Bloom and L. D. Bloom, 1989, I.75 n. 9).

Richard Brocklesby

WEDNESDAY 21 JULY 1784

MS: Hyde Collection.

ADDRESS: To Dr. Brocklesby in London.

POSTMARKS: ASHBORNE, 24 IY.

Dear Sir: Ashbourne, Derbyshire, July 21, 1784

The kind attention which You have so long shown to my health and happiness, makes it as much a debt of gratitude as a call of interest, to give you an account of what befals me, when accident removes me from your immediate care.[1]

The journey of the first day was performed with very little sense of fatigue, the second day brought me to Lichfield without much lassitude,[2] but I am afraid that I could not have born such violent agitation for many days together. Tell Dr. Heberden that in the coach I read Ciceronianus, which I concluded as I entred Lichfield. My affection and understanding went along with Erasmus, except that once or twice he somewhat unskilfully entangles Cicero's civil or moral, with his rhetorical character.[3]

I staid five days at Lichfield, but, being unable to walk, had no great pleasure, and yesterday (19th) I came hither,[4] where I am to try what air and attention can perform.

Of any improvement in my health I cannot yet please myself with the perception. The water has in these[5] summer months[6] made two invasions, but has run off again with no very formidable tumefaction, either by the efficacy of the Squils, which I

1. SJ here begins a series of nineteen letters to Brocklesby, which combine with his medical diary (*Aegri Ephemeris* or "Sick Man's Journal," 6 July–8 Nov. 1784) to record "a relentless battle between his dropsy and his diuretics and purgatives" (L. C. McHenry, Jr., "Art and Medicine: Dr. Johnson's Dropsy," *Journal of the American Medical Association* 206, 1968, p. 2508).

2. *Ante* To John Taylor, 7 July 1784, n. 1.

3. SJ may have had in mind a speech by Bulephorus ("Dialogus Ciceronianus," ed. Pierre Mesnard, in *Erasmi Opera Omnia*, 1971, Part I, ii.618–19): *Nemo non fatetur fidem in oratore praecipuam esse. Eam conciliat probitatis et grauitatis opinio, eleuat artis aut intemperantiae suspicio. Habeatur sane Cicero vir bonus, quod vix illi Fabius, licet impendio fauens, audet tribuere: sed, quod dissimulari non potest, artem magis ostendat, de se plura gloriose commemorat, licentius in alios inuehitur quam Cato, Brutus, aut Celius, cui sanctitatem tribuit Quintilianus*: "Everyone will acknowledge that trustworthiness in an orator is the chief thing. A reputation for honesty and seriousmindedness gains this, while a suspicion of artfulness and lack of moderation lessens it. While Cicero may be considered a good man—a thing which Fabius, though a strong partisan of his, hardly dares to allow; yet we must admit that he makes a greater display of his skill, boasts more, and inveighs more freely against others than Cato, Brutus, or Caelius to whom Quintilian ascribes conscientiousness" (*Ciceronianus*, trans. Izora Scott, 1908, p. 38).

4. SJ's diary makes it clear that "19th" is a mistake for "20th" (*Works*, Yale ed. I.374).

5. MS: "these" altered from "this"

6. MS: "months" altered from "month"

have used very diligently, or because it is the course of the distemper, when it is at a certain height, to discharge itself.

The Asthma has no abatement. Opiates stop the fit, so as that I can sit and sometimes lie easy, but they do not now procure me the power of motion; and I am afraid that my general strength of body does not encrease. The weather indeed is not benign; but how low is he sunk whose strength depends upon the weather? I still pass the night almost without sleep.

I am now looking into Floyer, who lived with his asthma to almost his ninetieth year.[7] His book by want of order is obscure, and his asthma, I think, not of the same kind with mine.[8] Something however I may perhaps learn.

My appetite still continues keen enough, and what I consider as a symptom of radical health, I have a voracious delight in raw summer fruit, of which I was less eager a few years ago.

One of the most troublesome attendants on my Malady is costiveness, which is perhaps caused by the opiates, though I have not for some months taken any thing more potent than diacodium, and of that not more than twice an ounce at a time, and ⟨very⟩ seldom an ounce in twenty-four hours; but I can seldom go [to] the garden without a cathartick. The aloes mixed with the s⟨quils⟩ even when I exceed the quantity prescribed, has not any effect.

You will be pleased to communicate this account to dear Dr. Heberden, and if any thing is to be done, let me have your joint[9] opinion.

Now—abite curæ[10]—Let me enquire after the club. I hope you meet, and do not forget, Dear Sir, your obliged, humble Servant,

SAM. JOHNSON

7. *Ante* To Bennet Langton, 27 Mar. 1784 and n. 6. SJ borrowed Floyer's work from the Lichfield Cathedral Library 17 July and returned it 9 Nov. (information supplied by Dr. G. W. Nicholls).

8. Floyer suffered from spasmodic asthma, SJ from a bronchial infection accompanied by emphysema (John Wiltshire, *Samuel Johnson in the Medical World*, 1991, pp. 39–40, 72).

9. MS: "j" superimposed upon "c"

10. SJ may be remembering a line from Tibullus (III.vi.7), *ite procul durum curae genus, ite labores*: "go, far away go, toils and troubles, heartless tribe" (trans. J. P. Postgate, Loeb ed.).

Joshua Reynolds

WEDNESDAY 21 JULY 1784

MS: Hyde Collection.
HEADING in JB's hand: To Sir Joshua Reynolds.

Dear Sir: Ashbourne, Derbyshire, July 21, 1784

The tenderness with which I am treated by my friends makes it reasonable to suppose that they are desirous to know the state of my health, and a desire so benevolent ought to be gratified.

I came to Lichfield in two days without any painful fatigue, and on Monday came hither where I purpose to stay and try what air and regularity will effect. I cannot yet persuade myself that I have made much progress in recovery. My sleep is little, my breath is very much encumbred, and my legs are very weak. The water has encreased a little, but has again run off. The most distressing symptom is want of sleep. I am, Sir, with great affection, your most humble servant,

SAM. JOHNSON

James Boswell

MONDAY 26 JULY 1784[1]

PRINTED SOURCE: JB's *Life*, 1791, II.534, 555.

[Ashbourne]

[He wrote to me July 26:] I wish your affairs could have permitted a longer and continued exertion of your zeal and kindness.[2] They that have your kindness may want your ardour. In the mean time I am very feeble, and very dejected.

1. The sequence of letters between SJ and JB, July–Aug. 1784, has been analyzed in detail by R. W. Chapman (*TLS*, 2 Mar. 1946, p. 103). From the excerpts in JB's *Life*, corrected and supplemented with reference to JB's Register of Letters, Chapman argues persuasively that SJ wrote three letters: the first conclusively dated 26 July, the second and third conjecturally dated 5 and 7 Aug. (both responding to JB's letter of 3 Aug.: *Post* To JB, *c.* 5 Aug. 1784 and n. 2).

2. *Ante* To Joshua Reynolds, 8 July 1784 and n. 3.

[July 26, he wrote to me from Ashbourne;] On the 14th I came to Lichfield, and found every body glad to see me. On the 20th, I came hither, and found a house half built,[3] of very uncomfortable appearance, but my own room has not been altered. That a man worn with diseases, in his seventy-second or third year, should condemn part of his remaining life to pass among ruins and rubbish, and that no inconsiderable part, appears to me very strange.—I know that your kindness makes you impatient to know the state of my health, in which I cannot boast of much improvement. I came through the journey without much inconvenience, but when I attempt self-motion I find my legs weak, and my breath very short; this day I have been much disordered. I have no company; the Doctor is busy in his fields, and goes to bed at nine, and his whole system is so different from mine, that we seem formed for different elements; I have, therefore, all my amusement to seek within myself.

3. The alterations that discommoded SJ may have consisted of the addition of a pediment or the construction of a small wing at the west end of the house (Thomas Taylor, *Life of John Taylor*, 1910, p. 20; *Life* IV.548–49).

Richard Brocklesby

SATURDAY 31 JULY 1784

MS: Hyde Collection.

ADDRESS: To Dr. Brocklesby in Norfolk Street, Strand.

Dear Sir: Ashbourn, July 31, 1784

Not recollecting that Dr. Heberden might be at Windsor, I thought your letter long in coming. But, you know, *nocitura petuntur*,[1] the letter which I so much desired tells me that I have lost one of my best and tenderest friends.[2] My comfort is,

1. *nocitura toga, nocitura petuntur / militia*: "in camp and city alike we ask for things that will be our ruin" (Juvenal, *Satires* x.8–9, trans. G. G. Ramsay, Loeb ed.).

2. Edmund Allen died 28 July (*GM* 1784, p. 558).

that he appeared to live like a Man that had always before his eyes the fragility of our present existence, and was therefore, I hope, not unprepared to meet his Judge.

Your attention, dear Sir, and that of Dr. Heberden to my health is extremely kind. I am loath to think that I grow worse; and cannot fairly prove even to my own partiality that I grow much better. I have in part of the interval since the great discharge of urine, been much better than I am now. My breath is very short and the water encroaches and retires. I yesterday took 80 drops of the vinegar of squils at one dose. I am subject to great dejection, but am willing to impute part of my maladies to the chilness and wetness of the weather.

My great distress arises from want of sleep. In Bed I cannot yet get rest. This morning after having tossed myself almost all night, I had recourse to a chair between five and six. I then slept, though not quite easily, for about three hours.

The business of common life must likewise be attended to. When I left London, I consigned to Mr. Allen's care a box of plate, which I now wish to put into your custody, till I come back. This box as I would lodge with[3] you, I[4] have enclosed an order by which you may demand it, and beg that you will take it, as soon as you can. I am, Dear Sir, your most obliged, and most humble servant,

SAM. JOHNSON

3. MS: "it" del. before "with"
4. MS: "and" del. before "I"

Lucy Porter

SATURDAY 31 JULY 1784

MS: Hyde Collection.

ADDRESS: To Mrs. Lucy Porter in Lichfield. Turn at Derby.

My Dearest Love: Ashbourne, Derby shire, July 31, 1784

When We parted, I left You ill, and was ill myself. I am told that at least I do not grow worse, and hope to hear the same of You if I do not hear better. You have had my prayers and I intreat that I may have yours.

I take the air[1] from time to time in the carriage, and find it pleasant at least. But the pleasures of the sick are not great nor many. But let us thank God for the ease and comfort which he is pleased to grant us. If the Summer grows at last warm, it will bring[2] us some help. Let me know, my dear, how you are, and if writing be troublesome, get Mr. Pearson's kind assistance, or that of any other friend. I am, Madam, your most humble servant,

SAM. JOHNSON

Direct to Ashbourne (Turn at Derby).

Make my compliments and return my thanks to Mrs.[3] Cobb to whose kindness I have great obligations.

1. MS: "air" superimposed upon undeciphered erasure
2. MS: "bring" written above one word del.
3. MS: "dear" del. before "Mrs."

Charles Burney

MONDAY 2 AUGUST 1784

MS: Wellcome Historical Medical Library.

ADDRESS: To Dr. Burney, Leicester Fields.

ENDORSEMENTS: From Dr. Johnson, Augst. 2d 1784, No. 10. Ashbourne, Augt. 2, 1784, No. 10.

Dear Sir: Ashbourne, Aug. 2, 1784

The Post at this devious town goes out so soon after it comes in, that I make haste to tell you, what I hope You did not doubt, that you shall certainly have what my thoughts will supply, in recommendation of your new book.[1] Let me know when it will be wanted.

1. SJ provided the dedication to the King for Burney's *An Account of the . . . Commemoration of Handel* (1785) (Hazen, pp. 30–33; Roger Lonsdale, *Dr. Charles Burney*, 1965, p. 285; *Post* To Charles Burney, 23 Aug. 1784; 28 Aug. 1784; 4 Sept. 1784).

My Journey has at least done me no harm, nor can I yet boast of any great good. The weather, you know, has not been very balmy. I am now reduced to think, and am at last content to talk of the weather. Pride must have a fall.

I have lost dear Mr. Allen,[2] and wherever I turn the dead or the dying meet my notice, and force my attention upon misery and mortality. Mrs. Burneys Escape from so much danger, and her ease after so much pain, throws however some radiance of hope upon the gloomy prospect, may her recovery be perfect, and her continuance long.[3]

I struggle hard for life. I take physick, and take air. My Friend's chariot is always ready. We have run this morning twenty four miles, and could run forty eight more. *But who can run the race with Death?* I am, Dear Sir, your most humble Servant,

SAM. JOHNSON

2. *Ante* To Richard Brocklesby, 31 July 1784, n. 2.

3. Elizabeth Burney, who suffered from recurrent bouts of hypochondria, had "gone to Hastings, to try Sea Air" (*The Letters of Dr Charles Burney, 1751–1784*, ed. Alvaro Ribeiro, SJ, 1991, p. 431).

James Boswell

c. THURSDAY 5 AUGUST 1784[1]

PRINTED SOURCE: JB's *Life*, 1791, II.555.

[Having written to him, in bad spirits, a letter filled with dejection and fretfulness, and at the same time expressing anxious apprehensions concerning him, on account of a dream which had disturbed me;[2] his answer was chiefly in terms of reproach, for a supposed charge of] affecting discontent, and

1. See below, n. 2.

2. In his Register, JB summarizes a letter he sent to SJ 3 Aug. The date and the description of this letter tally with the references in the *Life*: "Dr. Samuel Johnson, at Ashbourne. A long melancholy letter, quite in misery from my ambitious project of going to the English bar, being impracticable, at least for some time" (JB's Register of Letters, MS: Beinecke Library).

indulging the vanity of complaint. [It however proceeded,] Write to me often, and write like a man. I consider your fidelity and tenderness as a great part of the comforts which are yet left me, and sincerely wish we could be nearer to each other.—* * * * * * * *.—My dear friend, life is very short and very uncertain; let us spend it as well as we can.—My worthy neighbour, Allen, is dead.[3] Love me as well as you can. Pay my respects to dear Mrs. Boswell.—Nothing ailed me at that time; let your superstition at last have an end.

3. *Ante* To Richard Brocklesby, 31 July 1784, n. 2.

Richard Brocklesby

THURSDAY 5 AUGUST 1784

MS: Hyde Collection.

ADDRESS: To Dr. Brocklesby in Norfolk Street, Strand.

Dear Sir: Ashbourn, Aug. 5, 1784

I have just begun to try the tincture of canthrides, and yesterday took eight drops in the morning and ten in the evening. I have this morning taken twenty more, and a purge. I do not perceive that my Strength either encreases or diminishes, or that my nights grow better or worse, or my breath easier or straiter. I have sometimes taken of the acet. squill.[1] 120 drops in the day with no sensible effect either upon the stomack or urinary passage. I have now a mind to use the cantharides, and will proceed with caution.

My diacodium is almost gone, and I have never been able to get any that seems to admit comparison with Mr. Holders. I have taken now and then, indeed pretty frequently, a grain of opium, which being a cheap drug, is every where genuine. When You knew me first I took three grains, but now seldom more at a time than one.

1. *acetum scilliticum*: dried squills combined with vinegar (William Lewis, *Materia Medica*, 3d ed., 1784, p. 595).

To RICHARD BROCKLESBY, 5 *August* 1784

I return you thanks, dear Sir, for your unwearied attention both medical an[d] friendly, and hope to prove the effect of your care by living to acknowledge it. I am, Dear Sir, your most humble servant,

SAM. JOHNSON

James Boswell

c. SATURDAY 7 AUGUST 1784[1]

PRINTED SOURCE: JB's *Life*, 1791, II.555–56.

[He in two days after, July 28, wrote to me again, giving me an account of his sufferings, after which follows:] Before this letter, you will have had one which I hope you will not take amiss; for it contains only truth, and that truth kindly intended. * * * * * *. *Spartam quam nactus es orna*;[2] make the most and best of your lot, and compare yourself not with the few that are above you, but with the multitudes which are below you. * * * * * *. Go steadily forward with lawful business or honest diversions. "*Be* (as Temple says of the Dutchmen) *well when you are not ill, and pleased when you are not angry*."[3] * * * * * *. This may seem but an ill return for your tenderness; but I mean it well, for I love you with great ardour and sincerity. Pay my respects to dear Mrs. Boswell, and teach the young ones to love me.

1. *Ante* To JB, 26 July 1784, n. 1; *c.* 5 Aug. 1784 and n. 2.

2. In *Epistolae ad Atticum* (IV.6) Cicero quotes a line from Euripides' fragmentary *Telephus*: Σπάρταν ἔλαχες, ταύταν κόσμει ("Sparta has fallen to your lot, do it credit," *Epistolae*, trans. E. O. Windstedt, Loeb ed.). In his *Adagia* (1515, II.v.i) Erasmus renders this as *Spartam nactus es, hanc orna* ("You have obtained Sparta, adorn it") and comments, "This proverb tells us that whatever province we happen to have made our own, we must fit ourselves to it, and suit our behaviour to its dignity" (M. M. Phillips, *The 'Adages' of Erasmus: A Study with Translations*, 1964, p. 300 and n. 3).

3. In his *Observations on the United Provinces of The Netherlands* (1673), Sir William Temple claims that spleen "is a Disease too refin'd for this Countrey and People, Who are well, when they are not ill; and pleas'd when they are not troubled" (Temple, *Observations*, ed. G. N. Clark, 1972, pp. 96–97).

William Bowles

SATURDAY 7 AUGUST 1784

MS: Hyde Collection.

Dear Sir: Ashbourn, Derbyshire, August 7, 1784

I am never long without some proof of your kind attention, and am much obliged by the enquiries which You have lately made for my convenience and information. What I shall be able to do in the winter is yet uncertain.

I have been here now about three weeks, and do not neglect any of the means by which I may hope to grow better. Neither exercise, diet, nor physick are forgotten, but I cannot boast of much improvement. I hope, however, that I am not worse, and not to grow worse, as the weight of time encreases, is not nothing.

In the mean time I hope, dear Sir, that nothing like sickness or sorrow approaches Heale. That your amiable Lady, and lively children are gay and happy, that my little friend goes on successfully with his studies; and that the little Lady's tongue is now as nimble as her feet. I am, Dear Sir, yours most affectionately,

SAM. JOHNSON

William Forbes

SATURDAY 7 AUGUST 1784

MS: National Library of Scotland.

ADDRESS: To Sir William Forbes, Bart., in Edinburgh.

POSTMARK: ASHBORNE.

ENDORSEMENT: Saml. Johnston, Ashbourne, 7 Augt. 1784.

Sir: Ashbourne, Derbyshire, ⟨Aug. 7,⟩[1] 1784

When Mr. Boswel first communicated to me his design of re-

1. MS: mutilated along fold

moving his family to London, I thought of it like all the rest of his Friends; for a while it seemed possible that his desire might evaporate in talk, or that the trouble and difficulty of such a migration might overpower his inclination. I was therefore content to say little, but what I said, he will tell you, was all discouragement. By degrees however I found his ardour for English Honour, and English Pleasures so strong that, he would have considered all open and declared opposition, as envy or malignity, or distrust of his abilities. I therefore withdrew my prohibition[2] on these terms.[3]

That he should not come to London till he had money saved by himself, and unborrowed, sufficient for the removal and establishment of his Family.

That while he resides in London, he shall live[4] on what he receives from his estate, and gets by his practice, without anticipation, or contraction of debts.

To these conditions, he will own, that he has agreed, and if [he][5] keep his own stipulation, you see, Sir, that no great mischief can be incurred. He can lose nothing but his Scottish business in the Scottish courts, which the appeals, and other incidental employment may easily recompense.

The danger is, and that danger is very great, lest he should be driven by his passions beyond the bounds which[6] he has consented to fix. The mischief then may be such[7] as both You and I sincerely wish him to escape. I have told him, with as much energy as I could call to my assistance, that He is too rich for an Adventurer, and by a game so hazardous and daring, he stakes more than he can win.

Since I began this letter, I have received from him a gloomy account of his perplexity and irresolution;[8] and his present intention is to delay his removal.[9] To gain time is a great ad-

2. MS: "prohi" repeated as catchword

3. Cf. *Ante* To JB, 11 July 1784.

4. MS: "live" written above "lives" del.

5. MS: "he" added in JB's hand

6. MS: "which" altered from "the"

7. MS: "very" del. before "such"; "such" superimposed upon "great" partially erased

8. MS: "irresosolution"

9. *Ante* To JB, *c.* 5 Aug. 1784, n. 2.

vantage. Reason and the advice of his Friends will probably prevail. Every reason against his removal, will be stronger another year. I am, Sir, with great respect, your most humble servant,

SAM. JOHNSON

John Hoole

SATURDAY 7 AUGUST 1784

MS: Hyde Collection.

ADDRESS: To Mr. Hoole in great Queen's Street, Lincolns Inn.

POSTMARK: PENY POST PAYD.

ENDORSEMENTS: Dr. Johnson, Dr. Johnson to J. Hoole.

Dear Sir: Ashbourne, Derbyshire, Aug. 7, 1784

Since I was here I have two little letters from You, and have not had the gratitude to write. But every man is most free with his best friends, because he does not suppose that they can suspect him of intentional incivility.

One reason for my omission is, that being in a place to which You are wholly a stranger, I have no topicks of correspondence. If You had any knowledge of Ashbourne, I could tell you of two Ashbourne men who being last week condemned at Derby to be hanged for a robbery, went and hanged themselves in their cell.[1] But this, however it may supply us with talk is nothing to You.

Your kindness, I know, would make You glad to hear some good of Me, but I have not much good to tell, if I grow not worse, it is all that I can say.

I hope Mrs. Hoole receives more help from her migration.

1. "A Letter from Derby, dated August 5, says, Tuesday afternoon our Assizes ended, when the following Prisoners received Sentence of Death, . . . John and Benjamin Jones (Brothers) for a Burglary and Robbery. . . . The two Jones's have since hung themselves in the Cell.—They had tied themselves up to a Beam, with a Cord like Packthread, and were found hanging Face to Face in their Shirts" (*Public Advertiser*, 9 Aug. 1784, p. 4).

Make her my compliments, and write again to, Dear Sir, Your affectionate servant,

SAM. JOHNSON

Richard Brocklesby

THURSDAY 12 AUGUST 1784

MS: Hyde Collection.

ADDRESS: To Dr. Brocklesby in Norfolk street, Strand, London.

POSTMARKS: ASHBORNE, 14 AV.

Dear Sir: Ashbourn, Aug. 12, 1784

I have not much to say but what is included in a short wish, O for an efficacious Diuretick!

You may remember that when I left London in my armamentarium medicum[1] I took by your consent a bottle of Tincture of Cantharides, which though you seemed to be a little afraid [of] it, you considered as having great powers to provoke urine, and such are I believe generally allowed it. Of this dangerous Medicine you directed me to begin with five drops.

I had once suffered by my disobedient excess in the use of squils, and I considered Cantharides as far more formidable; for a long time I did not venture them, but thinking a powerful medicine necessary, I began the use of them this Month.

August. 4. I took Tinct. Cantharid. in the morning 8 drops in the evening, 10.

5. In the morning 10 drops, in the evening, 10.
6. I neglected the account.
7. In the day 60 drops, at night 20 more.
8. In the morning, 20. afternoon. 30. Evening 30.
9. In the morning at two doses. 80.

You see, dear Sir, that of this potent and drastick tincture I have taken 80 drops a day, for three days together, and You are expecting to be told the consequence of my temerity,

1. *armamentarium medicum*: "medicine chest" (literally, "medical arsenal").

which You suppose to be punished with a strangury,[2] or to be rewarded with a salutary flood of water. But the truth is, a very unpleasing truth, that this acrid and vigorous preparation, this *medicamentum anceps*,[3] has been as impotent as morning dew, and has produced[4] no effect either painful or beneficial. I have therefore for the present left it, and as the water daily seems to encrease shall[5] have recourse to squills, of which I have a box, and hope that, as they are mingled with soap, their virtue is not dried away.

It often comes into my mind that a vomit would give some freedom to my respiration, but I have not lately tried it. Let me know your opinion, and Dr. Heberden's, and tell me what emetick I should use. Akensyde speaks much of Ipecacuanha, as relaxing the angustiæ pectoris.[6] Have other Physicians found the same effects? Or would You and Dr. Heberden have me try it?

Pray be so kind as to have me in your thoughts, and mention my case to others as you have opportunity. I seem to myself neither to gain nor lose strength. I have lately tried Milk but have yet found no advantage, and am afraid of it merely as a liquid. My appetite is still good which I know is dear Dr. Heberden's criterion of the vis vitæ.[7]

I have no great confidence in rural pharmacy, and there[fore] wish to have all of my medicines from Mr. Holder. If you have nothing new to order, be pleased to direct a Box of Squil pils, a bottle of Squil vinegar, and a bottle of diacodium to be sent to me at the Rev. Dr. Taylor's in Ashbourne, by the Manchester and Ashbourne Coach at the Swan in Lud Lane. It will come quickly to me. They should be sent the day that You receive this.

2. *strangury*: "a difficulty of urine attended with pain" (SJ's *Dictionary*).

3. *medicamentum anceps*: "hazardous drug."

4. MS: "ced" repeated as catchword

5. MS: "shall" written above "would" del.

6. *angustiae pectoris*: "stricture of the chest." *Ante* To Hester Thrale, 15 Jan. 1777, n. 2; 23 Aug. 1777 and n. 2.

7. *vis vitæ*: "life force."

As we cannot now see each other, do not omit to write, for You cannot think with what warmth of expectation I reckon the hours of a post-day. I am, Dear Sir, Your most humble Servant,

SAM. JOHNSON

Humphry Heeley

THURSDAY 12 AUGUST 1784

MS: Hyde Collection.

ADDRESS: To Mr. Heely, No. 5 in Pye street, Westminster.

POSTMARK: PENY POST PAYD T TU.

Sir: Ashbourne, Derbyshire, Aug. 12, 1784

As necessity obliges You to call so soon again upon me, you should at least have told the smallest sum that will supply your present want: You cannot suppose that I have much to spare. Two Guineas is as much as You ought to be behind with your creditor.

If you wait on Mr. Strahan in New-street, Fetter lane, or in his absence on Mr. Andrew Strahan,[1] show this by which they are entreated to advance you two Guineas, and to keep this as a voucher.[2] I am, Sir, Your humble Servant,

SAM. JOHNSON

The name is STRAHAN.

1. Andrew Strahan (1750–1831), youngest son of William Strahan, worked in the family business, which he was to inherit on his father's death the following year (J. A. Cochrane, *Dr. Johnson's Printer*, 1964, pp. xiv, 131, 207).

2. Heeley presented the "voucher," which was duly preserved by Andrew Strahan and "obligingly communicated" to JB (*Life* IV.371).

Hester Maria Thrale

THURSDAY 12 AUGUST 1784

MS: The Earl of Shelburne.

ADDRESS: To Miss Thrale.

Dear Madam: Ashbourn, Derbyshire, August 12, 1784

Your last letter was received by me at this place, and being so remote from the other Guardians that I could not consult them, I knew not what a[n]swer to make. I take it very kindly that You have written again, for I would not have You forget me, nor imagine that I forget you. Our kindness will last, I hope, longer than our lives. Whatever advice I can give you you may always require; for I love you, I loved your father, and I loved your Mother as long as I could.

At present, I have nothing to impress but these two Maxims, which I trust You never will dismiss from your mind.

In every purpose, and every action, let it be your first care to please God, that awful and just God before whom you must at last appear, and by whose sentence all Eternity will be determined. Think frequently on that state which shall never have an end.

In matters of human judgement, and prudential consideration, consider the publick voice of general opinion as always worthy of great attention; remember that such practices can very seldom be right, which all the world concluded to be wrong.

Obey God. Reverence Fame.

Thus you will go safely through this life, and pass happily to the next.

I am glad that my two other dear Girls are well. I am, dearest Madam, your most humble servant,

SAM. JOHNSON

Richard Brocklesby

SATURDAY 14 AUGUST 1784

MS: Hyde Collection.

ADDRESS: To Dr. Brocklesby in London.

POSTMARKS: ASHBORNE, 16 AV.

Dear Sir: Ashbourn, Aug. 14, 1784

I have hitherto sent you only melancholy letters,[1] You will be glad to hear so[me] better account. Yesterday the as[t]hma perceptibly remitted, and I moved with more ease than I have enjoyed for many weeks. May God continue his mercy.

Of this Remission the immediate cause seemed to be a catharsis and a day's abstinence, but perhaps I have used as much of both often without any benefit.[2] If health encreases and continues, we will not distress our minds with causes.

I doubt not but Mr. Holder has sent his bottles for I dare not yet venture, to be without my weapons.[3]

This account I would not delay, because I am not a lover of complaints or complainers, and yet I have since we parted, uttered nothing till now but terror and sorrow. Write to me, Dear Sir. I am, Your most obliged, and most humble Servant,

SAM. JOHNSON

1. *Ante* To Richard Brocklesby, 21 July 1784; 31 July 1784; 5 Aug. 1784; 12 Aug. 1784.

2. "Johnson thought the cause of his easier breathing might be 'a catharsis and a day's abstinence'; but it is probable that the squills in such large doses had some digoxin-like effect upon his heart" (John Wiltshire, *Samuel Johnson in the Medical World*, 1991, p. 59). Cf. *Post* To William Scott, 10 Oct. 1784.

3. *Ante* To Richard Brocklesby, 12 Aug. 1784 and n. 1.

Thomas Davies

SATURDAY 14 AUGUST 1784

PRINTED SOURCE: JB's *Life*, 1791, II.548.

The tenderness with which you always treat me, makes me

culpable in my own eyes for having omitted to write in so long a separation; I had, indeed, nothing to say that you could wish to hear. All has been hitherto misery accumulated upon misery, disease corroborating disease, till yesterday my asthma was perceptibly and unexpectedly mitigated. I am much comforted with this short relief, and am willing to flatter myself that it may continue and improve. I have at present, such a degree of ease, as not only may admit the comforts, but the duties of life. Make my compliments to Mrs. Davies.—Poor dear Allen, he was a good man.[1]

1. *Ante* To Richard Brocklesby, 31 July 1784, n. 2.

Lucy Porter

SATURDAY 14 AUGUST 1784

MS: Hyde Collection.

ADDRESS: To Mrs. Porter at Green Hill, Lichfield. Turn at Derby.

ENDORSEMENT in an unidentified hand: 1784.

Dear Madam: [Ashbourne] August 14, 1784

This is the first day when I could give any good account of myself. My Asthma which has harrassed me very much, remitted yesterday in a degree which surprised me, and which I pray God to continue. I have been lately very much dejected, and am still very weak, but am more cheerful.

In this place I have every thing but company, and of company I am in great want. Dr. Taylor is at his farm, and I sit at home. Let me hear[1] from You again. And let me hear, if You can, that You[2] are better. Pray for me. I am, my Dearest, Your most humble Servant,

SAM. JOHNSON

1. MS: "hear" written above undeciphered deletion
2. MS: "Your"

Richard Brocklesby

MONDAY 16 AUGUST 1784

MS: Hyde Collection.

ADDRESS: To Dr. Brocklesby in London.

POSTMARK: 18 AV.

Dear Sir: Ashbourn, Aug. 16, 1784

Better, I hope, and better. My respiration gets more and more ease and liberty. I went to Church yesterday after a very liberal din[n]er, without any inconvenience. It is indeed no long walk, but I never walked it without difficulty, since I came, before. I have now no care about the vomit, of which the intention was only to overpower the seeming *vis inertiæ* of the pectoral and pulmonary muscles.

I am favoured with a degree of ease that very much delights me, and do not despair of another race upon the stairs of the Academy.[1]

If I were however of a humour to see or to show the state of my body on the dark side, I might say

Quid te exempta juvat spinis de pluribus una?[2]

the nights are still sleepless, and the water rises, though it does not rise very fast. Let us however rejoice in all the good that we have. The remission of one disease will enable Nature to combat the rest.

I do not think you chargable with the inefficacy of the Cantharides. You did not originally prescribe them, nor much encourage them, upon my proposal.

The squills I have not neglected. For I have taken more than a hundred drops a day, and one day took two hundred and forty, which according to the popular equivalence of a drop to a grain is more than half an ounce. I purpose to try the infusion of wood ashes, and indeed to try all the diureticks, and

1. *Ante* To Hester Thrale, 26 Apr. 1784.

2. *quid te exempta iuvat spinis de pluribus una*: "What good does it do you to pluck out a single one of many thorns?" (Horace, *Epistles* II.ii.212, trans. H. R. Fairclough, Loeb ed.).

therefore wish for as much intelligence as can be had, of as many as have been found at any time successful. I have now spirit to try any thing.

I thank you, dear Sir, for your attention in ordering the medicines. Your attention to me has never failed. If the virtue of medicines could be enforced by the benevolence of the Prescriber how soon should I be well.

Dr. Taylor charges me to send his Compliments. I am, dear Sir, your most humble servant,

SAM. JOHNSON

William Strahan

MONDAY 16 AUGUST 1784

PRINTED SOURCE: C. K. Shorter, *Unpublished Letters of Dr. Samuel Johnson*, 1915.

Sir, [Ashbourne] August 16, 1784

If I have been long without writing I have broken no laws of friendship. I have suppressed nothing that my friends could be glad to hear. My time has passed in the toil of perpetual struggle with very oppressive disorder, till I obtained about four days ago an interval of relief. My breath has become more free, and I can therefore move with less encumbrance.[1]

What has procured this alleviation, or how I may hope to enjoy it, I cannot tell, but it gives me great comfort, and the delight which I receive I am waiting[2] to communicate to those whose kindness has given me reason to think that they take part in my pains or pleasures. I flatter myself now with coming again to town and being again a member of society.

I have not now heard for a long time either of your health or that of dear Mrs. Strahan. I hope that you are well and that

1. *Ante* To Richard Brocklesby, 14 Aug. 1784 and n. 2.

2. R. W. Chapman suggests that "waiting" is a misreading of either "writing" or "willing" (Chapman III.200 n. 1).

she is better, and that we shall all have a little more enjoyment of each other. I am, Sir, your most humble servant,

SAM. JOHNSON

Richard Brocklesby

THURSDAY 19 AUGUST 1784

MS: Hyde Collection.

ADDRESS: To Dr. Brocklesby in London.

POSTMARKS: ASHBORNE, 21 AV.

Dear Sir: Ashbourn, Aug. 19, 1784

The relaxation of the As[t]hma still continues, yet I do not trust it wholly to itself, but soothe it now and then with an opiate. I not only perform the perpetual act of respiration with less labour, but I can walk with fewer intervals of rest and with greater freedom of motion.

I never thought well of Dr. James's compounded medicines. His ingredients appeared to me sometimes inefficacious and trifling, and sometimes heterogeneous, and destructive of each other. This prescription exhibits a composition of about 330 grains, in which[1] there are 4 gr. of Emetick Tartar, and 6 drops of Thebaick tincture.[2] He that writes thus, surely writes for show. The basis of his Medicine is the Gum Ammoniacum,[3] which dear Dr. Laurence used to give, but of which I never saw any effect. We will, if you please let this medicine alone. The Squills have every suffrage, and in the squills we will rest for the present.

The Water which I consider as *fundi nostri calamitas*,[4] has

1. MS: "w" superimposed upon "th"

2. *Thebaick tincture*: "laudanum" (*OED*).

3. *gum ammoniacum*: "a concrete gummy-resinous juice; brought from the East Indies. . . . Its principal virtue is that of resolving obstructions; in which intention, it is frequently made use of in asthmas" (William Lewis, *Materia Medica*, 3d ed., 1784, pp. 47–48).

4. SJ quotes part of a line from Terence (*Eunuchus* I.i.79) for the sake of an

made some encroachments, but does not seem just now to gain ground, my urinary discharges are in the night commonly copious.

I will take my vinegar of Squills which has come down safe with my other medicines, and will be careful to send an account of any change that may happen. My great distress is inability to sleep. I am, Dear Sir, your most obliged, and most humble servant,

SAM. JOHNSON

anatomical pun: *fundi nostri calamitas* can mean not only "the blight of our farm" or "mildew on our crops" but also "the disease of our bottom" (*Oxford Latin Dictionary*; Terence, *The Eunuch*, trans. John Sargeaunt, Loeb ed.). Three years before SJ had indulged in similar wordplay: "I say the *woman* was *fundamentally* sensible" (*Life* IV.99).

George Nicol

THURSDAY 19 AUGUST 1784

MS: Gerald M. Goldberg.

ADDRESS: To Mr. ⟨Ni⟩col, Bookseller in the Strand, London.

POSTMARKS: ASHBORNE, 21 AV.

Dear Sir: Ashbourne, Derbyshire,[1] Aug. 19, 1784

Since We parted I have been very much oppressed by my As[t]hma, but it has lately been less laborious.[2] When I sit I am almost at ease, and I can walk, though yet very little, with less difficulty for this week past, than before. I hope, I shall again enjoy my Friends, and that You and I shall have a little more literary conversation.

Where I now am, every thing is very liberally provided for me but conversation. My Friend is sick himself, and the reciprocation of complaints and groans affords[3] not much of either pleasure or instruction. What we have not at home this town

1. MS: "D" superimposed upon "St"
2. *Ante* To Richard Brocklesby, 14 Aug. 1784 and n. 2.
3. MS: "affords" repeated as catchword

does not supply, and I shall be glad [of] a little imported intelligence, and hope that you will bestow now and then a little time on the relief and entertainment of, Sir, Your humble servant,

SAM. JOHNSON

Joshua Reynolds

THURSDAY 19 AUGUST 1784

MS: Hyde Collection.

ADDRESS: To Sir Joshua Reynolds in London.

POSTMARKS: ASHBORNE, 21 AV.

ENDORSEMENT: Dr. Johnson.

Dear Sir: Ashbourn, Aug. 19, 1784

Having had since our separation little to say that I could please You or Myself by saying, I have not been lavish of useless letters, but I flatter myself that You will partake of the pleasure with which I can now tell you, that about a week ago, I felt suddenly a sensible remission of my Asthma, and consequently a greater[1] lightness of action and motion.[2]

Of this grateful alleviation I know not the cause, nor dare depend upon its continuance, but while it lasts, I endeavour to enjoy it, and am desirous of communicating, while it lasts, my pleasure to my Friends. I am, Dear Sir, Your most humble Servant,

SAM. JOHNSON

Hitherto, dear Sir, I had written before the post, which stays in this town but a little while, brought me your letter. Mr. Davies seems to have represented my little tendency to recovery in terms too splendid. I am still restless, still weak, still watry, but the asthma is less oppressive.

Poor Ramsay![3] On which side soever I turn, Mortality pre-

1. MS: "greater" altered from "greatness"

2. *Ante* To Richard Brocklesby, 14 Aug. 1784 and n. 2.

3. Allan Ramsay had died 10 Aug. "at Dover, on his return from the continent" (*GM* 1784, p. 638). *Ante* To Hester Maria Thrale, 26 Apr. 1783; 23 Aug. 1783.

sents its formidable frown. I left three old friends at Lichfield, when I was last there, and now found them all dead. I no sooner lose sight of dear Allen, than I am told that I shall see him no more.[4] That we must all die, we always knew, I wish I had sooner remembred it. Do not think me intrusive or importunate if I now call, dear Sir, on You to remember it.

That the President of the Academy founded by the King, should be the King's painter is surely very congruous. You say the place ought to fall into your hands *with asking for*, I suppose You meant to write *without asking for*. If You ask for it I believe You will have no refusal, what is to be expected *without* asking, I cannot say. Your treatment at court has been capricious, inconsistent, and unaccountable. You were always honoured, however, while others were employed. If You are desirous of the place, I see not why You should not ask it. That sullen pride which expects to be solicited to its own advantage, can hardly be justified by the highest degree of human excellence.[5]

4. *Ante* To Richard Brocklesby, 31 July 1784, n. 2.

5. Reynolds had expected immediately to succeed Ramsay as Painter to the King. However, "he [Reynolds] was unwilling to solicit it, as was usual. But at last he complied with the custom, and received the appointment" (C. R. Leslie and Tom Taylor, *The Life and Times of Sir Joshua Reynolds*, 1865, II.448; James Northcote, *The Life of Sir Joshua Reynolds*, 1818, II.187). Reynolds was sworn in 1 Sept. 1784 (Leslie and Taylor, *Reynolds* II.448). *Post* To Joshua Reynolds, 2 Sept. 1784.

William Windham

c. FRIDAY 20 AUGUST 1784[1]

MS: Hyde Collection.

ENDORSEMENT: Doct. Johnson, Augt. 1784.

HEADING in JB's hand: To the Right Honourable William Windham.

NOTE in JB's hand: No date—but marked by Mr. Windham August 1784.

1. Dated with reference to SJ's "Remission" (*Ante* To Richard Brocklesby, 14 Aug. 1784).

Dear Sir: [Ashbourne]

The tenderness with which You have been pleased to treat me through my long ilness, neither health nor sickness can, I hope, make me forget; and You are not to suppose that after we parted, You were no longer in my mind. But what can a sick man say, but that he is sick, his thought[s] are necessarily concentred in himself, he neither receives nor can give delight; his enquiries are[2] after alleviations of pain, and his efforts are to catch some momentary comfort.

Though I am now in the neighborhood of the peak, You must expect no account of its wonders, of its hills, its waters, its caverns, or its mines; but I will tell you, Dear Sir, what I hope You will not hear with less satisfaction, that for about a week past my Asthma has been less afflictive. I am, Dear sir, Your most humble servant,

SAM. JOHNSON

Be pleased to make my compliments to the Burkes.

2. MS: "a" superimposed upon "?m"

Richard Brocklesby

SATURDAY 21 AUGUST 1784

MS: Hyde Collection.

ADDRESS: To Dr. Brocklesby in London.

POSTMARKS: ASHBORNE, 23 AV.

Dear Sir: Ashbourn, Aug. 21, 1784

My Breath continues still more lax and easy. The history of this commodious remission you shall now have. Having been long wearisomely breathless, On thursday the 12th I took a purge which operated with more violence than is common. I took no din[n]er at all. I took 240 drops of acet. squill.[1] The

1. *Ante* To Richard Brocklesby, 5 Aug. 1784, n. 1.

Squils seemed to do little. After I had been in bed some hours I took two grains of opium, and in the morning, I believe, I slept. When I rose, I find my breath easier and my limbs lighter. I walked to church, and returned, with unexpected facility. My breath from that time has been, though not equal, yet always easier than when we parted.

Yesterday, I repeated the experiment of purging without eating, but in my purge I poured so much of my new vinegar that after some struggle the stomach rejected it, and I underwent, in some degree, the operation of an emetick. I resolved however not to quit my purpose, and when a little rest had appeased my stomach took another cathartick, and with very little din[n]er waited the event. The cathartick took its natural course, and the squills, though I did not repeat them, paid me for my sickness, for I think the discharge of urine was encreased, which I am now endeavouring to promote. My Stomach is good, but I have taken no flesh yesterday or to day.

The kindness which you show by having me in your thoughts on all occasions will I hope allways fill my heart with gratitude. Be pleased to return my thanks to Sir George Baker[2] for the consideration which he has bestowed upon me.

Is this the Ballon that has been so long expected this Ballon to which I subscribed, but without payment? It is pity that Philosophers have been disappointed, and shame that they have been cheated; But I know not well how to prevent either. Of this Experiment[3] I have[4] read nothing, where was it Exhibited? and who was[5] the man that ran away with so much money?[6]

Continue, dear Sir, to write often and[7] more at a time; for none of your prescription[s] operate to their proper uses more

2. Sir George Baker (1722–1809), Bt. (1776), M.D., F.R.S., a socially prominent physician with literary inclinations; his patients included King George III, Queen Charlotte, and Sir Joshua Reynolds.

3. MS: "Experiment" altered from "Experiments"

4. MS: "have have"

5. MS: "was was"

6. *Ante* To Hester Maria Thrale, 31 Jan. 1784, n. 2; *Ante* To William Bowles, 3 Feb. 1784.

7. MS: "an" superimposed upon "w"

certainly than your letters operate as cordials. I am, Dear Sir, Your most humble Servant,

SAM. JOHNSON

Francesco Sastres

SATURDAY 21 AUGUST 1784

PRINTED SOURCE: Piozzi, *Letters* II.405–7.

Dear Sir, Ashbourne, August 21, 1784

I am glad that a letter has at last reached you; what became of the two former, which were directed to *Mortimer* instead of *Margaret* Street, I have no means of knowing, nor is it worth the while to enquire; they neither enclosed bills, nor contained secrets.[1]

My health was for some time quite at a stand, if it did not rather go backwards; but for a week past it flatters me with appearances of amendment, which I dare yet hardly credit. My breath has been certainly less obstructed for eight days; and yesterday the water seemed to be disposed to a fuller flow. But I get very little sleep; and my legs do not like to carry me.

You were kind in paying my forfeits at the club;[2] it cannot be expected that many should meet in the summer, however they that continue in town should keep up appearances as well as they can. I hope to be again among you.

I wish you had told me distinctly the mistakes in the French words. The French is but a secondary and subordinate part of your design;[3] exactness, however, in all parts is necessary, though complete exactness cannot be attained; and the French are so well stocked with dictionaries, that a little attention may easily keep you safe from gross faults; and as you work on,

1. Sastres lived at No. 14 Margaret Street, Cavendish Square (*Post* To Francesco Sastres, 17 Nov. 1784).

2. *Ante* To Hester Maria Thrale, 31 Jan. 1784, n. 7.

3. There is no record that Sastres's lexicographic project ever came to fruition (*Post* To Francesco Sastres, 2 Sept. 1784; 16 Sept. 1784; 20 Oct. 1784).

your vigilance will be quickened, and your observation regulated; you will better know your own wants, and learn better whence they may be supplied. Let me know minutely the whole state of your negotiations. Dictionaries are like watches, the worst is better than none, and the best cannot be expected to go quite true.

The weather here is very strange summer weather; and we are here two degrees nearer the north than you. I was I think loath to think a fire necessary in July, till I found one in the servants hall, and thought myself entitled to as much warmth as them.

I wish you would make it a task to yourself to write to me twice a week; a letter is a great relief to, Dear Sir, Your, etc.

Charles Burney

MONDAY 23 AUGUST 1784

MS: Hyde Collection.[1]

ADDRESS: To Dr. Burney in St. Martins Street, Leicester Fields, London.

POSTMARKS: ASHBORNE, 25 AV.

ENDORSEMENTS: Ashburne, Augt. 23, 1784, No. 9. From Dr. Johnson, a fragment, Augst. 23d 1784. No. 11.

Dear Sir: [Ashbourne] August 23, 1784

When I came to think on this,[2] I had quite forgot what we had said to the Queen,[3] and as it was natural to say the same again on the same subject, I was forced to look out for some remote track of thought, which I believe, you will think I have found; but it has given me some trouble, and perhaps may not please at last so well. But necessity must be obeyed.

⟨ ⟩

1. MS: mutilated; first paragraph (with address, postmarks, and endorsements on verso) and last paragraph have been recovered

2. *Ante* To Charles Burney, 2 Aug. 1784 and n. 1.

3. SJ had provided the dedication to the Queen in Burney's *History of Music* (vol. I, 1776) (Hazen, pp. 23–30; Roger Lonsdale, *Dr. Charles Burney*, 1965, p. 168).

I hope Mrs. Burney is quite recovered,[4] and that my naughty Girl is well. I am very poorly, but I think better to day than yesterday. I am, Dear Sir, Your most humble servant,

SAM. JOHNSON

4. *Ante* To Charles Burney, 2 Aug. 1784 and n. 3.

John Ryland

MONDAY 23 AUGUST 1784

MS: Hyde Collection.

Dearest Sir: [Ashbourne] Aug. 23, 1784

I sent You last post an idle letter, which could mean only to provoke you to write. I am indeed in a place whence You cannot expect much entertainment, and my thoughts You will easily believe turn much upon myself. My health has its vicissitudes. The Asthma has been for some time very considerably relieved, but last night it attacked me again, but is now milder. The water has taken possession of my legs and thighs, but does not encrease very fast, and I flatter myself from time[1] to time with its diminution, but in fact since I came hither, I cannot say that it is less. My legs are miserably weak, a few step[s] tires them, and my nights are miserably sleepless. And this being a very miserable account shall not be longer.

I find that poor dear Payne is a little better, and cannot but hope that, as his ilness is to a great degree superinduced and accidental, he may yet recover.[2] I love him much.

The Letter and Verses I received at Oxford, and brought them with me I suppose to London, but am afraid I shall hardly find them. If there was any thing in them which required particular notice let me have them again.

I am here in a clear air rather too keen, in a house where I want nothing but company, but I want company so much, that

1. MS: "t" superimposed upon "d"

2. *Post* To John Ryland, 2 Sept. 1784; 29 Sept. 1784; 6 Oct. 1784.

I often languish in dejection, which probably I should not feel, if I had you to talk with. I am, Dear Sir, Your most affectionate servant,

SAM. JOHNSON

Richard Brocklesby

THURSDAY 26 AUGUST 1784

MS: Hyde Collection.

ADDRESS: To Dr. Brocklesby in London.

POSTMARKS: ASHBORNE, 28 AV.

Dear Sir: [Ashbourne] Aug. 26, 1784

I suffered You to escape the last post without a letter, but You [are] not to expect such indulgence[1] very often, for I write not so much because I have any thing to say, as because, I hope for an answer, and the vacancy of my life here makes a letter of great value.

I ply the squills hard commonly taking an hundred drops of the vinegar a day, but I am not certain of any sensible effect. The Water however does not encrease, and the asthma continues in its milder state. My legs are miserably weak, and my nights restless and tedious, but *Spes alit.*[2]

I believe your intelligence of Dr. Taylors return to London, is mistaken. I shall certainly not stay here behind him, but what to do with myself who can tell me?

I have here little company and little amusement, and thus abandoned to the contemplation of my own miseries, I am sometimes gloomy and depressed, this too I resist as I can, and find opium, I think useful, but I seldom take more than one grain. The diacodium has not agreed with me, perhaps its fermentation makes it flatulent.

1. MS: "i" superimposed upon "s" partially erased

2. *Spes alit agricolas*: "Hope sustains the husbandmen" (*Cree's Dictionary of Latin Quotations*, 1978, p. 204).

Is not this strange weather? Winter absorbed the spring, and now autumn is come before we have had summer.

But let not our kindness for each other imitate the inconstancy of the seasons.

Have You ever known Ol. ter. do any good. It will I know, scent the urine strongly,[3] so will asparagus.[4] If it has ever produced bloody urine, it is a strong proof of its stimulating powers, and would raise hopes; I have no unwillingness to[5] try whatever is recommended by adequate authority. I am, Dear Sir, Your most humble Servant,

SAM. JOHNSON

3. Oil of terebinth, or turpentine, is "a most potent stimulating detergent diuretic"; it acts "in a peculiar manner on the urinary organs, impregnating the water with a violet smell" (William Lewis, *Materia Medica*, 3d ed., 1784, pp. 639–40).

4. Asparagus does have the effect ascribed to it by SJ (information supplied by Dr. B. L. Levinson).

5. MS: "to" repeated as catchword

Bennet Langton

THURSDAY 26 AUGUST 1784

MS: Hyde Collection.

ADDRESS: To Benet Langton, Esq., at Rochester, By London.

POSTMARKS: ASHBORNE, 28 AV.

Dear Sir: Ashbourn, August 26, 1784

The kindness of your last letter, and my omission to answer it, begins to give you even in my opinion a right to recriminate, and to charge me with forgetfulness of the absent.[1] I will therefore delay no longer to give an account of myself, and wish I could relate what would please either myself or my Friend.

On July 13. I left London, partly in hope of help from new air and change of place, and partly excited by the sick man's

1. *Ante* To Bennet Langton, 12 July 1784.

impatience of the present. I got to Lichfield in a stage vehicle, with very little fatigue in two days, and had the consolation to find that since my last visit, my three old acquaintance were all dead.

July 20. I went to Ashbourne where I have been till now, the house in which we live is repairing.[2] I live in too much solitude, and am often deeply dejected; I wish we were nearer and rejoice in your removal to London.[3] A friend at once cheerful and serious is a great acquisition. Let us not neglect one another for the little time which Providence allows us to hope.

Of my health I cannot tell you what my wishes persuaded me to expect, that it is much improved by the season or by remedies. I am sleepless; my legs grow weary with a very few steps, and the water breaks its boundaries in some degree. The Asthma, however, has remitted, my breath is still much obstructed, but is more free than it was. Nights of watchfulness produce torpid days. I read very little though I am alone, for I am tempted to supply in the day what I lost in bed.

This is my history, like all other histories, a narrative of misery. Yet am I so much better than in the beginning of the year, that[4] I ought to be ashamed of complaining. I now sit and write with very little sensibility of pain or weakness. But when I rise, I shall[5] find my legs betraying me.

Of the money which you mentioned I have no immediate need, keep it however for me, unless some exigence requires it.[6] Your papers I will show You certainly when You would see them, but I am a little angry at You for not keeping minutes of your own *acceptum et expensum*,[7] and think a little time might

2. *Ante* To JB, 26 July 1784 and n. 3.

3. It is possible that Langton planned to take up residence again in the Fleet Street lodgings he had engaged in March, "in order . . . to devote himself" to SJ (William Roberts, *Memoirs of the Life and Correspondence of Mrs. Hannah More*, 1834, I.178).

4. MS: "there were any hopes ⟨this recovery⟩," del. before "that"

5. MS: "shall" repeated as catchword

6. It seems unlikely that SJ refers to the £750 he had on deposit with Langton at the time of his death (*Life* IV.402 n. 2).

7. *acceptum et expensum*: "receipts and expenditure."

be spared from Aristophanes,[8] for the *res familiares*.[9] Forgive me, for I mean well.

I hope, dear Sir, that You and Lady Rothes, and all the young people, too many to enumerate, are well and happy. God bless you all. I am, dear Sir, Your most humble Servant,

SAM. JOHNSON

8. Langton was an accomplished classical scholar, with a special interest in Greek literature.

9. *res familiares*: "patrimony, domestic estate."

Unidentified Correspondent

LATE SUMMER 1784

MS: Hyde Collection.

⟨ ⟩ any help, for she would see no physical man.[1] Mrs. Gastrel is brisk and merry. Since I was at Lichfield last time three of my old acquaintances are dead. This is frightful.

1. The presumption is that SJ refers to Elizabeth Aston.

Charles Burney

SATURDAY 28 AUGUST 1784

MS: Pierpont Morgan Library.

Dear Sir: Ashbourn, Augst. 28, 1784

You see that I am not a tardy correspondent, though I know not well how to comply with your desire. I have forgotten the series of the paragraphs and if I remembred them it is not easy to knead new matter into a composition.[1]

Of the two additions proposed, relating to the Countenance

1. SJ refers to the dedication for Burney's *Commemoration of Handel* (*Ante* To Charles Burney, 2 Aug. 1784 and n. 1).

given to Musick by his name, and, the evidence which he has given of his taste, the first has been expressed in the last paragraph,[2] I think, as if we had foreknown it, so that nothing more can properly be said. The other has more difficulty.

After, *the most elegant of their pleasures* suppose we added something like this. "But that this pleasure may be truly elegant Science[3] and Nature must assist each other; a quick sensibility of melody[4] (or harmony) is not always originally bestowed, and those who are born with nice susceptibility of modulation, are often ignorant of its principles and must[5] therefore be in a great degree delighted[6] by chance; but when Your Majesty is pleased to be[7] present at Musical performances, the artists may congratulate[8] themselves upon the attention of a judge in whom all[9] requis[i]tes concur, who hears them not with instinctive emotion, but with rational approbation, and whose praise[10] of Handel is[11] not the effusion[12] of credulity, but the conviction[13] of science."[14]

I hope this may serve, or may awaken something in your own thoughts that may do better.

2. *Post* To Charles Burney, 4 Sept. 1784 and n. 2.

3. MS: "it must be Art" del. before "Science"

4. MS: "melo" repeated as catchword

5. MS: "must" written above "are" del.

6. MS: "delighted" written above "pleased only" del.

7. MS: "honour" del. before "be"

8. MS: "congratulatate"

9. MS: "are" del. before "all"

10. MS: "praise" altered from "praises"

11. MS: "is" written above "are" del.

12. MS: "effusion" altered from "effusions"

13. MS: "dictate" written above "conviction"; "conviction" altered from "convictions"

14. The published version of this paragraph reads: "But that this pleasure may be truly elegant, science and nature must assist each other; a quick sensibility of Melody and Harmony, is not always originally bestowed, and those who are born with this susceptibility of modulated sounds, are often ignorant of its principles, and must therefore be in a great degree delighted by chance; but when Your Majesty is pleased to be present at Musical performances, the artists may congratulate themselves upon the attention of a judge in whom all requisites concur, who hears them not merely with instinctive emotion, but with rational approbation, and whose praise of HANDEL is not the effusion of credulity, but the emanation of Science" (Hazen, p. 33).

I am, I think, not better, nor worse. I am often very much dejected, and wish for something to make me cheerful, to which the letters of my Friends always contribute. I am, Dear Sir, Your most humble Servant,

SAM. JOHNSON

Richard Brocklesby

MONDAY 30 AUGUST 1784

MS: Hyde Collection.

ADDRESS: To Dr. Brocklesby in London.

POSTMARKS: ASHBORNE, 1 SE.

Dear Sir: Ashbourn, Aug. 30, 1784

Mr. Wyndham has called to day, to take[1] up my writing time,[2] however I snatch a moment to tell You that every thing[3] seems to go on better and better. My Water has lately run away, my Man tells me that my legs are grown less; and my breath is much less obstructed. I think the Squils have been a very useful medicine. My two last nights have been better. I registred one of them in my medical journal, nox jucunda,[4] which it is long since I could say of a night before. I am, Dear Sir, your most humble Servant,

SAM. JOHNSON

1. MS: "take" altered from "taken"

2. William Windham stayed two nights in Ashbourne, leaving on the afternoon of 1 Sept. (*Life* IV.544).

3. MS: "things"

4. *nox jucunda*: "a pleasant night" (*Works*, Yale ed. I.390).

Richard Brocklesby

THURSDAY 2 SEPTEMBER 1784

MS: Hyde Collection.

Dear Sir: Ashbourne, Sept. 2, 1784

If nothing is better than when I wrote last, nothing is worse.

But I think every thing grows gradually better. By a pertinacious use of the squils, or by some other cause while I used them, the flux of water has encreased. My thighs are no longer hard, nor are my legs now in any remarkable degree tumid. The Asthma, I think, continues to remit, and my breath passes with more freedom to day than yesterday. I have since the *nox jucunda*,[1] set down *nox felix somno*[2] and *nox placida cum somno*.[3] Such Nights it is long since I have known.

Mr. Windham has been here to see me, he came I think, forty miles out of his way, and staid about a day and[4] a half, perhaps I make the time shorter than it was.[5] Such conversation I shall not have again till I come back to the regions of literature, and even there Windham is—inter stellas—Luna minores.[6]

Your squil pils, are perfect bullets, I commonly divide one into four. They begin now to purge me, which I suppose you intended, and that they produce their effect is to me another token that Nature is recovering[7] its original powers, and the functions returning to their proper state. God continue his mercies, and grant me to use them rightly. I am, dear sir, your most obliged and most humble servant,

SAM. JOHNSON

1. *Ante* To Richard Brocklesby, 30 Aug. 1784, n. 4.

2. *nox felix somno*: "a night made happy by sleep" (*Works*, Yale ed. I.391).

3. *nox placida cum somno*: "a placid night with sleep" (*Works*, Yale ed. I.391).

4. MS: "and" repeated as catchword

5. *Ante* To Richard Brocklesby, 30 Aug. 1784, n. 2.

6. *velut inter ignes / luna minores*: "As the moon among the lesser lights" (Horace, *Odes* I.xii.47–48, trans. C. E. Bennett, Loeb ed.).

7. MS: "tur" del. before "covering"

Joshua Reynolds

THURSDAY 2 SEPTEMBER 1784

MS: Hyde Collection.

ENDORSEMENT: Dr. Johnson.

Dear Sir: Ashbourne, Sept. 2, 1784

I am glad that a little favour from the court has intercepted your furious purposes.[1] I could not in any case have approved such publick violence of resentment, and should have considered any who encouraged it, as rather seeking sport for themselves, than honour for You. Resentment gratifies him who intended an injury, and pains him unjustly who did not intend it. But all this is now superfluous.

I still continue, by God's Mercy, to mend. My Breath is easier, my nights are quieter, and my legs are less in bulk, and stronger in use. I have however yet a great deal to overcome, before I can yet attain even an[2] old Man's health.

Write, do write to me now and then. We are now old acquaintance, and perhaps few people have lived so much and so long together, with less cause of complaint on either side. The retrospection of this is very pleasant, and I hope we shall never think on each other with less kindness. I am, Dear Sir, Your affectionate Servant, SAM. JOHNSON

1. Reynolds had contemplated resigning his position as President of the Royal Academy, "finding, . . . on the death of [Allan] Ramsay, that the place of King's Painter was not, as it should have been, at once given to him" (C. R. Leslie and Tom Taylor, *The Life and Times of Sir Joshua Reynolds*, 1865, II.448; *Ante* To Joshua Reynolds, 19 Aug. 1784 and n. 5). He had been sworn in as Painter to the King the previous day (*Ante* To Joshua Reynolds, 19 Aug. 1784, n. 5).

2. MS: "an" repeated as catchword

John Ryland

THURSDAY 2 SEPTEMBER 1784

PRINTED SOURCE: Chapman III.213–14.

Dear Sir: Ashbourne, Sept. 2, 1784

Your jealousy of opium I consider as one more evidence of your kindness, and as it is reasonable, I think the laws of friendship require, that it should be pacified.

When I first began to take opium, my usual dose was three

grains, which I found was in the opinion of physicians a great quantity. I know not however that it ever did me harm for I did not take it often; yet that the demands of my constitution might not encrease, I tried to satisfy it with less, and the event is, that I have sometimes attained my purpose of appeasing spasms or abating chilness by half a grain, sometimes by a grain, and have now perhaps for six Months never taken more than two. My dose at present is one grain, taken not habitually but occasionally, for it is by frequent intermissions that so small a dose can preserve its efficacy. In the last six days I have taken only two grains of opium.

My health is indeed very much improved. My breath which ⟨was⟩ extremely straitened, is now, though far from free, yet much less encumbred, and my thighs which began to swell very formidably, are by discharge of the water again shrunk almost to the size of health. God has been pleased to give me another warning by another reprieve; May he make the warning efficacious. Surely every hour convinces a thinking man how little he does, how little he has done, how little he can do for himself.

You are without female attention, and you have my sympathy, I know the misery of that vacuity in domestick life. The loss of Mrs. Williams who had been my inmate for about thirty years is not likely to be repaired, such another cannot easily be found, and I am not now qualified to beat the field of life. She was always at hand for conversation, and in almost all conversation was able to take part.

From the retrospect of life when solitude, leisure, accident, or darkness turn my thoughts upon it, I shrink with multiplicity of horrour. I look forward with less pain. Behind, is wickedness and folly, before, is the hope of repentance, the possibility of amendment, and the final hope of everlasting mercy. In all endeavour of amendments, and in the hope of mercy, let us, for the remaining days whether few or more, support and encourage one another. This is the true use of friendship.

My opinion is that as poor Payne's ilness,[1] was superinduced

1. *Ante* To John Ryland, 23 Aug. 1784.

by too much labour, it will be in a great measure alleviated by rest freely indulged, and properly continued. I should count his death a great loss. I am, dearest Sir, Your affectionate,

SAM. JOHNSON

Francesco Sastres

THURSDAY 2 SEPTEMBER 1784

PRINTED SOURCE: Piozzi, *Letters* II.407–8.

Dear Sir, Ashbourne, Sept. 2, 1784

Your critick seems to me to be an exquisite Frenchman;[1] his remarks are nice; they would at least have escaped me. I wish you better luck with your next specimen; though if such slips as these are to condemn a dictionary, I know not when a dictionary will be made.[2] I cannot yet think that *gourmander* is wrong;[3] but I have here no means of verifying my opinion.

My health, by the mercy of God, still improves; and I have hope of standing the English winter, and of seeing you, and reading Petrarch at Bolt-court; but let me not flatter myself too much. I am yet weak, but stronger than I was.

I suppose the club is now almost forsaken;[4] but we shall I hope meet again. We have lost poor Allen; a very worthy man, and to me a very kind and officious[5] neighbour.

Of the pieces ascribed by Bembo to Virgil,[6] the *Dirce* (ascribed I think to Valerius Cato), the *Copa* and the *Moretum* are,

1. *Frenchman*: "a (good, etc.) French scholar" (*OED*).

2. *Ante* To Francesco Sastres, 21 Aug. 1784 and n. 3.

3. Émile Littré's *Dictionnaire de la langue française* lists six meanings for *gourmander.* Although the first of these, "se livrer à la gourmandise," is attested in Malherbe, it does not appear in the French Academy's *Dictionnaire* (Littré, *Dictionnaire*, 1957, IV.165).

4. SJ refers to the Essex Head Club.

5. *officious*: "full of good offices." Cf. SJ's "On the Death of Dr. Robert Levet": "Officious, innocent, sincere" (*Poems*, l. 7, p. 234).

6. The ascription occurs in "Petri Bembi ad Herculem Strotium De Virgilii Culice," in *Opere del Cardinale Pietro Bembo* (Venice, 1729), IV.307.

together with the *Culex* and *Ceiris*, in Scaliger's *Appendix ad Virgilium*.[7] The rest I never heard the name of before.

I am highly pleased with your account of the gentleman and lady with whom you lodge; such characters have sufficient attractions to draw me towards them; you are lucky to light upon them in the casual commerce of life.

Continue, dear Sir, to write to me; and let me hear any thing or nothing, as the chance of the day may be. I am, Sir, Your, etc.

7. The *Appendix Virgiliana*, a collection of poems ascribed to Virgil, includes *Dirae* (not *Dirce*), a pastoral in hexameters; *Copa*, an elegiac poem about a dancing girl; *Moretum*, a georgic in hexameters; *Culex*, a hexameter poem about a gnat; and *Ciris*, an epyllion that tells the tale of Scylla. All these poems appear in a work by Joseph Scaliger (1540–1609), *P. Virgilii Maronis Appendix* (1572), described by Anthony Grafton as "an edition of and commentary on the *Appendix Vergiliana*, along with an assortment of Latin epigrams, some dealing with or attributed to Virgil and others anonymous but appealing for literary reasons" (Grafton, *Joseph Scaliger: A Study in the History of Classical Scholarship*, 1983, p. 120). SJ remembers correctly: Scaliger does attribute *Dirae* to Valerius Cato.

Hester Maria Thrale

THURSDAY 2 SEPTEMBER 1784

MS: The Earl of Shelburne.

ADDRESS: To Miss Thrale at John Cator's, Esq.

Dearest Madam: Ashbourne in Derbyshire, Sept. 2, 1784

I am glad that after your storm you have found a port at Mr. Cator's.[1] You may now make a pause in life, and gather your scattered thoughts together. I cannot but wish you would practice, what I recommended in our little pretty lecture room at Streatham, the registry of your course of thinking, and accidents of life. It will require little time, for thoughts or things of frequent occurrence are not worth a memorial, and the time which it takes it will liberally compensate. If you began to

1. *Ante* To Hester Maria Thrale, 6 July 1784, n. 1; *Ante* To Hester Thrale, 13 Aug. 1777, n. 3.

practice it when I recommended it, you have already derived pleasure from it. If by hurry or negligence, you should for a time omit it, do not therefore leave it off, but begin again, and be always careful to set down dates exactly.

I am, though still at a great distance from health and vigour, yet much better than when I left London, and flatter my self that I still gain ground of my disorders. As I have always wished you well, I hope, I am sometimes remembered in your prayers. I am, Dear Madam, your most humble servant,

SAM. JOHNSON

Charles Burney

SATURDAY 4 SEPTEMBER 1784

MS: Gerald Coke Handel Collection.

ADDRESS: To Dr. Burney in St. Martin's Street, Leicester Fields, London.

POSTMARKS: 6 SE, 145 ASHBOURN.

ENDORSEMENTS: From Dr. Johnson, Septr. 4th 1784, No. 13. Ashbourne, Sept. 4, 1784, No. 11.

Dear Sir: Ashbourne, Sept. 4, 1784

I have not the least objection to the little insertion in the last paragraph,[1] but am really sorry that there should be any need of recalling our Master's thoughts to his native country.[2] Nothing deserves more compassion than wrong conduct with good meaning; than loss or obloquy suffered by one who as he is conscious only of good intentions, wonders why he loses that kindness which he wishes to preserve, and not knowing his own faults, if as may sometimes happen, nobody will tell him, goes on to offend by his endeavours to please.

1. *Ante* To Charles Burney, 2 Aug. 1784 and n. 1.

2. The final paragraph of the published dedication reads: "How near, or how distant, the time may be, when the art of combining sounds shall be brought to its highest perfection by the natives of Great Britain, this is not the place to enquire; but the efforts produced in other parts of knowledge by Your Majesty's favour, give hopes that Music may make quick advances now it is recommended by the attention, and dignified by the patronage of our Sovereign" (Hazen, p. 33).

Of your *formulas* You may find one in every book dedicated to your patron or his predecessors. I do not like—*I have the honour etc.*[3] Chambers's Dictionary has a dedication, and Dr. Hoadley's Play[4] and forty more. I am delighted by finding that You like so well what I have done.

You will do me a real kindness by continuing to write, a post-day has now been long a day of recreation. I am, Dear Sir, Your most humble Servant,

SAM. JOHNSON

3. The dedication closes: "I am, With the most profound Humility, Your MAJESTY's most dutiful And devoted Subject and Servant" (Hazen, p. 33).

4. Both Ephraim Chambers's *Cyclopaedia* (1728) and *The Suspicious Husband* (1747) by Benjamin Hoadly (1706–57) were dedicated to George II.

William Cruikshank

SATURDAY 4 SEPTEMBER 1784

MS: Hyde Collection.

ADDRESS: To Mr. Cruikshank.

Dear Sir: Ashbourne, Derbyshire, Sept. 4, 1784

Do not suppose that I forget You. I hope I shall never be justly accused of forgetting my benefactors. I had till very lately nothing to write but complaints upon complaints of miseries upon miseries, but within this[1] fortnight, I have received great relief. My asthma which was exasperated by the smallest effort, and which scarcely permitted me to take twenty quick steps, on a sudden remitted;[2] afterwards the water ran away and my thighs have shrunk almost to their natural size, but what affords me still a greater present comfort, is that my nights are now easy. Of easy nights I have indeed had but, I think, five, but they give me hope of more.

Have your lectures any Vacation? If you are released from

1. MS: "this" altered from "the"

2. *Ante* To Richard Brocklesby, 14 Aug. 1784.

the necessity of daily study, You may find time for a letter to me.

The medicine to which I owe this help, if I owe it to any medicine is the Squil, of which I have taken the vinegar and powder with great diligence though for a long time without any discernable effect, but diureticks, you know, are of inconstant and uncertain operation. Of the vinegar I sometimes took more than an hundred drops in the day.

In return for this account of my health, let me have a good account of yours, and of your prosperity in all your undertakings. I am, Dear Sir, Your most humble servant,

SAM. JOHNSON

John Hoole

SATURDAY 4 SEPTEMBER 1784

MS: Hyde Collection.

ADDRESS: To Mr. Hoole.

ENDORSEMENT: Dr. Johnson to J. Hoole.

Dear Sir: Ashbourn, Sept. 4, 1784

Your Letter was indeed long in coming, but it was very welcome; Our acquaintance has now subsisted long, and our recollection of each other involves a great space, and many little occurrences, which melt the thoughts to tenderness. Write to me therefore as frequently as You can.

It has pleased God to grant me a[1] very wonderful recovery. My Water has again run away, my breath is no longer distressfully strait, and I have for a few nights past lain quietly[2] in Bed; when I came hither, I slept much in a chair; but for some days past, having rested in the night, I have been more capable of enjoying the day. This account will I hope, be welcome to

1. MS: "a" altered from "any"
2. MS: "q" superimposed upon "l"

dear Mrs. Hoole, and my reverend Friend, your son, as well as to your self. Make my compliments to them both.

I hear from Dr. Brocklesby and Mr. Ryland, that the club is not crouded,[3] I hope we shall enliven it when winter brings us together. I am, Dear Sir, Your most affectionate Servant,

SAM. JOHNSON

3. SJ refers to the Essex Head Club.

?George Nicol[1]

SATURDAY 4 SEPTEMBER 1784

MS: Hyde Collection.

Sir: Ashbourn, Sept. 4, 1784

I am pleased that You have been able to adorn the royal library with a Book which I believe to be very rare,[2] for I have not seen it. I have a very good copy,[3] and did not know that it had been printed on two kinds of paper.[4] The Polyglot Bible is

1. R. W. Chapman conjecturally identifies the recipient of this letter as William Strahan (Chapman III.218). While agreeing with Chapman that F. A. Barnard (R. B. Adam's candidate) is highly unlikely, I find George Irwin's suggestion of Nicol much more persuasive (Irwin, "Plump and Prospering Printer," *TLS*, 1 Apr. 1965, p. 255). On 19 Aug. SJ had requested "imported intelligence" from Nicol, the King's bookseller, who may well have responded with an account of his recent addition to the Royal Library. *Pace* Chapman, the postscript does not necessarily refer to franks: SJ may have enclosed two letters to be delivered by messenger or via the penny post.

2. SJ refers to Brian Walton's *Biblia Sacra Polyglotta* (1655–57), "the most accurate and best-equipped of the great Polyglots," published in six volumes folio (T. H. Darlow and H. F. Moule, *Historical Catalogue of the Printed Editions of Holy Scripture*, 1911, II.23).

3. SJ bequeathed his copy of the Polyglot Bible to Bennet Langton; it is now in the Hyde Collection (J. D. Fleeman, *A Preliminary Handlist of Copies of Books Associated with Dr. Samuel Johnson*, 1984, p. 4).

4. Twelve large-paper (or "royal paper") copies of the Polyglot Bible were printed; the large-paper copies measure approximately 19″ x 13½″, as compared with 16½″ x 11″ for the regular copies (W. T. Lowndes, *The Bibliographer's Manual*

undoubtedly the greatest performance of English typography, perhaps of all typography, and therefore ought to appear in its most splendid form among the books of the King of England. I wish you like success in all your researches.

The part of your letter that relates to a[5] writer whom You do not name, has so much tenderness, benevolence, and liberality, in language so unlike the talk of trade, that it must be a flinty bosom that is not softened into gratitude.[6]

It has now pleased God to restore my health to a much better state, than when I parted from London, if my strength encreases, indeed, if it does not grow less, I shall hope to concert measures with you, and, by your help, to carry on the design to considerable advantage.[7]

In the mean time accept, dear Sir, my sincere thanks for your generous offer, and friendly regard. Event is uncertain and fallacious, but of good intention the merit stands upon a basis that never can be shaken.

Add to your other favors that of writing often to, Sir, Your most humble Servant,

SAM. JOHNSON

I trouble you with two letters.

---

of English Literature [1834], rev. H. G. Bohn, 1864, p. 170; information supplied by Ms. C. A. Mackwell and Dr. John Morrison).

5. MS: "a" altered from "an"

6. MS: "titude" repeated as catchword

7. It is clear that the writer of the letter had expressed his affection for SJ ("an writer whom You do not name") and voiced the hope that SJ might embark upon a new literary project ("the design") commissioned by him.

Richard Brocklesby

THURSDAY 9 SEPTEMBER 1784

MS: Hyde Collection.

ADDRESS: To Dr. Brocklesby in London.

POSTMARKS: 145 ASHBORN, 11 SE.

Dear Sir: Ash[b]ourn, Sept. 9, 1784

I have not written to You very lately, because no alterations appeared. Every thing has run smoothly. My Breath grows easy, and the extraneous water is nearly at an end. But my Nights are not so placid and pleasing as they had begun to be. But we will not lose hope.

I now take no squills, lest they should lose their efficacy by custom. I take purges as they are wanted, and living where good milk is easily to be had I now breakfast upon milk.

I think, I gather strength, for having by accident taken lately several false steps, I have never fallen.

Do You know the Duke and Dutchess of Devonshire? and have you ever seen Chatsworth? I was at Chatsworth on Monday; I had indeed seen it twice before, but never when its owner[s] were at home.[1] I was very kindly received and honestly pressed to stay, but I told them that a Sick Man is not a fit inmate of a great house.[2] But I hope to go again sometime. I am, Dear Sir, Your most humble Servant,

SAM. JOHNSON

1. SJ had visited Chatsworth in 1772 and again in 1774 (*Ante* To Hester Thrale, 27 Nov. 1772; *Life* v.429).

2. Cf. *Post* To Joshua Reynolds, 9 Sept. 1784.

Joshua Reynolds

THURSDAY 9 SEPTEMBER 1784

MS: Hyde Collection.

ADDRESS: To Sir Joshua Reynolds in London.

POSTMARKS: 145 ASHBORN, 11 SE.

Dear Sir: Ashbourne, Sept. 9, 1784

I could not answer your letter before this day, because I went on the Sixth to Chatsworth and did not come back till the post was gone.

Many words I hope are not necessary between You and me

to convince You, what gratitude is excited in my heart, by the Chancellor's Liberality, and your kind offices. I did not indeed expect that what was asked by the Chancellor would have been refused, but since it has, we will not tell that any thing has been asked.[1]

I have enclosed a Letter to the Chancellor, which, when You have read it, You will be pleased to seal with a Head or other general seal, and convey it to him;[2] had I sent it directly to[3] him, I should have seemed to overlook the favour of your intervention.

My last letter told you of my advance in health, which, I think, in the whole still continues. Of the hydropick tumour there is now very little appearance; the Asthma is much less troublesome, and seems to remit something day after day. I do not despair of supporting an English winter.

At Chatsworth I met young Mr. Burke,[4] who led me very commodiously into conversation with the Duke and Dutchess.[5]

1. SJ responds to news in a letter of 2 Sept: the King had turned down Lord Thurlow's request that SJ's pension be increased in order to cover the expenses of a trip to Italy (*Ante* To Joshua Reynolds, 8 July 1784 and n. 3; *Boswell: The English Experiment*, ed. I. S. Lustig and F. A. Pottle, 1986, pp. 43–44; Fifer, pp. 172–73). "After all their expectations, Thurlow was embarrassed to report that no increase would be made . . . offering at the same time to provide £500 or £600 out of his own pocket as a 'mortgage' on Johnson's pension, a gift disguised as a loan" (*Later Years*, p. 262). *Post* To Lord Thurlow, 9 Sept. 1784.

2. This stratagem was intended to conceal from Thurlow the fact that SJ had allowed Reynolds to read his letter of thanks.

3. MS: "to" repeated as catchword

4. Through his father Edmund (whose political career with the Rockingham Whigs had begun under the patronage of Lord John Cavendish), Richard Burke associated with members of the Devonshire House Circle (Namier and Brooke II.146; Hugh Stokes, *The Devonshire House Circle*, 1917, pp. 83, 121).

5. On 6 Sept. the Duchess of Devonshire reported to her mother: "About one Dr Johnson and his friend Dr Taylor arriv'd; he look'd ill, but, they say, is wonderfully recover'd. He was in great good humour and vastly entertaining tho' his first *début* was dry. He sd upon young Burke's asking him if he was quite well—Sir, I am not half well, no nor a quarter well—and he talk'd in too high a strain about new friendships and Aristotle, but when he got more at his ease the Duke took him under the lime trees, and he was wonderfully agreeable indeed" (*Georgiana: Extracts from the Correspondence of Georgiana, Duchess of Devonshire*, ed. Earl of Bessborough, 1955, p. 92).

We had a very good morning. The Din[n]er was publick.[6] I am, Dear Sir, with great affection, Your humble Servant,

SAM. JOHNSON

6. According to Horace Walpole, at Chatsworth "the Duke of Devonshire keeps two public days in a week" (*The Walpole Society* 16, 1928, p. 29). SJ dined "very elegantly" on venison at one of these occasions, when "neighbouring gentry and clergy might present themselves as guests without invitation" (*Works*, Yale ed. I.393–94; *Life* IV.367 n. 3).

Lord Thurlow

THURSDAY 9 SEPTEMBER 1784

MS: Hyde Collection. A draft in SJ's hand. Collated with text in JB's *Life*, 1791, II.535.[1]

My Lord: [Ashbourne]

After a long and attentive[2] observation of Mankind, the generosity of your Lordship's offer excites[3] in me no[4] less wonder than gratitude.[5] Bounty,[6] so liberally bestowed (if my condition made it necessary) (I should gladly receive,)[7] for to such a Mind who would [not] be[8] proud to own his obligations? But it has pleased God to restore me such a measure of health,[9] that if I should now appropriate so much of a fortune destined to do good I should[10] not escape from myself the charge of advancing a false claim.[11]

My journey to the Continent though I once thought it necessary was never much encouraged by my Physicians, and I was

1. "I print it [the letter to Lord Thurlow] from the original draft in Johnson's own hand-writing" (JB's *Life*, 1791, II.535 n. 6).

2. "not inattentive" (*Life*) 3. "raises" (*Life*) 4. "not" (*Life*)

5. *Ante* To Joshua Reynolds, 9 Sept. 1784, n. 1.

6. MS: "Such" del. before "Bounty"

7. "Bounty, so liberally bestowed, I should gladly receive, if my condition made it necessary" (*Life*)

8. MS: "who would be" written above "it can give no" del.

9. "to so great a measure of health" (*Life*) 10. "could" (*Life*)

11. MS: "advancing a false claim" written above "getting money upon false pretences" del.

very desirous that your Lordship be told[12] of it by Sir Joshua Reynolds as an event very uncertain; for if I grew much better I should not be willing, if much worse, I should not be able,[13] to migrate.[14]

Your Lordship was solicited[15] without my knowledge, but when I was told that You were pleased to honour[16] me with your patronage,[17] I did not expect to hear of a refusal. Yet as I had little time to form hopes,[18] and have[19] not rioted in imaginary opulence, the[20] cold reception has been scarce a disappointment. And from your Lordship's kindness I have received a benefit which only Men like You can bestow,[21] I shall[22] live *mihi charior*[23] with a higher opinion of my own merit. I am.

12. "should be told" (*Life*)
13. "if much worse, not able" (*Life*)
14. *Ante* To Joshua Reynolds, 8 July 1784.
15. "first solicited" (*Life*)
16. MS: "honour" written above "favour" del.
17. MS: "intervention" del. before "patronage"
18. "as I have had no long time to brood hope" (*Life*)
19. MS: "had" del. before "have"
20. "this" (*Life*)
21. "are able to bestow" (*Life*)
22. "I shall now" (*Life*)
23. *mihi carior*: "dearer to myself." SJ alters the meaning of a phrase from Ovid, which occurs in both *Metamorphoses* (VIII.405, trans. F. J. Miller, Loeb ed.) and *Tristia* (IV.vi.46, trans. A. L. Wheeler, Loeb ed.). In the former, *mihi carior* refers to a friend who is "dearer" to the speaker "than my own self"; in the latter, it describes a wife, said to be "dearer than all."

Richard Brocklesby

SATURDAY 11 SEPTEMBER 1784

MS: Hyde Collection.

ADDRESS: To Dr. Brocklesby in London.

POSTMARKS: 145 ASHBORN, 13 SE.

Dear Sir: Ashbourn, Sept. 11, 1784

I think nothing grows worse but all rather better except sleep, and that of late has been at its old pranks. Last evening, I felt what I had not known for a long time, an inclination to walk for amusement, I took a short walk, and came back neither breathless nor fatigued. I just now take no physick except now and then a purge.

This has been a gloomy frigid ungenial Summer, but of late it seems to mend, I hear the heat sometimes mentioned, but I do not feel it.

> Præterea minimus gelido jam in corpore sanguis
> Febre calet solâ.—[1]

I hope however with good help to find means of supporting a winter at home, and to hear and tell at the club, what is doing, and what ought to be doing in the world.[2] I have no company here, and shall naturally come home hungry for conversation.

To wish You, dear Sir, more leisure would not be kind, but what leisure You have, You must bestow upon me. I am, Dear Sir, Your most humble servant,

SAM. JOHNSON

I took three squil pills last night.

1. *Praeterea minimus gelido iam in corpore sanguis / febre calet sola*: "Besides all this, the little blood in his now chilly frame is never warm except with fever" (Juvenal, *Satires* X.217, trans. G. G. Ramsay, Loeb ed.).

2. SJ refers to the Essex Head Club.

Lucy Porter

SATURDAY 11 SEPTEMBER 1784

MS: Hyde Collection.

ADDRESS: To Mrs. Lucy Porter in Lichfield. Turn at Derby.

POSTMARK: 145 ASHBORN.

My Dearest: Ashbourn, Sept. 11, 1784

By great perseverance in the use of medicines, it has pleased God that I am much better. The water is almost all run off, my breath is more free, and my legs grow stronger. My sleep was better for a few nights, but it has not staid with me. I purpose within a fortnight to be again at Lichfield,[1] and hope to find you likewise better. The summer has not been kindly, but it seems now to mend, and I hope will at last do us all good. I am, Dear Madam, your humble servant,

SAM. JOHNSON

1. SJ returned to Lichfield 27 Sept. (*Post* To Richard Brocklesby, 29 Sept. 1784).

William Bowles

MONDAY 13 SEPTEMBER 1784

MS: Hyde Collection.

ADDRESS: To W. Bowles, Esq., at Heale near Salisbury.

POSTMARKS: 145 ASHBORN, 15 SE.

Dear Sir: Ashbourn, Aug.[1] 13, 1784

To You the fortunate inhabitants[2] of the South west, a letter from Derbyshire is like a letter from Pontus, but the account which I have to send is not one of the Tristia.[3] I came hither with my Breath so strait, that every motion or effort distressed me; about a month ago the asthma remitted, and has never been very oppressive since. I came hither in some parts tumid with water, which has almost all run off by natural passages.

I hope You and your dear Lady, and all the younglings and all your Friends are well and happy. How soon I can be witness of that happiness I know not. I am now at a great distance, and though I purpose not a much longer stay in this place,

1. SJ misdated this letter; see postmark.

2. MS: "inhibitants"

3. In A.D. 8 Ovid was banished to Tomis, on the western shore of the Black Sea (called "Pontus," a name applied as well to the regions around it). In this place of exile he wrote the *Tristia* and the *Epistulae ex Ponto*. Cf. *Ante* To Hester Thrale, 3 Oct. 1767; 10 Oct. 1767.

where I have wanted no attention yet, as I have more places than one to call at, I fear, that I shall not reach Heale, while any fruit remains on the trees; Therefore eat it, and if Mrs. Bowles wishes me my part I shall be satisfied. I am, Dear Sir, Your most humble Servant,

SAM. JOHNSON

John Hoole

MONDAY 13 SEPTEMBER 1784

MS: Hyde Collection.

ADDRESS: To Mr. Hoole in Queens Street, Lincolns Inn, London.

POSTMARKS: 145 ASHBORN, ⟨15⟩ SE.

ENDORSEMENT: Dr. Johnson to J. Hoole.

Dear Sir: Ashbourn, Aug. 13,[1] 1784

I thank You for your affectionate letter. I hope we shall both be the better for each other's friendship, and I hope we shall not very quickly be parted. I have a better opinion of myself than I had reason to entertain when I left London. My Breath is more free, and my Water is again run off. But my legs are very weak, and my nights generally bad.[2]

Tell Mr. Nichols that I shall be glad of his correspondence when his business allows him a little remission, though to wish him less business that I may have more pleasure, would [be] too selfish.

Mr. Hastings's Packet I received, but do not know that I have a right to print it, or permit it to be copied.[3] You, Sir, shall see it, if you desire it, when I come to London.

1. The postmark points to the correct date; cf. *Ante* To William Bowles, 13 Sept. 1784.

2. Cf. *Ante* To Bennet Langton, 26 Aug. 1784.

3. JB quoted this sentence when in 1790 he wrote to ask Warren Hastings's cooperation with his biographical project. In their ensuing interview, Hastings may have explained the reference, but if so his explanation has not been recovered, and the entire paragraph relating to the "Packet" is deleted from the text printed in JB's *Life* (Waingrow, pp. 306–8; *Life* IV.359).

To pay for seats at the Ballon is not very necessary, because in less than a minute they who gaze at a mile's distance will see all that can be seen. About the wings, I am of your mind they cannot at all assist it, nor I think regulate its motion.[4]

I am now grown somewhat easier in my body, but my mind is sometimes depressed. I have here hardly any company, and at home poor Williams is gone[5]—but gone, I hope, to Heaven. May We, when we are called, be called to Happiness.

About the club I am in no great pain.[6] The forfeitures go on, and the house, I hear, is improved for our future meetings. I hope we shall meet often and sit long. I am, Dear Sir, your most humble servant,

SAM. JOHNSON

4. *Ante* To Hester Thrale, 12 Jan. 1784 and n. 3.

5. *Ante* To Hester Thrale, 20 Aug. 1783, n. 1.

6. SJ refers to the Essex Head Club.

David Barclay

THURSDAY 16 SEPTEMBER 1784

MS: Houghton Library.

ADDRESS: To Mr. Barclay in Red Lyon Square, London [*Readdressed in an unidentified hand*] Youngsbury, Near Wear, Herts.

POSTMARKS: 145 ASHBORN, 20 SE.

Sir: Ashbourn in Derbyshire, Sept. 16, 1784

As I have made some advances towards recovery, and loved Mr. Scot, I am willing to do justice to his memory. You will be pleased to get what account you can of his life, with dates, where they can be had, and when I return, We will contrive how our materials can be best employed.[1] I am, Sir, Your most humble servant,

SAM. JOHNSON

1. When John Scott died, 12 Dec. 1783, he left behind the manuscript of "Critical Essays on Some of the Poems, of Several English Poets." Scott's Quaker friends, David Barclay included, decided to preface the collection with a biog-

raphy of the author; Barclay then approached SJ, who did not live to undertake the project. Instead, John Hoole supplied the biographical account that accompanied the volume when it appeared in 1785 (L. D. Stewart, *John Scott of Amwell*, 1956, pp. viii–ix, 2–3).

Richard Brocklesby

THURSDAY 16 SEPTEMBER 1784

MS: Hyde Collection.

ADDRESS: To Dr. Brocklesby in London.

POSTMARKS: 145 ASHBORN, 18 SE.

Dear Sir: Ashbourn, Sept. 16, 1784

I have now let you alone a long time, having indeed little to say. You charge me somewhat unjustly with luxury. At Chatsworth You should remember that I have eaten but once,[1] and the Doctor with whom I live, follows a milk diet. I grow no fatter, though my stomack, if it be not disturbed by physick, never fails me.

I now grow weary of Solitude, and think of removing next week to Lichfield,[2] a place of more society, but otherwise of less convenience. When I am settled, I shall write again.

I had last night, many hours of continual sleep, and nothing I think grows worse. My legs still continue very weak. But I hope they likewise, if the water stays away will mend so far as to carry me a little about the town. But we are not to choose. I have already recovered to a wonder.

Of the hot weather that You mention, we have [not] had in Derbyshire very much, and for myself I seldom feel heat, and suppose that my frigidity is the effect of my distemper, a supposition which naturally leads me to hope that a better climate may be useful. But I hope to stand another English winter. I am, dear Sir, your most humble servant,

SAM. JOHNSON

1. *Ante* To Joshua Reynolds, 9 Sept. 1784, n. 6.
2. *Ante* To Lucy Porter, 11 Sept. 1784, n. 1.

Francesco Sastres

THURSDAY 16 SEPTEMBER 1784

PRINTED SOURCE: Piozzi, *Letters* II.409–10.

Dear Sir, Ashbourne, Sept. 16, 1784

What you have told me of your landlord and his lady at Brompton, has made them such favourites, that I am not sorry to hear how you are turned out of your lodgings, because the good is greater to them than the evil is to you.

The death of dear Mr. Allen gave me pain.[1] When after some time of absence I visit a town, I find my friends dead;[2] when I leave a place, I am followed with intelligence, that the friend whom I hope to meet at my return is swallowed in the grave. This is a gloomy scene; but let us learn from it to prepare for our own removal. Allen is gone; Sastres and Johnson are hasting after him; may we be both as well prepared!

I again wish your next specimen success.[3] *Paymistress* can hardly be said without a preface, (it may be expressed by a word perhaps not in use, Pay mistress).[4]

The club is, it seems, totally deserted; but as the forfeits go on, the house does not suffer; and all clubs I suppose are unattended in the summer.[5] We shall I hope meet in winter, and be cheerful.

After this week, do not write to me till you hear again from me, for I know not well where I shall be; I have grown weary of the solitude of this place, and think of removal.[6] I am, Sir, Your, etc.

1. *Ante* To Richard Brocklesby, 31 July 1784, n. 2.

2. *Ante* To Joshua Reynolds, 19 Aug. 1784.

3. *Ante* To Francesco Sastres, 21 Aug. 1784 and n. 3; 2 Sept. 1784.

4. The parenthetical sentence exemplifies the kind of prefatory statement SJ has in mind. In his *Dictionary* he includes *paymaster* but not *paymistress.*

5. SJ refers to the Essex Head Club.

6. *Ante* To Lucy Porter, 11 Sept. 1784, n. 1.

Joshua Reynolds

SATURDAY 18 SEPTEMBER 1784

MS: Hyde Collection.

ADDRESS: To Sir Joshua Reynolds in London.

POSTMARKS: 145 ASHBORN, 20 SE.

ENDORSEMENT: Dr. Johnson.

Dear Sir: Ashbourn, Sept. 18, 1784[1]

I flattered myself that this week would have given me a letter from You, but none has come. Write to me now and then, but direct your next to Lichfield.

I think, and, I hope, am sure, that I still grow better. I have sometimes good nights. But am still in my legs weak, but so much mended that I go to Lichfield in hope of being [able] to pay my visits on foot, for there are no coaches.

I have three letters this day, all about the ballon.[2] I could have been content with one. Do not write about the ballon, whatever else You may think proper to say. I am, Dear Sir, Your most humble Servant,

SAM. JOHNSON

1. MS: "1748"

2. The first successful balloon ascent in England was achieved by Vincenzo Lunardi (1759–1806), secretary to the Neapolitan Ambassador in London. On 15 Sept. Lunardi lifted off from the Artillery Ground, Moorfields, watched by a vast crowd that included the Prince of Wales and Lord North. His balloon traveled 24 miles before touching down safely near Ware, Hertfordshire (J. E. Hodgson, *The History of Aeronautics in Great Britain*, 1924, pp. 121–23).

John Ryland

SATURDAY 18 SEPTEMBER 1784

MS: Hyde Collection.

ADDRESS: To Mr. Ryland, Merchant in London.

POSTMARKS: 145 ASHBORN, [Undeciphered].

Dear Sir: [Ashbourne] Sept. 18, 1784[1]

1. MS: "4" del. before "8"; cf. *Ante* To Joshua Reynolds, 18 Sept. 1784

You are not long without an answer. I had this day in three letters three histories of the Flying Man in the great Ballon. I am glad that we do as well as our neighbours.[2] Lunardi, I find, forgot his barometer and therefore can [not report] to what height he ascended.[3]

Direct, if You please, your next letter to Lichfield. I am desirous of going thither; I live in dismal solitude and being now a little better and therefore more at leisure for external amusements, I find the hours sometimes heavy, at least for some reason or other I wish for change.

Mr. Wyndham was with me, a day here,[4] and tried to wheedle me to Oxford, and I perhaps may take Oxford in my way home.[5] I am Sir, Your most affectionate,

SAM. JOHNSON

2. *Ante* To Joshua Reynolds, 18 Sept. 1784 and n. 2; *Ante* To Hester Thrale, 22 Sept. 1783, n. 1.

3. Lunardi was to have been accompanied on the inaugural flight by his friend and financial backer, George Biggin, who carried a barometer in his pocket. When the balloon proved incapable of lifting off with two men in the car, Biggin disembarked, forgetting to give the barometer to Lunardi (James Trail to Jeremy Bentham, 16 Sept. 1784, *The Correspondence of Jeremy Bentham*, ed. Ian Christie, 1971, III.306–7).

4. *Ante* To Richard Brocklesby, 30 Aug. 1784, n. 2.

5. SJ stayed four nights in Oxford on his way back to London (*Post* To Edmund Hector, 17 Nov. 1784).

Richard Brocklesby

WEDNESDAY 29 SEPTEMBER 1784

MS: Hyde Collection.

ADDRESS: To Dr. Brocklesby in London.

POSTMARKS: LICHFIELD, 1 OC.

Dear Sir: Lichfield, Sept. 29, 1784

On one day I had three letters about the Air ballon.[1] Yours was far the best, and has enabled me to impart to my friends

1. *Ante* To Joshua Reynolds, 18 Sept. 1784 and n. 2.

in the country an Idea of this species of amusement. In amusement, mere amusement I am afraid it must end, for I do not find that its course can be directed, so as that it should serve any purposes of communication; and it can give no new intelligence of the state of the air at different heights, till they have ascended above the height of mountains, which they seem never likely to do.

I came hither on the 27th. How long I shall stay, I have not determined. My Dropsy is gone, and my Asthma much remitted, but I have felt[2] myself a little declining these two days, or at least to day, but such vicissitudes must be expected. One day may be worse than another; but this last month is far better than the former, if the next should be as much better than this, I shall run about the town on my own legs.

Was it by your means that a paragraph was in the papers, about my visit to Chatsworth?[3] It was like a trick of Boswel's, and I could hardly have suspected any body else.[4] It did indeed no harm, but what was the good?

I have since I left London been troubled with an inconvenience which I never knew in any great[5] degree before.[6] The fæces in the Rectum have concreted to such hardness, that I have been forced three times to dilute them by clysters, the last time there was a necessity of two injections before I was at ease. Think on this and tell me what should be done, for it is not a slight disorder, whether it be estimated by its immediate pain, or remoter consequence. I have made no change in my manner of living, except that I have taken more milk, than I have been used to take. I am, Sir, Your most obliged and most humble Servant,

SAM. JOHNSON

2. MS: "f" superimposed upon "m"

3. *Ante* To Richard Brocklesby, 9 Sept. 1784. "Within these ten days Dr. Johnson paid a visit to the Duke of Devonshire, at Chatsworth: He was a welcome guest to his Grace and the Duchess, who seemed much pleased with his company, and assured him that his visits would always be welcome to them" (*Public Advertiser*, 22 Sept. 1784, p. 4).

4. No evidence of JB's complicity has been recovered.

5. MS: "gread"

6. MS: "begree" del. before "before"

John Ryland

WEDNESDAY 29 SEPTEMBER 1784

MS: Beinecke Library.
ADDRESS: To Mr. Ryland, Merchant in London.
POSTMARKS: LICHFIELD, [Undeciphered].

Dear Sir: Lichfield, Sept. 29, 1784

At my return hither I had the gratification of finding two of my friends whom I left as I thought about two months ago, quite broken with years and diseases, very much recovered.[1] It is great pleasure to a sick man to discover that sickness is not always mortal; and to an old man, to[2] see age yet living to greater age. This is however, whatever Rochefoucault, or Swift may say, though certainly part of the pleasure, yet not[3] all of it.[4] I rejoice in the welfare of those whom I love and who love me, and surely should have the same joy, if I were no[5] longer subject to mortality. As a being subject to so many wants Man has inevitably a strong tendency to selfinterest; so I hope as a Being capable of comparing good and evil, he finds something to be preferred in good, and is therefore capable of benevolence, and supposing the relation of a good and bad man, as to his own interest the same, would rejoice more in the prosperity of the good.

I have for a little while past, felt, or imagined, some declension in my health, I[6] am still much better than I lately was, but I am a little afraid of the cold weather.

You have not lately told me of Payne, in whom I take a great interest. I think he may by indulgence recover, and that indulgence, since his employers allow it him, he will be very cul-

1. SJ refers to Elizabeth Aston and Lucy Porter (*Post* To Eva Maria Garrick, 2 Oct. 1784).

2. MS: "t" superimposed upon "s"

3. MS: "not" superimposed upon "all" partially erased

4. *Ante* To Hester Thrale, 29 Oct. 1777 and n. 10. The maxim in question is prefixed to "Verses on the Death of Dr. Swift."

5. MS: "no" altered from "not"

6. MS: "I" written above "but" del.

pable, if he denies himself.[7] I am, Dear Sir, Your affectionate, humble servant,

SAM. JOHNSON

7. *Ante* To John Ryland, 2 Sept. 1784.

William Strahan

THURSDAY 30 SEPTEMBER AND SATURDAY 16 OCTOBER 1784

PRINTED SOURCE: C. K. Shorter, *Unpublished Letters of Dr. Samuel Johnson*, 1915.[1]

ADDRESS: To William Strahan, Esq.

Sir, September 30, 1784

I have now spent the greatest part of the summer in quest of health, which, alas! I cannot boast of having found. I purpose to settle at my own home in a short time. Home has to a sick man a multitude of conveniences, and winter may be passed at London with more amusement and more assistance than at any other place.

My friends whom I have visited, and those whom I have left, have all contributed as they could to make my life more cheerful. I have had no complaint to make of neglect.

My living has not been without some expense, though not much, and I shall be glad of two bank notes of ten pounds each as soon as you can.

Be pleased to make my compliment to dear Mrs. Strahan, whom I hope to find better than I left her. Health and every other real good is sincerely wished you by, Sir, your most humble servant,

SAM. JOHNSON

Lichfield, October 16, 1784

1. Shorter has conflated two letters or parts of letters in such a way as to make it impossible to determine conclusively which paragraphs belong to which date. The page break after the first paragraph might indicate that the rest of the text comes from the letter of 16 Oct.

Eva Maria Garrick

SATURDAY 2 OCTOBER 1784

MS: Hyde Collection.

ADDRESS: To Mrs. Garrick at the Adelph, London.

POSTMARKS: LICHFIELD, 4 OC.

Madam: Lichfield, Oct. 2, 1784

I did not wonder that your heart failed you, when the journey to Lichfield came nearer, and indeed I love You the more for your tenderness and sensibility. I am now at Lichfield a second time, and am returned to it with some improvement of my health, in the two months for[1] which I staid away, and have the delight to find both Mrs. Aston and Mrs. Porter much mended in the same time. Mr. Garrick was with me lately, and is well.[2] Mr. Seward is very lame, and his daughter flourishes in poetical reputation.[3] What Lichfield affords more than this I hope to tell when I wait on You in London.

Please to make my compliments to dear Miss Moore.[4] I am, Madam, Your most humble servant,

SAM. JOHNSON

1. MS: "for" superimposed upon "sin"

2. SJ refers to Peter Garrick.

3. Anna Seward's *Louisa,* subtitled "A Poetical Novel in Four Epistles," had appeared the previous spring, and by the end of 1784 had gone through four editions (Margaret Ashmun, *The Singing Swan,* 1931, p. 123 n. 26). The many reviews of *Louisa* included one by JB, who praised its "genuine Sentiments" and "elegant Language" (*Public Advertiser,* 3 June 1784, p. 2).

4. SJ refers to Hannah More.

Joshua Reynolds

SATURDAY 2 OCTOBER 1784

MS: Houghton Library.

ADDRESS: To Sir Joshua Reynolds in London.

POSTMARK: 4 OC.

To JOSHUA REYNOLDS, 2 *October* 1784

Dear Sir: Lichfield, Oct. 2, 1784

I am always proud of your approbation, and therefore was much pleased that you liked my letter.[1] When You copied it, You invaded the Chancellor's right rather than mine.[2]

The refusal I did not expect, but I had never thought much about it, for I doubted whether the Chancellor had so much tenderness for me as to ask. He being keeper of the King's conscience ought not to be supposed capable of an improper petition.

All is not gold that glitters, as we have often been told; and the adage is verified in your place[3] and my favour,[4] but if what happens does not make us richer, we must bid it welcome, if it makes us wiser.

I do not at present grow better, nor much worse, my hopes however are some what abated, and a very great loss is the loss of hope. But I struggle on as I can. I am, Dear Sir, Your most humble Servant,

SAM. JOHNSON

1. *Ante* To Lord Thurlow, 9 Sept. 1784.

2. *Ante* To Joshua Reynolds, 9 Sept. 1784 and n. 2.

3. On 24 Sept. Reynolds had reported to the Duke of Rutland: "The place which I have the honor of holding, of the King's principal painter, is a place of not so much profit, and of near equal dignity with His Majesty's rat catcher. The salary is £38 per annum" (*Letters of Sir Joshua Reynolds*, ed. F. W. Hilles, 1929, p. 112).

4. MS: "favour" repeated as catchword

William Windham

SATURDAY 2 OCTOBER 1784

MS: Hyde Collection. Address and postmark, British Library (Add. MS: 37,914, f. 18).[1]

ADDRESS: To —— Wyndham, Esq., M.P., in Oxford.

POSTMARK: LICHFIELD.

HEADING in JB's hand: To The Right Honourable William Windham.

1. For a reconstruction of the circumstances leading to the separation of text and address, see G. J. Kolb, "The Address of Dr. Johnson's Last Letter to William Windham," *Notes and Queries* 202, 1957, p. 213.

Dear Sir: Lichfield, Oct. 2, 1784

I believe You have been long enough acquainted with the *phænomena* of Sickness, not to be surprised that a sick man wishes to be where he is not, and where it appears to every body but himself that he might easily be, without having the resolution to remove. I thought Ashbourne a solitary place, but did not come hither till last monday.

I have here more company but my health has for this last week not advanced, and in the languor of disease how little can be done. Whither or when I shall make my next remove, I cannot tell, but entreat you, dear sir, to let me know from time to time where You may be found, for your residence is a very powerful attractive to, Sir, Your most humble servant,

SAM. JOHNSON

John Perkins

MONDAY 4 OCTOBER 1784

MS: Hyde Collection.

ADDRESS: To Mr. Perkins in Southwark.

POSTMARKS: 119 LITCHFIELD, 6 OC.

ENDORSEMENT: 4 Octr. 1784.

Dear Sir: Lichfield, Oct. 4, 1784

I cannot but flatter myself that your kindness for me, will make you glad to know where I am, and in what state.

I have been struggling very hard with my diseases. My breath has been very much obstructed and the water has attempted to encroach upon me again. I past the first part of the summer at Oxford, afterwards I went to Lichfield, thence to Ashbourn in Derbyshire, and a week ago I returned to Lichfield.

My breath is now much easier, and the water is in a great measure run away, so that I hope to see you again before Winter.

To JOHN PERKINS, 4 *October* 1784

Please to make my compliments to Mrs. Perkins, and to Mr. and Mrs. Barclay.[1] I am, Dear Sir, Your most humble Servant,

SAM. JOHNSON

1. SJ refers to Robert Barclay and his wife.

Richard Brocklesby

WEDNESDAY 6 OCTOBER 1784

MS: Hyde Collection.

ADDRESS: To Dr. Brocklesby in London.

POSTMARKS: 119 LITCHFIELD, 8 OC.

Dear Sir: Lichfield, Oct. 6, 1784

The day on which I received your letter I sent for castor oil, having just a stoppage in the rectum, but being afraid in such an exigency to trust too much to a medicine of which I had no experience, I took near an ounce of the oil at night and followed it with another purge in the morning, and all passed without inconvenience.

My dropsy keeps down, my breath is much obstructed, and I do not get strength, nor in any great degree lose it. However I do not advance, and am afraid of winter. Give me what help and what hope you can.

The fate of the balloon I do not much lament.[1] To make new balloon[s] is to repeat the jest again. We now know a method of mounting into the air, and I think, are not likely to know more. The vehicles can serve no use, till we can guide them, and they can gratify no curiosity till we mount with them to greater heights than we can reach without, till we rise above the tops of the highest mountains, which we have yet not done. We know the state of the air [in] all its regions to the top of Teneriffe, and therefore learn nothing from those

1. SJ refers to the fiery demise of the Sheldon-Keegan balloon on 29 Sept. (*Ante* To Hester Maria Thrale, 31 Jan. 1784, n. 2).

[who] navigate a balloon below the clouds.[2] The first experiment however was bold, and deserved applause and reward. But since it has been performed and its event is known, I had rather now find a medicine that can ease an asthma. I am, Dear sir, Your most humble Servant,

SAM. JOHNSON

2. Cf. *Ante* To William Bowles, 3 Feb. 1784.

John Ryland

WEDNESDAY 6 OCTOBER 1784

MS: Historical Society of Pennsylvania.

ADDRESS: To Mr. Ryland, Merchant in London.

POSTMARKS: 119 LITCHFIELD, 8 OC.

Dear Sir: Lichfield, Oct. 6, 1784

I am glad that so many could yet meet at the club, where I do not yet despair of some cheerful hours.[1] Your account of poor dear Payne makes me uneasy,[2] if his distemper were only the true sea scurvey, it is on land easily, and I believe infallibly curable. But I am afraid it is worse, not a vitiation of particular humours, but a debilitation of the whole frame, an effect not of casualty but of time. I wish his recovery, and hope that he wishes, and prays for mine.

I have for some days, to speak in the[3] lightest and softest language made no advances towards health. My[4] breath is much obstructed, and my limbs are weak, of water however I have little reason to complain.

My mind, however, is calmer than in the beginning of the year, and I comfort myself with[5] hopes of every kind, neither despairing of ease in this world, nor of happiness in another.

1. SJ refers to the Essex Head Club.
2. *Ante* To John Ryland, 2 Sept. 1784; 29 Sept. 1784.
3. MS: "th" superimposed upon "li"
4. MS: "My" repeated as catchword
5. MS: "with" altered from "in the"

I shall, I think, not return to town worse than I left it, and unless I gain ground again, not much better. But, God, I humbly hope, will have mercy on me. I am, Dear Sir, Your most humble servant,

SAM. JOHNSON

William Scott

SUNDAY 10 OCTOBER 1784

MS: Estate of Sir John Colville.

ADDRESS: To Dr. Scot in the Commons, London.

POSTMARKS: LITCHFIELD, 13 ⟨OC⟩.

Dear Sir: Lichfield, Oct. 10, 1784

Considering that the excursion of this Summer was made with your assistance, I cannot think the better of my own attention, for having neglected to give You an account of what has befallen me.

July 13. I left London, very asthmatick, and in some degree, I think, hydropical, and found no help from the air of Staffordshire. I was not however very weak, for I came to Lichfield in two days with little fatigue.

Having languished at Lichfield a few days, I went (July 20) to Ashbourne in Derbyshire, where for some time the asthma harrassed me with great pertinacity, and the Water rose till I dressed myself with difficulty. But in the night between the 12th and 13th of August, after a day of great evacuation by abstinence and purges, by the help of an opiate taken about midnight, the asthma remitted, so that I went to Church with less labour than for some time before; and though the same freedom of respiration has not uniformly continued, and has now[1] for a week been interrupted, yet I have never drawn my breath with that struggle and straitness as before the remission.

1. MS: "not" del. before "now"

The water, by the use, I think, of squils, was in about five weeks driven through the urinary passages and left me in appearance totally free. I remain therefore Asthmatical though not in the extreme. Of the dropsy if it keeps the truce I have little complaint to make. But my limbs are very weak, my legs would not carry me far, if my breath would last, and my breath would not last if my legs would carry me. How I shall pass the winter I know not, but hope to pass part of it with You, and do not despair of a cheerful hour. I am, Dear Sir, Your most humble Servant,

SAM. JOHNSON

William Heberden

WEDNESDAY 13 OCTOBER 1784

MS: Houghton Library.

ADDRESS: To Dr. Heberden in London [*Readdressed in an unidentified hand*] Windsor.

POSTMARKS: 119 LITCHFIELD, 15 OC, 16 OC.

ENDORSEMENT in an unidentified hand: frm Dr. Johnson.

Dear Sir: Lichfield, Oct. 13, 1784

Though I doubt not but Dr. Brocklesby would communicate to you any incident in the variation of my health which appeared either curious or important, yet I think it time to give you some account of myself.

Not long after the first great efflux of the water, I attained so much vigour of limbs and freedom of breath that, without rest or intermission, I went with Dr. Brocklesby to the top of the Painter's academy.[1] This was the greatest degree of[2] health that I have obtained, and this, if it could continue, were perhaps sufficient; but my breath soon failed and my body grew weak.

At Oxford (in June) I was much distressed by shortness of

1. *Ante* To Hester Thrale, 26 Apr. 1784.

2. MS: "of" superimposed upon "h"

breath, so much that I never attempted to scale the library.[3] The water gained upon me, but by the use of squills was in a great measure driven away.

In July I went to Lichfield, and performed the journey with very little fatigue in the common vehicle, but found no help from my native air. I then removed to Ashbourn in Derbyshire where for some time I was oppressed very heavily by the Asthma, and the dropsy had advanced so far that I could not without great difficulty button me at my knees.

Something was now to be done; I took opium as little as I could, for quiet, and squills, as much as I could, for help; but in my medical journal Aug. 10. I find these words. Nec opio, nec squillis quidquam sensi effectum. Animus jacet.[4] But I plied the vinegar of Squills to an hundred drops a day,[5] and the powder to four grains. From the vinegar I am not sure that I ever perceived any consequence.[6] August 12. I took a cathartick, and finding [it] not active, took another, and the same day drank 240 drops of Squil vinegar, I had no dinner, and therefore went to bed much evacuated, for the double Physick had operated[7] powerfully. In the night I felt myself disturbed, and took two grains of opium, twice as much as I generally use. I rose in the morning with my Asthma perceptibly mitigated, and walked to church that day with less struggle than on any day before.

The water about this time ran again away, so that no hydropical tumour has been lately visible. The relaxation of my breath has not continued as it was at first. But neither do I breath with the same *angustiæ*[8] and distress as before the remission. The summary of my state is this.

I am deprived by weakness and the Asthma of the power of walking beyond a very short space.

3. The staircase to the Bodleian consists of 65 steps.

4. *Nec opio, nec squillis quidquam sensi effectum. Animus jacet*: "I did not feel any [beneficial] effect from opium or squills. Spirits low" (*Works*, Yale ed. 1.382).

5. MS: "day" superimposed upon "drops"

6. MS: "quence" repeated as catchword

7. MS: "operated" altered from "operati[ng]"

8. *Ante* To Richard Brocklesby, 12 Aug. 1784 and n. 6.

I draw my breath with difficulty upon the least effort, but not with suffocation or pain.

The dropsy still threatens, but gives way to Medicine.

The Summer has passed without giving me any strength.

My appetite is, I think, less keen than it was, but not so abated, as that its decline can be observed by any but myself.

Be pleased to think on me sometimes. I am, Sir, Your most obliged and most humble Servant,

SAM. JOHNSON

George Strahan

SATURDAY 16 OCTOBER 1784

MS: Houghton Library.

ADDRESS: To the Revd. Mr. Strahan at Islington, London.

POSTMARKS: 119 LITCHFIELD, 18 OC.

ENDORSEMENT: Answered Octr. 21, 1784.

Dear Sir: Lichfield, Oct. 16, 1784

I have hitherto omitted to give You that account of myself, which the kindness with which You have treated me, gives You a right to expect.

I went away feeble, asthmatical, and dropsical. The asthma has remitted for a time, but is now very troublesome, the weakness still continues, but the dropsy has disappeared, and has twice in the summmer yielded to medicine. I hope to return with a body somewhat, however little, relieved and with a mind less dejected.

I hope your dear Lady and dear little ones are all well, and all happy.[1] I love them all. I am, Dear Sir, Your Most humble servant,

SAM. JOHNSON

1. George Strahan and his wife Margaret had two daughters, Margaret and Maria Isabella (J. A. Cochrane, *Dr. Johnson's Printer*, 1964, p. xiv).

John Taylor

SATURDAY 16 OCTOBER 1784

MS: Hyde Collection.

ADDRESS: To the Revd. Dr. Taylor in Ashbourn, Derbyshire.

POSTMARK: 119 LITCHFIELD.

Dear Sir: Lichfield, Oct. 16, 1784

When I came to this place I found with some wonder and much delight that Lucy was much better than I had left her. Of Mrs. Astons recovery I had been informed, and found it equal to my expectation. All this was pleasant, but this is all the good that I have to tell, for since I left Ashbourn, I have not grown stronger, but seem to myself to have lost ground. My Breath has been very short, and my limbs are weak. The water, however makes no encroachments, or very little.

One pleasant thing more I have to tell. Lucy's behaviour is in the highest degree amiable and kind. I do not purpose to stay long here, but shall stay long enough to hear how [you] are in your health, and what are your designs, which I desire You to tell me. I am, Sir, yours affectionately,

SAM. JOHNSON

Pray let me know how Mrs. Longdon does.[1]

1. SJ may refer to the wife of Robert Longden.

Richard Brocklesby

WEDNESDAY 20 OCTOBER 1784

MS: Hyde Collection.

ADDRESS: To Dr. Brocklesby in London.

POSTMARKS: 119 LITCHFIELD, 22 OC.

Dear Sir: Lichfield, Oct. 20, 1784

I should continue my frequency of letters, if I had any thing pleasing to communicate, but the plain truth is that I have rather gone backwards these three weeks. I sometimes fancy that I eat too much, though I have no suppers, and am now trying to live more sparingly. My nights are wretched, and though opiates still the asthma, they give no sleep.

The oil of castor I have tried, and it seems particularly fitted for our intention.[1] It has no great power of stimulation, but seems to mingle itself with the matter in the intestines, and by hindering its concretion, to facilitate its ejection. Perhaps it does something[2] by lubricating the passage.

My limbs are very weak, my breath is very short, and the water begins to threaten, and I have begun to oppose by squil pills, which I think have prevailed over it twice this Summer. I purpose to ply them diligently and have great hope of Success, though I am sometimes very much dejected. I am, Dear Sir, your most humble servant,

SAM. JOHNSON

1. *Ante* To Richard Brocklesby, 29 Sept. 1784.

2. MS: "thing" repeated as catchword

William Gerard Hamilton

WEDNESDAY 20 OCTOBER 1784

MS: Hyde Collection.

ADDRESS: To Gerard Ha⟨milton, Esq., M.P⟩., in London.

POSTMARKS: 119 LITCHFIELD, 22 OC.

HEADING in JB's hand: To The Right Honourable William Gerard Hamilton.

Dear Sir: Lichfield, Oct. 20, 1784

Considering what reason You gave me in the spring, to conclude that You took part in whatever good or evil might befal me,[1] I ought not to have omitted so long the account which I am no[w] about to give you.

1. It is possible that SJ, telescoping time, refers to Hamilton's proffered benefaction of the previous November (*Ante* To Susanna Thrale, 18 Nov. 1783). However, Hamilton may well have renewed his offer of assistance.

My diseases are an Asthma and a Dropsy, and, what is less curable, seventy five. Of the dropsy in the beginning of the summer, or in the spring, I recovered to a degree which struck with wonder both me and my Physicians. The Asthma was likewise for a time very much relieved. I went to Oxford where the Asthma was very tyrannical, and the Dropsy began again to[2] threaten me, but seasonable physick stopped the inundation. I then returned to London, and in July took a resolution to visit Staffordshire and Derbyshire where[3] I am yet struggling with my diseases. The Dropsy made another attack, and was not easily ejected, but at last gave way. The asthma suddenly remitted, in bed on the 13th of august, and though now very[4] oppressive, is, I think, still something gentler than it was before the remission. My limbs are miserably debilitated, and my nights are sleepless and tedious.

When You read this, dear Sir, you are not sorry that I wrote no sooner. I will not prolong my complaints. I hope still to see You *in a happier hour*,[5] to talk over what we have often talked, and perhaps to find new topicks of merriment, or new incitements to curiosity. I am, dear sir, your most obliged and most humble servant,

SAM. JOHNSON

2. MS: "to" repeated as catchword

3. MS: "where" written above "which" del.

4. MS: "very very"

5. "Seen him [Sir Robert Walpole] I have, but in his happier hour / Of Social Pleasure, ill-exchang'd for Pow'r" (Pope, *Epilogue to the Satires (One Thousand Seven Hundred and Thirty Eight)* I.29–30).

John Nichols

WEDNESDAY 20 OCTOBER 1784

MS: British Library.

ADDRESS: To Mr. Nicol in Red lion Court, Fleetstreet, London.

POSTMARKS: 119 LITCHFIELD, 22 OC.

Sir: Lichfield, Oct. 20, 1784

When You were here, you were pleased, as I am told, to think my absence an inconvenience; I should certainly have been very glad to give so skilful a lover of antiquities, any information about my native place, of which however I know not much, and have reason to believe that not much is known.

Though I have not given you any amusement, I have received amusement from You. At Ashbourne, where I had very little company, I had the luck to borrow Mr. Boyer's Life[1] a book so full of contemporary History, that a literary Man must find some of his old Friends. I thought that I could now and then have told you something[2] worth your notice, and perhaps we may talk[3] a life over.[4] I hope, We shall be much together, You must now be to me, what you were before, and what dear Mr. Allen was besides. He was taken unexpectedly away,[5] but I think he was a very good man.

I have made little progress in recovery. I am very weak, and very sleepless. But I live on and hope. I am, Sir, Your most humble Servant,

SAM. JOHNSON

1. *Ante* To John Nichols, 12 Aug. 1782, n. 2.
2. MS: "sometime"
3. MS: "and then" del. before "talk"
4. MS: "over" repeated as catchword
5. *Ante* To Richard Brocklesby, 31 July 1784, n. 2.

John Paradise

WEDNESDAY 20 OCTOBER 1784

MS: Hyde Collection.

ADDRESS: To —— Paradise, Esq., near the Middlesex Hospital, London.

POSTMARKS: 119 LITCHFIELD, 22 OC.

HEADING in JB's hand: To John Paradise, Esq.

Dear Sir: Lichfield, Oct. 20, 1784

Though in all my summer's excursion I have given You no account of my self, I hope You think better of me than to imagine it possible for me to forget You, whose kindness to me has been too great and too constant, not to have made its impression on a harder breast than mine.

Silence is not very culpable when nothing pleasing is suppressed. It would have alleviated none of your complaints, to have read my vicissitudes of evil; I have struggled hard with very formidable[1] and obstinate maladies, and though I cannot talk of health think all praise due to my Creator and Preserver for[2] the continuance of my life. The Dropsy has made two attacks and has given way to medicine, the Asthma is very oppressive but that has likewise once remitted. I am very weak and very sleepless, but it is time to conclude the tale of misery.

I hope, dear sir, that You grow better, for you have likewise your share of human evil, and that your Lady and the young Charmers are well.[3] I am, Dear sir, Your affectionate, humble servant,

SAM. JOHNSON

1. MS: "f" superimposed upon "v"

2. MS: "for" repeated as catchword

3. Lucy Ludwell (1751–1814), daughter of Philip Ludwell (1716–67), a prosperous Virginia plantation owner, married John Paradise in 1769. Their two daughters were Lucy (1771–1800) and Philippa (1774–87) (A. B. Shepperson, *John Paradise and Lucy Ludwell*, 1942, pp. 455–56).

Francesco Sastres

WEDNESDAY 20 OCTOBER 1784

PRINTED SOURCE: Piozzi, *Letters* II.410–11.

Sir, Lichfield, October 20, 1784

You have abundance of naughty tricks; is this your way of writing to a poor sick friend twice a week? Post comes after post, and brings no letter from Mr. Sastres. If you know any thing, write and tell it; if you know nothing, write and say that you know nothing.

What comes of the specimen?[1] If the booksellers want a

1. *Ante* To Francesco Sastres, 21 Aug. 1784 and n. 3; 2 Sept. 1784.

specimen, in which a keen critick can spy no faults, they must wait for another generation. Had not the Crusca faults?[2] Did not the Academicians of France commit many faults? It is enough that a dictionary is better than others of the same kind. A perfect performance of any kind is not to be expected, and certainly not a perfect dictionary.

Mrs. Desmoulines never writes, and I know not how things go on at home; tell me, dear Sir, what you can.

If Mr. Seward be in town tell me his direction, for I ought to write to him.[3]

I am very weak, and have bad nights. I am, dear Sir, Your, etc.

2. SJ refers to the *Vocabolario degli Accademici della Crusca* (1612). His library included Giulio Ottonelli's *Annotazioni sopra il Vocabolario degli accademici della Crusca* (1698), which identified and corrected various mistaken references (Sledd and Kolb, pp. 42, 211 n. 83).

3. SJ refers to William Seward.

John Taylor

WEDNESDAY 20 OCTOBER 1784

MS: Houghton Library.

ADDRESS: To the Reverend Dr. Taylor.

ENDORSEMENTS: 1784, 20 Octr. 84.

Dear Sir: Lichfield, Oct. 20, 1784

I can hardly think that the bearer of this comes from you, for You would surely have written. I am in one of my bad fits, and having been driven by my Asthma to an opiate last night, have, I think, never closed my eyes. I should however have been glad to have heard of your health, and your house, and whatever belongs to You. I begin now to think of returning to London, but am in no great haste. I have attention enough here, and ease, I am afraid, I shall not easily find, but I go on hoping and hoping, and trying and trying. I am, Dear Sir, affectionately yours,

SAM. JOHNSON

John Taylor

SATURDAY 23 OCTOBER 1784

MS: Hyde Collection.

ADDRESS: To the Reverend Dr. Taylor in Ashbourn, Derbyshire.

POSTMARK: 119 LITCHFIELD.

ENDORSEMENTS: 1784, the Last; 23d Octr. 84, last Letter. This is the last Letter; My Answer which were the Words of advice, He gave to Mr. Thrale the day He dyed,[1] He resented extremely from me.[2]

Dear Sir: Lichfield, Oct. 23, 1784

Coming down from a very restless night, I found your letter which made me a little angry. You tell me that recovery is in my power. This indeed I should be glad to hear, if I could once believe it. But you mean to charge me with[3] neglecting or opposing my own health. Tell me therefore what I do that hurts me, and what I neglect that would help me. Tell it as soon as You can.

⟨*One to three lines*⟩[4] I would do it the sooner for your desire, and I hope to do it now in no long time, but shall hardly do it here. I hope soon to be at London. Answer the first part of this letter immediately. I am, dear sir, Your most humble Servant,

SAM. JOHNSON

1. SJ had urged Henry Thrale to obey his doctor's warning against "full meals" (*Works*, Yale ed. I.304). According to Hester Thrale, SJ told her husband, "such [voracious] eating is little better than Suicide" (*Thraliana* I.488).

2. "He [SJ] quarrelled with his truest friend Dr. Taylor of Ashbourne, for recommending to him a degree of temperance, by which alone his life could have been saved, and recommending it in his own unaltered phrase too, with praiseworthy intentions to impress it more forcibly" (Piozzi, *Letters* II.381).

3. MS: "with" altered from "without"

4. "Some person has torn off the Bottom" (Taylor's MS note).

Richard Brocklesby

MONDAY 25 OCTOBER 1784

MS: Hyde Collection.

ADDRESS: To Dr. Brocklesby in London.

POSTMARKS: 119 LITCHFIELD, 27 OC.

Dear Sir: Lichfield, Oct. 25, 1784

You write to me with a zeal that animates, and a tenderness that melts me. I am not afraid either of a journey to London or a residence in it. I came down with little fatigue, and I am now not weaker. In the smoky atmosphere I was delivered from the dropsy, which I consider as the original and radical disease. The town is my element, there are my friends, there are my books to which I have not yet bidden farewel, and there are my amusements. Sir Joshua told me long ago that my vocation was to publick life,[1] and I hope still to keep my station, till God shall bid me *Go in peace*.[2]

I have not much to add of medical observation. I believe some vigorous pill must be contrived to counteract the costiveness which opiate[s] now certainly produce, and to which it is too troublesome to oppose a regular purge. If You can order such a pill send me the prescription next post.

I now take the squils without the addition of aloes from which I never found other effect, than that it made the pill more bulky and more nauseous, but if it be of any use I will add it again. I am, Sir, Your most obliged and most humble servant,

SAM. JOHNSON

1. SJ's paraphrase of Reynolds repeats the substance of his own observation, "The town is my element": *publick* in this case has the force of *urban*.

2. "Go in peace" (Mark 5:34).

John Perkins

MONDAY 25 OCTOBER 1784

MS: Hyde Collection.
ADDRESS: To Mr. Perkins.

Dear Sir: Lichfield, Oct. 25, 1784

The experience which I have often had of your kindness is now bringing another trouble upon You. I beg that You will be pleased to employ some proper agent to do for me what this summons, which I have this day received, requires.

I am little better, and I flatter myself little worse, than when I left London. Please to make my compliments to Mrs. Perkins, and to all my friends about the Brew house. I hope soon to see You all again. I am, Dear sir, Your most humble servant,

SAM. JOHNSON

John Ryland

SATURDAY 30 OCTOBER 1784

MS: Hyde Collection.
ADDRESS: To Mr. Ryland, Merchant in London.
POSTMARKS: 119 LITCHFIELD, ⟨1⟩ NO.

Dear Sir: Lichfield, Oct. 30, 1784

I have slackened in my diligence of correspondence certainly not by ingratitude or less delight to hear from my friends, and as little would I have it imputed to idleness, or amusement of any other kind. The truth is that I care not much to think on my own state. I have for some time past grown worse, the water makes slow advances, and my breath though not so much obstructed as in some former periods of my disorder, is very short. I am not however heartless. The water has, since its first great effusion, invaded me twice, and twice has retreated.

Accept my sincere thanks for your care in laying down the stone;[1] what You and young Mr. Ryland have done, I doubt not of finding well done, if ever I can make my mind firm enough to visit it.

I am now contriving to return, and hope to be yet no disgrace to our monthly meeting.[2] When I shall be with you, as my resolution is not very steady, and as chance must have some part in the opportunity, I cannot tell. Do not omit to write,[3] for your letters are a great part of my comfort. I am, Dear Sir, Your most humble Servant,

SAM. JOHNSON

Pray write.

1. *Ante* To Thomas Bagshaw, 12 July 1784 and n. 3; *Ante* To John Ryland, 12 July 1784.

2. *Ante* To John Hawkins, 22 Nov. 1783 and n. 1; *Post* To John Ryland, 4 Nov. 1784.

3. MS: "w" superimposed upon "y"

Charles Burney

MONDAY 1 NOVEMBER 1784

MS: Hyde Collection. Address and postmarks, Pierpont Morgan Library.[1]

ADDRESS: To Dr. Burney in St. Martin's Street, Leicester Fields, London.

POSTMARKS: 119 LITCHFIELD, 3 NO.

ENDORSEMENTS: Litchfield, Nov. 1, 1784. No. 12. From Dr. Johnson, Novr. 1st 1784. No. 14.

Dear Sir: Lichfield, Nov. 1, 1784

Our correspondence paused for want of topicks, I had said what I had to say, on the matter proposed to my consideration,[2] and nothing remained but to tell you that I waked or

1. SJ used only half of his sheet for the letter to Charles Burney; he then folded the paper, wrote to Frances on one blank side (p. 3), and addressed the letter to Charles on the other (p. 4). *Post* To Frances Burney, 1 Nov. 1784.

2. *Ante* To Charles Burney, 2 Aug. 1784, n. 1.

slept, that I was more or less sick. I drew my thoughts in upon myself, and supposed yours employed upon your book.

That your book has been delayed I am glad, since you have gained[3] an opportunity of being more exact.[4]

Of the caution necessary in adjusting narratives there is no end. Some tell what they do not know, that they may not seem ignorant, and others from mere indifference about truth. All truth is not indeed of equal importance, but if little violations are allowed, every violation[5] will in time be thought little, and a writer should keep himself vigilantly on his guard against the first temptations to negligence or supineness.

I had ceased to write because, respecting You I had no more to say, and respecting myself could say little good. I can not boast of advancement, and in cases of convalescence it may be said with few exceptions, *non progredi, est regredi.*[6] I hope I may be excepted.

My great difficulty was with my sweet Fanny who by her artifice of inserting her letter in yours had given me a precept of frugality which I was not at liberty to neglect, and I knew not who was in town under whose cover I could send my letter. But I can now do to her as she did to me.[7]

I rejoice to hear that You are all so well, and have a delight particularly sympathetick in the recovery of Mrs. Burney.[8] I am, Dear Sir, Your most humble servant,

SAM. JOHNSON

3. MS: "gainend"

4. "While waiting for the engravers to finish the plates for his book [*An Account of the . . . Commemoration of Handel*] . . . Burney came across important additional information about Handel's early life, which obliged him to revise his biography extensively" (Roger Lonsdale, *Dr. Charles Burney*, 1965, p. 306).

5. MS: "violation" repeated as catchword

6. *non progredi est regredi*: "not to go forward is to go backward" (proverbial).

7. See above, n. 1.

8. *Ante* To Charles Burney, 2 Aug. 1784 and n. 3.

Frances Burney

MONDAY 1 NOVEMBER 1784

MS: Pierpont Morgan Library.

HEADING: To Miss Burney.

NOTE: Written on half a Letter to Dr. Burney, from Litchfield—only the Month previous to his Death—which took place the 14 of the following December, 1784.

Dear Madam: [Lichfield] Nov. 1, 1784

My heart has reproached me with my ingratitude to you, and my vanity has been mortified with the fear of being thought to want a due sense of the honour conferred on me by such a correspondence. I am obliged to Dr. Burney for the opportunity that he has given me of surmounting all difficulties.

Yet now I am enabled to write, what can I say? only one melancholy truth, that I am very ill, and another more chearful, but, I hope, equally sincere, that I wish You, dear Madam, to be better. I am now scheming to come home, but the schemes of the sick are dilatory, and then You must try what comfort you can give, to, Dear Madam, Your most humble servant,

SAM. JOHNSON

Francesco Sastres

MONDAY 1 NOVEMBER 1784

PRINTED SOURCE: Piozzi, *Letters* II.412.

Dear Sir, Lichfield, Nov. 1, 1784

I beg you to continue the frequency of your letters; every letter is a cordial; but you must not wonder that I do not answer with exact punctuality. You may always have something to tell: you live among the various orders of mankind, and may make a letter from the exploits, sometimes of the philosopher, and sometimes of the pickpocket. You see some ballons succeed and some miscarry, and a thousand strange and a thousand foolish things. But I see nothing; I must make my letter from what I feel, and what I feel with[1] so little delight, that I cannot love to talk of it.

I am certainly not[2] to come to town, but do not omit to write; for I know not when I shall come, and the loss of a letter is not much. I am, dear Sir, Your, etc.

1. Chapman (III.245) emends "with" to "will."

2. Chapman (III.245 n. 3) postulates a "slip," suggesting the possibility that SJ wrote "certainly soon."

Mrs. White[1]

TUESDAY 2 NOVEMBER 1784

MS: Birthplace Museum, Lichfield.

ADDRESS: To Mrs. White at Dr. Johnson's, in Bolt court, Fleetstreet, London.

POSTMARKS: 119 LITCHFIELD, 5 NO.

Mrs. White: Lichfield, Nov. 2, 1784

Wait on Mr. Strahan with my request that he will let you have three Guineas, for you, and Betsey Barber, and Mrs. Desmoulins, and leave this Note with Mr. Strahan. I am, Your etc.

SAM. JOHNSON

1. Mrs. White, SJ's housekeeper, to whom he left £100 in his will, where she is described as "my female servant" (*Life* IV.402 n. 2). It was customary for her to receive money for household expenses from William Strahan, who was continuing to act as SJ's banker (*Life* V.505; *Works*, Yale ed. I.336, 352).

James Boswell

WEDNESDAY 3 NOVEMBER 1784

PRINTED SOURCE: JB's *Life*, 1791, II.556.

Dear Sir, Lichfield, Nov. 3, 1784

I have this summer sometimes amended and sometimes relapsed, but upon the whole, have lost ground very much. My legs are extremely weak, and my breath very short, and the water is now encreasing upon me. In this uncomfortable state your letters used to relieve; what is the reason that I have them no longer? Are you sick, or are you sullen?[1] Whatever be the reason, if it be less than necessity, drive it away, and of the short life that we have, make the best use for yourself and for your friends * * * * * *[2] I am sometimes afraid that your omission to write has some real cause, and shall be glad to know that you are not sick, and that nothing ill has befallen dear Mrs. Boswell, or any of your family. I am, Sir, your, etc.

SAM. JOHNSON

1. From his return to Scotland in July until the beginning of the Winter Session, JB was "under a cloud of inactivity," suffering from "a long affliction of bad spirits" (JB's Register of Letters, Aug.–Nov. 1784, MS: Beinecke Library).

2. "His last letter to me then came, and affected me very tenderly. . . . Yet it was not a little painful to me to find, that in a paragraph of this letter, which I have omitted, he still persevered in arraigning me as before, which was strange in him who had so much experience of what I suffered. I, however, wrote to him two as kind letters as I could; the last of which came too late to be read by him" (*Life* IV.380).

John Ryland

THURSDAY 4 NOVEMBER 1784

MS: Hyde Collection.

ADDRESS: To Mr. Ryland, Merchant in London.

POSTMARKS: 119 LITCHFIELD, 8 NO.

Dear Sir: Lichfield, Nov. 4, 1784

I have just received a letter in which You tell me that You love to hear from me, and I value such a declaration too much to neglect it. To have a friend, and a friend like You, may be numbered among the first felicities of life, at a time when weakness either of body or mind loses the pride and the confidence[1] of self-sufficiency, and looks round for that help which perhaps human kindness cannot give, and which we yet are willing to expect from one another.

I am, at this time very much dejected. The water grows fast upon me, but it has invaded me twice in this last half year, and has been twice expelled,[2] it will, I hope give way to the same remedies. My Breath is tolerably easy, and since the remission of asthma about two months ago, have never been so strait and so much obstructed as it once was.

I took this day a very uncommon dose of squills, but hitherto without effect, but I will continue their use very diligently. Let me have your prayers.

I am now preparing myself for my return, and do not despair of some[3] more monthly meetings. To hear that dear Payne is better gives me great delight.[4]

I saw the draught of the stone. I am afraid the date is wrong. I think it should be 52.[5] We will have it rectified. You say nothing of the cost but that You have paid it. My intention was that[6] Mr. Payne should have put into your hands fifteen pounds which he received for me at Midsummer.[7] If he has not done it, I will order You the money, which is in his hands.

Shall I ever be able to bear the sight of this stone? In your company, I hope, I shall. You will not wonder that I write no more. God bless you for Christs sake. I am, Dear sir, Your most humble servant,

SAM. JOHNSON

1. MS: "confidence" altered from "confidences"
2. MS: "expelled" repeated as catchword
3. MS: "s" superimposed upon "m"
4. *Ante* To John Ryland, 2 Sept. 1784.
5. *Ante* To Thomas Bagshaw, 12 July 1784 and n. 1.
6. MS: "the"
7. *Ante* To John Ryland, 12 July 1784.

Richard Brocklesby

SATURDAY 6 NOVEMBER 1784

MS: Hyde Collection.

ADDRESS: To Dr. Brocklesby in London.

POSTMARKS: 119 LITCHFIELD, 8 NO.

Dear Sir: Lichfield, Nov. 6, 1784

Nothing now goes well, except that my Asthma is not oppressive to the degree that I have sometimes suffered. The water encreases almost visibly and the squills which I get here are utterly inefficacious. My Spirits are extremely low. Yet I have recovered from a worse state. I have supported myself with opiates til they have made me comatous. I have disobeyed Dr. Heberden, and taken Squills in too great a quantity for my Stomach. My Stomach at least is less vigorous, and the Squills I have taken in great quantities.

I am endeavouring to make haste to town.[1] Do not write any more hither. I am, Dear Sir, Your most humble Servant,

SAM. JOHNSON

1. SJ returned to London 16 Nov. (*Post* To Charles Burney, 17 Nov. 1784).

John Hawkins

SUNDAY 7 NOVEMBER 1784

PRINTED SOURCE: Hawkins, p. 576.

[Lichfield] 7 Nov. 1784

I am relapsing into the dropsy very fast, and shall make such haste to town that it will be useless to write to me;[1] but when I come, let me have the benefit of your advice, and the consolation of your company.

1. *Ante* To Richard Brocklesby, 6 Nov. 1784, n. 1.

Elizabeth Aston & Jane Gastrell

c. MONDAY 8 NOVEMBER 1784[1]

MS: Pembroke College, Oxford.

[Lichfield]

Mr. Johnson sends his compliments to the Ladies at Stowhill, of whom he would have taken a more formal leave, but that he was willing to spare a ceremony, which he hopes would have been no pleasure to them, and would have been painful to himself.

1. As L. F. Powell indicates (*Life* III.455), the chronology of SJ's return trip, via Birmingham and Oxford, makes 8 Nov. the likeliest departure date.

Charles Burney

WEDNESDAY 17 NOVEMBER 1784

MS: John Comyn.

ADDRESS: To Dr. Burney in St. Martins Street, Leicester Fields.

ENDORSEMENTS: Dr. Johnson's last rem[em]brance, 17 Novr. 1784. No. 13. Dr. Johnson's last remembrance; Novr. 17th 1784. No. 15.

Nov. 17

Mr. Johnson who came home last night, sends his respects to Dear Doctor Burney,[1] and all the dear Burneys little and great.

1. MS: "Burney" altered from "Burneys"

Edmund Hector

WEDNESDAY 17 NOVEMBER 1784

MS: Hyde Collection.

ADDRESS: To Mr. Hector in Birmingham.

POSTMARK: 17 NO.

Dear Sir: London, Nov. 17, 1784

I did not reach Oxford till friday morning, and then I sent Francis to see the Ballon fly,[1] but could not go myself. I staid at Oxford till Tuesday, and then came in the common vehicle easily to London. I am as I was, and having seen Dr. Brocklesby, am to ply the squils. But whatever be their efficacy, this world must soon pass away. Let us think seriously on our duty.

I send my kindest respects to dear Mrs. Careless. Let me have the prayers of both. We have all[2] lived long, and must soon part. God have mercy on us for the Sake of our Lord Jesus Christ. Amen. I am, Dear Sir, Your most humble Servant,

SAM. JOHNSON

1. The first successful ascent by an English balloonist, James Sadler (1751–1828), took place on 4 Oct. in Oxford. On 12 Nov. Francis Barber joined an "immense crowd of all ranks" that "thronged the streets, the buildings, the towers, the trees, and the fields" to observe Sadler's second ascent, from the University Botanic Garden (J. E. Hodgson, *The History of Aeronautics in Great Britain*, 1924, pp. 140–44, 199 n. 1).

2. MS: "all" repeated as catchword

Philip Metcalfe

WEDNESDAY 17 NOVEMBER 1784

MS: Princeton University Library.

ADDRESS: To Philip Metcalf, Esq., in Saville Row.

Nov. 17

Mr. Johnson came home last night, and hopes that Mr. Metcalf will favour him with a kind visit.

Francesco Sastres

WEDNESDAY 17 NOVEMBER 1784

MS: British Library.

ADDRESS: To Mr. Sastres, No. 14 Margaret Street, Cavendish Square.

Novem. 17

Mr. Johnson is glad to inform Mr. Sastres that he came home last night.

William Windham

WEDNESDAY 17 NOVEMBER 1784

MS: Sarah Markham.

ADDRESS: To —— Wyndham, Esq., in Queen Anne's Street West.

Nov. 17

Mr. Johnson missed his hope of sharing academical pleasures with Mr. Wyndham,[1] but hopes to make himself amends here. He came hither last night.

1. *Ante* To Edmund Hector, 17 Nov. 1784.

Elizabeth Way

TUESDAY 23 NOVEMBER 1784

PRINTED SOURCE: Chapman III.339.

Nov. 23, 1784

Dr. Johnson is very ill, but returns his thanks with great sense of Mrs. Way's kindness, and with true wishes for her happiness.

?*John Hollyer*[1]

SATURDAY 27 NOVEMBER 1784

MS: Current location unknown. Transcribed from a photograph in the Hyde Collection.

Sir: Bolt court, Fleetstreet, Nov. 27, 1784

I desire Y⟨ou will let me⟩ know, what Children of our ⟨*two or three words*⟩[2] are now living, what are their name⟨s and what⟩ is their condition. Be pleased to make ⟨all⟩ possible haste.[3] I am, Sir, Your most humble Servant,

SAM. JOHNSON

1. This letter descended through the Hollyer family; in the 1930s it belonged to Frederick Thomas Hollyer. Both A. L. Reade (*Johns. Glean.* IX.71) and R. W. Chapman (Chapman III.249) identify the probable addressee as SJ's cousin, with whom he had corresponded about Thomas Johnson (*Ante* To John Hollyer, 6 Dec. 1774).

2. "The tearing off of a portion of the letter has removed the name of the person whose children he [SJ] was enquiring after, but there can scarcely be a doubt that it was his cousin Tom Johnson. . . . Johnson was within little more than a fortnight of his death, and his thoughts were centred on making some provision for his needy kinsfolk" (*Johns. Glean.* IX.71–72).

3. On 9 Dec. SJ added a codicil to his will, in which he included as legatees Thomas Johnson's daughter Ann Whiting, her daughter Sarah, and any other surviving granddaughters (*Life* IV.403; *Johns. Glean.* IV.36).

Thomas Cadell

LATE NOVEMBER 1784[1]

MS: Houghton Library.
ADDRESS: To Mr. Cadel.
ENDORSEMENT: Dr. Johnson.

Sir:

I desire you will make up a parcel of the following Books, and

1. See below, n. 2.

send them to Oxford directed to Dr. Adams at Pembroke College.[2]

Johnson's Dictionary Fol.
— — 8vo
— Rambler 2 Sets
— Idler
Political tracts
Hebrides
Rasselas
Lives of the Poets.[3]

Irene a tragedy (if it can be easily got at Dodsley's else leave it out)

and please to let me know the whole of my debt[4] to You. I am, Sir, Your most humble Servant,

SAM. JOHNSON

2. On 8 Feb. 1785 Adams reported to one of SJ's executors, William Scott, "We have received a most agreeable Token of our Friend Dr. Johnson's Regard for his College in a Present of his Books and of his Publications of every kind which he sent us a little before his Death" (MS: Hyde Collection).

3. The only presentation copies still in the Pembroke College Library are a tenth edition (1784) of SJ's *Rambler* and a second edition (1775) of his *Journey* (*Life* I.527; J. D. Fleeman, *A Preliminary Handlist of Copies of Books Associated with Dr. Samuel Johnson*, 1984, pp. 28, 37).

4. MS: "debt" altered from "debts"

Bennet Langton

MONDAY 29 NOVEMBER 1784

MS: Hyde Collection.

NOTE in an unidentified hand: To Mr. Langton.

Dear Sir: November 29, 1784

I earnestly beg the favour of seeing You this Afternoon, do not be hasty to leave me, for I have much to say.[1] I am, Dear Sir, Your most etc.

SAM. JOHNSON

1. In his narrative of SJ's last days, John Hoole reported that on the evening

of 29 Nov. he found Langton engaged "on business" with SJ (*Johns. Misc.* II.152). It is likely that the two men discussed the publication of SJ's Latin poems, to which Langton "added a few notes, [and] sold them to the booksellers for a small sum, to be given to some of Johnson's relations" (*Life* IV.384).

William Strahan

MONDAY 29 NOVEMBER 1784

PRINTED SOURCE: C. K. Shorter, *Unpublished Letters of Dr. Samuel Johnson*, 1915.

ADDRESS: To William Strahan, Esq.

Dear Sir, November 29, 1784

I am very weak. When I am a little better I will beg your company; in the meantime, I beg you to inform me in two lines, when you shall have received my pension to Michaelmas, how much will be coming to me.[1] I am, Sir, your most humble servant,

SAM. JOHNSON

1. On 10 Dec. SJ signed a receipt for £88 5*s*., "being in full for my Pension to Michaelmas last" (MS: Berg Collection, New York Public Library).

William Vyse

MONDAY 29 NOVEMBER 1784

MS: Hyde Collection.

ADDRESS: To the Reverend Dr. Vyse in Lambeth.

POSTMARKS: PENY POST PAYD T MO, 3 OCLOCK S.

ENDORSEMENT in an unidentified hand: Novbr. 29th 1784.

Sir: Bolt court, Fleetstreet, Nov. 29, 1784

I am desirous to know whether Charles Scrimshaw of Woodsease (I think) in your Father's neighbourhood,[1] be now living,

1. William Vyse the elder came from Standon, Staffordshire (*Johns. Glean.* V.210). Standon is approximately six miles northeast of Woodseaves.

what is his condition, and where he may be found.[2] If You can conveniently make any enquiry about him, and can do it without delay, it will be an act of great kindness to me, he being very nearly related to me. I beg to pardon this trouble. I am, Sir, Your most humble Servant,

SAM. JOHNSON

2. Charles Skyrmsher (1688–1762), of Woodseaves, High Offley, Staffordshire, was probably SJ's first cousin—the son of his father's sister (*Johns. Glean.* IX.112–13). As he was about to draw up his will, SJ was seeking information about various relations (cf. *Ante* To ?John Hollyer, 27 Nov. 1784). According to Edmond Malone, SJ told Vyse "'he [SJ] was disappointed in the inquiries made after his relations'" (JB's *Life*, ed. Malone, 1804, IV.437–38 n. 3).

Richard Greene

THURSDAY 2 DECEMBER 1784

MS: Beinecke Library. The transcript (in the hand of Richard Greene) used as copy for JB's *Life*.

HEADING: To Mr. Green, Apothecary, at Lichfield.

Dear Sir, Decem. 2d 1784

I have enclosed the epitaph for my Father, Mother, and Brother, to be all engraved on the large size, and laid in the Middle Isle in St. Michael's Church, which I request the Clergyman and the Church-Wardens to permit.[1]

The first care must be to find the exact place of interment, that the stone may protect the bodies. Then let the Stone be deep, massy and hard, and do not let the difference of ten pounds or more defeat our purpose.

I have enclosed ten pounds, and Mrs. Porter will pay you ten more, which I gave her for the same purpose. What more is wanted shall be sent, and I beg that all possible hast may be made, for I wish to have it done while I am yet alive. Let me

1. For the text of the epitaphs, see *Life* IV.393 n. 2. It is unclear whether the stone was ever laid (*Life* IV.393 n. 3).

know, dear sir, that you receive this. I am, Sir, Your most humble Servant,

SAM. JOHNSON

To Mrs. Porter. Madam, be pleased to pay to Mr. Greene ten pounds. Sam. Johnson. £10.0.0. Decem. 2d 1784.

Lucy Porter

THURSDAY 2 DECEMBER 1784

MS: Hyde Collection.

Dear Madam: Dec. 2, 1784

I am very ill, and desire your prayers. I have sent Mr. Green the epitaph, and a power to call on You for ten pounds.[1]

I laid this summer a stone over Tetty in the Chapel of Bromley in Kent.[2] The Inscription is in Latin of which this is the English.

Here lie the remains of Elizabeth, descended from the ancient house of Jarvis at Peatling in Leicestershire; a Woman of beauty, elegance, ingenuity, and piety. Her first Husband was Henry Porter; her second, Samuel Johnson, who having loved her much, and lamented her long, laid this stone upon her.

She died in March. 1752.

That this is done, I thought it fit that You should know; what care will be taken of us, who can tell? May God pardon and bless us, for Jesus Christs sake. Amen. I am, Madam, Your most humble Servant,

SAM. JOHNSON

1. *Ante* To Richard Greene, 2 Dec. 1784 and n. 1.

2. *Ante* To Thomas Bagshaw, 12 July 1784; *Ante* To John Ryland, 12 July 1784; 30 Oct. 1784.

John Nichols

MONDAY 6 DECEMBER 1784

MS: British Library.
ADDRESS: To Mr. Nicholls.

6th Dec. 1784

The late learned Mr. Swinton of Oxford[1] having one Day remarked that one Man, meaning I suppose no Man but himself, could assign all the Parts of the ancient universal History to their proper Authors.[2] At the Request of Sir Robt. Chambers or of myself gave the Account which I now transmit to you in his own Hand, being willing that of so great a Work[3] the History should be known and that each Writer should receive his due Proportion of Praise from Posterity.

I recommend to you to preserve this Scrap of literary Intelligence in Mr. Swinton's own Hand, or to deposit it in the Museum, that the Veracity of this Account may never be doubted.[4] I am, Sir, Your most humble Servant,

SAM. JOHNSON

1. John Swinton (1703–77), F.R.S., historian and Keeper of the Archives, Oxford University (1767–77) (*Alum. Oxon.* II.iv.1378).

2. *Ante* To Samuel Richardson, 3 Feb. 1755 and n. 1.

3. MS: "History" del. before "Work"

4. On 15 Dec. (*Life* IV.550), Nichols presented both this letter and the accompanying list of authors to the British Museum (Add. MS: 5159). As Nichols remarked of the letter, "the date of it will shew that, amidst the pangs of illness, the love of truth, and an attachment to the interests of Literature, were still predominant" (*Lit. Anec.* II.554).

William Strahan

TUESDAY 7 DECEMBER 1784

MS: Berg Collection, New York Public Library.
ADDRESS: To Mr. Strahan.

To WILLIAM STRAHAN, 7 *December* 1784

Sir: Dec. 7, 1784

I was not sure that I read your figures right, and therefore must trouble you to set down in words how much of my pension I can call for now,[1] and how much will be due to me at Christmas.[2] I am, sir, your most humble servant,

SAM. JOHNSON

1. *Ante* To William Strahan, 29 Nov. 1784, n. 1.

2. On 13 Dec. SJ acknowledged receipt of £75, "for three Months Pension" (MS: Hyde Collection).

William Strahan

FRIDAY 10 DECEMBER 1784

PRINTED SOURCE: C. K. Shorter, *Unpublished Letters of Dr. Samuel Johnson*, 1915.

ADDRESS: To William Strahan, Esq.

Sir, Bolt Court, December 10, 1784

I am very unwilling to take the pains of writing, and therefore make use of another hand to desire that I may have whatever portion of my pension you can spare me with prudence and propriety.[1] I am, Sir, your humble servant,

SAM. JOHNSON

1. *Ante* To William Strahan, 7 Dec. 1784, n. 2.

INDEX

This is an index of proper names alone; the comprehensive index to the entire edition appears in Volume v. The following abbreviations are used: Bt. (Baronet), Kt. (Knight), ment. (mentioned). Peers are listed under their titles, with cross-references from the family name.

Entries for each of SJ's correspondents begin with a comprehensive listing of all letters to the individual in question. Page numbers for footnotes refer to pages on which the footnotes begin, although the item which is indexed may be on a following page.

The index was compiled mainly by Phyllis L. Marchand with the assistance of Marcia Wagner Levinson and Judith A. Hancock.

B

C

E

F

G

H

M

R

S

V

W

X

Y